# Behavioral Assessment and Case Formulation

# Behavioral Assessment and Case Formulation

Stephen N. Haynes,
William H. O'Brien, and
Joseph Keawe'aimoku Kaholokula

WILEY

John Wiley & Sons, Inc.

*Library of Congress Cataloging-in-Publication Data:*

Haynes, Stephen N.

Behavioral assessment and case formulation / Stephen N. Haynes, William H. O'Brien, Joseph Keawe'aimoku Kaholokula.

p. ; cm.

Includes bibliographical references and index.

ISBN 978-1-118-01864-4 (alk. paper); 978-1-118-09976-6 (eMobi); 978-1-118-09977-3 (ePub); 978-1-118-09975-9 (ePDF)

1. Psychodiagnostics. 2. Behavior modification. I. O'Brien, William Hayes. II. Kaholokula, Joseph Keawe'aimoku. III. Title.

[DNLM: 1. Mental Disorders—diagnosis. 2. Behavior. 3. Mental Disorders—therapy. 4. Personality Assessment. WM 141]

RC473.B43H39 2011

616.89'075—dc22                                                                                         2011008895

Printed in the United States of America

10 9 8 7 6 5 4 3 2 1

*To Megumi*
*—S. H.*

*To my parents Patricia Hayes O'Brien and William John O'Brien,*
*who blended heart and science*
*and my brothers, Daniel, Timothy, Michael, and Joseph O'Brien,*
*who taught creative thinking and how to take a punch*

*—W. H. O.*

*A Hawaiian proverb states,*
*'A'ohe pau ka 'ike i ka hālau ho'okahi*
*(not all knowledge is obtained from one school).*
*To my parents, Lawrence and Beverly Kaholokula,*
*whose schooling set a solid foundation.*
*To friends and family, whose schooling is lifelong.*
*—J. K. K.*

# Contents

# Preface

Clinicians face many challenges in the clinical assessment process. Several questions of particular importance arise: What is the best assessment strategy to use with a particular client? What assessment methods will best capture a client's unique strengths, limitations, behavior problems, and intervention goals? How can data from multiple sources be integrated in order to yield a valid and clinically useful case formulation? What procedures should be enacted in order to ensure a positive clinician-client relationship and be sensitive to the unique aspects of each client? How should intervention processes and outcomes be monitored?[1]

Behavioral assessment is a science-based paradigm that guides the clinician as he or she faces these assessment challenges. This book outlines the underlying principles of the behavioral assessment paradigm. It also provides guidelines for the application of behavioral assessment strategies and methods that can strengthen the validity and utility of clinical judgments.

In Chapter 1, we discuss behavioral assessment within the broader contexts of clinical and psychological assessment and measurement. Although we emphasize clinical applications of behavioral assessment, the principles and methods of this paradigm are important elements of measurement in psychopathology, education, organizational psychology, cognitive neuroscience, social psychology, and other areas of inquiry that rely on behavioral data.

---

[1] We often use the term *intervention* rather than *treatment* because many behavioral interventions are more broadly focused than the term treatment implies. For example, behavioral interventions can focus on changing the behavior of psychiatric staff members and teachers, strengthening the supervision and training of service providers, simplifying a home environment, or providing a support group for parents of children with disabilities.

We emphasize a science-based approach to clinical assessment. Without a scientific foundation, clinical judgments are more likely to be incomplete, less informative, and/or invalid. As a result, clients are less likely to receive optimal intervention benefits. Throughout the book we draw attention to the importance of (a) the client-clinician relationship; (b) being sensitive to the cultural and other unique aspects of a client; (c) the role of the clinician as a behavioral scientist; (d) using methods that can reduce biases in assessment and clinical judgments; (e) using a constructive and positive orientation in the assessment process; (f) using multiple assessment methods, instruments, contexts, and informants to enhance the validity of clinical judgments; (g) using time-series assessment strategies throughout the assessment process in order to evaluate changes in behavior over time; (h) including observation methods in clinical assessment; (i) using measures with strong psychometric evidence appropriate for the client; (j) using measures that are sensitive to change; (k) specifying the key dimensions of behavior problems beyond those associated with a diagnosis; (l) assessing functional relations associated with client behavior problems and goals; and (m) considering the influence of broader contextual and social systems factors that may be affecting a client.

In Chapter 2 we introduce the functional analysis as a paradigm for clinical case formulation. The functional analysis is a product of behavioral assessment—the integration of important, modifiable, causal variables and causal relations associated with a client's behavior problems and intervention goals. A clinical case is used to illustrate the applications of behavioral assessment methods and to show how data obtained in the assessment process can be integrated into a functional analysis. Functional Analytic Clinical Case Diagrams (FACCDs), which are causal diagrams of a functional analysis, are also introduced. The functional analysis and FACCD are designed to parsimoniously communicate the functional analysis to others, as an aid in teaching case formulations, and to assist in selecting the most cost-beneficial intervention focus with a client. We also examine assessment contexts that affect the cost-benefits of the functional analysis.

In Chapter 3 we present the functional analysis and the Functional Analytic Clinical Case Diagram in greater detail. We discuss the applications of causal diagrams and describe the elements of the FACCD. Elements of a functional analysis and FACCD include: (a) behavior problems and intervention goals; (b) the relative importance and sequelae of a client's behavior problems and intervention goals; (c) the type, strength, and direction of effects of their functional interrelations; (d) causal variables associated with behavior problems and intervention goals; (e) the modifiability, strength, and directionality of causal relations; (f) the interrelations, multiple causal paths, and interactions among causal variables; and (g) moderator, mediator, and hypothesized causal variables.

In Chapters 4, 5, and 6 we present the conceptual and empirical foundations of behavioral assessment. In Chapter 4, we note how the strategies of behavioral assessment are guided by research on the unique characteristics of a client's behavior problems. Most clients present with multiple behavior problems and we consider several causal models that can account for comorbidity. The same behavior problem can also differ in important aspects across clients, in terms of the most important attribute, response mode, or dimension. Further, the characteristics of a behavior problem will often vary across contexts and time. Recognizing the complexity and idiographic nature of behavior problems, behavioral assessment strategies emphasize measurement in multiple settings, with multiple methods, including multiple informants, across multiple times, using sensitive and precise measures, and the integration of idiographic and nomothetic assessment strategies.

In Chapter 5, we review causal models of behavior problems that further guide behavioral assessment strategies and the functional analysis. We first review the key conditions that are required for causal inference: covariation, temporal precedence, the exclusion of alternative explanations, and a logical connection. The mechanism of causal action is highlighted as particularly important because it can point to intervention strategies. We also consider sources of measurement and judgment error in the assessment process and strategies that can be used to minimize them.

In Chapter 6, we discuss causal relations that are particularly relevant for understanding clients' behavior problems. We consider how causal variables can have multiple attributes that differ in their causal effects and how a behavior problem can be affected by multiple causal variables. Further, a causal variable can have direct and indirect effects through different paths and can change across time and settings. The idiographic nature of causal relations is an especially important characteristic of causal models of behavior problems and underlies many of the assessment strategies that we discuss in this book. We discuss types of causal variables and causal relations that are most useful in clinical assessment: contemporaneous causal relations, differences in causal relations across contexts and settings, modifiability of causal variables, and social systems factors.

In Chapter 7, we summarize the principles and strategies of behavioral assessment. The chapter reviews how the conditional nature of behavior problems leads to collecting data from multiple sources; how the dynamic nature of behavior problems leads to time-series assessment; and how the heterogeneous nature of behavior problems leads to an emphasis on using well-specified variables in clinical assessment. Behavioral assessment strategies also emphasize a focus on contemporaneous functional relations, the assessment of clients in their natural environment, the use of idiographic strategies, and a scholarly approach to clinical assessment. Finally, in this chapter we present another case to illustrate these principles and strategies.

Chapters 8 and 9 focus on self-report and direct methods of assessment. In Chapter 8, we discuss the assets and liabilities of functional behavioral interviews, behavioral questionnaires, and self-monitoring. Ecological momentary assessment is highlighted as a particularly promising method of gathering self-report data on clients in their natural environment. In Chapter 9, we review direct methods of assessment, including naturalistic behavioral observation, analog behavioral observation, and psychophysiological assessment.

In Chapter 10, we integrate material from previous chapters and outline how causal relations can be identified and evaluated in clinical assessment. The chapter presents the assets and liabilities of rational derivation, the use of interviews and questionnaires to estimate causal relations, the use of experimental manipulations, and multivariate time-series regression methods. The chapter ends with specific recommendations for behavioral assessment strategies that are science-based and reflect our understanding of the nature of behavior problems and their related causal relations.

Finally, in Chapter 11, we return to the concepts presented in the first seven chapters and present 22 steps that can be used to construct a functional analysis.

Overall, the goal of this book is to provide graduate students, clinical researchers, and clinical supervisors and practitioners in the social sciences with an educational, science-based, practical, and informative resource for conducting behavioral assessments, as well as generating valid and useful functional analyses and clinical judgments. As we emphasize throughout this book, the clinician's ability to select the best intervention for a client, and the ability to monitor the intervention process and outcomes, depends on the degree to which he or she adheres to science-based assessment principles and strategies and collects valid assessment data that allow for the specification of the client's behavior problem(s) and related causal variables and relations.

CHAPTER

# 1

# Introduction to Behavioral Assessment and Case Formulation

Clinicians and clinical researchers face many measurement and clinical judgment challenges that emphasize explanation and prediction. Will a client harm himself or others? Can a parent provide a loving and safe living environment for a child? To what degree is a client's daily functioning affected by a traumatic brain injury? What learning environment would be most helpful for an elementary school child with developmental delays? Clinicians must also make judgments focused on determining what intervention strategies can, and should, be used for a particular client. Here, the central question is: What intervention will be most effective for a client's behavior problem and have the greatest impact on his or her quality of life? This latter intervention-focused judgment requires an integration of many lower-level judgments. What are the client's specific behavior problems and intervention goals? What variables affect his or her problems and goals? What variables might affect intervention outcome? How can intervention process and outcome be best measured? The aforementioned judgments are all elements of the clinical case formulation. The clinical case formulation, and the concepts and methods of behavioral assessment upon which it is based, is a major focus of this book.

In the following sections of this chapter, we first consider broader issues of psychological assessment and measurement. We then discuss the behavioral assessment paradigm, particularly as applied in case formulation and in other applications of psychological assessment. Throughout, we emphasize the importance of a thoughtful, scholarly, science-based approach to clinical assessment.

## CLINICAL ASSESSMENT AND PSYCHOLOGICAL ASSESSMENT PARADIGMS

A psychological assessment paradigm is a set of assessment-related principles, beliefs, values, hypotheses, and methods advocated in a discipline or by its adherents. A psychological assessment paradigm includes beliefs and hypotheses about: (a) the relative importance of specific behavior problems (e.g., the relative importance of insight versus behavior change as a focus of assessment for a person who reports experiencing significant levels of depression), (b) the relative importance of a particular response mode subsumed within a behavior problem (e.g., emphases on the relative importance of behavioral, cognitive, or emotional aspects of depression), (c) the most important causal variables associated with a behavior problem (e.g., emphases on the relative importance of early learning experiences, genetic factors, relationship factors, or contemporaneous cognitive variables as causes of domestic violence), (d) the mechanisms of causal action that are presumed to underlie behavior problems (e.g., learning processes, neurotransmitter systems and functions, intrapsychic processes and conflicts), (e) the importance of assessment in the intervention process (e.g., a diagnostic approach versus a functional approach to intervention design), (f) the best strategies for interacting with clients during the assessment-intervention process (e.g., degree of structured versus unstructured interviewing), and (g) the best assessment strategies and methods for obtaining information (e.g., the extent to which interviewing, self-report inventories, observation, rating scales, projective tests, etc., relevant to particular paradigms are used).

Because psychological assessment paradigms vary in the beliefs and hypotheses outlined above, their assessment goals can also differ. For example, the goals of assessment could include diagnosis, the identification of neuropsychological deficits, or the identification of personality traits. The goals of behavioral assessment are unique in that they emphasize the specification and measurement of a client's target behaviors[1] in relation to ongoing intraindividual (e.g., internal processes such as cognitive experiences or physiological responses), interindividual (e.g., social relationships), and nonsocial environmental (e.g., temperature, noise levels, etc.) events that can have causal and noncausal relations with them.

There are many psychological assessment paradigms and some assessment methods are congruent with multiple paradigms. *The Handbook of Psychological Assessment* by Goldstein and Hersen (1999) includes chapters on intellectual assessment, achievement testing, neuropsychological assessment, projective assessment, personality assessment, computer-assisted assessment, and behavioral assessment. Books by Butcher (2009), Corsini and Wedding (2010), Hunsley and Mash (2008), and a four-volume series on psychological assessment edited by Hersen (2004) present various psychological assessment paradigms applied to a variety of behavior problems and assessment goals. A comparative review of these paradigms is beyond the scope of this book, but interested readers are referred to these sources.

## EVALUATING PSYCHOLOGICAL ASSESSMENT PARADIGMS

It can be difficult to evaluate the relative strengths and weaknesses of psychological assessment paradigms because they differ in the principles, strategies, and criteria used to guide the evaluation. For example, a demonstration that behavioral assessment methods are superior to projective methods in measuring the situational specificity of a client's social anxiety may not be persuasive to adherents of a psychodynamic paradigm who presuppose that dispositional factors, rather than situational factors,

---

[1] By *target behaviors*, we mean the objects of measurement in behavioral assessment, which can include behavior problems, intervention goals, and the variables that affect them.

are the central determinants of this disorder. Additionally, adherents of a psychodynamic paradigm may not value the more molecular level information (as opposed to more generalized traits) that results from behavioral assessment and may fault behavioral assessment for its failure to sufficiently emphasize critical early learning experiences in parent-child interactions. However, all assessment paradigms can be evaluated in terms of clinical utility and validity—the degree to which they facilitate specific goals of assessment. For example, assessment methods from different paradigms (more specifically, the measures derived from an assessment method and associated instruments) can be evaluated on the basis of predictive validity—the degree to which they are correlated with the future occurrence of relevant behaviors such as tantrums, suicide, panic attacks, manic episodes, or child abuse. Similarly, different assessment methods can be evaluated on the degree to which they help identify important causal variables for behavior problems and/or evaluate the immediate and ultimate effects of intervention. One difficulty with such psychometric evaluations of assessment data, which we discuss in later chapters, is that the utility and validity of a measure can vary according to the goals of assessment (e.g., diagnosis versus risk assessment versus case formulation) and client characteristics.

Selecting an assessment strategy based on the goals of assessment is a key element of the *functional approach to psychological assessment*. That is, the utility and validity of a particular assessment strategy is always conditional. Consequently, an assessment method or instrument can be valid and useful in some assessment contexts and not in others. Additionally, it is important to note that utility and validity evidence applies to the *measure* derived from an assessment process, rather than to the instrument itself. For example, some instruments provide multiple measures that can differ in their utility and validity.

## ADOPTING A SCHOLARLY AND SCIENCE-BASED APPROACH TO CLINICAL ASSESSMENT

Because there are important relationships between assessment paradigms and assessment strategies, a clinician should carefully consider the conceptual implications of any assessment strategy that he or she uses. If, for example, a clinician chooses to use projective assessment instruments, he or she is embracing a paradigm that emphasizes the primacy of unconscious processes in the expression of behavior problems and the need to use highly inferential measures that are interpreted as markers (e.g., responses to ink blots) of these processes. A projective assessment strategy also deemphasizes the importance of the conditional nature of behavior problems and undervalues the identification of specific, minimally inferential, and modifiable behavioral and environmental variables in clinical assessment.

Under some circumstances it can be useful to blend assessment strategies from different assessment paradigms. In 1993, the journal *Behavior Modification* (vol. 17, no. 1) published a series of articles that examined the integration of behavioral and personality assessment strategies. It is clear, for example, that clients often differ in the likelihood that they will exhibit problem behaviors (e.g., social avoidance) that are associated with certain traits (e.g., neuroticism) across settings. Further, there are data indicating that self-report personality inventories can help the clinician identify such behaviors and their corresponding traits. In a further discussion of integration across paradigms, Nelson-Gray and Paulson (2004) discussed how behavioral assessment and psychiatric diagnosis can be used collaboratively. Although diagnosis is based on a syndromal taxonomy (i.e., matching behavioral symptoms and signs to criteria designated in a diagnostic category) and does not address many important aspects of client functioning, the authors argued that psychiatric diagnoses provide a means for systematically organizing and communicating the outcomes of assessment data.

The selection of assessment strategies from conceptually divergent paradigms is sometimes described as an eclectic approach to assessment. However, the use of conceptually incompatible assessment strategies often reflects the clinician's lack of familiarity with the conceptual foundations and underlying assumptions of the assessment paradigm. For all assessment strategies, the assessor should consider "What assumptions about behavior problems and their causes am I making by using this assessment strategy?"

## BEHAVIORAL ASSESSMENT, CLINICAL CASE FORMULATION, AND MEASUREMENT

One of the principle challenges faced by clinicians early in the assessment and case formulation process is that many clients have multiple interacting behavior problems. Complicating matters further is the very real probability that each behavior problem is influenced by multiple interacting causal factors. Clinical case formulations, and the assessment strategies upon which they are based, are designed to help clinicians integrate data on these multiple interacting variables. Additionally, clinical case formulations can be used to help the clinician design and evaluate interventions.

As the title of our book indicates, we describe one of several psychological assessment paradigms—the behavioral assessment paradigm—and emphasize its application in clinical case formulation. We also discuss behavioral assessment strategies applied to the monitoring of intervention processes and outcomes that are often based on the clinical case formulation. Because they emphasize the importance of precise multimethod assessment, behavioral assessment principles and strategies are also applicable to psychopathology, the study of the characteristics and causes of behavior problems. Before we discuss the behavioral assessment paradigm, we review the challenges faced by clinicians in making the intervention decisions for their clients.[2] We review the context in which clinical cases are formulated and consider several models of clinical case formulation in cognitive-behavior therapy (CBT). We also introduce the functional analysis as a useful clinical case formulation model for describing and explaining clients' behavior problems and intervention goals and for guiding intervention decisions. In Chapter 2, we introduce Functional

---

[2] We use the term *intervention* rather than *therapy* because the focus and methods of an intervention are often more broad than those considered as therapy. Interventions can focus on meeting a client's positive goals; helping a client change his or her thoughts, behavior, and emotions; and reducing the impairments to a client's more positive quality of life. Interventions can also focus on improving such extended systems as classrooms, psychiatric units, couple and family interactions, systems of treatment supervision, and administration policies at mental/behavioral health centers. The term *client* can refer to an individual, couple, family, group, classroom, hospital, or other extended system that is receiving psychological assessment or treatment services.

Analytic Clinical Case Diagrams (FACCDs) as a strategy for visually organizing and communicating the functional analysis. Subsequent chapters discuss the conceptual foundations of behavioral assessment and case formulation and strategies of behavioral assessment.

## THE CONTEXT OF CLINICAL CASE FORMULATION: THE CHALLENGE OF MAKING INTERVENTION DECISIONS

As indicated earlier, one of the most challenging tasks faced by clinicians is to design the best intervention plan for a client. Several factors make intervention planning for persons with behavior problems challenging. In the following section we review these factors.

The first challenge faced by a clinician is that most clients present to a clinician with multiple target behaviors and intervention goals. For example, in Krueger, Kristian, and Markon's (2006) review of comorbidity research, they noted that it is not uncommon for clients to present with three or more behavior disorders. Consider the not-unusual example of a client who comes to a mental health center with a major depressive disorder, excessive alcohol use, and marital discord. Where should the clinician focus his or her interventions? This target behavior selection decision partially depends on the clinician's judgment of the relative importance of each behavior problem. Relative importance, in turn, may be based on the degree of distress associated with each behavior problem or the extent to which each behavior problem affects quality of life. However, this target behavior selection decision can also be based on the interactions among these multiple behavior problems. For example, it may be that the client's depressed mood leads to overuse of alcohol and marital discord. Alternatively, it may be the case that marital discord leads to alcohol use and depressed mood. Notice how the intervention foci and strategies are likely to be different, depending on judgments about relative importance and causal interrelations (i.e., their *functional relations*). These are difficult judgments to make but are essential elements of a clinical case formulation. Importantly, the validity of these judgments depends on the validity of data obtained in clinical assessment. Inadequate assessment strategies or invalid clinical assessment data will diminish the validity of the case formulation and the consequent benefits of an intervention.

A second challenge to the clinical judgment process is that a client's multiple behavior problems can be influenced by many causal variables. Additionally, a single causal variable can influence a behavior problem through many causal pathways. For example, panic disorder has been associated with a diverse set of causal factors, including genetic influences, family modeling, traumatic life events, social reinforcement, classical conditioning, operant conditioning, threat processing, intrusive thoughts, physiological hyperreactivity, serotonin dysregulation, and medical conditions (Beidel & Stipelman, 2007). As we discuss in Chapter 6, identifying causal variables and the causal relations relevant to a client's target behaviors and intervention goals is an important aspect of behavioral case formulations. This is because behavioral interventions often attempt to modify the variables and pathways hypothesized to influence a client's behavior problems. Thus, behavioral case formulations, particularly the functional analysis model of case formulation, emphasize the identification of important and modifiable causal variables.

From our discussion thus far, it should be apparent that case formulation and the strategies for measuring treatment process and outcome are closely related. For example, if a clinician designs an intervention aimed at decreasing the frequency or intensity of a client's depressive mood states, an intermediate outcome of the intervention and a target of measurement should be changes in the key causal variables contained in the case formulation. Of course, the ultimate outcome variable would be the frequency and intensity of depressed moods. Thus, it is expected that changes in the causal variables identified in a functional analysis (i.e., immediate and intermediate outcomes) will affect the behavior problem (ultimate outcome).

This example illustrates the treatment utility of measuring immediate, intermediate, and ultimate treatment goals in behavioral assessment. If an intervention brings about significant changes in a hypothesized causal variable (an immediate and/or intermediate target of assessment) but not in the ultimate outcome, it is possible that the initial case formulation was incorrect. Suppose for example, a clinician generates a case formulation in which it is hypothesized that presleep worry about negative life events inhibits sleep onset for a particular client. An intervention targeting presleep worry is subsequently designed and implemented for the client. If preliminary intervention assessment data indicate that presleep worry had decreased as a function of the intervention without a corresponding improvement in sleep onset, it is likely that the case formulation was incorrect or underspecified and that other important causal variables are exerting important effects on sleep onset. We discuss immediate, intermediate, and ultimate assessment goals further in Chapter 7 when we discuss strategies of behavioral assessment.

Figure 1.1 illustrates the characteristics of an assessment paradigm, strategies of assessment, information obtained in a clinical assessment, case formulation, intervention decisions that result from these data, and how additional data on intervention process and outcome can affect a refinement in the case formulation. There are a few additional inferences that can be derived from Figure 1.1. First, measurement is an ongoing process during intervention. Second, the case formulation is informed by idiographic information (i.e., data from a specific client) and nomothetic information (i.e., findings from the research literature). Third, different assessment strategies will produce different types of data, different case formulations, and different intervention decisions.

Thus far we have argued that complex interactions can occur among multiple target behaviors and multiple causal variables for a given client. The complexity of these interactions creates a sizable challenge in judgment and decision making for a clinician. Clinical case formulations are designed to help the clinician organize and communicate complex arrays of assessment data in order to aid in the design of interventions. They also help the clinician assess the processes and the effects of interventions. Although they are principally based on idiographic data, clinical case formulations can and should be informed by relevant research in psychopathology and assessment. Failure to draw from the relevant research can place the client at risk for reduced benefits from the assessment-intervention process.

In addition to important differences between clients in their arrays and interactions among behavior problems, goals, and causal variables, a third challenge faced by a clinician has to do with the notion that clients invariably have differing life contexts. For example, clients with the same behavior problem can differ in the quality of their intimate relationships,

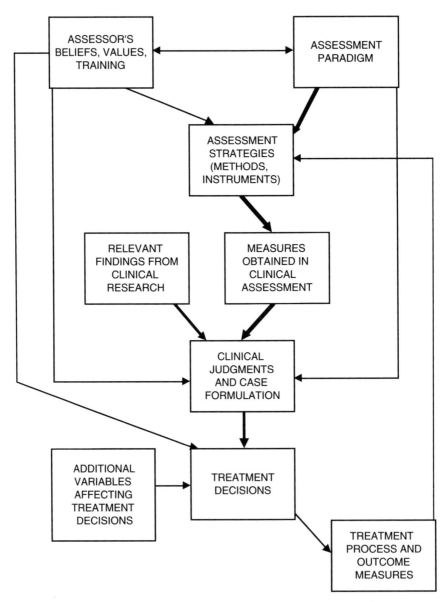

**Figure 1.1** The interactions among the clinician's assessment paradigm, the assessment strategies used in clinical assessment, the measures obtained, the clinical judgments and case formulation informed by these measures and relevant research, intervention decisions, and the impact of intervention process and outcome measures on additional assessment strategies (which can result in a refinement in the case formulation, intervention, and so forth).

*Source: Adapted from Haynes and O'Brien, 2000.*

cognitive impairments and abilities, physical health problems, level of family support, current exposure to life stressors, verbal expressive skills, cultural beliefs and attitudes, and economic resources. All of these life contexts can affect how well a particular intervention might work and are often elements in a clinical case formulation. Recall our example of a client experiencing depressed mood states. What contextual factors might affect a clinician's case formulation and intervention decision? If the client is a recent immigrant to the United States from Western Samoa, acculturative stressors, such as language barriers and perceived discrimination, might be contributing to his depressed mood and he may be using alcohol to cope with these stressors. A younger client might be affected more strongly by rejection experiences with peers, or a client's economic strains associated with a job loss might be affecting his mood, alcohol use, and marital relationship.

A fourth challenge is that the features of a behavior problem can vary from client to client. For example, one person with a depressive disorder can differ from other persons with the same disorder in the degree to which he experiences fatigue, or difficulty concentrating, loss of interest in pleasurable activities, and sleep disturbance. The causes of the specific depression symptoms, and thus the best intervention, can also be different. A careful examination of Axis I and II disorders in DSM-IV TR (APA, 2004) reveals that most disorders contain multiple and heterogeneous arrays of symptoms and behaviors.

A fifth challenge faced by clinicians has to do with the selection of an intervention for a specific behavior problem, for which there are often several empirically supported interventions strategies. This is particularly true in behavior therapy and cognitive-behavior therapy (CBT)[3] where many alternative interventions for a behavior problem may have received empirical support (e.g., Farmer & Chapman, 2008; Gallagher-Thompson et al., 2008; Kazdin, 2001; McKay & Storch, 2009). For example, Chorpita and Daleiden (2009) reported that there were 84 empirically based treatment protocols for children and adolescents with anxiety problems, 68

---

[3] We use the term *behavior therapy* or *CBT* (cognitive-behavior therapy) to refer to a range of behavioral, cognitive-behavioral, cognitive, emotionally focused, behavior analytic, and behavior modification treatment strategies.

for oppositional and aggressive problems, and 39 for delinquent problems. Chorpita and Daleiden (2009) also noted over 40 treatment "elements" and specific foci within treatments (e.g., communication skills, response prevention, stimulus control) that could address the causal relations contained in a functional analysis of a child's behavior problems.

Even when a clinician selects a specific empirically supported intervention available for a behavior problem, it is likely that the effectiveness of the intervention will vary across persons. For example, Compton Burns, Egger, and Robertson (2002) noted that although there is strong empirical support for CBT with childhood anxiety disorders, 20–40% of children do not evidence clinically significant change. When measures of intervention outcome indicate intervention failure, the clinician must refine the intervention using the empirical literature and a modified case formulation to better address the idiosyncratic aspects of the client's problems, goals, and life contexts.

These examples illustrate the importance of science-based assessment strategies and clinical case formulations. To develop the best intervention strategy for a client, the clinician must acquire valid and useful data on the client, have a specific understanding of the client's problems and goals, identify causal relations, and frequently evaluate the effects of the intervention over time and across contexts.

In summary, a clinician's primary assessment task is to design an intervention that will have the greatest *magnitude of effect* for a client. This task is challenging because there are multiple behavior problems and intervention goals often presented by clients, multiple factors that can lead to and affect those behavior problems, multiple ways in which clients can differ in aspects of behavior problems and in their life contexts, multiple empirically supported intervention strategies available, and variation in treatment response even when the best available interventions are used. All of the decisions and assessment data collected within this complex decisional environment must then be integrated in a clinical case formulation that, in turn, can help the clinician design interventions that will yield the greatest potential benefit for the client.

Because of its central role in intervention decisions, the clinical case formulation is one of the most important products of preintervention assessment. The clinical case formulation is an integrated set of clinical judgments and hypotheses about the *functional relations*[4] among target behaviors and the variables affecting them. It reflects data and inferences from clinical assessment with the client and is also guided by empirical research in psychopathology and therapy. Essentially, the clinical case formulation guides the clinician in making the best intervention decision in a challenging clinical context. As we discuss later, the clinical case formulation has other goals, such as indicating areas where additional data are needed, communicating intervention rationales to clients and other professionals, and helping trainees clarify their clinical judgments about a client.

Although it is an important element in the assessment-intervention-evaluation process, the clinical case formulation is only one of many variables that affect intervention decisions. Some of these other important variables include: (a) time limitations of the clinician or client; (b) the cost of intervention; (c) the skills, theoretical orientation, and biases of the clinician; (d) the degree to which the proposed intervention is acceptable to the client, the client's family, or the service delivery agency (e.g., school, mental health center, hospital); (e) the policies within the service delivery agency (e.g., that may restrict or encourage the use of some types of interventions); and (f) the level of cooperation from important persons involved in the care of the client.

In summary, we discussed in this section the many difficult judgments a clinician must make in the assessment process that are essential elements of a clinical case formulation. Most important, the validity of a clinician's judgments about a client's behavior problem depends on the validity of the data obtained in clinical assessment. Inadequate assessment strategies or invalid clinical assessment data will diminish the validity of the case formulation and diminish the ultimate benefits of intervention for the client.

## THE ROLE OF CLINICAL CASE FORMULATION ACROSS INTERVENTION PARADIGMS

This book focuses on clinical case formulation in behavior therapy, but the clinical assessment principles we propose are applicable across

---

[4] A *functional relation* exists when two variables demonstrate shared variance: Some dimension (e.g., rate, magnitude, length, age) of one variable is associated with some dimension of another.

assessment and intervention paradigms. The most important feature of this approach is the advocacy of a science-based strategy of clinical assessment and clinical case formulation. Clinicians who do not follow a science-based "best practice" model for assessment and intervention place their clients at risk for less-than-optimal benefits. Broadly based scientific foundations of clinical assessment have been presented in Haynes, Smith, and Hunsley (2011) and diverse models of clinical case formulation, some science-based and some not, have been presented in edited books by Eells (2007), Sturmey (2009), and Tarrier (2006).

The presumed clinical utility of case formulations is based on the assumption that they help the clinician focus the intervention on modifiable causal variables and causal relations that exert the strongest effects on target behaviors. Because there are many potential target behaviors and intervention strategies in behavior therapy, the case formulation can also facilitate the selection of target behaviors and interventions that are likely to have the greatest probability of success and the greatest magnitude of effects.

Clinical case formulations are less important for intervention paradigms with a narrower array of intervention strategies. For example, if a clinician operates primarily from a client-centered humanistic framework, the intervention strategy (e.g., supportive and empathic listening, unconditional acceptance) is similar across clients. Although the focus of the therapy sessions will differ as a function of the unique issues raised by each client, the same intervention strategy will tend to be used for all clients, whether they are anxious, depressed, have an eating disorder, experience intrusive thoughts, or are confronted with marital conflicts.

### Box 1.1 Behavioral Assessment and the Client-Clinician Relationship

The client-clinician relationship is a central aspect of all behavioral assessments and behavioral interventions. A client's progress in assessment and treatment, or the benefits he or she receives, is diminished in the absence of a positive relationship between the clinician and the client, parent, staff person, teacher, or spouse. The goal of establishing and maintaining a positive client-clinician relationship is facilitated if the clinician uses Rogerian, person-centered principles and methods of clinical interactions during the assessment process (e.g., active and empathic listening to the client, respect for the client's values and goals, sensitivity to individual differences among clients).

The assessment data collected, the case formulation based on those data, and intervention outcome can be significantly affected by the interpersonal relationship between the clinician and client (see Howard, Turner, Olkin, & Mohr, 2006 for a treatment example). Rogerian, person-centered strategies can provide an excellent foundation for that relationship. Client dissatisfaction with the clinical assessment process or the clinician, regardless of how well the clinician attends to science-based assessment strategies, can affect the degree to which the client cooperates with the assessment process, feels understood and respected, provides valid information, and even agrees to continue with the assessment-intervention process. A Rogerian, person-centered orientation is also the basis of a collaborative approach to clinical assessment and is consistent with the emphasis in behavioral assessment on respect for individual differences. Carl Rogers forcefully articulated a client-centered approach to clinical interactions in his 1951 book *Client-Centered Therapy: Its Current Practice, Implications, and Theory*. See Leahy (2008) for additional discussion of the therapeutic relationship in behavior therapy.

Similarly, Gestalt-based therapies include a set of strategies that are designed to increase a client's awareness of his or her momentary thoughts and feelings, especially as they occur within the therapeutic relationship. The goal of the therapy, which is consistent across a range of presenting problems, is to identify and remove internal, historically generated "psychological blocks" so that the client can enhance his or her functioning in their current life context.[5]

---

[5] One focus of Gestalt therapy is similar to a method in behavioral assessment: The clinicians' monitoring of the client's reactions to discussion topics. In the behavioral interview process (see Chapter 7), the clinician attends to not only the content of the client's verbal responses, but paralinguistic cues such as facial expressions, verbal tone, and body movements that signal possible anxiety responses or avoidance associated with the topics being discussed (see Kohlenberg and Tsai (2007) for a discussion of these strategies in functional analytic psychotherapy).

Clinicians who use humanistic, client-centered, and Gestalt-based interventions are also less likely to conduct formal preintervention assessments. For example, many client-centered clinicians believe that preintervention assessment undermines the client-clinician relationship, results in invalid information, and impedes therapeutic progress. Consequently, clinicians using these approaches are not confronted with the need to formally integrate sometimes-conflicting information from multiple sources on multiple behavior problems and multiple causal variables and functional relations. Further, it is not necessary for them to match these complex arrays of data with the most appropriate interventions. During intervention sessions, they can react "in the moment" to issues raised by the client and to the dynamics of the client-clinical relationship (see Corsini & Wedding, 2010, for an overview of several systems of psychotherapy).

In contrast, a clinician operating within a behavioral paradigm more often relies on preintervention clinical assessment data and nomothetic research, integrated into a clinical case formulation, to select the best intervention foci and strategies for a particular client. Furthermore, a behavioral clinician is less likely to assume that an intervention focus and strategy will be equally effective across clients with the same behavior problems or diagnoses.

## CLINICAL CASE FORMULATION IN BEHAVIOR THERAPY

We have already emphasized that formidable challenges confront the behavioral clinician in deriving a clinical case formulation. For example, even a seemingly limited problem, such as difficulty initiating and maintaining sleep, can result from different combinations of multiple causal variables and can be differentially amenable to multiple intervention strategies. Sleeping difficulties can be affected by the client's sleeping environment (e.g., noise, temperature, bed, lighting, partner's movements), pain, circadian rhythm disruption, schedule of napping, medication use, alcohol and drug use, ruminative thoughts and worry when in bed, neuroendocrine and neurophysiologic factors, amount and timing of aerobic conditioning and exercise, diet and eating schedules, physical health problems, and conditional responses associated with the sleeping environment. Given the many potential causal relations associated with a client's insomnia, the clinician can select different intervention strategies, such as relaxation training, aerobic exercise, stimulus-control intervention, modification of medication use, gradual shifts in sleep-wake cycles, and addressing the stressors in the client's life, depending on the most important and modifiable causal variables for a client's sleeping problem (see Savard & Morin, 2002, for discussions about the causes, assessment, and treatment of insomnia).

Further complicating the case formulation tasks is the high likelihood that a client seeking help for a sleep disorder is apt to be concurrently experiencing other problems such as depressed mood, mood shifts, anxiety, panic episodes, nightmares, distress in his or her interpersonal relationships, negative life events, or substance use—all of which may affect sleep, be affected by sleep, and/or be affected by other causal variables. The fact that many clients have multiple interrelated behavior problems, with multiple interacting causal relations, points to the importance of clinical case formulation in organizing data and inferences and in helping the clinician select the intervention strategy that is most likely to benefit the client. Although we advocate for the importance and utility of clinical case formulation in intervention planning, we also understand that there are contexts in which it is not cost-beneficial. We discuss these costs and benefits next.

Within cognitive-behavior therapy, which is the most empirically based intervention paradigm, intervention strategies differ in the degree to which they are individualized across clients with the same behavior problem. In some behavioral intervention protocols, the intervention is similar for all clients with the same behavior problem or diagnosis. This would be illustrated by a 12-week, standardized intervention program for children with anxiety disorders that involved a set sequence of sessions involving gradual exposure, desensitization, and self-talk strategies.

However, in other circumstances, a behavioral intervention for a specified behavior problem can be based on a molar-level (i.e., less detailed or less specific) causal model and still differ across clients in their specific application. For example, interventions for many children with self-injurious behaviors can be similar in that they attempt to manipulate response contingencies or substitute more adaptive behaviors for the less adaptive behaviors. However, the interventions can also differ in their specific applications, depending on whether the behavior is considered to be maintained by positive reinforcement (such as attention) or by negative reinforcement (such as withdrawal from an unpleasant situation or termination of an aversive task). We refer the reader to Koegel, Valdez-Menchaca, Koegel, and Harrower (2001) for more details about the treatments for persons with autism syndrome behaviors.

## THE COSTS AND BENEFITS OF CLINICAL CASE FORMULATION

Although we discuss this issue in greater depth in later chapters, we note here that a clinical case formulation can require many hours on the part of the client and clinician. It is reasonable to ask whether the benefits to the client are worth the time and effort to develop a clinical case formulation. The answer to this question reflects the emphasis in behavioral assessment on the conditional nature of all assessment evidence: "It depends."

Recall that the main goal of the clinical case formulation is to increase the benefits of a clinical intervention. When an empirically supported intervention protocol has been shown to be effective for a substantial majority of clients who present with a specific disorder, the costs of developing an individualized case formulation and designing an individualized intervention for a client may outweigh the potential benefits. Alternatively, if no empirically supported intervention is available, the client presents with a complex array of behavior problems, or the empirically supported interventions have variable outcomes, the benefits of developing an individualized case formulation may outweigh the costs. (For further discussion of intervention research methods, designs, assessments, outcomes, and challenges, see Chambless & Ollendick, 2001; McKay, & Storch, 2009; Sturmey, 2009, Nezu & Nezu, 2008; Steele, Elkin, & Roberts, 2008; see also http://www.therapyadvisor.com.)

For example, Mitte (2005) conducted a meta-analysis of cognitive-behavior therapy (CBT) for generalized anxiety disorder. Using data from

65 intervention outcome studies, she determined that CBT was superior to no treatment control conditions (Hedges $g$ = .86 for anxiety measures, .76 for depression measures) and placebo therapy conditions (Hedges $g$ = .57 for anxiety measures, .52 for depression measures). These results suggest that CBT can be an effective intervention for anxiety symptoms and depression symptoms. Further, the favorable comparisons with placebo treatments suggest that it confers benefits that exceed common therapy factors. However, it is important to note that the large effect sizes observed in CBT versus no treatment control comparisons and the moderate effect sizes observed for the CBT versus placebo therapy comparisons also indicate that a sizable percentage of clients did not demonstrate a measurable improvement as a function of CBT (approximately 20% in the CBT versus no treatment comparisons and 30% in the CBT versus placebo comparisons). This variation in intervention outcomes suggests that additional causal factors are affecting the anxiety symptoms for some persons with GAD and that these causal factors are not being fully addressed in the standardized programs.

## ALTERNATIVE MODELS OF CLINICAL CASE FORMULATION IN COGNITIVE-BEHAVIOR THERAPY

Several models for behavioral clinical case formulation have been proposed. For an in-depth review of these models, we refer the reader to Haynes and O'Brien (2000) and Sturmey (2009). In this section we summarize the models articulated by Nezu and Nezu (2004), Persons (2008), and Linehan (1997). In subsequent chapters, we describe the functional analysis and the importance of scientifically based behavioral assessment strategies for all CBT models of case formulation.

### A Problem-Solving Approach to Case Formulation

Nezu and Nezu (2004) outlined a "problem solving" approach to clinical case formulation. From their perspective, the "problem" to be solved by the clinician is to determine what intervention strategy is likely to be the most effective for a client. The offered solution is to use a decisional algorithm similar to those used in problem-solving therapy.

Nezu and Nezu emphasize the important role the clinician plays in clinical case formulation as a problem-solver. They recognize that clinicians operate within different paradigms and that the beliefs, expectations, and values embedded within a given paradigm affect how the clinician approaches the clinical case formulation process. Clinicians also differ in their clinical problem-solving skills—their abilities to solve problems presented by a client. The key problem-solving skills identified by Nezu and Nezu include defining problems, generating possible solutions to problems, identifying the positive and negative outcomes associated with possible solutions, and implementing the solutions.

In Nezu and Nezu's case formulation paradigm, the best intervention strategy for a client is derived from three sequential clinical judgments (i.e., three specific problems to be addressed). Each is outlined below.

1.  *Determining what the main problems are and whether they are amenable to intervention.* In this initial component of case formulation, the clinician must translate the client's complaints into specific, measurable problems and intervention goals that can then be used for intervention planning. As we discuss further in the chapters on assessment (Chapters 7 to 10), this first step begins with the process of gathering information about the client's concerns using a "funnel approach"—beginning with a broadly focused assessment across many domains (e.g., home, work, and marital relation) of the client's life and gradually narrowing the assessment focus to more specific factors (e.g., what is happening at work that influences a client's depressed mood).

2.  *Analysis of the client's problems and determining intervention goals for the client.* Nezu and Nezu presume that there are multiple possible causal variables for a behavior problem, that the permutations of causal variables can differ across clients with the same disorder, and that there are reciprocal influences among multiple *response modes* (which they label a *general systems approach*). Thus, a major focus of this area of formulation is the identification of the factors that trigger or maintain the client's behavior problems.

In addition to the problem analysis noted earlier, and consistent with the functional analysis discussed later in subsequent chapters, this formulation step also is concerned with the identification of important outcomes for the client. These outcomes can be immediate, intermediate, or ultimate. Immediate and intermediate outcomes can also operate as causal variables for the client's main behavior problems.

3. *Determination of the best intervention strategy.* Decisions about the best intervention strategy are affected by the first two steps in the formulation and are also informed by research on the effects, cost-effectiveness, moderator variables (i.e., variables that can alter the intervention outcomes), and incremental validity and utility of potential intervention strategies. Here is where the clinician needs to integrate assessment data from various sources, which can often be contradictory, with the findings of empirical research. The goal of this integration is to increase the validity of clinical judgments in order to maximize intervention benefits.

Nezu and Nezu recommend that the clinical case formulations be summarized in a *Clinical Pathogenesis Map.* The Clinical Pathogenesis Map is similar to the Functional Analytic Clinical Case Diagrams presented in Chapter 3, in that both illustrate idiographic aspects of client behavior problems and the factors that affect them. Nezu and Nezu also recommend that the clinician generate a *Goal Attainment Map,* which identifies optimal strategies for reaching each clinical goal. The Clinical Pathogenesis Map and the Goal Attainment Map are evaluated and revised as intervention proceeds by examining the degree to which case formulation's predicted outcomes match the observed outcomes.

## Persons' Cognitive Behavioral Case Formulation

Persons (2008) presented a rationale and strategy for Cognitive Behavioral Case Formulation, which, like other models of behavioral case formulation, is designed to facilitate decisions about the best intervention strategy for an individual client. Cognitive Behavioral Case Formulations include the attributes of a client's behavior problems, the factors that may be affecting the behavior problems, and the functional relations among behavior problems and causal factors.

Given Persons' clinical focus on depression and anxiety disorders, CBCF is especially congruent with cognitive models of behavior problems, which emphasize the central importance of core beliefs and the life events that activate those core beliefs as causal factors of behavior problems. Thus, CBCFs can be used to help the clinician understand and explain a client's behavior problems and their relation to situations and events.

According to Persons, a CBCF should include the following seven components:

1. *Behavior problems list*: The clinician generates a specific list of the client's behavior problems.
2. *Core beliefs list*: A list of the client's beliefs about self and the world that may be related to the behavior problems. These core beliefs are considered the primary causal variables and can be suggested by a diagnosis, results from research, or clinical assessment (e.g., a "Thought Record" in which the client self-monitors the situation, behaviors, emotions, thoughts, and responses to the situation relevant to a problem behavior).
3. *Activating events and situations:* These are the external events (e.g., the presence of a teacher) that activate core beliefs (e.g., I'm a failure), which lead to the behavior problems (e.g., poor academic performance).
4. *Working hypotheses:* The clinician generates a model of the interrelations between the client's problems, core beliefs, and activating events.
5. *Other components:* The clinician also identifies and integrates: (a) the origins of core beliefs (the early learning history that explains the core beliefs), (b) the intervention plan, and (c) anticipated intervention obstacles.
6. *Treatment plan:* Although this component is not part of the Cognitive Behavioral Case Formulation, Person includes this component to demonstrate how the working hypothesis is central to treatment planning.

7. *Predicted obstacles to treatment:* Predictions are made, based on the information gathered, regarding problems that may surface during therapy.

The product of these seven components is a written clinical case formulation, designed to guide intervention decisions and intervention strategies. Examples of Cognitive Behavioral Case Formulations are provided in Persons and Davidson (2001).

## Dialectical Behavior Therapy Clinical Case Formulation

Linehan (Koerner & Linehan, 1997) outlined a model for the clinical case formulation that is compatible with Dialectical Behavior Therapy. Her clinical case formulation approach focuses on Borderline Personality Disorder but is applicable to other disorders as well. Linehan's case modeling approach integrates a biosocial and learning-based theory of the factors that affect the onset and maintenance of borderline personality disorder and includes behavior problems that are likely to be barriers to effective intervention. Dialectical Behavior Therapy Clinical Case Formulations emphasize the importance of the client's behavior problems in the context of the client's community. They include variables affecting the clinician and presume that the interactions among multiple factors affecting the client are dynamic (see Ebner-Priemer et al., 2007, for recent research on the high level of daily instability in Borderline Personality Disorder clients).

Several aspects of Dialectical Behavior Therapy Clinical Case Formulations emphasize the importance of using an idiographic approach to intervention design, including these seven steps.

1. *Borderline Personality Disorder can result from different permutations of causal factors.* Consistent with the multimodal concepts of causality discussed in Chapter 6, they stress the importance of biological vulnerability, high sensitivity to emotional stimuli, high emotional reactivity, and the *moderating effects* of the client's social environment. A moderator variable such as "an invalidating social environment" (e.g., when other persons teach the individual that their emotional responses are pathological) can help trigger or exacerbate dysfunctional emotional reactions to emotional stimuli.

2.  *It is important to identify functional relations relevant to the client's behavior problems.* The clinician and client identify chains of environmental events, thoughts, actions, emotional reactions, and responses by the client and others that precede and follow each problem behavior. This analysis of *causal chains* allows the clinician to identify multiple places where alternative responses by the client might be helpful.

3.  *Contexts are important.* The client's responses and capabilities are likely to vary across different settings and contexts. For example, emotional responses to environmental events may be stronger in the context of sleep deprivation or as a function of recent life stressors.

4.  *Some causal relations are bidirectional.* There can be reciprocal influences between the client's responses and environmental events. For example, a client with Borderline Personality Disorder might respond frantically to an intimate partner's withdrawal from the room during an argument, and the client's frantic behavior leads the partner to withdraw entirely from the home to escape the situation. Thus, the client plays an active role in shaping his or her contexts and the responses of other persons.

5.  *An important causal variable can be the client's insufficient skills in managing environmental challenges.* Among many Borderline Personality Disorder clients, these skills deficits may be a result of several factors such as: (a) a lack of learning key behaviors, (b) a history of reinforcement for dysfunctional behavior, (c) interference in the implementation of skilled responses due to heightened emotionality, and (d) inhibition of skill use by faulty beliefs.

6.  *The behavior problems of persons with Borderline Personality Disorder can interact, affect the process and outcome of therapy process, and affect decisions about the best strategy and focus of therapy.* Negative self-statements, inhibited grieving, avoidance of painful thoughts, an inability to control intense emotional reactions, and overly active or passive responses to life events are examples of important behavior problems that are observed among many persons with borderline personality disorder. These problems can, and

oftentimes do, interact. In some circumstances, the interactions among these behaviors can result in high-risk behaviors such as self-injury. They can also produce behavioral patterns that affect how the clinician and client interact during sessions. Finally, they can also affect clinical decision making in that the behaviors that are most urgent or severe will need to be prioritized in treatment.

7. *It is important to conduct task analyses relevant to the client's problems.* Basing judgments on the identification of causal chains for dysfunctional behaviors, the clinician and client construct situation-specific step-by-step sequences of behaviors necessary to acquire desired behavioral responses to environmental challenges.

Dialectical Behavior Therapy Clinical Case Formulations are summarized in a written format and flow chart (see an example of this on page 363 of Koerner & Linehan, 1997) that integrates data collected to highlight antecedents and precipitating events, specific thoughts, contexts, emotional stimuli, actions, causal mechanisms, their "links," primary target behaviors, and consequent events. Consistent with our discussion of the cost-benefits of clinical case formulation presented earlier, Linehan suggests that a standardized intervention program that addressed all components of the model would result in clinically meaningful benefits for many clients (acknowledging that many other factors contribute to intervention outcome). However, a standardized intervention program would not be as effective or cost-efficient as an individually tailored intervention program that included components that match the most significant behavior problems and associated causal variables for a particular client. For a discussion on the importance of matching intervention mechanisms and causal variables for a client, we refer the reader to Haynes, Kaholokula, and Nelson (1999).

## Common Features of Alternative Clinical Case Formulation Models

The models presented by Nezu and Nezu, Persons, and Linehan differ in terms of causal model assumptions and which elements of the clinical case formulation are emphasized. However, they have many commonalities and are similar in some ways to the functional analysis model of clinical case formulation we present in the next chapter. All the aforementioned models emphasize that:

- Preintervention assessment is critical for clinical case formulation. Further, all assert that the validity and utility of clinical case formulations depend on the quality of assessment data.
- Clinical case formulations are needed to develop the most effective intervention strategy for a client. An associated assumption here is that intervention effectiveness can be enhanced if the intervention targets modification of causal relations that exert significant effects on the client's problems and intervention goals.
- There are important individual differences in the attributes of clients' behavior problems.
- There are multiple interacting causes of behavior problems and individual differences in the organization and influence of such causal variables.
- Behavior problems and causal variables can be multimodal— involving emotions, thoughts, physiology, and actions.
- Careful specification of clients' behavior problems is crucial for a clinical case formulation.
- The clinician's attitudes and beliefs about preintervention assessment can affect assessment strategies and the data acquired in clinical assessment.
- There is utility in providing a written report or visual display of the clinical case formulation to organize and summarize inferences made based on the assessment data.

## INTRODUCTION TO BASIC CONCEPTS IN BEHAVIORAL ASSESSMENT

In Chapter 7 we discuss the principles and strategies of behavioral assessment in greater detail. In this section we introduce the basic concepts and principles of behavioral assessment to show how they advance the focus and goals of all models of behavioral case formulation, guide the measurement of treatment outcome and process, and are applicable to a wide array of settings, populations, and assessment goals.

## Applicability of Behavioral Assessment

We have emphasized the applicability of behavioral assessment concepts and strategies in behavioral case formulation. Because it includes an array of science-based assessment strategies, behavioral assessment can be used in many settings, such as mental/behavioral health clinics, hospitals, homes, school settings, and residential and workplace settings. Behavioral assessment can also be applied across many populations (e.g., infants, children, families, dyads, older and younger adults), and across DSM diagnostic categories. Compare the extensive applicability of behavioral assessment with the more restrictive applicability of projective, personality, cognitive, or neuropsychological assessment paradigms—most nonbehavioral assessment paradigms can provide valid and useful data, but in a much more limited array of assessment contexts.

Haynes and O'Brien (2000) and Haynes and Kaholokula (2007) outline the numerous research, educational, occupational, institutional, and program evaluation applications of behavioral assessment. Some of these include the following.

**Intervention Outcome Research**. Behavioral assessment has been used to measure: (a) immediate, intermediate, and ultimate intervention outcome and side-effects of intervention; (b) intervention process variables (e.g., intervention adherence and the client-clinician interactions); (c) moderators and mediators of intervention outcome; (d) the generalizability and transportability of an intervention; (e) temporal factors such as the time-course and maintenance of intervention effects; and (h) postintervention lapse and relapse and functionally related variables.

**Experimental Functional Analysis.** Because of its emphasis on the use of science-based assessment strategies, particularly behavioral observation, behavioral assessment is the primary measurement paradigm used in *experimental functional analyses*. The experimental functional analysis is rooted in the behavior analytic tradition and involves the systematic manipulation of environmental independent variables (e.g., attention from peers, task avoidance, or tangible rewards) in order to evaluate their effects on one or more behavior problems. The methodology is typically conducted using a well-controlled within-subject design. Perhaps the most common design in experimental functional analysis is the replication or reversal ABAB design, where phase A is the baseline condition and phase B is the introduction of a key independent variable (e.g., social attention). For a more detailed discussion of the experimental functional analysis, see Hanley, Iwata, and McCord (2003) and Lattal and Perone (1998).

**Psychopathology.** Psychopathology involves the study of behavior disorders and problems—in particular, the variables that affect their onset maintenance, duration, and severity. Because behavioral assessment emphasizes the use of specific, precise, science-based measures, it is especially useful in psychopathology research. For example, Blechert et al. (2010) tracked eye movements of persons diagnosed with anorexia nervosa and bulimia nervosa in order to investigate attentional bias to self-photos; they found a significant correlation between attentional biases and degree of body dissatisfaction for persons diagnosed with anorexia nervosa. Ditre et al. (2010) acquired observer measures of the smoking behavior of participants (e.g., from video recordings of latency to light a cigarette, number of puffs taken, and total time spent smoking) following a laboratory stressor (a cold-pressor test to elicit pain) in their investigation of a social-cognition causal model of the relations among pain, smoking motivation, smoking-related outcome expectancies, and pain coping behaviors. Trull and Ebner-Priemer (2009) edited a special section in *Psychological Assessment* on the use of ecological momentary assessment (EMA; real-time samples of participants' behavior in their natural environment; see Chapters 8 and 9) in the study of mood disorders and mood dysregulation, anxiety disorders, substance use disorders, and psychosis. Measurement methods consistent with a behavioral assessment paradigm (e.g., observation, self-monitoring, psychophysiological measurement, narrowly focused self- and other-report questionnaires) are included in almost all articles published in the premier journals of psychopathology, *The Journal of Abnormal Psychology* and *Journal of Abnormal Child Psychology*.

**The Differential Applicability of the Conceptual Elements of Behavioral Assessment.** The behavioral assessment paradigm offers guiding principles for clinical assessment. The paradigm suggests that examination of particular types of variables and functional relations, using particular measurement strategies and methods, will often result in valid and clinically useful case formulations, intervention selection, and intervention outcome evaluation.

The conceptual and methodological elements of the behavioral assessment paradigm have been widely applied, but differ in the degree to which they are useful across populations, behavior problems, and settings. For example, there is convincing evidence that social response contingencies, such as the immediate responses of parents and teachers to children's behavior, can significantly affect the rate of self-injurious behaviors of many individuals with developmental disabilities (e.g., Kahng et al., 2002). However, it is illogical to presume that response contingencies such as social attention are an important causal factor for all behavior problems or for all persons with the same behavior problem. Consider, for example, Iwata's research on the experimental functional analysis that indicated that 20–35% of clients with self-injurious behaviors are minimally influenced by manipulation of response contingencies, such as social attention (Iwata et al., 1994).

Of course, social response contingencies are often important causal factors for behavior problems and can be used to weaken maladaptive behaviors and to strengthen more positive alternative behaviors. The assessor's mandate is to use the conceptual elements of the behavioral assessment paradigm to guide the assessment focus. For example, when selecting assessment targets, it is important to presume that response contingencies (among other potential causal variables) *may* be an important causal variable for a client's behavior problems and goals. This presumption will guide the assessor toward a careful consideration of the potential role of response contingencies in a client's behavior problem that will frequently, but not invariably, lead to a more clinically useful behavioral case formulation. In Chapter 6, we consider in greater detail the types of causal variables and relations that have often been found useful in clinical assessment.

A frequent conceptual and methodological error, even among behavior therapists, is the adoption of a univariate or excessively narrow causal model of behavior problems. This error is exhibited in some clinicians who presume that a wide range of behavior problems can be accounted for by causal models that emphasize mostly response contingencies, cognitive processes, genetic predisposition, experiential avoidance, or interpersonal processes. Such a limited view of potential causal factors increases the risk that the clinician will fail to identify important causal factors during clinical assessment, thereby reducing the potential impact of intervention. As we discuss in Chapter 10 and as is outlined in many books on psychopathology, the clinician must be familiar with the multiple possible causal variables, causal paths, and causal mechanisms that can be relevant for a particular behavior problem and for a particular person.

**Differential Applicability of the Methods of Behavioral Assessment.** A similar caveat applies to the applicability of specific behavioral assessment methods. For example, behavioral observation in analog settings can be a powerful method of assessing social interactions of psychiatric inpatients, dyadic interactions of couples, and other adults with interpersonal difficulties (see review in Heyman, Smith Slep, 2004). However, analog observation may be less useful in the assessment of some persons who are experiencing problems with sleep, worry, or obsessive thoughts because such behaviors are difficult to observe in contrived settings.

We have emphasized that the multiple strategies, methods, and instruments of behavioral assessment paradigm are some of its strengths. However, as with behavioral concepts of causality, the clinical utility of each strategy, method, and instrument differs across behavior problems, assessment goals, populations, and settings. For example, the assessment of social response contingencies for a client's behavior problem might best be approached with analog observation (e.g., using an ABAB strategy) when the focus is on parent- or staff-child interactions of high-frequency behaviors such as communication behaviors, with a parent-report questionnaire when the focus is on parental responses to a child's headaches, and with self-monitoring when the focus is on how a client responds to his or her spouse during the course of a day. The decisions about the best assessment method depend on the characteristics of the client's behavior, assessment setting, goals of assessment, and available resources. The clinician must consider which assessment strategy will provide the most valid and useful data for a particular assessment goal.

The applicability and utility of individual methods of behavioral assessment can be affected by several variables:

- *Developmental level of the client.* For example, Ollendick and Hersen (1993) commented that cognitive abilities affect the applicability of self-monitoring with children; very young children may not be able to accurately track their behaviors.
- *Level of cognitive functioning.* Data from self-monitoring, interviewing, and questionnaire assessment methods can also be affected by a client's medication use, substance use, neurological impairment, attention abilities, and delusional intrusive thought processes.
- *Reactive effects of the assessment method.* When applied to some behavior problems, clients, or in some assessment settings, assessment instruments can affect the variables being measured or affect the behavior of others in the client's environment.
- *Availability of, and cooperation from, persons in the client's social environment.* Behavioral assessment methods often involve cooperation by the clients' spouse, teacher, supervising staff member, school and hospital administrator, or family members.
- *Characteristics of the target behaviors and causal variables.* We commented earlier that some behavior problems and causal variables are more amenable to measurement with some methods than with others. Important characteristics include: (a) whether the variable is currently occurring, (b) the frequency of the variable (e.g., is the frequency sufficiently high that a clinician could observe it), (c) the setting in which the variable occurs (e.g., home, school, social versus nonsocial contexts), and (d) the response mode (e.g., overt activity versus physiological event). For example, early traumatic life experiences can be a powerful causal variable for later behavior problems but can be assessed only through behavioral interviews or self-report inventories. Conversely, some important causal variables can be observed by others but not readily reported by a client. For example, a parent may not accurately recollect and/or report how he or she responds to the oppositional behavior of a teenager, although the responses are observable during an analog naturalistic observation.

- *Costs of an assessment method and resources of the assessor.* As we noted earlier in this chapter, some behavioral assessment methods, such as observation in the natural environment and ambulatory monitoring of psychophysiological responses, can be expensive. For example, the use of a few trained observers to collect data on family interactions in a client's home may require scores of hours for observer training, coding, and data analysis. The expense of some assessment methods may explain their more frequent use in well-funded clinical research settings than in less well-supported clinical settings. However, as we will discuss in Chapter 7, there are strategies to reduce the costs of acquiring data in a client's natural environment.
- *Constraints and contingencies on the assessor.* Sometimes assessment strategies and methods are dictated by contingencies and restrictions operating on the assessor. For example, a comprehensive behavioral case formulation of self-injurious behavior (e.g., to determine if the self-injurious behaviors are affected by social reinforcement, termination of demands, etc.) using systematic manipulation of possible functional variables in a clinic office is difficult in a clinic or school setting where the clinicians are allotted a limited amount of time with the clients or where such methods are not financially reimbursed.

## SUMMARY

The clinical case formulation is composed of many judgments, such as the identification of a client's behavior problems and intervention goals and the variables that affect them. Behavioral assessment is a multifaceted, scholarly, science-based conceptual and methodological paradigm designed to aid the clinician in gathering valid and useful assessment data. It is a *functional approach to psychological assessment* in that the best assessment strategy for any occasion depends on the goals of assessment and the characteristics of the client and his or her context.

The clinical assessment process and case formulation are often difficult because clients frequently present with multiple behavior problems and intervention goals, which can be complexly interrelated, with multiple interacting causal variables influencing each. Interventions based on case formulations can be beneficial because there are important differences among clients in the characteristics and causal relations relevant to their behavior problems and goals, and often there are multiple empirically supported interventions available. A clinician's ultimate task is to design an intervention that will have the greatest *magnitude of effect* for a client.

We focus on the functional analysis in this book but there are alternative models of clinical case formulation within the cognitive-behavioral paradigm. The models presented by Nezu and Nezu, Persons, and Linehan have common emphases: (a) the importance of clinical case formulation for intervention selection, (b) the importance of evidence-based clinical assessment strategies, (c) individual differences in the attributes of clients' behavior problems and intervention goals, (d) multivariate causality and the multiple attributes of causal variables and relations, (e) the role of the clinician's attitudes and beliefs about preintervention assessment, and (f) the importance of providing a record of the clinical case formulation.

We emphasize the applicability of behavioral assessment for intervention outcome evaluation, psychopathology, and experimental functional analysis. Because it is a methodologically diverse system, different methods and elements are differentially applicable across goals and across assessment contexts within those goals.

CHAPTER

# 2

—=◆◇◆=—

# Introduction to the Functional Analysis as a Paradigm for Behavioral Case Formulation

In this chapter we introduce the functional analysis as a paradigm for clinical case formulation in behavior therapy. First, we present a clinical case to serve as a basis for discussion of the functional analysis, *Functional Analytic Clinical Case Diagrams*, and the behavioral assessment methods used to acquire data for the functional analysis and evaluate the interventions based on it. Subsequent chapters discuss these topics in greater detail, including (a) how we use causal diagrams to illustrate the functional analysis, (b) the attributes, assets, and limitations of the functional analysis, (c) empirical and conceptual foundations of the functional analysis, (d) behavioral assessment strategies to develop the functional analysis, and (e) the importance of valid clinical assessment data in the construction of the functional analysis. Throughout these chapters we explain how the principles and methods of behavioral assessment are central to the construction of the functional analysis and also guide strategies for measuring the processes and outcomes of interventions and for conducting basic research on behavior disorders.

## DEFINITION OF FUNCTIONAL ANALYSIS

The functional analysis is defined as:

> The identification of important, controllable, causal, and noncausal functional relations applicable to specified behaviors for an individual. (Haynes & O'Brien, 1990; 2000)

Similar to the models for clinical case formulation that we present in Chapter 1, the functional analysis is the clinician's (a) hypothesized and *dynamic* working model of a client's behavior problems and goals, (b) the functional relations among the behavior problems, (c) the variables that affect and are affected by the client's behavior problems and goals, (d) the strength and form of causal and noncausal relations relevant to the client's behavior problems and intervention goals, and (e) important attributes and facets of all of these variables. The *Functional Analytic Clinical Case Diagram* is a *causal diagram* that visually illustrates the aforementioned components of the functional analysis. In elaborating on its definitions, we highlight here five important aspects of the functional analysis.

1. The functional analysis emphasizes *functional relations* between and among behavior problems and causal variables for an individual client. As we mention in Chapter 1, there are many interactions that typically occur among a set of behavior problems, causal variables, and goals for a particular client. These many *idiographic* functional relations can be causal or noncausal. However, *causal relations* are particularly important in the functional analysis because they are often targeted for change in behavioral interventions.

2. For considerations of parsimony and clinical utility, the functional analysis emphasizes *important* behavior problems, causal variables, and functional relations. By important, we are referring to (a) behavior problems that are identified by the client or clinician as being the most distressing and/or socially significant, (b) causal variables that are most relevant to the behavior problem, and (c)

causal relations that are presumed to have the strongest effects on a client's behavior problem.

3. The functional analysis emphasizes causal variables that are *controllable*. Many important causal variables associated with a behavior problem are important but cannot be modified (e.g., genetic factors, childhood abuse and neglect, neurological damage, or traumatic life experiences). As such, they are not targeted for change in typical behavioral interventions. However, the sequelae associated with these historical and/or unmodifiable causal variables may exert important contemporaneous (i.e., *proximal*) causal effects on current behavior (e.g., memories of trauma, conditioned emotional reactions, avoidance behaviors, and social skills deficits). Importantly, these contemporaneous causal effects are more apt to be modifiable and are therefore included in a functional analysis. Consequently, the original and/or unmodifiable causal variables are de-emphasized in the functional analysis. Alternatively, important causal variables that (a) are currently operating in the client's life *and* (b) can be changed, are emphasized in the functional analysis.

4. Functional analyses are *idiographic*. There are likely to be important differences in the functional analyses among clients with the same behavior problem or intervention goal. This idiographic emphasis stands in contrast to nomothetic models of behavior disorders that are derived from groups of people with similar behavior problems. Nomothetic models provide information about the expected or average relationships among variables (see Loehlin, 2004). Many manualized treatment programs are based on the outcome of nomothetic research.

Empirically supported nomothetic models of behavior disorders are an important part of clinical science and are applicable to the functional analyses. These models and the studies upon which they are based can help the clinician narrow his or her search for causal variables to a smaller array of possibilities for an individual client. Using Beck's model of depression as an example, Persons

(2005) noted how nomothetic models could serve as a guide for the development of idiographic functional analyses.

5.  The conceptual foundations of the functional analysis and the assessment methods for the construction of a functional analysis are broadly applicable across psychological assessment paradigms and within behavioral subparadigms. We emphasize empirically supported and clinically useful classes of variables and methods of behavioral assessment. However, the functional analysis is not restricted to a particular class of variables and assessment strategies. For example, functional relations can be estimated through experimental manipulation (e.g., presenting and withdrawing putative causal variables), multivariate time-series assessment strategies (e.g., measuring multiple variables repeatedly across time and examining their time-lagged correlations), ambulatory monitoring (e.g., measuring cardiovascular or physical activity throughout the day), and self-report methods (e.g., interviews and questionnaires that query about functional relations).

---

### Box 2.1 Contrasting Definitions of "Functional Analysis"

Haynes and O'Brien (1990) reviewed the various definitions of functional *analysis* and related terms, such as functional assessment and functional behavioral assessment. The term *functional analysis* has been defined in many different ways. It is used in rehabilitation and neuropsychology to refer to the evaluation of a client's functional capabilities (e.g., ability to work, exercise, and manage daily responsibilities). The term is also used in different ways in mathematics, ecology, dentistry, and other disciplines.

In psychology, the most common definition is associated with applied and experimental behavior analysis, derived from the work of B. F. Skinner, and refers to establishing a functional relation between the occurrence of a behavior and antecedent and/or consequent environmental events using systematic manipulation and direct observation.

Our definition of functional analysis is more broadly based and is closely associated with the mathematical concept of *the identification of functional relations* (the identification of shared variance between variables; see Chapter 1, footnote 4). Functional relations for a behavior can include multiple types of variables, such as environmental settings, antecedent stimuli, behavior consequences, diet, social contexts, cognitive processes, conditioned emotional responses, genetically based factors, neurophysiologic processes, and extended social systems, among many others. *Functional analysis*, as used in this book and in applied behavior analysis, emphasizes the importance of learning-based functional relations: Response contingencies are an important factor in functional relations, but in our use of the term, functional analyses often includes other events, processes, and contexts that demonstrate shared variance with the target behavior.

With a focus on a wider range of variables and functional relations, a broader set of assessment strategies are also applicable. In addition to ABAB or interrupted time-series designs, which are primarily used in applied and experimental behavior analysis, functional relations can also be estimated through multivariate time-series regression analyses, self-monitoring, real-time measurement in the natural environment, and a variety of self-report methods.

The following section presents a clinical case, Mrs. Sanchez, to illustrate the components, attributes, rationales, and assessment strategies and methods associated with behavioral assessment and the functional analysis.

## MRS. SANCHEZ: A CLINICAL CASE EXAMPLE OF THE FUNCTIONAL ANALYSIS AND FUNCTIONAL ANALYTIC CLINICAL CASE DIAGRAM, AND METHODS OF BEHAVIORAL ASSESSMENT

To illustrate the components, attributes, and assessment strategies and methods associated with the functional analysis, we present the clinical case of Mrs. Sanchez (adapted from Haynes, Yoshioka, Kloezeman, &

Bello, 2009). The case illustrates how the validity of a clinical case formulation depends on the validity of the measures upon which it is based and also reflects many judgments by the clinician. In the case description, we also explain the rationale for the assessment methods used to gather data for the functional analysis and the sensitivity of the behavioral assessment paradigm to dimensions of individual difference.

### Referral and Initial Assessment Session

Mrs. Lynda Sanchez, a married 38-year-old female immigrant from Malaga, Spain, was referred to an outpatient mental health clinic for a behavioral assessment after she failed to make significant progress in a standardized outpatient therapy program following a 10-day psychiatric hospitalization. She had been seeing a therapist weekly for 6 months and was admitted to the hospital after she expressed suicidal ideation to her husband and therapist on a number of occasions. The primary goals of the first assessment session were to specify Mrs. Sanchez's behavior problems, positive intervention goals, and to develop a preliminary functional analysis of her behavior problems.[1]

An important goal of all behavioral assessment sessions is to establish and maintain a positive relationship with the client (see Box 1.1 and Chapter 10 for an extended discussion of the clinician-client relationship). As we explained earlier, the clinician does this by discussing with clients the methods and purpose of all assessment strategies, by using client-centered interview methods such as open-ended questions, behavioral reflections, and empathic and supportive comments. The clinician also attempts to identify and address potential barriers to adherence with the assessment process (e.g., transportation problems, concerns about the potential negative consequences of the assessment and treatment process).

*Self-Reported Behavior Problems.* During the initial semistructured interview, Mrs. Sanchez reported feelings of sadness, excessive fatigue,

---

[1] Functional analyses often emphasize the reduction of behavior problems. However, functional analyses can also emphasize positive intervention goals such as increasing a child's positive social interactions with her peers, improving the quality of a couple's sexual intimacy, helping a client increase his artistic enjoyment and output, and assisting a client to identify important life values and ways to approach those values.

and sleepiness, increased appetite, and lack of energy during the previous several months. Mrs. Sanchez stated that her symptoms of depression had recently worsened and that she and her husband were having more marital conflicts. After episodes of marital conflict, which were occurring several times a week, Mrs. Sanchez would often feel severely depressed and isolate herself in her bedroom for several hours.

Mrs. Sanchez's depressed mood was characterized by feelings of guilt about her role as a mother and wife, sleep disturbances, worry about impending failure and stressors, and a decrease in physical activity. During her depressive episodes, she reported difficulty getting out of bed and would sometimes spend the entire day watching television, eating, and sleeping in her bedroom. On days when Mrs. Sanchez did leave the house and engage in her parental and household activities, she experienced a lessening in her depressive symptoms and feelings of guilt. Mrs. Sanchez also mentioned that she often felt more depressed in the evenings.

Four months prior to the initial visit, Mrs. Sanchez quit her job as a bilingual administrative assistant in an accounting firm due to an increase in her depressive symptoms. At work she had been feeling fatigued, had difficulty concentrating, and had begun to miss work 1 or 2 days every week. Mrs. Sanchez also reported difficulties attending to and caring for their 6-year-old son, Frank. Frank had missed a number of days of school (1 to 2 days per week) in the past several months because Mrs. Sanchez had been unable to get him ready for school in the mornings. Frank was becoming increasingly noncompliant and oppositional at home, often yelling at his mother, "not hearing," refusing her requests, and "throwing tantrums" nearly every day.

Mrs. Sanchez also reported being increasingly concerned with her husband's drinking. Many of the marital arguments and disagreements focused on the amount of money that Mr. Sanchez was spending on alcohol and how alcohol affected his behavior toward her and Frank. After these arguments, Mrs. Sanchez would often feel guilty and ruminate about her inability to be a good mother and wife. These ruminations and feelings of guilt became so severe that Mrs. Sanchez began to seriously entertain thoughts of suicide. As a result, she was subsequently admitted to an inpatient psychiatric facility and was discharged 8 weeks prior to this intake interview. After discharge from the hospital, Mrs. Sanchez had not experienced suicidal thoughts but her depressive symptoms had remained severe enough to significantly impair her functioning.

*Personal Intervention Goals.* Mrs. Sanchez's goals for therapy included feeling less depressed, having a more affectionate and positive communicative relationship with her husband, improving the quality of her sleep, experiencing more enjoyment in her daily activities (such as a more positive relationship with Frank, less dread of household chores, more recreational activities and time with friends, and more positive time with her husband), and being able to resume work outside the home. She also wanted to be more physically active by returning to her routine of jogging several times a week.

*Self-Report Questionnaires.* Information obtained from the initial interview is often used to plan additional assessment strategies. As we discuss in Chapter 7, clinical judgments are most likely to be valid when derived from multiple assessment methods (such as interviews, self-report questionnaires, self-monitoring, and behavioral observation), multiple instruments that target the same construct (such as more than one self-report questionnaire on depression), and when they attend to multiple response modes. Based on information from the initial interview, Mrs. Sanchez was asked to complete a number of self-report questionnaires at the end of the interview. The Beck Depression Inventory-II (Beck, Steer, & Brown, 1996) and Scale of Suicidal Ideation (Beck, Kovacs, & Weissman, 1979) were administered to quantify depressed mood and past suicidal behaviors. Mrs. Sanchez also completed the Marital Satisfaction Inventory–Revised (Snyder, 1997), the Dyadic Adjustment Scale (Hunsley, Best, Lefebvre, & Vito, 2001), and the Communication Patterns Questionnaire (Christensen, 1987) to assess marital satisfaction and marital communication styles.[2]

*Self-Monitoring.* Because clients will behave differently in different contexts and because the assessment process can have strong *reactive effects*,[3] the clinician cannot know the degree to which data obtained in a clinic setting are representative of the behavior of clients in their natural

---

[2] Haynes et al. (2011) discuss the rationale and psychometric foundations of multisource assessment.

[3] *Reactive effects* of assessment refer to the observation that the assessment process often affects targeted behaviors or the behavior of other persons in the client's environment.

environments. Therefore, it is beneficial to acquire information about the client's behavior in their natural environments. To capture behaviors in their natural environments, clinicians can use *self-monitoring diaries* and other *ambulatory assessment methods* (see Chapters 8 and 9).

Self-monitoring diary and ambulatory assessment methods have been used in several studies to provide real-time data on diurnal mood and emotions (Ebner-Priemer, 2007), marital interactions (Laurenceau, Barrett, & Rovine, 2005), and family interactions (Cummings, Goeke-Morey, Pap, & Dukewich, 2002). *Electronic diaries* utilize personal digital assistants (see review in Piasecki, Hufford, Solhan, & Trull, 2007), which are handheld computers used to monitor specific behaviors and events such as activities, mood, marital conflicts, drinking, social interactions, and environmental stressors. In this case study, Mrs. Sanchez was given a small handheld computer to record her moods several times throughout the day, as well as her sleep patterns each morning, and physical activity at the end of each day, over a period of one week.

There are several different strategies for recording behavior using self-monitoring. One strategy is *event-contingent recording*. In event recording, the client records behavior, thoughts, emotional states, and/or physiological symptoms whenever a particular event (e.g., problem behavior, causal variable) occurs. Since Mrs. Sanchez reported frequent marital conflicts, she was asked to answer a series of questions on the handheld computer about events, experiences, and feelings preceding and following these conflicts. In addition, Mrs. Sanchez was asked to wear an *actigraph* at night to measure nocturnal movements (Haynes & Yoshioka, 2007; Tryon, 2006) to supplement the self-report measures of her sleep patterns.

*Initiating Couple Assessment and Inspecting Records.* Because Mrs. Sanchez was concerned about her marital relationship and marital conflicts seemed to trigger or exacerbate some of her problems, Mrs. Sanchez was asked to have her husband accompany her to the second assessment session. The clinician also obtained written permission to access copies of her medical records from the psychiatric facility where she had received inpatient care and from her former outpatient clinical social worker for review prior to the second assessment session. Her medical records were sought to gather information about Mrs. Sanchez from additional sources.

Information from these records indicated a history of depression and suicide in her family but no identifiable medical problems. As is the case with many psychiatric records, they focused on describing her symptoms, providing a psychiatric diagnosis, but did not report on the functional relations associated with her behavior problems.

## Second Assessment Session

*Couple Assessment.* In the second session the following week, the clinician interviewed Mr. and Mrs. Sanchez together and then separately. The goals of the second assessment session were to (a) identify the couple's marital problems and their causes, (b) establish positive intervention goals for their marriage, (c) assess Mr. Sanchez's behavior problems and goals, and (d) continue to explore functional relations among Mrs. Sanchez's depression and the couple's individual behavior and marital problems.

Individual interviews were conducted in addition to the couple's conjoint interview because past research has suggested that conjoint interviews can reduce the validity of self-reports of "sensitive" issues such as sexual problems or domestic violence (see reviews of couple assessment strategies in Snyder, Heyman, & Haynes, 2007). In the conjoint interview, the couple was queried about the problems in their relationship, goals for their marriage, and commitment to maintaining the marriage. Additionally, the data obtained from Mrs. Sanchez's handheld computer were downloaded into the clinician's computer and the information collected on the couple's marital conflicts and Mrs. Sanchez's mood was reviewed with them.

The interview with the couple revealed that Mr. Sanchez had recently been consuming large quantities of alcohol (such as six to eight 12-ounce bottles of beer) every night. When drinking, Mr. Sanchez often (three to five times a week) became loudly critical of Mrs. Sanchez's role as mother and wife, and her lack of an income. A review of Mrs. Sanchez's diary of marital interactions revealed that the couple had experienced five marital conflicts over the previous week and, consistent with Mrs. Sanchez's report, that these marital conflicts often preceded a worsening in her mood and depressive behaviors. The conflicts were related to either Mr.

Sanchez's drinking or his complaints about Mrs. Sanchez's inability to maintain a clean house, prepare meals, and supervise their son.

Mr. Sanchez had also begun yelling at Frank on many occasions when he perceived him to be noncompliant or playing roughly around the house. Mrs. Sanchez feared that her husband's behavior towards Frank was becoming increasingly aggressive, although he had never hit Frank. Mr. Sanchez agreed that Frank had been displaying aggressive, inattentive, and oppositional behaviors at his elementary school and at home. His teachers had threatened to hold Frank back a grade due to his "lack of social readiness" and inability to complete his schoolwork.

*Analog Behavioral Observation of Couple Interaction.* As we discuss in Chapters 9 and 10, behavioral assessment strongly emphasizes the direct *observation* of behavior, and researchers as well as clinicians have often used observation methods to assess marital interaction (see Gottman & Notarius, 2000, and Snyder et al., 2008, for a review). Since Mr. and Mrs. Sanchez reported having frequent disagreements about problems in their relationship, the clinician conducted two 10-minute analog observations of Mr. and Mrs. Sanchez as they discussed their marital problems. The goals of these analog observation sessions were to identify specific communication strengths and problems that could be contributing to their relationship difficulties or could be relevant to improving their communication skills and relationship satisfaction (Heyman & Smith Slep, 2004).

The couple was first asked to role-play a situation in which Mr. Sanchez came home after he had stayed out late at night drinking. In the second analog situation, the couple was asked to discuss how to best handle Frank's behavior problems at school. While directly observing their role-play, the couple's interactions were coded using the Marital Interaction Coding System (Weiss & Summers, 1983). As indicated by Heyman, Eddy, Weiss, and Vivian (1995), the observation codes were collapsed into the following four categories: (1) hostility, (2) constructive problem discussion, (3) humor, and (4) responsibility discussion. During the analog observations Mr. and Mrs. Sanchez displayed high levels of hostility and low levels of constructive problem discussion, humor, and responsibility discussion.

*Marital and Child Behavior Problem Questionnaires.* While the individual interview sessions with one partner were conducted, the other partner completed self-report questionnaires. Since studies have found alcohol abuse to be related to the perpetration of marital violence (such as Murphy & O'Farrell, 1994), Mr. and Mrs. Sanchez were asked to independently complete the Conflict Tactics Scale 2 (Straus, Hamby, Boney-McCoy, & Sugarman, 1996) to measure events that may occur during their disagreements. Mr. Sanchez also completed the Dyadic Adjustment Scale, the Marital Satisfaction Inventory–Revised, and the Communication Patterns Questionnaire to gather more information about the couple's relationship. In addition, Mr. and Mrs. Sanchez each completed a parent report form of the Child Behavior Checklist (Achenbach & Rescorla, 2001) to provide their evaluation of Frank's behavior problems and a measure of social support (the Perceived Social Support Scale–Revised, Blumenthal et al., 1987).

*Interview with Mrs. Sanchez.* The clinician met with Mrs. Sanchez individually and interviewed her about her mood and feelings of guilt and the contexts in which they occurred during the previous week. Since Mrs. Sanchez scored in the severe range on the BDI-II and the mild–moderate range on the SSI, the clinician focused the interview on Mrs. Sanchez's depressive symptoms (e.g., thoughts, activities), the contexts in which her symptoms were most likely to occur, how she behaved during depressed and nondepressed states, and the possible mediator (e.g., self-deprecating thoughts) and moderators (e.g., Frank's presence, talking with her sisters in Spain) of changes in her mood.[4]

The data obtained from the handheld computer suggested that Mrs. Sanchez experienced some diurnal variability in her moods over the previous week. It showed that her mood ratings were significantly worse after 5 P.M. compared to the morning. Mrs. Sanchez was also queried about her sleeping patterns and physical activity. The sleep data obtained from the actigraph revealed that Mrs. Sanchez had an average sleep-onset latency of 68 minutes and an average total time in bed of 10.3 hours a night (a measure of sleep "efficiency"). The actigraph also revealed a distinct 2-hour period each afternoon (i.e., 2 P.M. to 4 P.M.) during which

---

[4] A *mediating variable* (*intervening variable*) explains the relations between other variables. It provides a causal link between other variables.

A *moderating variable* affects the form or strength of relation between two or more other variables (see Glossary in Haynes et al., 2011).

time Mrs. Sanchez stayed in bed and her activity level was very low. Mrs. Sanchez had very little physical activity over the previous week. Her diary data showed that there were 3 days of the week during which she did not leave the house and reported no participation in aerobic activity. Mrs. Sanchez was instructed to continue using the handheld computer diary and the actigraph.

*Interview with Mr. Sanchez.* During his individual interview, Mr. Sanchez, a 40-year-old male, also from Malaga, stated that he was recently under a great deal of stress and worked long hours managing the family's restaurant. A number of the restaurant's employees had been failing to show up for their work shifts. In response to these stressors, Mr. Sanchez had started staying out late after work and drinking with his friends. His drinking had been the source of a number of recent marital conflicts between the couple. He was given the Short Michigan Alcohol Screening Test (Selzer, Vinokur, & van Rooijen, 1975) to assess the severity of his drinking (he scored an 8, indicating a probable problem with alcohol). To obtain a measure of his daily drinking in his natural environment, Mr. Sanchez was given a handheld computer and instructed to record the number and type of alcoholic beverages that he consumed every day, his daily workload, and his stress level, to identify the settings and triggers associated with his drinking and marital conflicts.

*Information about Frank.* An important behavioral assessment strategy is to obtain information about an individual's behavior across *multiple settings and sources.* This reflects the facts that different informants have different experiences with a client; that a client's behavior problems and functional relations can vary in important ways across contexts; and that data from each source can reflect idiosyncratic errors and biases. Thus, in addition to obtaining information about Mr. and Mrs. Sanchez's son Frank through their responses to questionnaires and interviews, the clinician contacted Frank's teacher between the second and third sessions to obtain information about Frank's behavior in his school setting. During the telephone interview, Frank's teacher reported that over the past few months, Frank had been engaging in more aggressive, oppositional, and inattentive behaviors, which were having a negative effect on his performance at school and impairing his social relationships with other students. She stated that Frank would often (one or two times a day) push other children or try to take toys or school materials away from them. In addition, Frank frequently failed to complete his schoolwork and often did not follow classroom rules. As a result, Frank was often placed in "time-out," which had little effect on his behavior according to his teacher. Frank's teacher also pointed out that Frank had missed about 13 days of school over the past 2 months. His absences were having a negative effect on his schoolwork and she was considering having him repeat the first grade. The teacher agreed to ask her assistant to record Frank's aggressive behavior, on-task behavior, and positive and negative social interactions with peers every 2 hours for 1 week.[5] Frank's teacher also completed a Child Behavior Checklist regarding Frank's behavior at school.

On a weekly basis, beginning with the second assessment session, Mr. and Mrs. Sanchez each completed short-form questionnaires that were idiographically constructed using the most salient items from the previously administered questionnaires (marital satisfaction questionnaire for both, depression questionnaire for Mrs. Sanchez, and alcohol use questionnaire for Mr. Sanchez; see discussion of idiographic behavioral assessment in Haynes, Mumma, & Pinson, 2009). They were also asked to bring Frank with them to the next assessment session.

## Third Assessment Session

*Goals and Review of Data.* The goals of the third assessment session were to (a) continue to specify the form, sequences, and contexts of Mr. and Mrs. Sanchez's marital problems, (b) gather more data on Mr. and Mrs. Sanchez's individual behavior problems and goals, and to (c) specify the form and strength of functional relations relevant to Frank's behavior problems.

The results from the marital questionnaires that Mr. and Mrs. Sanchez completed during the previous sessions were reviewed with them. On the Marital Satisfaction Inventory–Revised, the couple scored high (indicating problems) in global distress, disagreement about finances, role orientation, and conflict over child-rearing. The couple scored low

---

[5] *Momentary time sampling* (Hartmann, Barrios, and Wood, 2004) is an observation procedure in which the observer notes the status of the target behavior at the end of preset intervals (such as once every 2 hours).

(indicating problems) on the affective communication, problem-solving communication, and time-together scales. The information obtained from the Communication Patterns Questionnaires indicated high levels of demanding, withdrawal, and avoidance communication patterns as perceived by the couple. The couples' perceptions of constructive communication and woman demand/man withdraw were low. Results of the CT2 showed that both Mr. and Mrs. Sanchez demonstrated high levels of psychological aggression. In contrast, both spouses endorsed a zero or low score (indicating no major problems) on the physical aggression, injury, and sexual coercion subscales of the CT2. Mr. and Mrs. Sanchez both scored in the distressed range on the four subscales of the DAS (cohesion, satisfaction, consensus, and affectional expression).

A review of Mr. and Mrs. Sanchez's diaries of marital interactions showed that the couple had experienced four marital conflicts during the previous week. All of the conflicts were related to Mr. Sanchez's coming home after drinking with friends. A worsening in Mrs. Sanchez's mood followed each episode of conflict. After the conflicts ended, Mrs. Sanchez would usually go to bed while Mr. Sanchez remained angry and would stay up late drinking more beer and watching television. The couple did not discuss these conflicts in the morning and were uncommunicative the following day. On the Perceived Social Support Scale-Revised, Mrs. Sanchez scored very low on measures of social support from family, friends, and significant others.

*Frank's Behavior Problems and Parent-Child Interactions.* As requested, Mr. and Mrs. Sanchez brought Frank to the third session with them. Many studies have found significant relations between the number and types of children's behavior problems and marital conflict between their parents (Cummings & Davies, 2002). Other research has found that parents' negative emotionality and negative conflict tactics are related to children's insecure emotional and behavioral responses (Cummings, Goeke-Morey, Pap, & Dukewich, 2002). Knowing this literature, the clinician reviewed the results of the Child Behavior Checklists that Mr. Sanchez, Mrs. Sanchez, and Frank's teacher had completed to provide an estimate of the rate and severity of Frank's behavior problems at home and at school. Mr. and Mrs. Sanchez both rated Frank in the clinical range on attention problems. Frank's teacher reported that Frank's behavior at school was in the clinical range on attention problems, social problems, delinquency, and aggression.

The couple was then queried about the functional relations between Mr. Sanchez's drinking and depression, the couple's marital problems, and Frank's behavior problems. The clinician inquired about the situations and contexts in which Frank was more and less likely to exhibit his behavior problems (that is, the clinician gathered data on the *conditional probabilities* of behavior problems to obtain important information about possible causal relations), how they responded to his positive and negative behaviors, and their attributions (e.g., blaming the other) about his oppositional and inattention behaviors.

Mrs. Sanchez attributed Frank's behavior problems at school to Mr. Sanchez's drinking and the family's financial instability, while Mr. Sanchez thought that Frank's problems were a reaction to Mrs. Sanchez's lack of attention and consistent discipline during her depressive episodes. Both stated that Frank would often lock himself in his room or throw his toys after being yelled at by Mr. Sanchez. The couple would usually leave Frank alone after these episodes, which often occurred in the middle of their own marital conflicts.

*Analog Behavior Observations of Parent-Child Interactions.* Analog observations have been used as a method to assess child behavior problems (Mori & Armendariz, 2001) and parent-child interaction (Roberts, 2001) in clinic settings. Given the concerns about Frank's behavior problems, the clinician wanted to observe Frank's behavior and his interactions with his parents. Therefore, during the third session the clinician conducted analog observations of Frank's attention to academic tasks and aggressive behavior during interactions with his parents. The first clinic analog observation involved placing Frank in a simulated academic setting (i.e., desk, workbook materials) and asking him to complete schoolwork for 10 minutes. Frank's behavior was coded for on-task and off-task behavior. Results from the first analog observation indicated that Frank was on-task for 25% of the observation period.

The second analog observation involved child-directed play and a "chore" situation in which Mr. and Mrs. Sanchez were asked to first play a game of Frank's choosing for 10 minutes and then to instruct Frank to put the toys away in a toy box. The clinician observed Frank and his parents to gather qualitative data on Frank's behavior and parent-child interactions (e.g., how Frank's parents responded to his positive and noncompliant behaviors). Frank's behavior was coded for compliance and aggressive behavior. Frank was compliant with 40% of his parents' requests and demonstrated one act of aggressive behavior in which he threw a toy across the room (the parents did not respond when he threw the toy). During the "play" situation, the parents made no positive comments and engaged in no positive physical contact with Frank.

*Additional Assessments and Feedback.* The clinician again met individually with Mr. and Mrs. Sanchez. Self-monitoring logs and ambulatory assessment data were independently reviewed with Mr. and Mrs. Sanchez. The sleep data obtained from the actigraph and self-monitoring revealed that during the previous week Mrs. Sanchez had an average sleep-onset latency of 65 minutes and an average total "in bed" time of 10.1 hours a night, with frequent (6–15) awakenings during the night (i.e., a low "sleep efficiency" score). These sleep patterns were not meaningfully different than her sleep patterns during the previous week. Also, there were no significant changes in Mrs. Sanchez's activity level from the previous week.

Since Mr. Sanchez had scored in the high range on the Short Michigan Alcohol Screening Test, the clinician focused this interview on Mr. Sanchez's alcohol drinking and the stressors he was experiencing at work. According to the data obtained from Mr. Sanchez's handheld computer, he had consumed four to nine bottles of beer per night during the previous week. Review of his daily workload and stress level recorded on the handheld computer indicated that Mr. Sanchez drank less (i.e., an average of five beers) on days when his stress levels were lower than on days when his stress levels were higher. All of the nights when the couple experienced marital conflicts were nights when Mr. Sanchez had reported higher levels of stress at work and consumed a large quantity (more than eight beers) of alcohol prior to returning home from work.

The couple was instructed to continue handheld computer diary recordings of their marital conflicts, Mrs. Sanchez's mood, and Mr. Sanchez's drinking; and Mrs. Sanchez was instructed to continue to wear the actigraph. Mr. and Mrs. Sanchez were also asked to provide a daily behavior rating on their handheld computers of Frank's aggressive and noncompliant behaviors during the upcoming week.

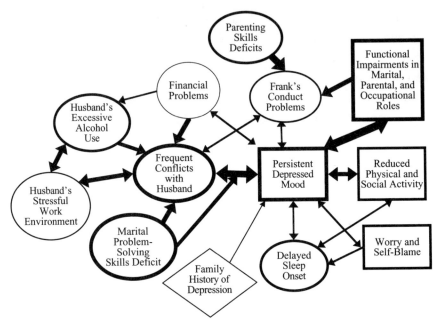

**Figure 2.1** FACCD of Mrs. Sanchez and her family that illustrates several behavior problems with different levels of importance, their functional relations, multiple causal variables with different degrees of modifiability, and functional relations between causal variables and behavior problems.

*Source: Adapted from Haynes et al., 2009.*

At the end of the third assessment session, the clinician presented a preliminary case formulation in the form of a Functional Analytic Clinical Case Diagram (FACCD) (see Figure 2.1). The goals of this presentation were to solicit feedback about the behavior problems and their causes summarized in the functional analysis, to assess commitment for therapy, and to secure informed consent about the focus and methods of intervention.

## BRIEF FUNCTIONAL ANALYSIS CASE FORMULATION AND FUNCTIONAL ANALYTIC CLINICAL CASE DIAGRAM

The functional analysis for Mrs. Sanchez, in the form of a *Functional Analytic Clinical Case Diagram*, is illustrated in Figure 2.1 and its legend is explained in Figure 2.2. In this section, we briefly discuss elements and

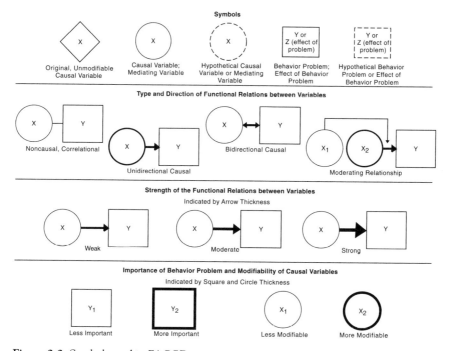

**Figure 2.2** Symbols used in FACCDs.

underlying concepts of the functional analysis and address them in more depth in subsequent chapters.

The Functional Analytic Clinical Case Diagram in Figure 2.1 depicts a *higher-order case formulation* (see Haynes & O'Brien, 2000, for more on levels of specificity in functional analysis). It is considered "higher-order" because each causal variable, behavior problem, and functional relation can be broken down to more specific elements for the purpose of developing more focused intervention strategies. Figure 2.2 identifies the symbols used in the Functional Analytic Clinical Case Diagram, which we discuss in depth in Chapter 11.

To summarize some elements of the functional analysis, Mrs. Sanchez was experiencing multiple problems, including depressed mood, decreased levels of physical activity, worry, and feelings of guilt (represented in the square boxes in Figure 2.2). In addition, her depressed mood was affected by distressing interactions with her husband and son and vice versa.

The frequent arguments with Mr. Sanchez often led to a worsening of Mrs. Sanchez's depressed mood, which then led to increased conflicts among her, her husband, and their son. Deficits in marital problem-solving skills, financial stressors, and her husband's work stress and alcohol intake were also contributing factors to Mrs. Sanchez's depressed mood.

During periods when Mr. Sanchez was consuming large amounts of alcohol, partially in response to work and family stressors, the financial status of the family further eroded, leading to increases in the rate of the couple's arguments and level of marital distress. Frank's increasing levels of aggressive and oppositional behaviors were affected by his parent's poor behavior management skills. For example, they paid little attention to his positive and negative behaviors and were inconsistent in their responses.

We noted earlier that past research has found that increased levels of marital discord can have a negative effect on a child's adjustment (see Cummings & Davies, 2002, for a review). These findings are consistent with the clinician's hypothesis that the couple's relationship distress might be contributing to their son's behavior problems. Additionally, one study on mediators and moderators in the relationship between a parent's problem drinking and their child's adjustment found that maternal depressive symptoms partially mediated the relationship between parental drinking and child social problems (El-Sheikh & Flanagan, 2001). Alcohol use has also been found to be associated with severe marital distress and higher levels of male aggression (e.g., Halford & Osgarby, 1993). These studies have demonstrated the bidirectional relations among paternal problem drinking, marital conflict, maternal depressive symptoms, and child behavior problems, and point to the potential benefits of behavioral marital and family therapy.

Based on the preliminary case formulation, the clinician and Mr. and Mrs. Sanchez agreed on individual and family behavioral intervention plans. Mrs. Sanchez agreed to continue with her individual cognitive behavioral treatment for depression, with an emphasis on addressing her negative self-attributions and increasing her prosocial behaviors, communication skills, and problem-solving abilities. After discussion and review of the treatment options available for him, Mr. Sanchez decided to join a substance abuse program to reduce his alcohol consumption. Mr. and Mrs. Sanchez agreed to continue with their daily self-monitoring logs. The couple decided to begin attending behavioral marriage counseling to address the problems in their relationship. The couple also agreed to eventually find a family psychologist to help them reduce Frank's behavior problems and enhance the positive aspects of their family relationships.

## AN OVERVIEW OF THE COMPONENTS OF THE FUNCTIONAL ANALYSIS AND FUNCTIONAL ANALYTIC CLINICAL CASE DIAGRAM

The functional analysis and Functional Analytic Clinical Case Diagram of Mrs. Sanchez illustrate several components of the functional analysis. We discuss these and additional components in Chapter 11, but introduce them here. We start by emphasizing that all components contribute to the main goal of the functional analysis, which is to estimate the *relative magnitude of effect*[6] of various causal factors on the client's behavior problems or intervention goal attainment. Further, there is an emphasis on estimating the extent to which modifying a given causal variable would exert a positive impact on a behavior problem or intervention goal.

The functional analysis, illustrated by the FACCD, includes the following 17 components.

1. *The client's behavior problems and/or intervention goals.* The ultimate focus of the functional analysis is on the major behavior problems or intervention goals of the client. In the case of Mrs. Sanchez, several problems and goals were identified: Her "Depressed Mood" was most notable, and depressed mood is also associated with several other problems and goals. As we will discuss later, it is often helpful to characterize behavior problems in a functional analysis in terms of *response modes* and *dimensions*[7]

---

[6] In this context, *magnitude of effect* refers to the strength of a causal relation between two variables—the degree to which change in a causal variable is associated with change in the behavior problem or another variable.

[7] A *dimension* is a quantifiable attribute of a variable, such as its rate, severity, duration, cyclicity, and latency.

(such as rate, severity; note "persistent" depressed mood for Mrs. Sanchez), which can sometimes be affected differently by causal variables.

2. *The relative importance of the client's behavior problems and goals.* Consider the difference in Figure 2.1 between the importance of "Depressed Mood" and "Decreased Social Activity." Most clients have multiple behavior problems, which often differ in importance. As we discuss in Chapters 4 and 7, the relative importance of a behavior problem can reflect risk to the client or others, the degree of personal distress experienced by the client or others, or the extent to which it interferes with effective functioning in important life domains (e.g., interpersonal relationships, family relationships, work, academic performance, etc.).

3. *The form of functional relations among a client's behavior problems.* The functional relations among a client's behavior problems have many attributes. Behavior problems can be unrelated or related. The functional relation, if it exists, can be causal or noncausal. Their valence can vary (i.e., a positive or inverse relationship). Finally, functional relations can be unidirectional or bidirectional. As we discuss in subsequent chapters, *bidirectional causal relations* are particularly important for intervention targets because changes in one variable can lead to reciprocal changes in the other variable. And, under certain conditions, such reciprocal relations can promote changes across time.

4. *The strength of functional relations among behavior problems.* Strength reflects the estimated magnitude of effect or, in this case, the degree to which change in one behavior is associated with change in another.

5. *The effects of a client's behavior problems.* Many behavior problems have important *sequelae*.[8] Specifically, a behavior problem can have adverse consequences for occupational, social, legal, medical, or family aspects of the client's life or the lives of

---

[8] *Sequelae* in this sense are problems or events that occur as a consequence of a behavior problem. As a medical term, it refers to medical conditions that arise from a disease or injury.

others. Additionally, a given behavior problem can lead to other behavior problems. The effects of behavior problems are important components of a functional analysis because they influence the estimated magnitude of effect of a particular intervention focus. For example, a child's physical aggression can harm peers and siblings, increase marital distress between his or her parents, increase the child's social isolation, interfere with academic performance, and lead to dismissal from school. Any intervention that reduces the child's physical aggression could also produce improvements in these other areas of functioning.

6. *Causal variables.* An important focus of the functional analysis is the identification of important causal variables for a client's behavior problems. There are many classes of causal variables, as we discuss in Chapter 6, but the functional analysis emphasizes contiguous antecedent behaviors, environmental events, situations, contexts, response contingencies (which can be external or experiential), and cognitive antecedent and consequent variables. The emphasis on these variables is based on research that indicates they can exert important triggering or maintaining effects on behavior problems.

7. *The modifiability (clinical utility) of causal variables.* Causal variables differ in the degree to which they are amenable to modification in an intervention program. Sometimes, important causal variables are not readily modifiable. Therefore intervention efforts directed at them would be less effective or cost-beneficial for the client than focusing on more modifiable variables.

8–9. *The form and strength of functional relation between causal variables and behavior problems.* Similar to relations that occur among behavior problems, the relations between causal variables and behavior problems vary in strength, valence, and directionality.

10–11. *The form and strength of functional relations among causal variables.* As is the case between causal variables and behavior problems, causal variables can affect each other in terms of strength, valence, and directionality.

12–15. *Additional types of causal variables and relations.* Causal variables can act as moderators or mediators. *Moderator variables* affect the strength or direction of relation between two other variables. *Mediator variables* explain "how" or "through what means" a causal variable affects a behavior problem. Causal variables (as well as behavior problems) can also be hypothesized. *Hypothetical causal variables* are potential causal variables that are inferred, but unmeasured. They can be targeted for future measurement or suggested by the results from nomothetic research. *Interactive causal relations* suggest that the magnitude of effect of each variable depends on its interactions with other causal variables. Interactive causal relations illustrate how causal relations can be synergistic.

16. *Chains of causal variables.* Behavior problems are often the end point of (or imbedded in, or downstream of) chains of causal variables and other behavior problems. Chains can include environmental events and client behaviors. Chains are important elements of the functional analysis because they can point to several possible intervention points.

17. *Direction of functional relations.* Two variables can be positively or negatively related. When positively related, increases in one variable are associated with increases in the other. When negatively related, increases in one variable are associated with decreases in the other. Similarly, moderating variables can have a positive or negative effect on the functional relation between two variables. An example of a negative relation would be when an increase in emotional support from friends (the moderator variable) leads to a decrease in the strength of relation between marital conflict and depressed mood.

## ADDITIONAL CHARACTERISTICS OF THE FUNCTIONAL ANALYSIS

With the case of Mrs. Sanchez, we introduced concepts of the functional analysis, illustrated strategies and methods of behavioral assessment used to develop the functional analysis, and showed how the functional analysis can be illustrated with a Functional Analytic Clinical Case Diagram.

In Chapter 11 we expand upon this introduction and discuss other important attributes of the functional analysis. Here, we briefly mention eight of these attributes:

1. The functional analysis always includes measurement and judgment errors and is *hypothesized* and *tentative*. This is the case because of limitations in our ability to measure causal variables, behavior problems, and functional relations and limitations imposed by the cognitive abilities and biases of clinicians (in Chapter 7 we discuss errors in clinical judgments).

2. The functional analysis is *nonexclusionary*. A valid functional analysis does not preclude other valid functional analyses for the same client's behavior problems. For example, a strong functional relation between a client's work stress and management of type 2 diabetes does not exclude the possibility of a strong functional relation between marital conflict and management of type 2 diabetes, or equally valid functional analyses that emphasize cognitive, neurophysiological, or behavioral skills variable sets.

3. The functional analysis is *dynamic*. Because its many elements and relations among elements can change over time (as a result of additional assessment data or true changes in client behavior or causal relations), the functional analysis can change over time.

4. A functional analysis can have *limited domains of validity*. Its validity may be limited by factors such as setting (home versus work), psychological state or developmental stage of the client, and dimensions of behavior problems (e.g., valid for the onset but not the severity of panic episodes). Haynes et al. (2011) discuss further the conditional nature of psychometric evidence and clinical judgments.

5. Functional analyses can differ in their *level of specificity*. A functional analysis and FACCD can range in specificity from higher-order, more molar, variables (e.g., anxiety, marital distress) to lower-order variables (e.g., hypervigilance, hypersomnia, deficits in ability to communicate feelings) depending on how the functional analysis will be used. Higher-level functional analyses are most often useful for selecting initial treatment targets while

lower-level (more specific) functional analyses are more helpful for designing specific intervention strategies.

6. The functional analysis integrates findings from *nomothetic research* and *idiographic clinical assessment* of the client.

7. A functional analysis can include *extended social systems*. Important sources of variance in a client's behavior problems and the achievement of intervention goals can be associated with the behaviors of other people and in distal variables. For example, a client's chain of causal variables affecting a behavior problem can be affected by factors that affect the behavior of a teacher, psychiatric aide, or spouse as well as by a life stressor and workplace and hospital policies.

8. The functional analysis is congruent with and amenable to a goal-oriented *constructional approach* to assessment as well as to an approach that emphasizes intervention with a client's behavior problems.

## SUMMARY

The functional analysis is one model of clinical case formulation and overlaps in goals with other models of behavioral clinical case formulation. The functional analysis is defined as "the identification of important, controllable, causal and noncausal functional relations applicable to specified behaviors for an individual." The functional analysis emphasizes important, controllable, causal relations relevant to a client's behavior problems and intervention goals. It is a clinical case formulation whose validity and utility is strengthened by multiple methods of science-based assessment strategies and the integration of nomothetic research.

There are several components of the functional analysis: (a) the client's behavior problems and/or intervention goals and their relative importance, sequelae, and interrelations; (b) the importance, modifiability, and interrelations among contiguous social/environmental antecedent and consequent causal variables; and (c) the actions of moderator, mediator, and hypothetical variables and causal chains.

The functional analysis includes different types of functional relations and is a "best estimate" derived from multiple clinical judgments by the clinician. A valid functional analysis does not preclude the possibility of other valid functional analyses. It can also change over time, be expressed at different levels of specificity, and have limited domains of validity. A functional analysis is an integration of nomothetic and idiographic data and can also include extended social systems. It is congruent with and amenable to a goal-oriented, constructional approach to assessment.

The Functional Analytic Clinical Case Diagram is a causal diagram that illustrates all components of the functional analysis. It can be a cost-beneficial method of facilitating treatment decisions with complex cases, communicating a functional analysis to others, and teaching clinical assessment and clinical judgment skills.

# 3

# Illustrating the Functional Analysis With Functional Analytic Clinical Case Diagrams

## INTRODUCTION TO THE FUNCTIONAL ANALYTIC CLINICAL CASE DIAGRAM

In the first chapter, we introduce the case formulation challenges faced by clinicians that arise from the large number of clinical judgments that must be integrated and the multiple sources of error in the process of arriving at those judgments. In Chapter 2, we introduce the concepts and goals of the functional analysis as a clinical case formulation paradigm. We emphasized that a primary goal of the functional analysis is to facilitate the identification of important, modifiable causal variables relevant to a client's behavior problems and the attainment of his or her intervention goals. In turn, the clinician can use this information to select intervention targets with the greatest potential benefit or magnitude of effect for the client.

Because of the complexities inherent to the clinical assessment and judgment processes, it can be difficult for the clinician to effectively and efficiently organize assessment data. It is also difficult to clearly communicate clinical case formulations to clients and other professionals. The traditional method of describing a case formulation is through a written text, usually in the form of lengthy social, psychiatric, educational, and occupational history narratives. However, written case descriptions can be long and often contain information that may be interesting, but is mostly irrelevant to the clinical case formulation. Visual presentations of case formulations convey information in an alternative format and can communicate complex information more effectively and efficiently. A series of books by Edward Tufte, titled *Visual Explanation* and *Visual Display of Quantitative Information*, provide excellent overviews of the benefits and problems associated with the visual presentation of concepts, relations, and data.

In this chapter, we describe how a form of visual case formulations, which we label Functional Analytic Clinical Case Diagrams (FACCD), can be an efficient and effective way of organizing and describing a functional analysis. We present the elements of the FACCD, first illustrated in Figure 2.1. We also discuss the benefits and limitations of an FACCD.

## INTRODUCTION TO CAUSAL DIAGRAMS

Causal diagrams (also called *graphical diagrams, directed graphs, path diagrams*, and *path analysis*) are visual summaries of causal relations relevant to a particular phenomenon.[1] As such, they graphically depict a phenomenon and the factors associated with it. Causal diagrams have become a common way to present complex data in many disciplines. They have been used to explain and predict crop yields (as a function of amount of pesticide use or rainfall), hurricane rate and severity (as a function of ocean temperatures and currents), death rates (as a function of malnutrition or disease), infection rates (such as a function of sexual activity or hygiene conditions), and economic output (as a function of government fiscal policies). Judea Pearl (Pearl, 2000) provides an excellent review of the use of causal diagrams, along with concepts of causality, in several disciplines. Figures 3.1 and 3.2 illustrate causal diagrams from two different disciplines. Note the amount of information that is efficiently displayed in

---

[1] A *causal model* is a generalizable, simplified, and hypothetical description of a complex phenomenon, usually involving multiple inputs (causes) and outputs (effects) and their interrelations.

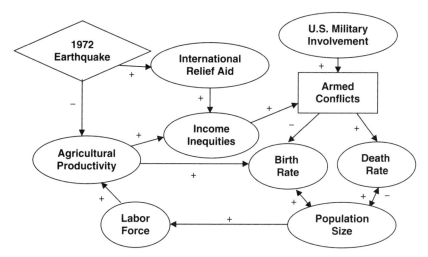

**Figure 3.1** A causal diagram for armed conflict in Nicaragua in the l980s.

*Source: Adapted from www.americanedu/TED/ice/Nicaragua/htm.*

each diagram and the amount of text that would be required to describe elements of the diagram.

The Functional Analytic Clinical Case Diagram is a form of causal diagram that visually represents a functional analysis of a client's behavior

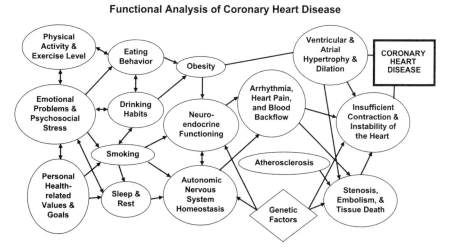

**Figure 3.2** A causal diagram for coronary heart disease.

*Source: Adapted from Tampere Hypertension Study; M. T. Tuomisto & R. Lappalainen, personal communication.*

problems and intervention goals. All causal diagrams have several central elements: (a) input variables, (b) output variables, and (c) connections among variables.

As Figures 2.1 and 2.2 illustrate, input, output, and their connections are depicted in an FACCD. Input variables are typically conceptualized as the causal variables associated with a client's behavior problems. Output variables are those whose values vary as a function of changes in the input variables. In functional analysis, the output variables are usually the likelihood, frequency, duration, and intensity (i.e., the "dimensions") of a client's behavior problems. They can also include the effects of the behavior problems on other behaviors. At times, it can be difficult to distinguish or disambiguate input and output variables (or causal variables and behavior problems). This is particularly true when bidirectional relations are involved.

The lines and arrows of a causal diagram depict the form and strength of relations among input and output variables. Thus, an input variable for a client who is having trouble falling asleep at night could be physiological arousal associated with presleep ruminative thoughts (e.g., worry about daily stressful events). The connection between physiological arousal and the latency to sleep onset could be unidirectional or bidirectional. Input and output variables and their connections could also be weak, moderate, or strong depending on the operation of other variables that affect the client's sleep-onset, such as alcohol use, diet, exercise, health problems, and room environment. We illustrate how the strength of a functional relation between variables can be depicted by the thickness of the line that connects them in Figure 2.1, provided a legend in Figure 2.2, and further illustrate this relationship in Figure 3.4. We illustrate in Figure 3.3 how the input (causal) and output variables (behavior problems) can also be depicted by the boldness of its symbol (i.e., diamond, circle, or square shapes).

As we note in Chapter 2 and discuss further at the end of this chapter, the FACCD can help the clinician organize and communicate his or her clinical judgments and assists in testing the validity, utility, and limits of the functional analysis. Most important, the FACCD allows the clinician to estimate the relative effects of interventions that can be focused on different causal variables and connections. Specifically, within an FACCD, the clinician can estimate the extent to which an intervention targeting one hypothesized causal variable exerts an effect on a problem behavior relative to the effects of intervening with other hypothesized causal variables.

## ILLUSTRATING THE ELEMENTS OF A FUNCTIONAL ANALYSIS IN A FUNCTIONAL ANALYTIC CLINICAL CASE DIAGRAM

The following schematic diagrams illustrate how the FACCD depicts important information about the functional analysis. We discuss elements and principles of the functional analysis and FACCDs (such as multiple behavior problems, causal relations, and moderator variables) in greater detail in subsequent chapters. Note how all 18 elements of the FACCD contribute to the main goal of the functional analysis, which is to estimate the relative magnitude of effect of focusing intervention efforts on each causal variable identified in the functional analysis.

### Elements of Causal Diagrams in the FACCD

1. *Multiple behavior problems.* Recall that most clients who seek behavioral health services present with more than one behavior problem or intervention goal. Behavior problems are depicted by boxes in an FACCD and they are sometimes labeled with a "Y" (see Chapter 3). It is important to note that the boxes can also be used to denote "negative" maladaptive behaviors (e.g., self-injury) or "positive" adaptive behaviors (e.g., calling a friend) and/or intervention goals.

   Behavior problems can be directly observed and measured or "hypothetical." Observed and measured behavior problems are depicted by solid lines. Hypothetical variables are depicted by a box with dotted lines (see Figure 3.3). We provide a more detailed discussion about the nature of behavior problems in Chapter 4.

2. *The relative "importance" of behavior problems.* The *importance* of a behavior problem is depicted by the border boldness of the box (see Figure 3.3). Behaviors that are considered more important

have thicker borders than those with thinner borders. We noted in Chapter 2 that the degree of "importance" of a behavior problem or intervention goal can be based on a number of factors such as degree of risk of harm to self or others, the degree of distress, degree of impairment, degree of deviation from normative behavior, or on qualitatively based ratings of importance by the client, therapist, researcher, or others. An important principle of the functional analysis and FACCD is that interventions targeting the most important behavior problems will result in the most substantial benefits for the client.

As depicted in Figure 3.3, we restrict estimates of all elements in the FACCD to three levels of differentiation, based on the qualitative nature of the clinical judgments and ability of clinicians to reliably discriminate among multiple levels.

3.  *The forms of functional relations among behavior problems.* Any given behavior problem can be associated with many other behavior problems. The *forms of functional relations* can be correlational and noncausal or they can be causal. If they are causal, the relations can be unidirectional or bidirectional (see Figures 2.2 and 3.4).

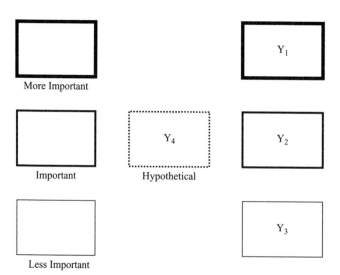

**Figure 3.3** A causal diagram that illustrates multiple behavior problems, levels of relative importance, and a hypothetical behavior problem, indicated by border boldness of the boxes.

Functional relations among behavior problems are important because if an intervention affects a behavior problem that, in turn, affects another behavior problem, the magnitude of effect of the intervention will be increased.

4. *Strength of functional relations among behavior problems.* Causal relations can vary in their relative *strength* and an FACCD can depict three levels of strength (weak, moderate, strong), indicated by the boldness of the connectors (see Figures 2.2 and 3.4). Estimates of the strength of relations can be determined quantitatively (e.g., correlational analysis, conditional probability analysis, time-lagged correlations, ANOVA) or qualitatively (e.g., estimating based on research literature, client reports, clinicians' intuitive estimates). Both of these strategies have strengths and limitations that we discuss in Chapter 10.

5. *The effects of behavior problems.* A behavior problem often has an adverse impact on other areas of a client's life. These adverse *effects* can include health risks, functional impairment, economic problems, legal risks, and problems for others. These effects are depicted by boxes that can vary in degree of importance. The magnitude of intervention impact is increased when improvement in the problem behavior also promotes improvement in important effects of behavior problems. Figure 3.5 illustrates the effect of

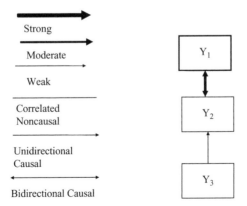

**Figure 3.4** A causal diagram that illustrates multiple behavior problems, their relative importance, and the form and strength of their functional relations, indicated by line boldness of the directional indicators.

behavior problems ($Z_1$) as well as the relative importance of the behavior problems ($Y_1$–$Y_3$) and the form and strength of their functional relations.

6. *Causal variables.* There are many different types of *causal variables.* In behavioral assessment, causal variables are generally defined, as situational (e.g., antecedent stimuli, settings, response contingencies) or intrapersonal events (e.g., expectations, biological responses) associated with changes in problem behavior. In the FACCD, causal variables are indicated by circles or ovals as illustrated in Figure 3.5.

7. *Modifiability of causal variables.* Causal variables have different degrees of modifiability, and some cannot be modified. *Modifiable causal variables* are those that can be changed by a clinical intervention, whereas unmodifiable variables are those that cannot be readily changed with a clinical intervention. Commonly encountered unmodifiable causal variables include brain injury, early traumatic life experiences, genetic vulnerability, early learning, system-level barriers to effective intervention, marital distress with an uncooperative partner, or unavoidable life stressors. As we illustrated earlier in Figure 2.2, modifiable causal variables are represented as a circle in an FACCD and unmodifiable variables are depicted by a diamond shape. The degree of modifiability is illustrated by three levels of borders boldness (see Figures 3.8 and 3.9).

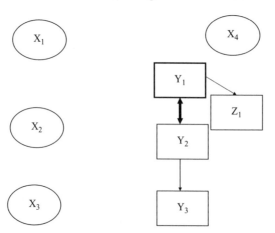

**Figure 3.5** A causal diagram that illustrates multiple behavior problems, their relative importance, the form and strength of their functional interrelations, their effects, and causal variables (indicated by circles or ovals).

8–9. *The form and strength of functional relations between causal variables and behavior problems.* Causal variables can differ in the form of their relations with behavior problems. They can be unidirectional or bidirectional. They can also exert weak, moderate, or strong causal effects (see Figure 3.6).

10–11. *The form and strength of relations among causal variables.* A causal variable can have effects in many ways. For example, causal variables can form chains, a causal variable can affect multiple behavior problems, and a causal variable can affect a behavior problem through multiple causal paths. Like other functional relations depicted in an FACCD, the causal relations among causal variables can be unidirectional or bidirectional and weak, moderate, or strong. Figure 3.7 illustrates the form and strength of relations among causal variables as well as other elements of a causal diagram reviewed thus far.

12–15. *Additional types of causal relations.* Causal relations can also be characterized by the manner in which they exert their effect. A *moderating causal relation* affects the strength of relation between two other variables. A *mediating causal relation* "explains" or accounts for the relation between two other variables. A

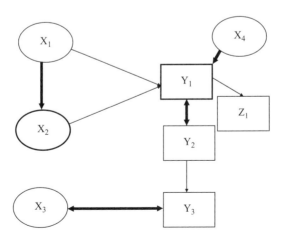

**Figure 3.6** A causal diagram (FACCD) that illustrates multiple behavior problems, their relative importance, the form and strength of their functional relations, their effects, causal variables and their modifiability, the form and strength of relations among causal variables and behavior problems, and multiple causal paths.

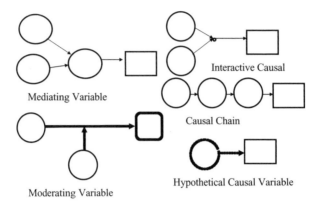

**Figure 3.7** Different types of causal variables and relations (FACCD).

*hypothetical causal relation* is one that is unmeasured, has yet to be measured, or is inferred from nomothetic research. *Interactive causal relations* occur when two variables combine (multiply) to exert a causal impact that is greater than their individual impact (additive impact) on a causal relationship. Figures 3.7 and 3.8 illustrate these additional types of causal variables, along with a chain of causal relations.

17. *The direction of causal relations.* The direction of causal relations can be either positive or negative. In a positive causal relation, increases in one variable are associated with increases in another variable and vice versa. In contrast, a negative (inverse) causal relation is one in which an increase in one variable is associated with a decrease in the other variable or vice versa. The direction of a causal relation is independent from its form and magnitude. In a causal diagram, the direction of causal relations are assumed to be positive unless indicated by the "−" sign, as we illustrate in Figure 3.9 between causal variables $X_1$ and $X_2$.

18. *The functional response class of behavior problems.* Sometimes several behavior problems that differ in their form can be grouped together when they are maintained by the same response contingencies (e.g., when different behavior problems all help the client escape from an aversive emotional state). A functional response class is illustrated in Figure 3.10.

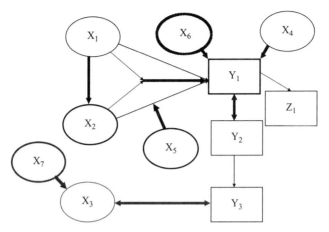

**Figure 3.8** A causal diagram (FACCD) that illustrates multiple behavior problems, their relative importance, the form and strength of their functional relations, their effects, causal variables and their modifiability, the form and strength of relations among causal variables and behavior problems, moderating variable ($X_5$), mediating variable ($X_3$), interactive causal relation ($X_1$–$X_2$), hypothetical causal variable ($X_6$), and causal chains ($X_1 \rightarrow X_2$).

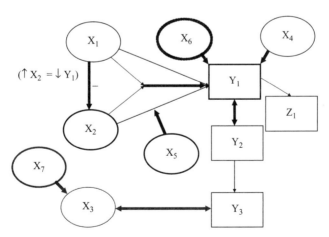

**Figure 3.9** A causal diagram that illustrates multiple behavior problems, their relative importance, the form and strength of their functional relations, their effects, causal variables and their modifiability, the form and strength of relations among causal variables and behavior problems, moderating, mediating, and hypothetical causal variables, causal chains, and the direction of functional relations (negative relation indicated by a "–" sign between $X_1$ and $X_2$).

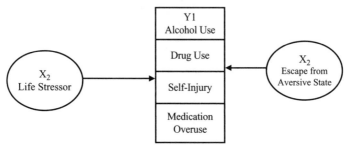

Functional Response Class

**Figure 3.10** A functional response class in which several different behavior problems are maintained by the same causal variables.

## EXAMPLES OF CAUSAL DIAGRAMS APPLIED TO THE FUNCTIONAL ANALYSIS: EXAMPLES OF THE FACCD

On the following pages we provide several examples of the FACCD applied to various behavior problems (see Figures 3.11 through 3.15). Each depicts elements of the FACCD and illustrates their utility for synthesizing many complex clinical judgments about a client.

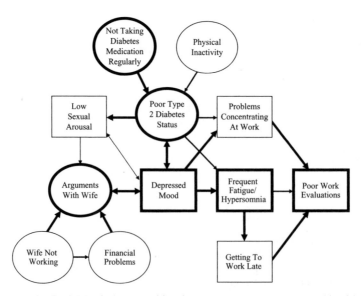

**Figure 3.11** An FACCD of a 38-year-old male seen at an outpatient mental health clinic, with complaints of fatigue, poor concentration, and depressed mood. Many causal variables were associated with poorly controlled diabetes and marital conflict.

*Source: From Kaholokula et al., 2009.*

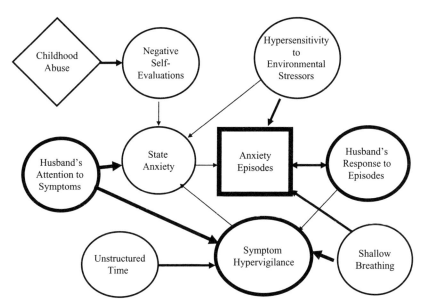

**Figure 3.12** An FACCD of a 45-year-old woman reporting frequent anxiety/panic episodes. Causal variables were associated with cognitive factors (such as hypervigilance to symptoms, negative self-evaluations), environmental stressors, high states of anxious arousal, and reinforcement by spouse.

*Source: From Haynes et al., 1998.*

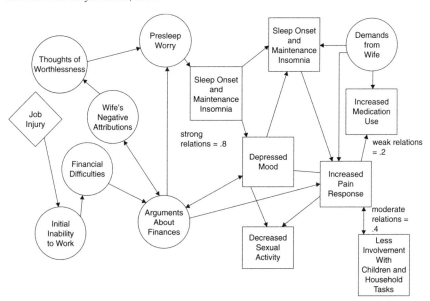

**Figure 3.13** FACCD of 46-year-old male with chronic pain complaints. Pain behavior associated with depressed mood, medication use, and withdrawal from family interactions. Worry, sleep, marital conflict contributed to pain responses.

*Source: From Haynes et al., 2001; Haynes and Williams, 2003.*

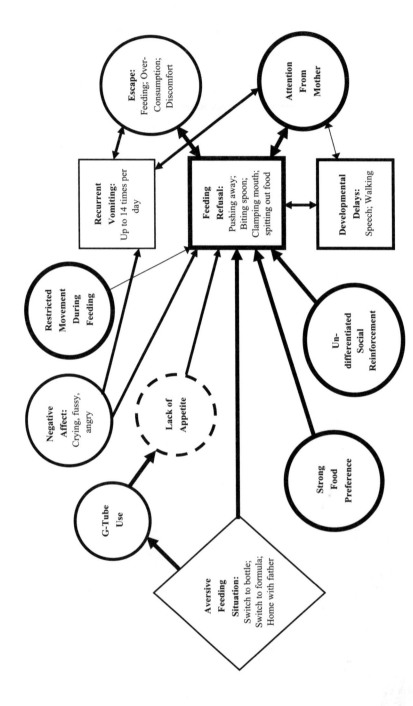

**Figure 3.14** FACCD of 16-month-old girl with eating problems and developmental delays. Associated with a history of aversive eating experiences, social reinforcement, with probable biological mediators.

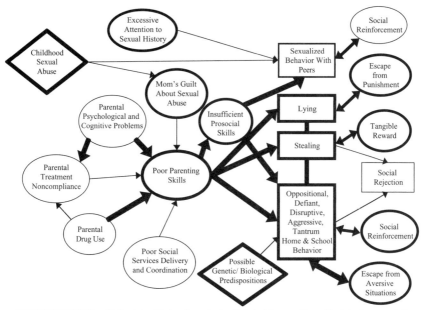

**Poor Parenting Skills:** Use of bribes, inconsistent contingencies, insufficient reinforcement for positive behaviors, rewards for oppositional and defiant behaviors, few negative contingencies for aggressive behaviors, frequent instructions, no follow-through with expressed contingencies

**Figure 3.15** FACCD of eight-year-old girl with severe oppositional, defiant, aggressive, tantrum, and conduct/antisocial behaviors. Most causal variables were associated with poor parenting skills and deficiencies in services provided to the family.

Most of the preceding FACCDs illustrate "higher level, less specific" functional analyses, which can be most useful for making broad intervention decisions. Also notice the many different potential intervention targets and how targeting the most important causal variables could have the greatest magnitude of effect for the client. More specific functional analyses are often necessary to guide more specific intervention strategies (see Chapter 11).[2]

## BENEFITS AND GOALS OF FACCDS

Throughout this book we comment on the costs and benefits of the functional analysis and of constructing an FACCD. In this section, we

---

[2] Many Functional Analytic Clinical Case Diagrams in the following pages were initially constructed by advanced graduate students enrolled in a course on behavioral assessment. Identifying information has been removed.

summarize eleven benefits of using an FACCD to illustrate the functional analysis. We summarize their limitations in the subsequent section.

1.  *Communication of the clinician's case formulation*. The main benefit of an FACCD is that it allows the clinician to construct, examine, and communicate to others a visual model of the hypothesized causal variables and causal relations applicable to the behavior problems or intervention goals of a client. The complex clinical judgments that are efficiently depicted in the FACCD are the integration of data derived from clinical assessment with relevant nomothetic research findings.

2.  *The ultimate goal of the FACCD is to help the clinician estimate which intervention focus would have the greatest magnitude of effect (the greatest benefit) for the client*. All elements of the FACCD contribute to this overall estimate. Essentially, the FACCD allows the clinician to "model" and estimate the effects of different interventions.

3.  *To assist in the identification of causal variables, behavior problems, and functional relations that require additional assessment*. The FACCD can indicate where additional assessment is needed. Recall that an FACCD sometimes includes hypothetical behavior problems, causal variables, and paths. These are often potentially important variables that have been suggested by the results of nomothetic research with persons who have behavior problems similar to those of the client. The findings of such research can provide support for exploring the possibility that an important causal variable may be operating, which is not initially reported by the client or identified in the initial assessment.

    Variables can also be "hypothetical" when there is conflicting information obtained about them during the assessment, or the clinician has assessment-based hypotheses that have not been sufficiently evaluated. Thus, hypothetical variables in the FACCD can also suggest that there is a potentially important behavior problem that requires additional assessment.

4.  *To encourage parsimony in the clinical case formulation*. Parsimony is a goal of all causal models and causal diagrams. A parsimonious

account of a phenomenon will provide an optimal balance between degree of explanation and number of variables. A parsimonious FACCD is one that includes all important causal variables and behavior problems and excludes those that are less relevant or important. This makes it easier to communicate a functional analysis to other professionals, service providers, and clients and increases its potential clinical utility. In Chapter 11, we discuss ways of making complex functional analyses more parsimonious by using functional response classes and different levels of specificity.

5. *To encourage a scientific and scholarly approach to clinical assessment and case formulation.* The construction of an FACCD requires that the clinician carefully consider the judgments he or she is making about the client. For example, the clinician must estimate the relative importance of behavior problems and consider the magnitude and direction of causal relations among behavior problems. We outline the steps and sequence of clinical judgments in the construction of an FACCD in Chapter 11. Also, clinicians are less likely to introduce their biases, derive premature clinical case formulations, omit important variables, and omit important assessment strategies, if they follow a careful, sequential, clinical science-based approach to constructing a functional analysis and an FACCD.

6. *To increase the clinical case formulation skills of supervisees.* Doctoral, and MSW (Masters of Social Work)—level clinicians frequently function as clinical supervisors for those in training or those providing direct service. Encouraging supervisees to construct an FACCD of their client's behavior problems and positive intervention goals can help them approach clinical case formulation more systematically and thoughtfully. It can help them examine the thoroughness of their assessment methods and the scientific and logical bases of their clinical judgments.

7. *To exclude common but irrelevant causal variables and functional relations in case formulations.* The FACCD can indicate when potentially important causal variables or functional relations (often suggested by the results of nomothetic research) are not applicable for a client. Although a behavior problem can have

multiple causes and comorbidities, only a subset of these causes and comorbidities is likely to operate for any client and be represented in the FACCD.

By omitting potential but less relevant variables and relations, the FACCD reduces the chance that an intervention will focus on them. For example, some studies have suggested that a critical family environment (e.g., "expressed emotion") can sometimes trigger depressive episodes for persons who experience bipolar mood swings (see review in Miklowitz, 2007). Under these conditions, the family interactions of some clients with a bipolar diagnosis can be supportive and uncritical and a family interaction causal variable would not appear in such an FACCD. Therefore, for such a client, a family-focused intervention on critical exchanges could improve the quality of their family interactions but may not be as beneficial for the client as an intervention directed at more important causal variables.

8. *To emphasize the importance of science-based assessment strategies.* The ultimate benefit of a functional analysis for the client is better intervention outcome. Intervention outcome, in turn, is affected by the validity of the functional analysis. Clinicians who use science-based assessment strategies to derive their clinical judgments are more likely to develop valid and clinically useful functional analyses. The use of invalid measures in clinical assessment places the client at risk for reduced benefits by increasing the risk of an invalid case formulation. Other discussions of science-based approaches to clinical assessment have been presented by Haynes and Heiby (2004), Haynes et al. (2011), Hersen (2006), and Hunsley and Mash (2008).

9. *To encourage a positive goal approach to clinical case formulation.* Although we often orient our discussion of functional analysis in terms of causal models for clients' behavior problems, the functional analysis and FACCD can be used in a *constructive and positive goal-oriented assessment context* to identify important, modifiable causal variables for clients' *positive intervention goals*. The FACCD can identify those variables, for example, that affect a client's goal of having more fulfilling and enjoyable friendships, becoming a better

parent, making significant contributions to community welfare, being more resilient to stressors in his or her life, adapting a healthier diet or exercise patterns, or enhancing his or her involvement in spirituality. In these cases, the elements of the functional analysis are similar: The clinician identifies causal variables and causal relations applicable to achieving those positive goals.

10. *To help match the causal variables and relations applicable to a client's behavior problem with the mechanisms of intervention programs.* An FACCD has two important implications for the clinician's understanding of intervention mechanisms. First, it requires that the clinician understand the mechanisms of action for applicable interventions (see treatment mechanisms described in Farmer & Chapman, 2008, and Chorpita et al., 2008). Second, knowledge of the mechanisms of potential interventions can suggest to the clinician which potential causal variables and relations should be assessed. If the clinician knows, for example, that an empirically supported treatment includes a focus on increasing interpersonal communication skills, the clinician must estimate the degree to which a client's problems or goals are a function of communication skills deficits.

11. *To guide intervention process and outcome assessment strategies.* The FACCD indicates: (a) important intervention outcome variables, which are the main variables upon which the success of the intervention is to be judged, (b) immediate and intermediate outcome variables that predict the main outcome variables, and (c) the operation of moderator and mediator variables.

## LIMITATIONS OF THE FUNCTIONAL ANALYSIS AND OF FACCDS

Although we emphasize the benefits of FACCDs, they also have the following four limitations, in particular.

1. Functional analyses and FACCDs *are not always cost-beneficial.* Functional analyses and FACCDs take time to develop and

can delay intervention initiation. Consequently, they are more beneficial in some clinical assessment contexts than in others. The development of an FACCD is more beneficial when: (a) applied with complex cases, (b) applied to cases that are failing in intervention, (c) communicating about complex cases to other professionals, and (d) training new clinicians to approach clinical case formulation with their clients in a carefully structured, scholarly, and sequential manner.

2.  The assessment demands of constructing a valid functional analysis and the complexity of an FACCD make it less cost-beneficial for clients with few behavior problems or behavior problems that involve a small array of causal variables. In some cases, the most cost-beneficial strategy is to expose a client to a readily available, empirically supported intervention and to conduct a more extensive functional analysis with the client only if significant improvements are not observed after several sessions.

3.  An FACCD is *pseudo-precise*. The causal diagram, illustrating levels of importance, modifiability, and strength of functional relations, can suggest a level of measurement precision that is unwarranted, given current levels of clinical assessment technology. The clinician should remember, and communicate to others, that the functional analysis and FACCD are tentative, hypothesized, and unstable. They are only a summary of the clinician's clinical judgments at the time the assessment was conducted and in that assessment context. The elements of an FACCD are likely to change over time, differ across contexts, and reflect measurement errors and clinical judgment errors.

4.  *A functional analysis and FACCD do not include all variables necessary for intervention decisions.* The FACCD represents a causal model of the client's behavior problems or intervention goals. It may not include other important factors that affect intervention decisions, such as the acceptability of proposed interventions to the client or others, the skill of the therapist, financial and time constraints, the availability of appropriate

interventions, and policies at the treatment agency. For an expansion of the FACCD to include intervention variables, we direct the reader to Mueller (2011).

## SUMMARY

In summary, the functional analysis includes many complex clinical judgments about a client that can be challenging to efficiently and effectively organize for the clinician and to communicate to others. We introduced the FACCD as an efficient and effective alternative to the traditional method of communicating about a case formulation through a written case history.

The FACCD is a diagram of the functional analysis and of the important and modifiable causal relations relevant to a client's behavior problems. The elements of an FACCD include boxes, circles, lines, and arrows that represent essential information about the functional analysis. These elements convey information about the behavior problems, causal variables, and functional relations that account for the onset, rate, duration, or severity of a behavior problem.

The causal diagrams presented in this chapter illustrate how the FACCD visually conveys important information about the functional analysis. Its elements include: (a) multiple behavior problems, (b) the relative importance of behavior problems, (c) the forms, strength, and direction of functional relations among behavior problems, (d) the effects of behavior problems, (e) causal variables and their modifiability, (f) the forms, strength, and direction of relations between causal variables and behavior problems and among causal variables, (g) types of causal variables—hypothetical, moderating, and mediating, and (h) interactive causal relations. Several examples of FACCDs were presented.

An FACCD can help the clinician: (a) estimate the relative magnitude of effect of focusing intervention on causal variables within the model, (b) identify areas where additional assessment is needed, (c) develop parsimonious clinical case formulations, (d) adopt a more careful approach to clinical case formulation, (e) communicate more effectively the case formulations to others, (f) indicate where potential causal variables do not operate for a client, (g) adhere to best-practice assessment strategies, and (h) attend to the mechanisms of action of potential interventions.

There are also limitations to an FACCD. The functional analysis and FACCD are most likely to be cost-beneficial with complex or failing cases, but less so for clients who present with limited behavior problems or few causal variables. Also, the FACCD can imply an unwarranted degree of precision in clinical judgments.

# Conceptual and Empirical Foundations of Behavioral Assessment and the Functional Analysis I

## The Complex Nature of Behavior Problems

**CHAPTER OVERVIEW**

In Chapters 1–3, the role, basic strategies, challenges, limitations, and benefits of behavioral assessment and clinical case formulation were introduced. We also presented several models of clinical case formulation, emphasized the clinical utility of the functional analysis, and illustrated how multimethod behavioral assessment strategies can enhance the validity of a case formulation. We then presented a clinical case example to illustrate the functional analysis, the Functional Analytic Clinical Case Diagram (FACCD), and the close relations between the functional analysis and behavioral assessment strategies. Finally, we discussed the elements, benefits, and limitations of the functional analysis and the FACCD.

In this chapter, we examine the complex nature of behavior problems. We also show how the characteristics of behavior problems influence the focus and structure of the functional analysis. Finally, we review how characteristics of behavior problems guide assessment strategies used to develop the functional analysis and measure intervention process and outcome.

## OVERVIEW OF THE COMPLEX NATURE OF BEHAVIOR PROBLEMS

One of the goals of behavioral assessment and the functional analysis is to describe the multiform behavior problems experienced by a client. This is an important, albeit difficult, goal to achieve in both clinical and research contexts. The difficulty in this endeavor arises from several sources. First, clients often present with multiple behavior problems that have varied attributes. Second, there are often complex interrelations occurring among the many behavior problems and attributes. Third, each behavior problem typically involves several response modes that cut across cognitive, physiological, affective, and motor systems. Finally, each response mode can be measured on a number of *dimensions* (e.g., rate, severity, duration) that can vary according to context (e.g., home versus school setting), time (e.g., day-to-day changes in mood), state (e.g., level of fatigue, medication state), and the unique characteristics (e.g., age, gender, ethnicity, learning history, biobehavioral capacities) of a given client.

Consider, for example, two hypothetical clients with a diagnosis of Posttraumatic Stress Disorder. Each client will present with a set of behavior problems that can be manifested in distinct cognitive, physiological, and motor response modes. Further, the attributes of the behavior problems are unique for each client. For example, the content of a thought or flashback is specifically tied to each individual's history. Adding to this already complex scenario, we further assume that the onset, rate, severity, and duration of each behavior problem are idiosyncratic. Finally, we assume that these complex behavior problems vary as a function of the many contexts each client experiences. The characteristics of behavior problems that are relevant to the functional analysis and strategies of assessment (see Chapter 7) are summarized in Table 4.1.

**Table 4.1 Characteristics of Behavior Problems Relevant to the Functional Analysis and Behavioral Assessment**

| Characteristics | Description/Example | Implications for Behavioral Assessment and Functional Analysis |
|---|---|---|
| • Clients often have multiple behavior problems | • Clients seeking treatment for substance dependence often have mood, anxiety, psychophysiological, and interpersonal problems. | • The initial assessment process should avoid a premature focus on a single problem. Understanding the relative importance and interrelations among behavior problems is a critical assessment goal. |
| • Behavior problems have multiple response modes | • Anxiety disorders have cognitive, motor, emotional, and physiological response modes. The relative importance of these response modes differs across persons with an anxiety disorder. | • A goal of assessment and case formulation is to identify and measure the most important response modes for a client's behavior problems using multimodal assessment strategies. |
| • Behavior problems have multiple dimensions | • A specific behavior problem, such as catastrophic thinking, can be characterized by its rate, magnitude, duration, cyclicity, and latency to onset. The relative importance of these dimensions will differ across persons with similar behavior problems. | • A goal of assessment and case formulation is to identify and estimate the relative importance of the various dimensions of a client's behavior problems. Each dimension can be associated with different causal variables. |

*Continued*

**Table 4.1** *Continued*

| Characteristics | Description/Example | Implications for Behavioral Assessment and Functional Analysis |
| --- | --- | --- |
| • Conditional nature of behavior problems | • The rate of a child's aggressive behaviors will vary across social contexts (e.g., school versus home), interpersonal context (e.g., friends versus family), and states (e.g., medicated versus unmedicated state). | • Assessment of behavior problems should occur in different contexts and states. Additionally, a functional analysis can be valid in some contexts but not others. |
| • Dynamic nature of behavior problems | • The pattern, modes, and/ or dimensions of a set of interrelated behavior problems such as panic disorder often change over time. | • The assessor should use time-sampling assessment strategies that most accurately capture the rate of change of a behavior problem. Assessment should be ongoing throughout the assessment-treatment process. The validity of the functional analysis will vary across time. |

*Source: Table adopted from Haynes et al., 2007.*

## WHY A FOCUS ON BEHAVIOR PROBLEMS RATHER THAN BEHAVIOR DISORDERS?

The terms "*behavior disorder*," "*mental disorder*," and "*behavior problem*" usually refer to a specified set of behaviors or a covarying set of thoughts, emotions, psychophysiological states, affective states, and observable actions. In the United States and many other countries, the primary source for defining behavior (or mental) disorders is the Diagnostic and Statistical Manual (American Psychiatric Association, 2000). The DSM conceptualizes a mental disorder as a set of psychological, affective, and behavioral responses that create subjective distress, disability, and/or increased risk for adverse life outcomes (e.g., injury, death, loss of important social roles, loss of freedom) (American Psychiatric Association, 2000).

The terms "behavior disorder," "mental disorder," and "behavior problem" have different meanings. "Behavior disorders" or "mental disorders" refer to a formally specified set of signs and symptoms that may often occur together and form a "clinical syndrome" that meets formal diagnostic criteria. Posttraumatic Stress Disorder is an example. Currently, a DSM diagnosis of Posttraumatic Stress Disorder requires that several criteria be met: (a) a person must have been exposed to a severe traumatic event (such as physical assault), (b) the traumatic event is re-experienced (such as through intrusive thoughts), (c) the person experiences avoidance or emotional numbing (such as avoiding activities or settings associated with the traumatic event), (d) the person experiences symptoms of hyperarousal (such as exaggerated startle responses to noises), and (e) the symptoms must be present for at least one month.

In many cases, a behavior disorder or mental disorder diagnosis is also dependent on exclusionary and temporal criteria. For example, a diagnosis of a Delusional Disorder can be given only if the symptoms are not the result of some other medical condition (e.g., encephalopathy, urinary tract infection) or substance abuse. Similarly, a diagnosis of Schizophrenia requires that symptoms (such as delusions, disorganized speech) be present for at least one month.

In contrast to "mental disorders" and "behavior disorders," a "behavior problem" refers to any behavior (i.e., thought, emotion, physiological response, or observable action) that is associated with harm, distress, impairment, or concern, *regardless* of whether or not it meets criteria for a psychiatric diagnosis. Examples of common behavior problems that are *not* represented as a diagnostic category in the DSM are nightmares, specific social skills deficits, depressed mood, threats of violence (such as bullying at school), hyperactivity, marital conflict, elevated blood pressure, interruptions during dyadic exchanges, oppositional behavior, failure to take prescribed medications, irritability, and repetitive unwanted thoughts.

The boundaries between behavior problems and behavior or mental disorders are fuzzy. However, compared to behavior disorders or mental disorders, behavior problems are more specific, homogeneous, and measurable. A focus on "behavior problems," however, also has limitations. One important limitation is that the operational definitions of behavior problems can vary across researchers and clinicians.

For the purposes of behavioral assessment and the functional analysis, as well as for clinical research and intervention, a focus on "behavior problems" is often more relevant and clinically useful. Mental health professionals often treat persons with important behavior problems that do not satisfy criteria for a formal diagnosis. A panic attack is an example (see Smits et al., 2006). A panic attack is one criterion for a formal diagnosis of Panic Disorder and can include symptoms such as pounding heart, chest pain, fear of dying, and feeling dizzy. However, experiencing panic attacks alone is not sufficient for a diagnosis of Panic Disorder. A diagnosis of Panic Disorder also requires temporal considerations (such as worry for at least one month), exclusion of alternative diagnoses, and exclusion of specified causes (such as panic attacks cannot be the result of substance use). A clinician working with a client experiencing panic attacks would likely develop a functional analysis to guide intervention for the client's unique behavior problems and their causes regardless of whether or not criteria for Panic Disorder were met.

Recall that in earlier chapters each behavior problem is shown to be amenable to varied operational definitions. The *level of specificity* is an important consideration in behavioral assessment. Briefly, the level of specificity of a behavior problem refers to the number of clinically useful lower-level components it subsumes (see Haynes & O'Brien, 2000, for a detailed discussion of specificity). For example, the higher-level behavior problem of "marital distress" can include many lower-level components, such as "marital conflict." In turn, marital conflict can include many lower-level components such as "problem-solving deficits," "negative attributions about partner's behavior," "selective attention to the partner's negative behaviors," and "verbal expressions of disapproval toward partner." Finally, problem-solving deficits can be decomposed into even lower-level behaviors such as "critical comments," "interruptions," and "withdrawal during disagreements."

Figure 4.1 illustrates several levels of specificity for a depressive disorder. Note that there are strategies for assessment at every level of specificity and that the "best" level of specificity would depend on the goal of

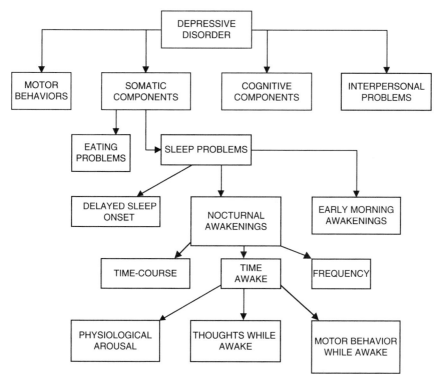

**Figure 4.1** An illustration of six levels of increasing specificity, starting with a major depressive disorder with four major components, each of which has multiple subcomponents, and so forth.

*Source: Reprinted with permission from Haynes, 2004; Haynes & O'Brien, 2000.*

the assessment (e.g., diagnosis, brief screening, multivariate intervention outcome evaluations, or initial functional analysis).

Because behavior problems can be reduced to increasingly more specific and lower levels of behavior, we use the term *functional specificity* to refer to the level of specificity that is most effective for clinical decision-making. Behavior problems that are operationally defined at an excessively molar level of specificity are too heterogeneous and thereby less helpful for clinical decision-making and a functional analysis. Common examples of insufficiently specific labels for behavior problems include "low self-esteem," "need for control," "manipulative," "depression," "insomnia," and "acting out." All of these global labels have multiple components that can differ across persons and contexts. Additionally, the many subcomponents within each label can be influenced by different causal variables.

It is important to note as well that if a behavior problem is defined at an excessively low (micro) level of specificity, it can be too narrowly focused to aid in clinical decision-making. Returning to the earlier example of panic, measurement of beat-to-beat variability in heart rate may incompletely capture the experience of "heart pounding," which is a key component of a panic attack.

Although behavioral assessment strategies and the functional analysis are applicable to both behavior disorders and behavior problems, we focus on behavior problems for several reasons. First, as already observed, mental health professionals often encounter persons with distressing behavior problems that do not meet formal diagnostic criteria. For example, although only 2% to 3% of the U.S. population meets DSM criteria for Obsessive-Compulsive Disorder (OCD), as many at 25% may experience some distressing obsessive and compulsive symptoms (see discussion in Zucker, Craske, Blackmore, & Nitz, 1996).

Second, many persons who seek treatment for various behavior problems receive a diagnosis of "Not Otherwise Specified," a diagnostic subcategory that reflects the heterogeneity and ambiguity of current diagnostic schemes. An example would be a client who receives a DSM diagnosis of "Eating Disorder, Not Otherwise Specified." This label could be applied if the client severely restricted his or her caloric intake, indulged in frequent eating binges, and induced vomiting after meals, but did not meet other criteria for the more specified diagnostic categories, such as Anorexia Nervosa, which requires that the person be at least 15% below expected weight and exhibit significant body image distortion. A careful behavioral assessment of this client would help the clinician understand the client's behavior problem and aid in intervention planning, even though the client did not meet formal diagnostic criteria.

Third, the multiple behavior problems that comprise the symptoms of most diagnostic categories often exhibit low-to-moderate levels of covariation. For example, fatigue, irritability, and sleep disturbance are all indicators for Generalized Anxiety Disorder, but they are only moderately correlated (Beidel & Stipelman, 2007). Thus, the specific behavior problems experienced by persons with a Generalized Anxiety Disorder diagnosis are likely to differ in important ways.

Given the heterogeneity in symptoms and signs of behavior disorders, data on functional relations that use a diagnostic category rather than specific behavior problems are difficult to interpret. For example, some of the specific behavior problems subsumed within the Generalized Anxiety Disorder diagnosis are related to alcohol use while others are not. Thus, one person with Generalized Anxiety Disorder may be using alcohol because it reduces his anxiety in social situations while another person with Generalized Anxiety Disorder may be using alcohol to reduce chronic worrisome thoughts. Similarly, intervention research that uses a global measure of Generalized Anxiety Disorder would not provide information about the effects of the intervention on specific components of Generalized Anxiety Disorder.

Fourth, most psychiatric diagnoses can result from multiple permutations of symptoms. Consequently, persons with the same diagnosis can exhibit vastly different combinations of behavior problems. Returning to our current example, a diagnosis of Generalized Anxiety Disorder can result from any three of the following behavior problems: restlessness, fatigue, difficulty concentrating, irritability, muscle tension, and sleep disturbance. In these examples, the elements within the functional analysis, and associated behavioral assessment strategies, would differ across clients as a function of the unique set of symptoms that contributed to the diagnosis for each client. Because of differences between persons with the same diagnosis, research participant samples with the same diagnosis are likely to differ in their composition across studies, leading to inconsistent findings regarding causal factors and intervention outcome.

A focus on diagnostic categories or behavior disorders that are composed of heterogeneous behavior problems can also hinder our ability to describe and explain the causes of behavior problems and to construct a valid and clinically useful functional analysis. The causal variables that affect one behavior problem within a diagnostic category, such as fatigue in Generalized Anxiety Disorder, can differ from the causal variables that affect another symptom, such as concentration difficulties. A functional analysis that focuses on a diagnostic category or behavior disorder when there is a low level of covariation among its component behavior problems leads to imprecise estimates of causal relations in research and clinical assessment. Consequently, the validity and clinical utility of the functional analysis and interventions based on it are also diminished.

Fifth, an emphasis on diagnoses leads a clinician to adopt a categorical labeling strategy (i.e., a person does or does not meet criteria for a particular behavior disorder diagnosis) that does not reflect the individual differences just noted. Additionally, many behavior problems can be more adequately thought of as falling on a continuum of severity rather than in dichotomous categories. As Widiger and Edmundson (2009) stated, the complex, conditional, and dynamic nature of behavior disorders are not well captured by a categorical diagnostic system because it makes distinctions at arbitrarily determined points along the continuum of behavior distributions.

Finally, if we focus our assessment efforts and a functional analysis on a client's categorically based diagnosis of a behavior disorder, we would be identifying factors that increase or decrease the likelihood of receiving a diagnosis. However, we would not be able to identify factors that lead to increases or decreases in the frequency, severity, or duration of the individual components of the diagnosis. Consider, for example, the treatment of "schizophrenia." A patient may begin taking an antipsychotic medication and have a significant reduction in the frequency and intensity of delusional thoughts and auditory hallucinations. However, at the conclusion of treatment, the patient would continue to be diagnosed as having "schizophrenia." Thus, the probability of having or not having the diagnosis can be unrelated to significant changes in the intensity and/or frequency of important components of the diagnosis. From a diagnostic perspective, improvement would be evident only when there is an elimination of all key symptoms subsumed within the diagnostic category of schizophrenia. If this were to occur, the client presumably would be "undiagnosed" and determined to be "not schizophrenic." Of course, the complete elimination of all subcomponents of many diagnostic categories in the DSM rarely occurs. This contributes to the pernicious tendency for diagnostic labels to persist even in the presence of significant improvement in client functioning.

Consider another example. Recall that the diagnosis of panic disorder requires that the client must also report that he or she experiences "recurrent" panic attacks that are operationally defined as "discrete" episodes where "at least four" of the following physiological responses occur in a short time span (10-minute or less onset to peak duration): nonpainful cardiac experiences (palpitations, pounding heart, increased heart rate); sweating, trembling, or shaking; shortness of breath; feeling of choking;

chest pain; abdominal distress; dizziness or lightheadedness; derealization; fear of losing control or going crazy; fear of dying; numbness or tingling sensations; and chills or hot flushes. Additionally, the client must report that he or she has experienced, for at least one month, persistent concern about having additional panic attacks, or persistent worry about the consequences of an attack, or a "significant change" in behavior due to the attacks. Finally, substance abuse, a medical disorder, or another psychiatric condition must be ruled out. Suppose, for example, that a client initially reports experiencing 10 of the 13 panic symptoms listed by the DSM and two "persistent worry" symptoms. After participating in a well-designed intervention based on interoceptive exposure and cognitive therapy focusing on attributions and labeling, the client learns that many of his or her panic symptoms are, in fact, benign indicators of sympathetic nervous system activity. Further, the client learns that he or she does not need to fear these symptoms. Consequently, the client may report that he or she experiences only four of the original 10 symptoms, and at a significantly reduced level of intensity. Despite the improvements in symptoms and clear evidence that the clinician has identified important functional relations in order to produce improvements, DSM diagnostic criteria would continue to classify the client as having panic disorder. There is no allowance for the clinician to denote in the diagnostic system itself the substantial improvements in client functioning. Additionally, there is no mechanism in a categorical approach to provide an index of which symptoms have improved and for what reasons.

To summarize, behavioral assessment and the functional analysis emphasize factors that strongly affect a client's specific behavior problems. Even though these behavior problems may not meet diagnostic criteria for a disorder, they are relevant intervention targets because they are often personally distressing for a client and associated with *functional impairment* (i.e., impairment in a person's life roles as a student, worker, parent, and spouse). The conceptual basis, reliability, social implications, costs and benefits, and measurement issues associated with diagnostic and classification systems in psychopathology have been the subject of intense debate. For further discussion of these issues, the reader can consult Hersen and Porzelius (2002), Hersen, Turner, and Beidel (2007), and Widiger and Edmundson (2009).

## CLIENTS OFTEN HAVE MULTIPLE BEHAVIOR PROBLEMS

As we illustrated with the case of Mrs. Sanchez, one of the early goals of behavioral assessment is to specify the behavior problems of a client and the functional relations among these problems. Persons who seek psychological services often have multiple behavior problems. For example, researchers have found that as many as 99% of adolescents diagnosed with Schizophrenia have at least one comorbid behavior disorder, such as depression (30%), oppositional defiant disorder (43%), and attention deficit hyperactivity disorder (84%; Ross, Heinlein, & Tregellas, 2006). Similarly, 51% of adolescents and 59% of adults with diagnosable anxiety-related disorders have comorbid psychiatric disorders such as depression (Essau, 2003). Finally, among persons who abuse inhaled substances (such as amyl nitrate and nitrous oxide) there is a high comorbidity of mood (48%), anxiety (36%), and personality disorders (45%; Wu & Howard, 2007). We refer you to Haynes and Kaholokula (2008), Krueger et al. (2006), and Lilienfeld, Waldman, and Israel (1994) for further discussions of comorbidity.

## WHY DO CLIENTS HAVE MULTIPLE BEHAVIOR PROBLEMS?

Haynes and O'Brien (2000) and Kaholokula et al. (2008) described several causal models that can account for comorbid behavior problems (see also Haynes et al., 2011). As illustrated in Figure 4.2, behavior problems can covary under several conditions. First, they can covary when they share the same antecedent or consequent causal variable (Functional Relations A and C). For example, chronic pain can affect both sleep disturbances and depressed mood (Davison & Jhangri, 2005). Second, they can covary when one behavior problem acts as the causal variable for another behavior problem (Functional Relation B). An example of this would be when a client's social anxiety leads to alcohol use to reduce anxiety (Morris, Stewart, & Ham, 2005). Third, they can covary when they are influenced by different, but covarying, causal variables (Functional

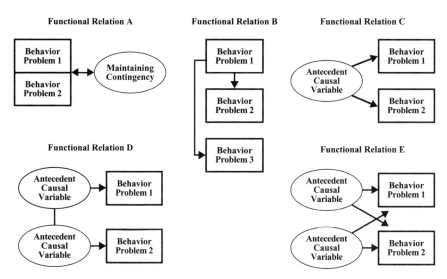

**Figure 4.2** Five examples of functional relations that can result in covarying behavior problems.

Relation D). An example of this would be when a person's recent divorce leads to depressed mood and a simultaneous change in residence leads to excessive worries about personal safety. Finally, they can covary when they are both affected by different but non-covarying causal variables (Functional Relation E). An example of this would be when a student's hypervigilance and fear of social evaluation are both influenced by the presence of a teacher and peers, independently of each other.

As we illustrate with the previous examples, it is not uncommon for a person to be exposed to multiple, co-occurring, and interrelated causal variables. Although each causal variable can affect different behavior problems, a causal relation between the causal variables, or their co-occurrence, can erroneously suggest a functional relation between the behavior problems. For example, a parent with a sick child may also be experiencing work-related stressors, personal health problems, marital conflict, and loss of social support. Each of these causal variables could lead to separate but covarying problems such as sleep loss, eating disorders, depressive symptoms, and anxiety.

Knowing that a client has multiple behavior problems and understanding the functional relations among them has an important impact on intervention decisions. Consider the intervention foci that would have the greatest magnitude of effect for each of the functional relations depicted in Figure 4.2. In Functional Relation B, the intervention target that would have the greatest magnitude of effect on all three behavior problems is behavior problem 1. Improvement in this behavior problem would lead to improvements in behavior problems 2 and 3. A concrete example would be if problem 1 represents food avoidance/excessive food restriction, problem 2 represents bingeing, and problem 3 represents purging. In this case, an intervention that targeted bingeing would have a lesser overall magnitude of effect for the client, assuming that all are equally important.

Contrast Functional Relation B with E in Figure 4.2, where the behavior problems have independent causes. An intervention focused on a single behavior problem would have minimal effect on the other behavior problem. In this scenario, a more broadly focused intervention targeting both causal variables would be necessary to achieve for maximum effects on the two behavior problems.

We have focused on the ways in which causal relations and the heterogeneous characteristics of diagnostic systems can account for the fact that many clients present with multiple behavior problems. Comorbidity also depends on how the behavior problems are defined as well as the assessment and decision-making strategies used by the clinician. To illustrate, Social Phobia, Panic Disorder, Agoraphobia, and Posttraumatic Stress Disorder include overlapping diagnostic criteria (i.e., *nonspecific diagnostic criteria*), such as subjective anxiety, physiological arousal, avoidance behaviors, and excessive worry. Consequently, a person who meets criteria for one of these disorders has an increased likelihood of meeting criteria for another.

Similar symptom overlap has been noted among other classes of behavior disorders, such as personality disorders (Clarkin and Sanderson, 2000), childhood anxiety disorders (Last, Strauss, & Francis, 1987), and severe childhood behavior disorders (Mash & Terdal, 1997). Essentially, many specific behavior problems are not uniquely associated with a particular behavior disorder. For example, sleep disturbances, a common behavior problem across all anxiety disorders, is also a problem for people with depression and drug dependence, for people taking prescription medications, and for people experiencing marital, work, and financial problems.

As we discuss in Chapter 7, the probability that multiple behavior problems will be identified by a clinician also depends on which assessment strategies the clinician uses. We discuss errors in clinical judgment in Chapter 10, but we note here that sometimes clinicians too quickly focus their clinical assessment on a particular problem and fail to query for additional problems. This is most likely to happen when initial problems are highly salient to the clinician or client, such as suicidal behaviors, major depressive episodes, debilitating panic episodes, or severe marital conflict.

A premature focus on a single behavior problem can also happen when a client reports a behavior problem that is consistent with the expectations of the clinician. For example, a clinician might prematurely focus on the compulsive behaviors, or social anxiety, of a client who appears rigid and constrained in his or her interactions with the clinician. Such a premature focus decreases the chance that the clinician will detect other, perhaps more important problems that could also have important functional relations to the initially identified problem. We also discuss the role of the clinician in clinical judgment in Chapter 5.

## BEHAVIOR PROBLEMS CAN HAVE IMPORTANT FUNCTIONAL INTERRELATIONS

Functional Relation B in Figure 4.2 illustrates that a behavior problem can influence other behavior problems. This is an important concept for behavioral assessment and functional analysis. Persons (2005) noted this in her causal diagram of "Jim," who was a depressed and anxious mechanical engineer. Her case formulation indicated that his anxiety affected his depression symptoms, alcohol use, and problems at work. We also provide examples of functional relations among multiple behavior problems in several figures in Chapter 3.

The causal model in Figure 4.3 illustrates several functional relations among four behavior problems for a client. Note that an intervention that reduced "Anxiety" would also reduce the client's depressive symptoms, social isolation, and alcohol use. Essentially, this intervention focus would have the greatest magnitude of effect, relative to interventions targeting any

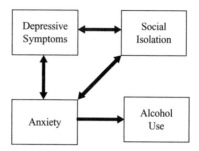

**Figure 4.3** A causal diagram illustrating unidirectional and bidirectional causal relations among a client's four behavior problems.

one of the other three behavior problems. Although interventions focusing on these other problems would also benefit the client, they would do so to a lesser degree because these behavior problems have less influence on the other behavior problems. Consider the relative magnitude of effect for an intervention that focused on the client's alcohol use versus his anxiety.

Figure 4.4 further illustrates how our estimate of the functional relations among behavior problems is an important element of a functional analysis. Given that most interventions involve multiple components, in this example the greatest magnitude of effect would be associated with an intervention that changes $Y_2$ for client A, $Y_1$ for client B, and $Y_3$ for client C. These examples illustrate why the functional relations among a client's multiple behavior problems affect intervention decisions.

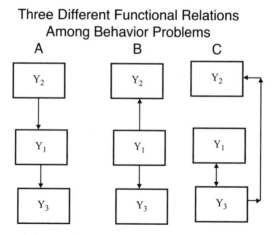

**Figure 4.4** A causal diagram illustrating three patterns of functional relations among multiple behavior problems.

# BEHAVIOR PROBLEMS DIFFER IN THEIR IMPORTANCE

In the previous sections, we discussed how the functional relations among a client's multiple behavior problems are essential elements of the functional analysis because they affect decisions about which intervention focus is likely to have the greatest magnitude of effect. However, we need to know more about a client's behavior problems in order to estimate the relative magnitude of effect of various intervention foci for that particular client. Thus, another essential focus of behavioral assessment, and an important element of the functional analysis, is the importance of the behavior problem, which we illustrated in Figure 3.2.

"Importance" is the relative weight or value associated with each behavior problem or intervention goal for a client. Judgments about importance can help the clinician estimate the relative benefits to the client if an intervention is effective. Simply stated, clients benefit more when a more important behavior problem is modified than when a less important behavior problem is modified. Think of the relative benefits to a client if we can help him or her reduce mildly distressing episodes of sleep disturbance relative to reducing severely distressing binge eating or panic episodes.

The impact of importance estimates on intervention decisions is illustrated in Figure 4.5. In this causal diagram, $Y_3$ was rated as more important than $Y_1$ and $Y_2$. This is depicted by bolder lines on the

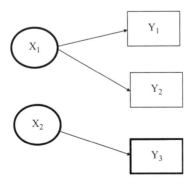

**Figure 4.5** A causal diagram illustrating differential magnitude of effect associated with changes in behavior problem $Y_3$ compared to behavior problems $Y_1$ and $Y_2$. Note that the relative magnitude of effect of changing $X_1$ versus $X_2$ depends on the relative importance of the three behavior problems.

box. If we assume that all other elements of the functional analysis were equal, such as strength of relations and modifiability of causal variables, the greatest magnitude of effect for this client would be associated with the modification of causal variable $X_2$. We complicated the causal diagram a bit by showing that $X_1$ causes two behavior problems. This illustrates that the relative magnitude of effect of $X_1$ and $X_2$ also depends on other elements of the functional analysis, such as the relative importance of $Y_3$ compared to $Y_1$ and $Y_2$ combined.

It can be difficult to estimate the relative importance of a client's behavior problems. One reason for this is that importance is a higher-order clinical judgment based on several interrelated lower-order assessment-based and value-based judgments. A second reason, consistent with the *idiographic nature of the functional analysis*, is that the same behavior problems can differ in relative importance across clients.

"Importance" is also relevant when an intervention focuses on the attainment of positive goals rather than the reduction of behavior problems. That is, the magnitude of effect would be greater when more important intervention goals are achieved than when less important intervention goals are achieved. For example, a client may rate the intervention goal of "communicating my feelings better with my spouse" much higher than "helping me deal with an intrusive co-worker."

Estimates of the relative importance of a client's behavior problems can be derived from multiple and overlapping sources of information. We outline five of them here:

1. *The rate and magnitude of a behavior problem.* For example, importance might reflect the relative rate or magnitude of a client's problem with alcohol use, panic episodes, and binge eating. A client might be using alcohol to the point of severe intoxication most days of the week to manage work-related stressors, while her panic episodes and binge eating happen less frequently and exert less disruption to her life roles and quality of life. Thus, her alcohol abuse would be given a higher importance rating relative to panic and binge eating.

2. *The adverse or negative effects of the behavior problem.* The relative importance of a client's behavior problem can be based on

judgments about the probability that the behavior problem will lead to harm to the client or others *independent from rate and magnitude*. An example of this would be infrequent unprotected sexual contact with a high-risk partner. Although the behavior occurs at a low frequency, it could still be considered an important behavior problem because of the possibility of acquiring a sexually transmitted disease.

3. *The degree of influence on the client's personal distress.* Clients differ in the degree to which they experience distress or believe their quality of life is affected by their marital or work distress, depressed moods, anxious thoughts, sleep and health problems, and substance use, to name a few. These relative estimates of importance are usually based on subjective reports of distress or concern by the client during the assessment process. Consider the earlier example in which the client who is drinking excessive amounts of alcohol might report her panic episodes as having a greater negative impact on her overall quality of life.

4. *The degree of functional impairment associated with a behavior problem.* The importance of a behavior problem can be based on the degree to which the problem is associated with impairment in his or her daily life. For example, behavior problems can differ in their impact on work, marital happiness, social relationships, or family functioning.

5. *Behavior problems that interfere with therapy progress.* A client's behavior problem can be important because it affects the attainment of other intervention goals. Behaviors that interfere with an intervention can vary widely in their form and can also be dependent on the focus, context, and strategies of the intervention. For example, an intervention targeting a child's self-injurious behavior could be hampered by his or her persistent escape behaviors during behavioral training sessions. In this example, the self-injurious behaviors may be more damaging but their modification is dependent on a prior reduction of the child's escape behaviors. In other examples, exposure interventions for a phobia could be hampered by a client's negative outcome expectancies. Similarly, intervention progress in cognitive-behavior therapy

with a variety of clients can be hampered by hyperreactive emotional responses of the client to the therapist (for a discussion of client resistance and strategies for coping in cognitive-behavior therapy, see Watson & McMullen, 2005).

To illustrate how the various means of estimating the relative importance of a client's multiple behavior problems could be applied, we review the work of Linehan (1993) and Koerner and Linehan (1997). They discussed how dialectic behavioral treatment (DBT) strategies, primarily with persons diagnosed with borderline personality disorders, focus on problems in a descending order of their importance. The importance ratings are based on degree of possible harm, functional impairment, and impairment of the therapy process. The first stage of therapy typically focuses on suicidal/homicidal or other life-threatening behavior. Subsequently, the focus turns to behavior that impairs the client's quality of life and behaviors necessary to promote positive changes in the client's life. Finally, Linehan's Dialectical Behavior Therapy addresses problem behaviors that interfere with therapy.

Our outline of the ways to estimate the importance of a client's behavior problem also illustrates that information from multiple sources is critically important. In many cases, the source of these estimates is the client. For example, after identifying behavior problems, a clinician can ask a client to rate on a 5-point scale (from "1" as being not at all important, to "5" being extremely important) the relative importance of each behavior problem. Persons and colleagues recommend generating a "problem list" as part of a clinical case formulation. Each problem on this list is then rated by the client on its level of importance (Persons, 2006).

In addition to client reports, judgments about the relative importance of behavior problems (and positive intervention goals) can also be based on information from informants, such as a spouse, teacher, psychiatric staff, parents, coworkers, and primary care physicians. Differences in importance ratings generated by other informants and the client are not uncommon. This is because the judgments from each are based on idiosyncratic considerations and biases. For example, a teacher may rate disruptive behavior as highly important because it interferes with his or her ability to conduct a class. Alternatively, the client (in this case a student) may rate disruptive behavior as a trivial concern because it allows him or her to escape from exposure to the aversive lesson material.

When disagreements in importance ratings occur, the clinician should consider how the client and other informants differ in their evaluation of the behavior problem. In some cases, it may be that the informant ratings are most relevant to the functional analysis. In other cases, it may be that the client ratings are most relevant.


## BEHAVIOR PROBLEMS HAVE MULTIPLE RESPONSE MODES

As we note in earlier chapters, a *response mode* of a behavior problem refers to its form or type. Response modes are organizational categories or taxonomies of behavior. There are many taxonomies of behavior. A well-developed taxonomy was presented by Arthur Staats who posited that behavior problems could be assigned to "language-cognitive," "sensory-motor," and "emotional-motivational" behavioral repertoires (Staats, 1986). However, the most frequently invoked response modes involve five overlapping categories: (a) overt action (observable motor behavior), (b) verbal behavior (such as subjective reports or verbal expressions of distress), (c) cognitive activity (such as thoughts or beliefs), (d) physiological responses (such as blood pressure changes), and (e) combinations of these, such as "emotional" behaviors (for examples of positive and negative emotional priming, see Lang, 1995).[1]

Response mode categories can also be specific to a particular behavior problem and overlap with the *components*, *facets*, or *elements* of a behavior problem. For example, anxiety, PTSD, and depression are often considered to have cognitive, behavioral, and psychophysiological modes (see reviews in Hersen et al., 2006, and Hersen & Thomas, 2006). The *tripartite model* of anxiety disorders refers to the cognitive, behavioral,

---

[1] Other authors sometimes refer to response modes as response *dimensions*, such as physiological, cognitive, motor, and emotional by Lang (1995). Response modes are also called *response systems*, or *response channels*. Definitions of *response mode* are also different in computer science and some areas of medicine, where the term can refer to responses to or by sound, sight, touch, and temperature. Cone (1998b) prefers the term *behavior content area*.

and emotional components of anxiety disorders (Bergman & Piacentini, 2005). What is important to note is that there are a number of response mode taxonomies and the most useful taxonomy can differ across behavior problems.

The concept of response mode is challenging because of the fact that different response modes tend to be measured in different ways. In Chapters 7–9, we discuss methods and strategies of assessment used to capture the response modes of behavior problems. Briefly, we can obtain objective data on motor activity and psychophysiological behaviors through the use of external observers (such as trained raters, using a validated behavioral observation system), activity monitoring instrumentation (such as pedometers, actimeters), and psychophysiological recording instruments (such as measuring blood pressure with ambulatory biosensors). In contrast, we measure thoughts and felt emotions primarily through self-report.

Because response modes are often measured in different ways, the measurement of response modes are confounded with the method of their measurement. Furthermore, the differences in assessment methods can account for apparent differences among and within response modes. Consider, for example, the source of differences that emerge between data based on retrospective self-report versus instrumentation-acquired measures of real-time physical activity or physiological arousal. Two articles by Cone (1979, 1998) provide an erudite overview of these conceptual and methodological issues.

Despite the aforementioned challenges, for many clients, the specification of response modes can be an important goal of behavioral assessment and a component of the functional analysis. This is because most behavior problems have multiple response modes. Additionally, and most important to the functional analysis, there are two important attributes of response modes: asynchrony and differential causality.

Response modes can be asynchronous across time. *Synchrony* is the degree of congruence in the time-course of two events. Asynchronous events differ in their time-courses (such as in periodicity, latency, or duration) and show low magnitudes of covariance or low degrees of congruence across time. Consider the differential response latencies of heart rate and diastolic blood pressure to a laboratory stressor. Heart rate can be affected within a second of stimulus onset while diastolic blood pressure can take many seconds to show a measurable response. Additionally, diastolic blood pressure may not show any measurable response to small and transient stimuli that can affect heart rate.

There are also individual differences in response mode asynchrony among persons with the same behavior problem. For example, some persons with anxiety problems experience intense subjective distress in some anxiety-provoking situations but do not avoid them, whereas other persons might avoid or escape these situations and therefore experience less distress. Clients with chronic pain can show asynchrony among response modes, such as differences in subjective reports of pain or fatigue, facial grimaces, mobility impairment, functional impairment (such as negotiating multiple work and household tasks), verbal complaints to others, and use of pain medication (see discussions in Turk & Melzack, 2001). Haynes and O'Brien (2000) discuss several explanations for response mode asynchrony, including measurement confounds, differences in underlying pathophysiology, and differential latency of causal effects.

An important concept for behavioral assessment and the functional analysis is that the most important causal variables and causal relations can differ across response modes for a client. For example, a client's frequent complaints to family members about his or her chronic pain may be more strongly affected by the responses of the family members (such as receiving supportive versus critical comments) than by the cognitive or biochemical causal factors underlying the pain. Essentially, the causal factors that affect the experience of pain can be different than the causal factors that affect complaints about pain or the functional impairment associated with it. The former may be more strongly affected by pain sensitivity catastrophic thoughts about the pain, and neurophysiologic factors, while the latter may be more strongly affected by social reinforcement and escape from aversive settings. Also consider how the different response modes of a behavior problem can lead to different problems for a client, such as when the client's physiological experience of pain may be causing work problems (such as being unable to sit for long hours), but the verbal expression of that pain may be causing marital problems. Interventions for reducing "pain" would differ according to which response modes and which causal relations were most relevant for a client.

In summary, when developing a functional analysis for a client, the clinician should be sensitive to the possibility of asynchrony among response modes. The emphasis on response modes is consistent with our emphasis on *functional specificity* of variables in the functional analysis, as we discuss in Chapter 2. The clinician should also remember that the importance of different response modes for a client's behavior problem can change over time. For example, for a person experiencing Posttraumatic Stress Disorder symptoms, intrusive images may be of greater concern early in intervention, while emotional numbing may be more important later. Also consider how a child identified as being oppositional and defiant might exhibit truancy and stealing after entering the seventh grade whereas he might have only been verbally disruptive and indifferent to the teacher's instructions in the classroom in earlier grades.

An ultimate goal of the functional analysis is to select an intervention that targets the causal mechanisms operating for a client. Thus, for example, if a problem behavior were being maintained by high levels of social reinforcement, then the most appropriate intervention would either remove social reinforcement or provide differential social attention for a response that competes with, or is an alternative to, the problem behavior. Similarly, if a problem behavior appears to be strongly affected by dysfunctional thoughts (e.g., negative outcome expectancies), then the most appropriate intervention would target the dysfunctional thoughts.

The relations between the predominant response mode of a client's behavior problem and the outcome of mode-specific interventions have been the focus of extensive research and discussion. There are several challenges to understanding the benefits of matching intervention mechanisms to causal mechanisms. One challenge is that we often do not know why an intervention works—the mechanisms of action have not been identified. Also, matching response modes to interventions does not mean that one has matched causal mechanisms to intervention mechanisms. Further, multiple interventions with the same focus are often available and some interventions often focus on multiple response modes (such as many cognitive-behavioral therapies for depression and anxiety).

Chorpita, Daleiden, and Weisz (2005) discussed a method of identifying mechanisms of various empirically supported treatments so that the treatment could be matched to the characteristics of a specific client. Doss and Atkins (2006) also discussed some of the methodological challenges of examining intervention mechanisms, which they term "treatment mediators." In an example of matching treatment to behavior problem components or response mode, Evers, Kraaimaat, van Riel, and de Jong (2002) provided customized cognitive-behavioral treatments to clients in the early stages of rheumatoid arthritis. Treatment components that targeted pain and functional disability, fatigue, negative mood, and impaired social relations were provided to patients based on their preferences and important aspects of their presenting problems.

Research on the incremental benefits of matching interventions to the predominant mode of a behavior problem for a client has provided mixed outcomes. The issue of response mode-treatment matching has been discussed by Shiffman (1993) for smoking, by Linehan (1993) for personality disorders, by Michelson (1986) for agoraphobia, by Ost, Jerremalm, and Johansson (1981) for social phobia, by Imber et al. (1990) for depression, by Haaga et al. (1994) for hypertension, and by McGlynn and Rose (1996) for anxiety and fear. We discuss this issue more thoroughly in later chapters.

We suggest that, for many clients, the validity and utility of a functional analysis will be strengthened (i.e., more effective interventions can be selected) by a consideration of specific response modes during clinical assessment. There will be benefits from attention to response modes to the degree that the response modes do not strongly covary, have different degrees of importance, and are differentially influenced by causal variables. If they covary strongly and are equally important, an intervention focus on any response mode would be equally effective. If they are influenced by the same causal relations, an assessment of any would identify the same causal paths and suggest the same intervention foci. Nevertheless, a functional analysis will allow for such clinical judgments to be made—judgments that are difficult to make solely on the basis of a client's diagnosis or identified set of behavior problems.

The clinician must consider if the benefits outweigh the costs of gathering separate data on different response modes associated with a client's behavior problems. For example, do the cost and time in gathering psychophysiological data add to our understanding of a client's self-reported anxiety symptoms? Findings from past research and information obtained from a clinician's initial assessments with a client can offer suggestions about whether or not response modes can differ in importance or are asynchronous and warrant multimodal measurement.

The examples of response modes we provided thus far also illustrate that response modes can differ in their magnitude of functional interrelations and have different levels of specificity and overlap. For example, the physiological, behavioral, and cognitive response modes in anxiety disorders are not independent. A client's overt behaviors, such as avoidance behaviors, often occur concurrently and have bidirectional causal relations with cognitive (such as thinking about negative outcomes) and physiological responses (such as increase in heart rate and palpitations).

Given these caveats, the clinician must decide if assessment data from individual response modes will strengthen the validity and utility of the functional analysis. The clinician should consider which response modes to measure and how to best measure them to facilitate the identification of important causal variables and aid in selecting the intervention that best helps the client.


## BEHAVIOR PROBLEMS HAVE MULTIPLE DIMENSIONS

Most behavior problems can be described on multiple dimensions ("dimensions" are sometimes called "parameters"). Recall that a *dimension* is a quantitative attribute of a behavior problem or other variable. The most important dimensions of behavior problems, and causal variables, are rate, probability, duration, severity, magnitude (intensity, number of symptoms), cyclicity (periodicity), variability, and latency. For example, we can measure manic episodes in terms of their rate, the severity of accompanying symptoms, duration, the time between a depressive and manic episode (latency), and the likelihood (conditional probability; such as the likelihood that one will occur following sleep disturbance). We elaborate more on the dimensions of behavior problems in Box 4.1.

## Box 4.1 Dimensions of Behavior Problems

*Rate:* The relation between a quantity and time, for example, the number of headaches per month, or tantrums per hour, or nightmares per week.

*Probability:* The likelihood that an event will occur, usually within the context of time or some other quantity. For example, the likelihood that a client will relapse within a year following successful therapy.

*Magnitude:* The numerical value of a variable associated with a particular scale of measurement. For example, the magnitude of blood pressure based on mmHg or magnitude of heart rate change based on beats per minute.

*Duration:* The length of time that elapses between the onset and end of an event. For example, the length of time that a manic episode occurs, the length of time a person lays awake at night thinking about the next day's work before falling asleep, or how long a child maintains a single tantrum.

*Severity/Intensity:* A qualitative or quantitative measure, usually subjectively estimated, of distress or impairment, often influenced by rate, magnitude, and duration. For example, a client's rating of the severity of a panic episode, depressed mood, or anxiety state.

*Latency:* The time between two events. For example, the time between the onset of a depressive phase to the onset of a manic phase for a client with bipolar disorder or the length of time between a positive statement by a person and a positive statement by his or her partner.

*Variability:* The range or degree to which values of an event change across time, context, or persons. For example, the range of a client's positive and negative mood states across a week, or the range of positive and negative exchanges of a couple at home relative to public settings.

*Cyclicity:* Systematic variation over the course of time; a period of time in which regularly occurring events occur; often measured in terms of rate or latency. For example, circadian patterns of melatonin production or the monthly pattern of a client's migraine headaches.

Several aspects regarding the multidimensional nature of behavior problems are particularly relevant for behavioral assessment and the functional analysis. First, the dimensions of a behavior problem can differ in their relative importance across clients. For example, one client can have depressive episodes or headaches that are frequent but short and severe in duration while another client can have depressive episodes or headaches that are less frequent and severe but longer in duration.

Second, the dimensions of a behavior problem can be asynchronous. That is, different dimensions of a behavior problem often do not strongly covary. For example, a reduction in the severity of a child's tantrum episodes may or may not be associated with a reduction in the rate of those episodes. Figure 4.6 illustrates individual differences and asynchrony in two dimensions (rate and intensity) of "hypervigilance," measured with two clients, before and during cognitive intervention.

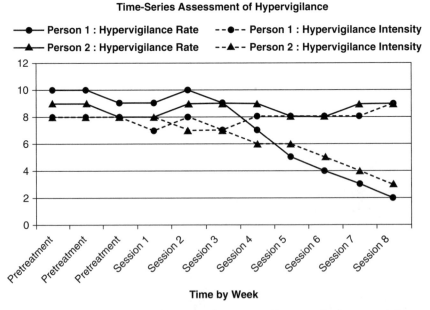

**Figure 4.6.** Time-series data of the rate and intensity of hypervigilance in two different persons with PTSD over the course of three assessment occasions and eight therapy sessions. The figure illustrates differences across time between persons and as a function of dimension of the behavior problem.

*Source: From Kaholokula et al., 2008.*

Perhaps most important in behavioral assessment, different dimensions of a behavior problem can be influenced by different causal variables. There are many examples of the differential effect of causal variables across dimensions of a behavior problem. For example, Barnett and Gotlib (1988) suggested that learned helplessness beliefs might affect the duration and magnitude, more than the latency to onset, of depressive episodes, which might more likely be triggered by environmental events. Similarly, catastrophic thoughts may affect the duration and severity of panic episodes more than their rate (see discussions in Smits et al., 2006). The responses of family members may affect the severity and duration of medical conditions, such as asthma, more than the onset of those conditions (Wicks-Nelson & Israel, 1997). The events that trigger paranoid delusions, such as a person being confronted with ambiguous social stimuli, may be different from the events that affect the duration and content of the delusions (such as responses of others to the client's behavior when delusional; Haynes, 1986).

As we continue to emphasize, an ultimate goal of the functional analysis is to facilitate a match between intervention mechanisms and the causal mechanisms operating for a specific client. Given that causal relations can differ across the dimensions of a behavior problem and the possible asynchrony of those dimensions, different behavioral interventions are likely to have varying effects across dimensions of behavior problems. These varying effects arise as a function of the degree to which the treatment mechanisms of action address the causal mechanisms affecting the behavior problem dimension. Referring to the previous examples of panic episodes, interventions that reduce catastrophic thoughts associated with the physiological sensations during a panic episode would be expected to have a stronger effect on the severity and duration of the episodes than on their rate.[2] If the clinician is interested in reducing the rate of the episodes, the identification of factors that increase the likelihood of the panic episodes would be more useful. The clinician must address the question "What is the most important dimension of this behavior problem for this client?" To answer that question requires a multidimensional behavioral assessment strategy.

---

[7] A reduction in rate might also occur for clients if they worried less about the panic episodes, which, in turn, decreased their sensitivity to life stressors.

## BEHAVIOR PROBLEMS ARE CONDITIONAL

An important concept that guides behavioral assessment strategies, informs the functional analysis, and imposes limits on its validity for each client, is that a person's behavior problems are often conditional. That is, for many clients, behavior problems vary systematically across contexts. By context, we are referring to social contexts (such as the presence of unfamiliar people versus familiar people), physical contexts (such as classroom versus home), and psychological or physiological contexts (such as emotional states). For example, a young child with autistic symptoms may be more likely to injure herself, or to engage in self-stimulatory behavior, in a classroom that includes structured academic demands relative to unstructured play (O'Reilly et al., 2005). A patient recovering from excessive alcohol use may be more likely to have a relapse in response to interpersonal conflict than to other types of life stressors (Walitzer & Dearing, 2006). A patient in a psychiatric hospital may be more likely to experience delusions during stressful interactions with a family member, than with other patients.

Consistent with our emphasis on idiographic strategies in behavioral assessment and individual differences in the functional analysis, the conditions that affect the aspects of a behavior problem can also differ across persons with similar behavior problems. For example, one person could be more likely to have an alcohol relapse as a way of reducing negative affect associated with interpersonal problems, while another is more likely to have an alcohol relapse in response to pressures from friends to drink (Walitzer & Dearing, 2006). One person with a diagnosis of panic disorder with agoraphobia may be at a higher risk of panic attacks in an open space while another person with the same diagnosis may be at a higher risk of panic attacks in stressful social settings. As these examples illustrate, a number of settings and contexts affects aspects of clients' behavior problems, including social contexts, physical settings, psychological or physiological states, and recent events.[3]

---

[3] In applied behavior analysis, settings and contexts are sometimes referred to as *establishing operations*: An event or condition that temporarily influences the effectiveness of a response contingency and the rate of behaviors affected by those contingencies or discriminative stimuli. *Discriminative stimuli* are those associated with differential probabilities that a particular response will be followed by a particular consequence.

These examples also illustrate how different contexts can serve as causal variables for behavior problems and how they can affect the dimensions and attributes of a behavior problem (see Chapter 5 on causal variables). Particular contexts associated with elevated conditional probabilities of a behavior problem serve as *markers* for the operation of specific causal variables. As we discuss later, the clinician should consider the *mechanism of action* of these causal relations: "How does a stressful interpersonal experience increase the likelihood of a patient's delusions?" "What is it about a specific event that leads to the patient's delusions?" "Why is a child more likely to injure himself at home than at school?" "What are the differences between school and home that might account for the difference in self-injury?" As a further example, consider how the delusional talk of a psychiatric patient can serve an escape or approach function. In the first case, he may engage in delusional talk in order to escape from an aversive social situation. In the second case, delusional talk brings about social attention from other patients.

### Box 4.2 Conditional Probabilities

*Conditional probability* is the likelihood that an event will occur, given that some other event has occurred. Consider two variables: A and B. The unconditional probability of A is the likelihood that A will occur without considering the occurrence of any other variable. In essence, this is the base rate of A. One can then compare the unconditional probability of A to the conditional probability of A given B. Specifically, one can determine whether the occurrence of A, given the occurrence of B, is different from the unconditional probability of A. This conditional probability can be higher (in which case B could be thought of as an event that increases the probability of A) or lower (in this case B could be thought of as an event that decreases the probability of A) than the unconditional probability of A. If the conditional probability of A given B is equal to the unconditional probability of A, then there is no functional relation between the two variables.

Behavior problems differ in the degree to which they are likely to vary across contexts. Some behavior problems have strong and reliable functional relations with contextual variables while others are more stable across contexts. For example, short-term memory deficits of persons following acquired head injury may vary somewhat across situations as a function of the stressfulness and stimulus complexity of the situation. However, for some persons, memory deficits associated with head injury are fairly invariant across contexts in which short-term memory plays an important role (see discussions in Cushman & Scherer, 1995).

Regardless of cross-contextual stability, the clinician should assume that a client's behavior problems can be at least partially context specific. Making this assumption during the behavioral assessment process is useful because it can often lead the clinician to discover clinically important sources of variance for the behavior problem, which can then strengthen the validity and utility of the functional analysis and point to more effective intervention strategies.

As we discuss in Chapters 7 and 8, the variation in the attributes of behavior problems across contexts highlights the need for context-specific assessment strategies. Although most self-report questionnaires do not provide context-specific information, assessment methods such as self-monitoring, functional interviews, and observation can provide useful context-relevant data, as we describe in Chapters 8 and 9.

## THE DYNAMIC NATURE OF BEHAVIOR PROBLEMS

The attributes of a client's behavior problem can also change across time. That is, there can be variability across time in the modes, importance, dimensions, and the functional relations of a client's behavior problems. For example, two people experiencing a major depressive episode may both experience early morning awakenings, decreased appetite, and concentration difficulty. While one of them shows a dramatic reduction in these aspects of depression across time, the other one can show steady or highly variable patterns across time. Or, some aspects of a client's behavior problem can change more than others. Further, as we discuss in

Chapter 6, a client's mood can be adversely affected by marital conflict at one time and by an accumulation of daily stressors at another.

The dynamic nature of behavior problems is also illustrated by daily and within-day changes in the frequency and content of a psychiatric patient's delusions, the blood pressure of a hypertensive patient, the pain reports and degree of functional impairment of a chronic pain patient, the activity rate of hyperactive children, the sleep patterns of persons with insomnia, caloric intake of persons diagnosed with anorexia nervosa, and the dyadic interactions of couples with distressed marriages. Individual differences in the time-course of attributes of a behavior problem are illustrated in Figure 4.6.

As with the conditional nature of behavior problems, changes in the time-course of a behavior problem suggest that a causal variable might be operating. For example, in Figure 4.6, the change in person 1's hypervigilance rate could be due to the presence of a new friend, while change in person 2's hypervigilance intensity could be due to a recent move to a new neighborhood. An increase in depressive symptoms, anxiety, or self-injurious behaviors suggests that causal variables or causal relations for those behaviors have changed—perhaps the client is experiencing new life stressors, the loss of a social support, a change in response contingencies, the side-effects of a prescribed medication, or the effects of another behavior problem.

Haynes and Kaholokula (2008) outlined several means through which behavior problems can change over time in response to changes in causal variables and their causal relations: (a) the repeated or prolonged exposure to a causal variable can result in the extinction, sensitization, or habituation of a behavior problem; (b) new causal variables can emerge while old causal variables cease to operate on a behavior problem; and/or (c) the actions of *mediators* and *moderators* can change over time.

The factors that can affect the dynamic nature of a behavior problem outlined above result from true changes in causal variables and relations that affect the client's behavior problem. A client's behavior problems can also only appear to change during the clinical assessment as the clinician gathers more information from the client. With additional assessment data, the clinician can change his or her judgments about the client's behavior problem. Adding to the impression of variability across time, clients often change their report of a behavior problem across assessment sessions, even though the behavior problem has not changed. These assessment-related changes in the clinician's judgments reflect our earlier point that the functional analysis is based on clinical judgments, which can be affected by numerous sources of error. A science-based approach to clinical assessment reduces the chance and impact of these errors.

The dynamic nature of a person's behavior problems has several implications for behavioral assessment, which we discuss in Chapter 7 with a particular emphasis on time-series assessment. The dynamic nature of behavior problems also indicates that the functional analysis is likely to be dynamic because its elements are likely to change across time. The dynamic and conditional nature of the functional analysis means that it has a *limited temporal domain of validity*—its validity is likely to erode over time. This is a particularly important consideration when a clinician is using medical, psychological, or other archived records to help construct a functional analysis.

## SUMMARY

The boundaries between the concepts of a behavior problem and psychiatric diagnosis overlap and both are amenable to a functional analysis. However, a more circumscribed term, behavior problem, is most clinically useful in behavioral assessment and the functional analysis because behavior problems can be more precisely defined, their measurement is less dependent on temporal and diagnostic exclusion criteria, they avoid some of the heterogeneity problems associated with formal diagnosis, and they are often the focus of clinical interventions.

Assessments can be conducted and functional analyses can be developed at different levels of specificity. We stress *functional specificity*: The best level of specificity depends on the goals of the assessment. For example, the goal of the initial assessment could be to determine the initial focus of intervention, to illustrate client's strengths and assets, to assist with strategic intervention planning with specific behavior problems, or to help communicate a clinical case formulation with other professionals. At any level of specificity, precise measurement is essential to the acquisition of valid data and the construction of a valid and clinically useful functional analysis.

The specification of behavior problems can be challenging because clients often have multiple and co-occurring behavior problems. Behavior problems covary because they are sometimes affected by a common causal variable. Additionally, one behavior problem can act as a causal variable for another behavior problem. Finally, two or more behavior problems may be influenced by different but covarying causal variables.

A clinician must also form judgments about the importance of behavior problems. Additionally, the effects of behavior problems for a client and the interrelations among behavior problems are important considerations in the functional analysis. Finally, the clinician must estimate the relative benefits to the client of focusing intervention on each causal variable within the functional analysis.

Many behavior problems have multiple response modes and dimensions. Response modes and dimensions of behavior problems can vary in importance across and within clients, can be asynchronous across time, can be affected by different causal variables and relations, and can respond differently to clinical interventions.

We emphasize the multivariate and interactive aspects of behavior problems because they guide behavioral assessment strategies and contribute to the ultimate goal of the functional analysis—to facilitate a match between intervention mechanisms and the causal mechanisms operating for the behavior problems of a specific client. Different behavioral interventions are likely to have differential effects across response modes and dimensions of behavior problems.

# 5

# Conceptual and Empirical Foundations of Behavioral Assessment and the Functional Analysis II

## The Complex Nature of Causal Variables and Causal Relations

### INTRODUCTION TO BASIC CONCEPTS OF CAUSALITY

In this chapter we discuss concepts of causality and the complex attributes of causal variables and causal relations in psychopathology. Causality is a particularly important topic because the behavioral assessment paradigm and the functional analysis emphasize the identification and specification of variables and causal relations that affect clients' behavior problems and the attainment of their intervention goals. Concepts of causality help the clinician to know what variables might be important and how they might be operating for a person's behavior problems. Decisions about the best assessment strategies, methods, instruments, and measures in clinical assessment are also influenced by how we think about the causes of behavior problems. For example, if we assume that the causes of Mrs. Sanchez's depressive episodes (our case example in Chapter 2) are stable biological processes, we are less likely to examine life events or interpersonal factors that may trigger the onset of her mood changes or to examine thoughts and actions that might affect the duration of her depressive episodes.

We begin this chapter with an examination of the basic concepts of causality that permeate the philosophy of science and the behavioral sciences. We then consider the necessary conditions for inferring a causal relation, with particular emphasis on causal inference in psychopathology and in formulating a functional analysis. Finally, we consider attributes of causal variables and causal relations that are particularly relevant to the functional analysis.

## DIVERSE CONCEPTS OF CAUSALITY

Causality has been discussed and debated among philosophers of science for centuries. The dialogues have centered on several fundamental questions. Does causality exist? What is the definition of "causality"? What is a "cause"? What are the types of causes? What conditions are necessary for inferring a causal relation? Can causal relations be bidirectional as well as unidirectional? What are the limitations of causal inferences? Of course, an in-depth presentation of these issues would require several chapters, but we will briefly review some of them to provide a historical context for the subsequent discussion of causal relations in the functional analysis.[1]

The question of whether causality exists independently from our perceptions of it has been an important, and continuing, debate in the philosophy of science. David Hume, an 18th-century Scottish philosopher, wrote extensively on this topic. Hume argued that we must base causal inferences on perceptions and that there is no reason to believe that

---

[1] See books by Blalock (1971; *Causal Models in the Social Sciences*), Bunge (2009; *Causality and Modern Science*), Haynes (1992; *Causal Models in Psychopathology*), James, Mulaik, and Brett (1982; *Causal Analysis*), Pearl (2000; *Causality*), and Shadish, Cook, and Campbell (2002; *Experimental and Quasi-Experimental Designs for Generalized Causal Inference*), which provide more extensive discussions of the concepts, issues, and background of causality concepts.

causality exists apart from our perceptions. To illustrate, Hume (1740) used the classic billiard ball example in his important work on causality entitled A *Treatise of Human Nature*.

Here is a billiard-ball lying on the table, and another ball moving towards it with rapidity. They strike; and the ball, which was formerly at rest, now acquires a motion. This is as perfect an instance of the relation of cause and effect as any which we know, either by sensation or reflection. Let us therefore examine it. It is evident that the two balls touched one another before the motion was communicated, and that there was no interval betwixt the shock and the motion. Contiguity in time and place is therefore a requisite circumstance to the operation of all causes. It is evident, likewise, that the motion which was the cause is prior to the motion which was the effect. Priority in time is therefore another requisite circumstance in every cause. But this is not all. Let us try any other balls of the same kind in a like situation, and we shall always find that the impulse of the one produces motion in the other. Here, therefore, is a third circumstance, viz. that of a constant conjunction betwixt the cause and effect. Every object like the cause produces always some object like the effect. Beyond these three circumstances of contiguity, priority, and constant conjunction, I can discover nothing in this cause. The first ball is in motion; touches the second; immediately the second is in motion: and when I try the experiment with the same or like balls, in the same or like circumstances, I find that upon the motion and touch of the one ball, motion always follows in the other. In whatever shape I turn this matter, and however I examine it, I can find nothing farther.

**"An Abstract of a Book Lately Published" (para. 9). The work is in the public domain and available at www.davidhume.org.**

A human observer, witnessing what Hume describes as one ball striking another, would invariably conclude that the action of the first billiard ball had, in fact, *caused* the second billiard ball to move. Hume, however, claimed that the causal relation between the first and second billiard ball cannot be directly observed, but only inferred or more specifically *induced* from an observation of *coincidence in time and space* and replication of the presumed cause-effect sequence with other similar objects and in other settings. According to Hume, a strict empiricist, knowledge based on inductive logic, rather than direct observation, was inherently tautological and therefore flawed. Specifically, Hume argued that the mere fact that two billiard balls acted in a specific way in the past, does not in any way necessitate that they should continue to act in the same way in the future.

The work of Hume and other philosophers of science make a strong case that causal relations cannot be directly observed nor empirically demonstrated. Instead, a causal relation is an inference based on inductive logic. Thus, in scientific and clinical assessment contexts, it is crucial to acknowledge that the demonstration of a causal relation is essentially a matter of persuasion using scientific methodology and careful data analysis. It is similar to *construct validity* in the sense that it is an inferred property based on multiple pieces of evidence.

John Stuart Mill, a 19th-century philosopher, also wrote extensively on the problem of demonstrating causal relations. Mill described conditions that would be persuasive in forming an inference of causality: (a) temporal precedence—the cause must precede the effect, (b) the cause and effect must be related (covariation), and (c) all other explanations of the cause-effect relation must be eliminated. Mill also provided strategies that could be used to rule out alternative explanations of cause-effect relations. The *Method of Agreement* states that an effect will be present whenever the presumed cause is present. The *Method of Difference* states that the effect will not occur when the cause is not present. Finally, the *Method of Concomitant Variation* states that when relations are observed using *both* the preceding methods, causal inferences are strongest (Shadish, Cook, & Campbell, 2002).[2]

---

[2] For clinical assessment purposes, note how there could be a causal relation without meeting Mill's three conditions if a causal relation was conditional on some other variable, as we discuss in Chapter 4.

Let us return for a moment to Hume's example of the billiard ball. Using the Method of Agreement, one sees that whenever the second ball moves, the first ball has also moved. In addition, using the Method of Difference, one sees that if the first ball does not move, the second ball does not move. Finally, the Method of Concomitant Variation indicates that the second ball will not move unless the first ball has struck it and whenever the first ball strikes the second ball, the second ball moves.

Given the aforementioned philosophical perspectives, it is clear that causation is an *idea* that is based on certain conditions including covariation, temporal order, and the ability to rule out plausible alternative explanations. Although the issue of whether causality exists apart from our perceptions of it remains an open question, most behavioral scientists are willing to assume that causal relations exist and are of critical importance in clinical assessment and intervention. Further, for behavioral scientist-practitioners, what may matter most is that certain variables are reliably associated with (or are likely to be associated with) certain outcomes, and that manipulating these variables often leads to important changes in these outcomes.

Philosophers of science have proposed several classes of causal variables. Some classes are more applicable to clinical assessment and the functional analysis than others. In considering the classes of causes listed below, assume that "Y" is a dimension of a behavior problem (e.g., frequency of binge eating or intensity of social anxiety) and that "X" is a potential causal variable (e.g., such as a life stressor or a discriminative stimulus).

The 10 classes of possible causal variables are as follows:

1. *Sufficient cause*: Y always occurs after X occurs. However, Y can occur without the prior occurrence of X. A practical example of this would be a fever (Y) and a severe bacterial infection (X). A fever will always (or almost always) occur when one has a severe bacterial infection. However, a fever can occur without the prior occurrence of a bacterial infection (e.g., other biological events, such as a virus, can cause fever).

2. *Necessary cause*: Y never occurs without the prior occurrence of X. However, X can occur without Y occurring. A practical

example of this would be alcohol intoxication (Y) and alcohol consumption (X). Alcohol intoxication never occurs without consumption of alcohol. However, alcohol consumption does not always lead to intoxication.

3. *Necessary and sufficient cause:* Y never occurs without the prior occurrence of X (necessary) and Y always occurs after X occurs (sufficient). A practical example of this would be gravity (Y) and the presence of an object (X). Specifically, gravity is never detected in the absence of an object and wherever there is an object, gravity is detected. Thus, there is no instance of one occurring without the other.

4. *Insufficient cause:* Y can occur when X occurs in combination with Z (another causal variable). However, Y does not occur when X occurs alone. An example of this would be combustion (Y), heat and fuel (X), and oxygen (Z). Combustion will occur when high heat and fuel are combined with oxygen. However, combustion will not occur as a result of heat and fuel alone. An insufficient cause need not be a necessary cause.

5. *Necessary but insufficient cause:* Y never occurs without X, but X is insufficient to cause Y; another variable must be involved.

6. *First cause:* That cause upon which all other causes depend; the earliest event in a causal chain.

7. *Immediate (proximal) cause:* That cause which produces the effect without any intervening events (i.e., there is a *temporal contiguity* between Y and X).

8. *Mediate (distal) cause:* That cause which produces its effect only through another causal variable.

9. *Principal cause:* That cause upon which the effect primarily, or most strongly, depends (the X among multiple causal variables with the strongest effect on Y).

10. *Secondary cause:* That cause upon which the effect partially, but not most strongly, depends (the X among multiple causal variables that has a detectable, but not principal effect on Y).

Many of the causal variables associated with clients' behavior problems are *insufficient* because they operate as causal variables in combination with other causal variables or only in certain contexts. For example, a client's high levels of anxiety, obsessions, and compulsive behaviors may be more likely when periods of relationship conflict occur together with major life stressors (i.e., *an interactive or additive causal relation*).

Functional analyses often include *distal* as well as more *proximal* (*mediate* and *immediate*) causes. For example, an immediate cause of a psychiatric patient's aggressive behavior on a psychiatric unit may be staff members' critical comments to the patient about his perseverative speech. However, these proximal causes may only influence the patient's behavior when more distal causes such as patient fatigue from sleeplessness or medication noncompliance are also present.

Several classes of causal variables outlined above are rarely elements of functional analysis or causal models of behavior disorders. For example, few variables are *necessary, sufficient,* or *necessary and sufficient* in psychopathology. Instead, most causal variables in psychopathology function as one among many. They exert causal effects in combination with other causal variables and can thus be classified as insufficient. Further, as we note in the previous chapters, the effects of these causal variables and the combinations of causal variables can differ across persons and can change for a person across time and contexts.

Concepts of causality have also been debated in the behavioral sciences. These debates have centered on (a) the competing definitions of causality; (b) whether causal concepts are relevant to the behavioral sciences (e.g., is consideration of "causality" necessary in order to design effective intervention programs or can these program be based on observations of intervention effects and/or functional relations only?); (c) the kinds of events that can serve as causes (e.g., can a person's thoughts or behavior serve as a cause of that person's other thoughts or behavior?); (d) the potential for infinite regress of causal inference (e.g., one can always ask what was the cause of a cause); (e) the subjective nature of causal inferences, especially in clinical settings because causal relations are essentially clinical inferences that are influenced by myriad cognitive biases; (f) the best level of specificity in causal inferences; (g) temporal aspects of causal relations (e.g., can events that happened years ago be considered as causes for a client's current behavior problem?); (h) the complex and challenging social implications associated with some causal inferences (e.g., can alcohol use "cause" domestic violence?); (i) the best methods of identifying causal relations in nomothetic research and in clinical assessment; and (j) the difficulties of ruling out alternative explanations for an apparent causal relation. We will discuss many of these issues as we continue to consider the principles and methods of behavioral assessment and the functional analysis.

## NECESSARY CONDITIONS FOR INFERRING A CAUSAL RELATION IN BEHAVIORAL ASSESSMENT, PSYCHOPATHOLOGY, AND THE FUNCTIONAL ANALYSIS

Several concepts of causality, methods of estimating causal relations, and limitations of causal inferences guide behavioral assessment strategies, inform our causal models in psychopathology, and are relevant to the functional analysis. We will briefly describe the following: (a) the necessary conditions for inferring causal relations for a client's behavior problems (e.g., What does the clinician have to do to be confident about his or her causal judgments?); (b) the subjective nature of causal judgments; (c) the domain (i.e., limitations and boundaries) of causal relations; (d) varying levels of specificity of causal judgments; (e) the dynamic nature of causal inferences (e.g., How can causal relations change over time?); (f) the nonexclusivity of causal relations (e.g., There can be more than one valid functional analysis for a client's behavior problems); and (g) the individual differences in causal relations across clients with the same behavior problem.

In estimating the causal relations that affect a client's behavior problems, the clinician must consider whether four essential conditions of causality have been met. Note also that these essential conditions guide many of the methods of behavioral assessment that we discuss in Chapters 7, 8, and 9. The main benefits of the four conditions we discuss below are that they guide the clinician's assessment foci and strategies and help the clinician avoid a false positive causal judgment: Falsely concluding that there is a causal relation between two variables when, in fact, there is none.

## Covariation

The most widely accepted condition for inferring a causal relation between two variables is that there must be evidence of a functional relation, that is, two variables must exhibit concomitant variation, covariation, correlation, elevated conditional probability, shared variance, or some other mathematical relation if they are to be considered to have a possible causal relation. Absence of a mathematical relation negates the possibility of a causal relation. For example, in order for "escape from an aversive situation" to function as a causal variable for a child's self-injurious behaviors, the behavior must be more likely to occur in aversive situations than in nonaversive situations (e.g., elevated conditional probability). If a client's "level of psychophysiological arousal" functions as a causal variable for panic episodes, measures of panic episodes and psychophysiological arousal (e.g., covariation between perceived fear and increased heart rate) must be correlated.

"Covariation" seems like a simple and logical requirement for a causal relation. However, there are several caveats and complications. First, sometimes a variable can be causally related to a client's behavior problem, but errors in the ways that they are measured will preclude the identification of a functional relation. For example, two variables that are causally related may be uncorrelated when they are measured outside of the *domain of their causal relation*. To illustrate, a child may exhibit oppositional behavior when asked to pick up his toys but only in the presence of one parent. Thus, there is covariation between the request to pick up toys (X) and oppositional behavior (Y) only in a particular context (a particular parent being present). If the clinician gathers information in the "wrong" context (e.g., when the other parent is present), no functional relation will be observed between the verbal request and the oppositional behavior.

Second, causal relations can exist within some but not other *values of variables*. For example, there can be a significant causal relation between the severity of a client's life stressors (e.g., work and school difficulties) and her sleeping problems, but only within certain ranges of frequency or intensity of life stressors. If we examine the relation between life stressors and sleeping problems when life stressors are infrequent, mild, or show little day-to-day variation, we may observe weak or no covariation. Alternatively, if we examine the same relation when life stressors are frequent or intense, we may observe very strong covariation (assuming daily variation).

Third, interaction effects among causal variables can mask a causal relation. For example, verbal aggression by other patients on a psychiatric unit could trigger a patient's delusional verbal behavior, but only when he has recently refused medication or experienced significant conflict with family members. If we measured the covariation between verbal aggression and delusional behavior during periods of low family conflict and good medication compliance, we may not observe significant covariation.

## Temporal Precedence

Another condition for inferring causal relations is temporal precedence. Temporal precedence requires that the *hypothesized causal variable must precede the behavior problem in time*. Assuming a functional relation exists between X and Y, X must precede Y in order for X to satisfy the requirement of temporal precedence. Remember that X does not have to *always* precede Y and that Y can occur without the prior occurrence of X because "necessary and sufficient relations" are uncommon in causal models of behavior problems. However, a causal relation between two variables is negated when there is a consistent lack of temporal precedence. Without establishing precedence between X and Y, it is difficult to rule out the possibility that (a) X is a result, rather than a cause, of Y, or (b) X and Y show covariation because they are both caused by another variable, "Z."

As with covariation, "precedence" seems to be a simple mandate for causal inference but it can be a difficult condition to establish in clinical assessment. First, precedence is a necessary but insufficient condition for excluding the possibility of a "third variable effect." For example, Z could function as a causal variable for X and Y but the effects of "Z" could have a shorter latency for X than for Y. This differential causal latency would result in covariation between X and Y (satisfying the first necessary condition for causality) and X would reliably precede Y (satisfying the second necessary condition for causality). Despite meeting the first two conditions for causality, X would not be a cause of Y (note that both could be true: Y could be influenced by both X and Z).

Consider a case in which a person's work stressors served as a causal variable for both her excessive use of alcohol and self-cutting, but that the work stressors affected alcohol use sooner than self-cutting. Suppose for example, that the person would go to a bar immediately after a stressful workday, but engage in the self-injurious behavior later in the evening after returning home. If we monitored alcohol use and self-injury, they would show covariation, and alcohol use would reliably precede self-injury. Consequently, it would appear that alcohol use served as a causal variable for self-injury. (We are assuming in this example that the likelihood of self-injury is not greater following alcohol use while controlling for the effects of work stressors.) The likelihood of this erroneous judgment might also be increased because of the clinician's knowledge that some research has found that alcohol and drug use increases the chance of self-injury for at-risk persons.

Notice the intervention implications for making an erroneous causal clinical judgment—if self-injury were the most important behavior problem, we would likely emphasize reducing alcohol use as one way to reduce self-injury. However, interventions more strongly focused on reducing work stressors or on moderating its effects may be more important for decreasing the likelihood of self-injury. An intervention focused on alcohol use could be beneficial for the client but would not result in the maximum intervention benefit for her, assuming all other elements of the functional analysis, such as modifiability of the causal variables, and strength of causal relations, are equal. As we have emphasized, a major goal of the functional analysis is to help select interventions with the *greatest magnitude of effect* and our assessment strategies have a strong effect on the validity of the functional analysis.

Prior research can be particularly helpful when we have difficulty gathering data on causal relations during clinical assessment and can help the clinician focus the behavioral assessment on potential causal relations for a client's behavior problems and goals. However, temporal precedence presents additional challenges to the clinician in interpreting published research. One challenge is that causal relations can sometimes only be accurately identified within *restricted temporal domains*. For example, the effects of a causal variable can be time-limited and differ across behavior problems. Consequently, measurement of a hypothesized causal relation outside of its temporal domain (e.g., before or after the causal effects) could suggest a lack of temporal precedence and covariation between two events when, in fact, there is a causal relation between them.

Measurement outside the temporal domain of a causal relation is a common problem in longitudinal research, such as research on the relations between depression and marital distress (see review of research in this area by Beach et al., 2006, and Rehman et al., 2008). In these longitudinal studies, depression and marital distress are often measured two or three times, perhaps a month or a year apart, to examine the degree to which depression (or marital distress) at time 1 predicts marital satisfaction (or depression) at time 2. This is a convenient time-sampling strategy for the researchers and research participants, but it is unlikely to capture the causal latency and dynamic qualities of the target variables. Given the normal variability in depressed mood and its effects on interpersonal behaviors, its strongest effects on marital satisfaction might occur within hours, days, or weeks, rather than a month or year away. Further, the latency of causal effects might be different for happy couples than for unhappy couples. If there are multiple causal variables that affect both depressed mood and marital satisfaction, many important events that could affect the strength of their functional relation are likely to occur within the time between measurement periods. Therefore, inappropriately timed longitudinal measurement would obscure temporal precedence and provide inaccurate estimates of the causal relations between two variables.

The requirement that a causal variable reliably precede the behavior problem in causal inferences is frequently violated in psychopathology research and in drawing causal inferences in clinical assessment. Although warnings against confusing a statistically significant correlation with causation are included in nearly every psychology research textbook, many competent researchers and clinicians interpret significant correlations or between-group differences based on cross-sectional data, as an index of a causal relation between variables. This inferential error is most likely when the correlations reported in the studies or observed in clinical assessment are congruent with the researchers' or clinicians' *a priori* expectations.

Examples of causal statements from such research take the form of: "If A functions as a cause of B, we would expect to find a significant correlation between A and B in our sample (or with our client), and the results confirmed our hypotheses."

Precedence cannot be established in cross-sectional research or in clinical assessment by simply measuring two variables at the same time and one time only. No matter how elegantly designed and analyzed (e.g., path analysis, structural equations modeling, or hierarchical regression strategies), the results of cross-sectional research and assessment can be consistent with, but never confirm, hypothesized causal relations. Similarly, it is difficult to draw inferences about causal relations for our clients by simply administering self-report questionnaires (e.g., self-report questionnaires on life stressors and anxiety level), unless there are temporal elements contained in the questionnaires themselves (such as, "I often feel anxious before meeting people I don't know").

Ward and Thorn (2006) emphasized the importance of temporal precedence in their critique of a study conducted by Cook, Brawer, and Vowles (2006). In the Cook et al. study, a structural equation model was developed that depicted the causal relations among catastrophizing, fear of re-injury, depression, disability, and pain severity. In this model, several potential causes were identified. Specifically, fear of re-injury was presumed to mediate the relation between catastrophic thoughts and perceived disability, depression, and pain severity among chronic pain patients (see Figure 5.1). In a finding that also relates to the *conditional nature of causal relations*, the functional relations were different for older than for younger patients. Their causal model is presented in Figure 5.1; note the temporal relations among the variables and the differing strengths of functional relations depicted.

While Cook et al.'s (2006) investigation provided important insights into the interactions among multiple variables in the experiencing of chronic pain, Ward and Thorn (2006) pointed out that temporal precedence could not be established because the study was cross-sectional (all of the measures were collected at a single point in time). Consequently, the various causal paths could potentially be reversed. For example, they argued that it could be the case that pain severity leads to depression, fear of reinjury, and catastrophic thoughts, which, in turn, lead to pain-related disability.

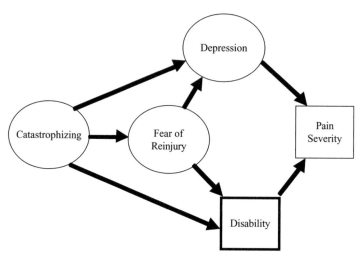

**Figure 5.1** A nomothetic causal model of disability associated with chronic pain, indicating the importance of fear as a mediator for the effects of catastrophizing. The strength of relations among variables will differ across clients.

*Source: Based on data from Cook et al., 2006.*

Because of the multidimensional nature of behavior problems, temporal precedence of a causal variable may hold for one dimension of the behavior problem and not another. For example, a client's poor ability to solve conflicts in his family relationships may affect the severity or duration of his depressive episodes but not their onset (see discussion in Nezu and colleagues, 1987 and 2004). Similarly, a client's erroneous attributions about physical sensations, such as believing that a rapid heartbeat indicates the start of a heart attack, may affect the duration or severity of the client's panic episodes, but not their onset (see review of panic disorder in Smits et al., 2006). Finally, a person who has experienced recent problems falling asleep may start to worry about being able to fall asleep when he or she goes to bed. In this case, the presleep worry could be a result of a person's prior sleeping difficulties (see book on cognition and sleep disorders by Bootzin et al., 1990).

Because causal relations can differ across dimensions of behavior problems, it is important that the clinician attend to the most important dimension during clinical assessment and to specify the targeted dimensions in functional analyses and emphasize this dimension in the Functional Analytic Clinical Case Diagram and for follow-up assessments. For example, failure to specify whether the functional analysis explains the onset, rate, likelihood, magnitude, or duration of a behavior problem can lead to erroneous causal inferences, less-than-optimal intervention foci based on the functional analysis, and the use of measures that are insensitive to changes in the targeted problems.

The previous examples we presented also highlight the importance of *individual differences* in the temporal aspects of causal relations. Recall that worry might function to prolong but not trigger sleep-onset difficulties. However, worry could be triggered by other events for some persons, such as the occurrence of a life stressor, that then lead to sleep-onset problems.

In some cases, a causal variable consists of patterns of interactions, such as those involving response contiguities rather than a simple "event." In such cases, the temporal relations between cause and effect are more complex. Take, for example, the causal variable "positive reinforcement," which includes a series of interactions between the client and environmental events. In the case of "positive reinforcement," the client's problem behavior is followed by a consequence that then increases the likelihood that the response will occur under similar circumstances (i.e., the response is "selected"). Because the consequence follows problem behavior, the temporal precedence requirement for establishing causality is not met. What then is the causal variable that can satisfy the temporal precedence requirement in the case of positive reinforcement?

Early behavioral psychologists, who eschewed the use of inferred psychological constructs such as expectations, memories, or anticipation of reinforcement, could not generate a logical causal argument for the relations between consequences and behavior because of the temporal precedence problem. More contemporary behavioral models, however, allow for the use of inferred psychological constructs. When such inferred constructs are used, a more coherent causal model of positive reinforcement can be offered. Specifically, the occurrence of the positive reinforcer after a behavior creates a response-consequence association in a person's cognitive representation of the environment (neuroscientists would further argue that biological interconnections are formed among neurons that process information pertaining to behavior and outcomes). Thus, when the person encounters a stimulus situation that is similar to the original positive reinforcement condition, cognitive events, such as expectations, memories, and anticipation of reinforcement are activated which, in turn, prompt the previously reinforced behaviors. Thus, the causal variables are cognitive states that are triggered by prior exposure to specific stimuli.[3]

*Bidirectional* (i.e., *circular*) *causation*, in which two variables affect each other, also presents additional measurement and conceptual challenges to establishing temporal precedence in clinical assessment and in psychopathology research. Covariation is easy to identify in bidirectional causal relations but the mechanisms of effect, the differential effects of each variable, and temporal precedence is more difficult to establish.

## The Exclusion of Alternative Explanations for the Functional Relation

As we noted in several prior examples, two variables can demonstrate significant covariation and one variable may reliably precede the other, not because of a causal relation between them, but because they are both affected by a third variable. Two variables can erroneously appear to be causally related in several ways, as illustrated in Figure 5.2. In each case, $Y_1$ covaries with, and precedes, $Y_2$. If the clinician or researcher measures only $Y_1$ and $Y_2$, and not X, he or she could erroneously infer that $Y_1$ had a causal relation with $Y_2$ when, in fact, their apparent causal relation is due to the differential effects of one or more third variables. Note the different causal latencies between X and $Y_1$ and $Y_2$ in Figure 5.2. Incorrectly inferring that there is a causal relation between two variables is especially likely under three conditions: (1) when the latency of causal effects of X are shorter for $Y_1$ than they are for $Y_2$ (which results in a reliable temporal precedence of the first variable over the second), (2) when the researchers or clinicians fail to measure X (an issue of the "*content validity*" of the causal model and diagram as we discuss in Chapter 3), and (3) when the functional relation observed between $Y_1$ and $Y_2$ is consistent with the investigator's beliefs.

Differences in causal latency have implications for clinical assessment strategies. When examining a possible causal relation between two behavior problems of a client, the clinician should consider the possibility that the observed covariance is due to the effects of a third variable.

---

[3] At a different level of analysis, the causal variable can be considered a *response-consequence contiguity*, which must precede any observed effect on the behavior.

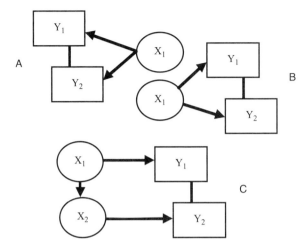

**Figure 5.2** Three ways in which two behavior problems ($Y_1$ and $Y_2$) can demonstrate reliable covariation and temporal precedence in the absence of a causal relation. In all cases, the latency of causal effect is different for the two behavior problems, which results in temporal precedence of one over the other.

The exclusion of alternative explanations for a hypothesized causal relation can be the most difficult-to-implement requirement for causal inference. Exclusion requires careful measurement of multiple variables in a carefully defined temporal sequence, combined with the application of empirically guided theoretical suppositions about what functional relations among the multiple variables are potentially relevant. Most, if not all, hypothesized causal relations in a functional analysis are open to many alternative explanations, and it is impossible within a clinical assessment context to consider them all. This limitation highlights our earlier statements that a functional analysis represents *subjective and tentative judgments* by the clinician, based on the best available evidence.

The strongest test of a causal relation ultimately relies on observing the effects of *systematic manipulation* of the hypothesized causal variable (see Kazdin, 2002, for a discussion of within-subject designs). However, the same caution in drawing causal inferences should be applied here. Systematic effects on $Y_1$ associated with the manipulation of $X_1$ are indicative of a causal relation only to the degree that alternative explanations for the apparent effects of the manipulation can be accounted for. Further, the operation of a third variable does not preclude a causal relation between X and Y. In these cases, as illustrated in Figure 5.1, the covariance between the behavior problems can only be partially accounted for by the action of a third variable.

## LOGICAL CONNECTIONS BETWEEN VARIABLES

Covariation, precedence, and the exclusion of (or controlling for) causal influence from a third variable are essential but incomplete conditions for causal inference in the functional analysis. For a variable to be considered "causal" it must also have a logical causal connection with the effect. The clinician must ask, "Does this causal relation have plausible theoretical or conceptual underpinnings?" or "How would X affect Y?" Eating an early breakfast may covary with, and always precede, a child's aggressive behaviors. But what is the *causal link* or *causal mechanism*? Perhaps aggression occurs only at school and early breakfasts occur only on school days. Or, perhaps a child's diet affects electrolyte balance or neurotransmitter reuptake and, thus, operates as the causal mechanism. For "early breakfast" to be considered a cause of the classroom aggression, the logic of such a connection, the mechanism of causal action, must be established or there must be a reasonable expectation that a causal connection can be established.

It is especially important to consider logical connections when higher-order, more abstract, and less specific causal variables are suggested in traditional case formulations. For example, how would "frustration" cause aggression or self-injury? How would "low self-esteem" lead to panic episodes or social avoidance? Consideration of the more specific pathways (i.e., *mediation*) between these causal variables and the target behavior problems can help the clinician develop a more clinically useful functional analysis. For example, intervention foci become more apparent when "frustration" is more specifically considered as "thoughts of being a failure as a parent" and "adversarial communication style with partner" or when "low self-esteem" is broken down to "self-deprecating thoughts about artistic skills" and "fear of negative evaluation by others."

We recognize that the four essential conditions for causal inference, although seemingly simple, can be difficult to evaluate in clinical assessment. For example, covariation can be difficult to detect when multiple causal variables affect a client's behavior problem and when other variables moderate or mediate the effects of a causal variable. Additionally, it can be difficult to identify and observe hypothesized causal relations when they occur in less accessible natural environments (e.g., between marital conflict and self-injury, between work stressors and depressed mood, or between a child's noncompliance and a parent's responses at bedtime). Finally, temporal precedence is difficult to establish when one is evaluating the relations between intraindividual variables such as thoughts and emotional states.

## MECHANISMS OF CAUSAL RELATIONS

As we just suggested, the mandate for a logical connection and the exclusion of alternative explanations in causal judgment requires that we identify the *causal mechanism*; the means through which a causal effect operates. When we think about causal mechanisms we are asking the question: "How, or in what way, does X influence Y?"

Causal inference can be based on the assumption that a causal mechanism between variables will eventually be identified. For example, the mechanisms of action of some psychotropic medications have not yet been identified but their beneficial actions for some patients have been (Bhuvaneswar, Baldessarini, Harsh, & Alpert, 2009). As we discuss in Chapter 10 (see Box 10.2), there are obvious benefits for the focus and outcome of interventions if we can identify the causal mechanisms underlying an apparent causal relation. In the case of psychotropic medications, new medications could be developed that more specifically, powerfully, or efficiently target the mechanism of action.

### Box 5.1 Causal Mechanisms and Bubonic Plague

The history of the bubonic plague provides an example of the importance of causal mechanisms. A causal relation between rats, fleas, and the bubonic plague (Black Death) was identified long before the mechanism of the causal connection, the way in which fleas harbored and transmitted the plague, was understood. For hundreds of years, through the European Dark and Middle Ages, the cause of the Plague was unknown. At different times, it was assumed to be poisoned wells, poisoned food, God's anger, astrological forces, "outside" groups (Jews, Gypsies, or beggars) and sinful behavior. It was not until the end of the 19th century that Alexandre Yersin isolated the causal bacterium *Yersinia pestis* that, in turn, enabled more effective prevention and treatment (see Biddle, 2002).

Note that the causal relation "rats cause the plague" can be supported by all tests of causation: (a) increases and decreases in the number of rats were followed by increases and decreases in the number of plague cases, (b) exterminating rats was followed by a reduction in plague cases, and (c) cities with more rats had more plague cases than cities with fewer rats. The rat-plague causal model was useful for municipal policies, in that it validly pointed to the conclusion that extermination of rats would lead to a reduction in plague cases. However, understanding the mechanism of causal action permitted many additional intervention strategies.

To further illustrate the benefits of understanding causal mechanisms, we offer another example taken from Haynes (1992)—the example of "turning a light switch to illuminate a lamp." A person turns a light switch (X) and a lamp illuminates (Y)—there is a strong functional relation between the two events and precedence (light switch → light). The question of causal mechanism can be stated as "How did the light switch cause the lamp to light?" We can infer that turning the light switch "caused" the light to go on because X preceded Y, the two events are highly correlated, temporally sequenced, and do not appear to be caused by a third variable. However, there are domains for this causal relation. Under some conditions, turning the light switch may be neither sufficient nor necessary for the lamp to illuminate, as in the cases of a broken switch, a burned-out filament, or an alternative switch.

The "turning a light switch to illuminate a lamp" example further illustrates the importance of the functional analysis, and of identifying causal mechanisms in clinical case models. If we understand the mechanisms underlying the causal relation between the operation of the light switch and the lamp illumination, a more diverse set of causal relations and opportunities to control the light becomes available. If we identify the relations among electron flow, amperage, wattage, types of conductive materials, and the internal atmosphere of the bulb, we can develop alternative ways of causing the light to go on. We can also control more dimensions of the effect, such as intensity or temperature of emitted light. More importantly, understanding causal mechanisms allows us to more effectively determine the possible reasons why the light sometimes fails to illuminate and to subsequently correct the problem. As with functional and dysfunctional behaviors, the same causal mechanisms can be responsible for both the normal operation of the light and its malfunctions.

This example again illustrates the concepts of *level* and *domain* of causal relations. At a higher, more molar level, we can think of the cause of the illumination as flipping a switch. At a lower, more micro level, we can consider the cause as the flow of electrons through resistant media. Both are valid and useful levels of causal relations in different contexts; that is, both are conditional in that they depend on other variables. For example, throwing the light switch causes illumination of the light only when there is sufficient outside power, an unbroken electric circuit, an appropriately sealed bulb, an intact filament, and a specific range of current and wattage.

Diversity in the *dimensions of causal effects* is also illustrated in our example. Dimensions of the light can include its latency until full illumination, brightness, duration of illumination, dispersion, color, variability (flicker frequency), or the amount of heat generated. As with a client's behavior problems, the various dimensions are likely to be differentially influenced by unique combinations of causal variables and paths. The amount of heat generated in the light bulb is more strongly affected by the resistant material than by the gaseous environment of the bulb. An important point we made earlier is that the dimensions of a client's behavior problem upon which we focus our assessment strategies and the functional analysis will affect the causal relations we identify. Given that behavior problems have multiple dimensions, we are likely to identify multiple causal relations that vary across dimensions of the behavior disorder.

# THE ROLE OF THE CLINICIAN IN CAUSAL INFERENCE

A functional analysis of a client's behavior problems is the integration of many judgments by the clinician and, as we have emphasized, is only a hypothesized causal model. The inference that the relation between variables meets the four requirements for a causal relation is influenced by clinical training, theoretical orientation, research findings, and prior experience of the clinician. It is also influenced by the intrinsic fallibilities of human judgment and reasoning. In the former case, these clinician characteristics have been characterized as presuppositions to the causal field (Einhorn, 1988, p. 57). In the latter case, these clinician characteristics have been labeled cognitive biases and/or cognitive heuristics (see, for example, Tverski & Kahneman, 1974).

Presuppositions to the causal field are a necessary, albeit limiting aspect of a clinician's reasoning. They are necessary because a clinician is presented with a great amount of highly complex information. Consider, for example, a typical initial interview wherein a client may report dozens of problem behaviors that can be represented in cognitive processes, overt-behavior, emotional states, beliefs, and physiological systems. Further, a client may speculate on myriad causal variables and consequences associated with each problem behavior. A clinician cannot realistically codify and analyze all of these behavior problems and potential causes. Hence, he or she will use *a priori* decision frames or presuppositions to narrow the scope of inquiry.

As noted earlier, some presuppositions arise from formal training and theoretical orientation, while others arise from more informal sources, such as prior clinical experience. It is clear that presuppositions influence the degree to which a hypothesized causal relation is considered logical, plausible, supported by data, and clinically useful. For example, some psychodynamic theorists posit that "repression" or "sublimation" are critically important causal variables for some behavior problems. Personality theorists often argue that behavior disorders are the result of broad traits, such as "degree of introversion" or "degree of agreeableness." Theorists from other orientations find these causal explanations to be cumbersome, dysfunctionally heterogeneous, and incongruent with scientific psychology. It is unreasonable to expect that a case formulation can be completely independent of the *a priori* schema of the clinician.

Covariation misestimation is one of the more serious errors that can arise from the noncritical use of presuppositions. As we discuss further in Chapter 10, when guided by presuppositions, clinicians tend to ask *only* about causal variables that are deemed to be relevant to the behavior problem according to their theoretical orientation and/or training. Additionally, there is a tendency for clinicians to selectively attend to, and recall, information that is consistent with their presuppositions and simultaneously ignore or discount information that is contrary to their presuppositions. (For excellent discussions of the role of presuppositions in clinical decision making, see Garb's 1998 book, *Studying the Clinician: Judgment Research and Psychological Assessment,* and Garb's 2005 review article, "Clinical Judgment and Decision Making.")

Covariation misestimation can also occur among behaviorally oriented therapists. For example, one of us (WHO) conducted an investigation in which graduate students who had completed coursework in behavioral assessment and therapy were provided with a contrived set of self-monitoring data presented on three problem behaviors: headache frequency, intensity, and duration (O'Brien, 1995). The data set also contained information about three potentially relevant causal variables: hours of sleep, marital argument frequency, and stress levels. The data were constructed so that only a single causal factor was strongly correlated (i.e., $r > .60$) with a single problem behavior (the remaining correlations between causal variables and target behaviors were of very low magnitude).

Students were instructed to (a) evaluate self-monitoring data as they typically would in an assessment setting, (b) estimate the magnitude of correlation between each causal factor and problem behavior, and (c) select the most highly associated causal factor for each problem behavior. Results indicated that the students consistently and significantly underestimated the magnitude of strong correlations and overestimated the magnitude of weak correlations. In essence, they demonstrated a central tendency bias by guessing that two variables were moderately correlated regardless of whether or not they *were in fact* correlated.

We further evaluated the potential limitations of intuitive data evaluation methods by surveying members of a large organization of behavior therapists (Association for Behavioral and Cognitive Therapies, ABCT). Similar to the O'Brien (1995) study, we created a data set that contained three problem behaviors and three potential causal variables in a 3 × 3 table. The correlation between a problem behavior and three causal factors was either low ($r = .1$), moderate ($r = .5$), or high ($r = .9$). Participants were instructed to identify which of the three possible causal variables was most strongly associated with each problem behavior. Results again indicated that the participants were largely unable to accurately discern the magnitude of correlation among the problem behaviors and causal variables (O'Brien, Kaplar, & McGrath, 2004).

Taken together, these results suggest that covariation misestimation is common among clinicians. Further, one reason for this misestimation is that confirmatory information or hits (i.e., instances in which the target behavior and *presupposed causal variable* co-occur) are overemphasized in decision making relative to disconfirming information (i.e., instances in which the target behavior and *presupposed causal variable* do not co-occur).

Heuristics, decision-making shortcuts, and biases are another set of errors in clinical judgment. Like presuppositions, they help the clinician narrow the quantity and range of data that are considered in an assessment. Unlike presuppositions, heuristics, shortcuts, and biases are usually not a result of formal training or research. Instead, they appear to be a component of ordinary human reasoning, judgment, and decision making. Six of the more well-researched heuristics, decision-making shortcuts, and biases are listed below:

1. *Availability heuristic:* Information that has recently occurred or is more accessible to the clinician influence decisions more than less recent and/or less salient information, *independent of its actual relevance or validity.*

2. *Anchoring:* Information received early in the assessment process (e.g., reason for referral information, the initial impressions of the clinician) will exert a larger impact on decisions relative to information gathered later, regardless of its relevance or validity.

3. *Representativeness:* Clinical judgments are unduly influenced by a small and select number of features of a client that are consistent with the clinician's schema about behavior problems. For example, a clinician may observe mood variability and risky behavior in an adolescent. These two behavior problems are key features of borderline personality disorder. The clinician may thereby make a diagnosis of borderline personality disorder based mainly on these features. The problem in this particular example is that although mood variability and risky behavior are closely associated with borderline personality disorder, they are also commonly observed in typical adolescents. Thus, the clinician may be generating a diagnosis based on the extent to which the two behavior problems "matched" a diagnostic category while simultaneously failing to consider the extent to which these behavior problems commonly occur in nondisordered populations (see also "Base-rate misjudgments").

4. *Base-rate misjudgments:* Clinical judgments are insufficiently influenced by data on base rates and likelihood ratios, such as overestimating the likelihood that a client with depression but no history of suicidal ideation will engage in suicidal behavior.

5. *Confirmatory bias:* Clinical judgments are more strongly influenced by data that are consistent with expectations than with data that are inconsistent with expectations.

6. *Insensitivity to measurement errors:* Clinical judgments are sometimes made without adequate consideration of the limitations of measures used (e.g., assuming that a measure is a "true" indicator of a behavior problem without fully considering the degree of error in it).

As is evident in our aforementioned coverage of presuppositions and biases, there are a number of ways that human decision makers can incorrectly appraise assessment information. One goal for writing this book is to promote a more systematic, conceptually and empirically based, logical, scientific approach to clinical assessment and case formulation. In effect, we aim to reduce the impact of idiosyncratic biases of the clinician and researcher on clinical judgments. As much as possible, the behavioral assessment strategies used by a clinician, the inference he or she derives from the clinical assessment measures, and the elements in a functional analysis should reflect the characteristics of the client rather than the *a priori* biases of the clinician. We further discuss the strategies that can be used to reduce the impact of these presuppositions and biases in Chapter 7.

## SUMMARY

Many classes of causal variables have been proposed by philosophers of science. The classes that are most applicable to the functional analysis include insufficient causes, proximal causes, and distal causes. For most behavior problems, there is no "necessary" cause. A necessary cause is where Y never occurs without the prior occurrence of X, but X can occur without Y occurring.

Although concepts of causality have been assertively debated in the behavioral sciences, there are four essential conditions for inferring a causal relation: (a) covariation, (b) temporal precedence, (c) the exclusion of alternative explanations for a hypothesized causal relation, and (d) the identification of a logical, or potentially logical, connection between variables.

There are several caveats and potential errors associated with causal inferences in clinical assessment: (a) errors in our measurement strategy can result in a failure to identify an existing causal relation; (b) causal relations can operate in some but not other contexts; (c) some causal relations operate only within some values, or for some dimensions, of the variables; (d) interactions can mask causal relations; (e) some causal relations can be identified only within a restricted range of temporal boundaries; (f) causal inferences sometimes reflect the biases of the clinician; (g) significant correlations are sometimes erroneously interpreted as indicative of a causal relation; (h) causation is sometimes inferred from temporally insensitive, cross-sectional research designs; (i) there can be important individual differences in causal relations relevant to a behavior problem; (j) bidirectional causal relations can be difficult to specify; (k) the validity of causal inference depends on the quality of the measurement strategy;

(l) it is difficult to preclude the operation of a third variable when specifying a causal relation; and (m) causal relations can be described at different levels of specificity.

Given that most interventions are presumed to target causal variables of a behavior problem, it is particularly important to identify the mechanism of a causal relation. If we understand the causal mechanisms, we can expand the options for intervention, increase an intervention's magnitude of effect, reduce iatrogenic effects of an intervention, make interventions more efficient, and better understand how a behavior problem develops.

The functional analysis is composed primarily of the clinician's causal inferences about a client's behavior problems or positive intervention goals. It is a hypothesized causal model composed of judgments by the clinician that often reflects the clinician's biases. The application of science-based, best-practice assessment strategies will reduce the degree to which the functional analysis reflects beliefs, expectations, and causal attributions of the clinician that are not based on sound empirical research and theory.

# Conceptual and Empirical Foundations of Behavioral Assessment and the Functional Analysis III

## Characteristics of Causal Variables and Causal Relations in the Functional Analysis

### INTRODUCTION TO BASIC CONCEPTS OF CAUSALITY IN BEHAVIORAL ASSESSMENT

The previous chapter presented basic concepts of causality. We made the argument that causal variables and causal relations are central components of behavioral assessment and the functional analysis. As we noted in previous chapters, behavioral interventions are often designed to modify the hypothesized causes of behavior problems. This means that the identification and measurement of causal variables and causal relations are vital goals in behavioral assessment.

The clinician's conceptions of causality and assumptions about what causal variables are relevant to a behavior problem will affect the selection of clinical assessment strategies and methods, the composition of a client's functional analysis, the intervention decisions based on the functional analysis, and how intervention outcome is measured. Recall that the functional analysis, illustrated by a Functional Analytic Clinical Case Diagram (FACCD), is the summation of a clinician's hypotheses about a client's behavior problems and goals and the many ways that various causal variables influence them. The clinician's hypotheses are informed by the results of clinical assessment with the client, often guided by relevant research about which causal relations are most likely to be important and clinically useful in reducing behavior problems and achieving intervention goals. We also acknowledged that the identification and measurement of causal variables and causal relations is a complex and challenging task.

In this chapter we examine additional concepts of causality that are critically important in the behavioral assessment paradigm. We turn our attention to the types of causal variables and causal relations that have often been the focus of behavioral assessment and behavioral case formulations. Throughout this chapter we emphasize 10 aspects of causal variables and causal relations:

1. *The Multiple Attributes and Dimensions of Causal Variables:* Causal variables have multiple attributes that can have different effects on behavior problems.
2. *Multiple causality:* A behavior problem can be affected by many causal variables acting concurrently or sequentially.
3. *The interactive and additive effects of multiple causal variables:* A behavior problem can be influenced by the interactive and additive effects of multiple causal variables.
4. *Individual differences in causality:* The influence of a causal variable on a specific behavior problem can differ across persons, as a function of many factors.
5. *Conditional nature of causal relations:* The influence of a causal variable can differ across settings and contexts.
6. *Dynamic nature of causal relations:* The influence of a causal variable can change over time.

7. *Bidirectional causation:* The relations between causal variables and behavior problems can be bidirectional—a causal variable can influence a problem behavior and the problem behavior can influence a causal variable.

8. *Causal variables can be described at different levels of specificity:* Any causal variable can be reduced to component elements or added to others to form a higher-level aggregated variable. More specific, molecular-level causal variables are often more useful in intervention planning than are less specific, molar-level causal variables. However, the most appropriate level of specificity depends on the goals of the assessment.

9. *Chains of causal variables:* Causal variables for a behavior problem can form chains.

10. *Change in a causal variable:* Causal effects can be associated with a "change" in, rather than absolute level of, a dimension of a causal variable.

These ten aspects of causal variables and causal relations affect the clinician's decisions about which assessment strategies to use with a client and how best to interpret and integrate the data. Because all possible causal relations cannot be assessed in a single assessment occasion, the most effective strategy is to combine idiographic (i.e., collect information for a specific behavior problem, from a specific client, under specific circumstances; see Haynes et al., 2009) and nomothetic approaches (i.e., collect information from relevant research). The overarching goals of combining idiographic and nomothetic strategies are to understand: (a) the most clinically important attributes and dimensions of the multiple causal variables that are influencing a client's behavior problem, (b) how the multiple causal variables interact with each other and the behavior problem, (c) the conditional and dynamic nature of the causal relations influencing the behavior problem, and (d) the level of specificity needed to yield a functional analysis that will aid in intervention design. As we discuss later in Chapters 7–10, the principles, foci, methods, and strategies of the behavioral assessment paradigm are consistent with the aspects of causal variables and causal relations that we discuss throughout this chapter.

## CAUSAL VARIABLES FOR BEHAVIOR PROBLEMS HAVE MULTIPLE ATTRIBUTES

Causal variables have multiple attributes that can differ in their causal effects. For example, persons experiencing a traumatic event can differ in the degree to which their conditioned fear responses are later triggered by the sounds, sights, or smells associated with the original traumatic event (e.g., Bryant, 2006; Keane et al., 2008; and Wilson & Keane, 1997). Because causal effects can differ across attributes of a causal variable, the mere identification of a causal variable may be insufficient to account for its effects. Thus, it is important to identify specific attributes of causal variables in order to design interventions with optimal benefits for a client. The essential question is "What is it about the causal variable that is exerting the most important effects on the behavior problem for this client?"

Important attributes of causal variables can include: (a) stimulus attributes (e.g., sounds, sights, smells, tactile features of a stimulus), (b) temporal attributes (e.g., how soon does a reinforcing event occur following a child's positive social behaviors), (c) degree of intrinsic or acquired reinforcement properties (e.g., how reinforcing is social attention for a child with autism syndrome behaviors relative to a child with separation anxiety), and (d) contextual features (e.g., the effects of a client's recent history of exposure to the causal variable).

Consider for example how the *conditional nature and context* of a potential reinforcer can affect the degree to which it affects a behavior. Immediate attention from a parent can reinforce a child's oppositional behavior to the degree that it is *differentially associated* with the behavior (Wahler, Vigilante, & Strand, 2004). That is, the attention will exert stronger reinforcement effects when it is more likely to occur after oppositional behavior relative to any other behavior. Alternatively, if attention from a parent occurs also after many other behaviors, then attention will have weaker reinforcement effects on oppositional behavior. Similarly, attention from a psychiatric hospital staff member will serve as a stronger reinforcer for delusional speech produced by a hospitalized patient to the degree that it is *differentially associated* with that behavior (Liberman, Teigen, Patterson, & Baker, 1973).

In both examples, the causal variable "attention" is not sufficiently specific for our case formulation and intervention design because it does not capture the conditional aspects of the variable—it does not explain the contexts in which "attention" is likely to exert its strongest effects. To be more clinically useful in these examples, the functional analysis should indicate that attention contingent *upon the problem behavior* is the causal variable, not attention per se.

The *temporal contiguity* between a causal variable and behavior also influences the magnitude of its effect. Many effective response contingencies are delayed (such as payment that is delayed following the completion of work; grades that are given days or weeks after the completion of academic tasks). However, response contingencies that more immediately follow a behavior typically exert stronger effects. Therefore, when evaluating the relation between a causal variable and problem behavior, it is important to evaluate temporal contiguity and bear in mind that response contingencies could be either delayed or immediate.

The influence of many causal variables can also be affected by the degree to which the variables have intrinsic or acquired reinforcing properties. Clients differ in the degree to which a particular causal variable is experienced as positive or negative and these individual differences are affected by many factors. For example, attention from a parent, teacher, staff member, or peer can strongly affect the rate of oppositional behavior for one child in a classroom, but not another (Northup et al., 1995). Therefore, in assessing the occurrence or nonoccurrence of a client's problem behavior, the clinician should examine the extent to which various potential causal variables have intrinsic or acquired reinforcing properties.

The aforementioned examples emphasize the *individual and conditional nature of causality* in the behavioral assessment paradigm. That is, a particular variable can have an important causal relation with a behavior problem or treatment goal for some persons, sometimes, and in some contexts. They further illustrate an important tenet of the behavioral assessment paradigm that we discuss in Chapter 4: Diagnosis, or the mere identification and quantification of a client's behavior problems, is insufficient to identify the factors that are causing those problems. Thus, the best clinical assessment strategy would be one that focuses on potential causal variable attributes and causal relations relevant to a specific client's behavior problems and intervention goals.

## BEHAVIOR PROBLEMS CAN BE AFFECTED BY MULTIPLE CAUSAL VARIABLES

*Multivariate causality* is an important concept in psychopathology and the behavioral assessment paradigm. Often, a client's behavior problem can result from a combination of many causal factors that act concurrently or sequentially. All of the behavior problems depicted in Figures 3.12 to 3.16 of Chapter 3 were affected by multiple, concurrently operating and/or sequentially operating causal variables. Multivariate causality has been well documented for virtually all behavior problems that clinicians encounter in outpatient and inpatient settings.

We note that an emphasis on multivariate causality does not preclude the possibility that a client's behavior problem can be most strongly affected by a single, important causal variable. A client's migraine headaches may be most strongly affected by the intake of foods containing tyramine. A client's panic attacks may be most strongly associated with social contexts involving the possibility that he or she will be negatively evaluated. However, hundreds of published studies have documented that a given behavior problem is most likely affected by multiple, concurrently operating and/or sequentially operating causal variables.

As we discuss in Chapter 10, the concept of multiple causality suggests that the clinician should refrain from making premature causal inferences during behavioral assessment. The clinician should be careful not to let the early identification of an important causal variable exclude the search for other important causal variables. Although a clinician may quickly identify presleep ruminations as an important causal factor for the sleep problems of a client, he or she should not let that knowledge preclude continuing the search for the concurrent or sequential operation of dietary, environmental, or psychosocial stressors and physiological causal factors. As we discuss in the chapters on assessment strategies and methods (Chapters 7–9 and 11), the clinician should always broadly survey for multiple possible causal variables.

## Box 6.1 Multivariate Causality and Causal Mechanisms

Although multivariate causal variables for behavior problems have been well documented, the *mechanisms* underlying their causal relations have less frequently been identified. How is it that dissimilar causal variables have similar effects on a behavior problem? For example, how can both caffeine and the cessation of a life stressor trigger a migraine headache? How can hormonal imbalances and excessive worry both lead to erectile failure? How can anxiety sensitivity and fear of negative evaluation both increase the chance of panic attacks? The answer to these questions resides with the *mechanisms* that underlie the causal relations.

Multivariate causal relations for a behavior problem can occur in three ways: (a) when different causal variables operate through a common causal mechanism, (b) when different causal variables operate through multiple independent causal mechanisms, and (c) when a single causal variable affects a behavior problem through multiple causal mechanisms.

**Shared Causal Mechanism.** Let us consider the problem of child abuse to illustrate the idea of a shared causal mechanism. Most models of child abuse hypothesize multiple causal variables and mechanisms: deficient parenting skills, low education level of parents, poor parent anger management skills, parent substance use, poor parent social support, insufficiently developed sense of empathy, challenging and aversive child behavior/misbehavior, a high frequency and magnitude of daily social/environmental stressors in the parents' lives, stressful family financial condition, marital distress and conflict, the experiences of parents with their parents, and deficient communications skills between parents (see discussion of child abuse in Wise, 2006).

If we focus our discussion of child abuse on one causal variable—a high level of social/environmental stressors acting on the parent—we can see how multiple causal variables can operate through a common mechanism. Because a "stressful environment" can increase the chance of child abuse, any stressful event for the parent can function as a causal variable for child abuse. Stressful events may include a noncompliant child, marital conflict, job-related stressors, or withdrawal from a psychoactive substance. These different causal variables can have similar effects for a client because they operate through a common causal variable or mechanism—social-environmental stress.

At a more specific or molecular level of analysis, we can further examine the mechanism through which social-environmental stressors affect parenting behaviors, as suggested by Wahler and Hann (1986). One explanation for child behavior problems is that social-environmental stressors disrupt a parent's ability to follow the behavior of his or her child. When tracking abilities are impaired, the parent cannot respond with appropriate behaviors at the appropriate times to a child's behavior. Positive behaviors by the child are more likely to go unrewarded and negative behaviors are more likely to go uncorrected. So, any event that disrupts the ability of the parent to attend to or track the child can increase the chance of child behavior problems or childhood abuse or neglect. In these examples, a common causal mechanism, or a common mediating variable, can account for the similar effects of dissimilar variables. Shared causal mechanisms are similar to the mediating variables illustrated in Figure 3.10, are further illustrated in Figure 6.1.

## MULTIPLE CAUSAL PATHS CAN EMANATE FROM A SINGLE CAUSAL VARIABLE

We discussed earlier how multiple causal variables could affect a behavior problem through multiple concurrent and/or sequential pathways. Additionally, a single causal variable can affect a client's behavior problems through multiple causal paths. For example, alcohol use by a parent could decrease prosocial and child behavior management skills, increase marital conflict, and increase parent-child conflict. Figure 6.2 illustrates several

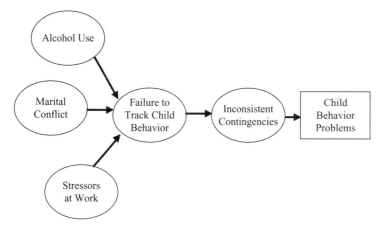

**Figure 6.1** A partial FACCD for a client that illustrates a shared causal mechanism for several causal variables associated with child behavior problems. Note that "Failure to Track" *mediates* the effects of the three antecedent causal variables on child behavior problems (see discussion of moderating and mediating variables in Box 6.2).

causal paths through which a client's alcohol use could increase the chance of aggression toward his children.

Consider another example. Chronic life stressors, such as poverty, chronic health problems, a demanding career, or prolonged family conflicts, could result in impaired immune system functioning and a

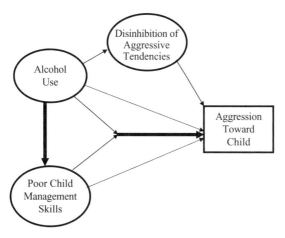

**Figure 6.2** An FACCD illustrating multiple paths through which alcohol use can increase the chance of aggression toward a child. Notice that "alcohol use" and "child management skills" have both direct and interactive effects on "aggression toward child" and that "child management skills" partially *mediates* (see discussion in Box 6.2 on the effect of "alcohol use" on "aggression toward child").

subsequent increased risk of illness through several mechanisms (for a review of the psychological, behavioral, and biological factors related to chronic life stressors, see Schneiderman, Ironson, & Siegel, 2005). Chronic life stressors can also lead to an increased risk for illness via other causal paths, such as increased alcohol and drug use, changes in diet, and sleep disruption. Yet another example is social isolation, which can increase the risk of depressed mood because it reduces exposure to social reinforcement, increases the likelihood of negative ruminations, increases dependency on reinforcement from a few persons, undermines social support networks that buffer the effects of negative life events, and reduces physical activity level.

Multiple causal paths can also be involved in the adverse effects of child abuse on the interpersonal functioning of the child later in life (e.g., Friesen, Woodward, Horwood, & Fergusson, 2010). Sexually abusive experiences as a child may have long-term effects on a client's expectancies as an adult regarding the consequences of attentive behaviors from others, and beliefs about the chance of being harmed in intimate interpersonal situations. These early abusive experiences can also lead to conditioned fear responses to physically intimate situations and a tendency to avoid some social situations that resemble the abusive situation. A child may also develop negative self-labels and become nonresponsive to the positive approaches of others. These are all *causal mechanisms* in that they explain *how* a history of sexual abuse (a *distal causal variable*) can lead to interpersonal difficulties as an adult through many *proximal causal variables*.

Finally, as we noted earlier, sometimes the mechanisms underlying a causal relation for behavior problems are assumed, but not identified. For example, Bentall, Haddock, and Slade (1994) proposed a multivariate causal model of hallucinations among psychiatric patients. They suggested that hallucinations were most likely to occur during periods of anxiety and during conditions of sensory deprivation or unpatterned auditory stimulation. They further suggested that hallucinations occur when a patient attributes mental events to external sources. However, the exact cognitive or neurophysiologic processes that account for the patient's failure to appropriately attribute self-generated mental events have not been identified. Thus, if Bentall and colleagues' model is valid, we know that some causal variables affect hallucinations, but not *how* they affect hallucinations.


## INDIVIDUAL DIFFERENCES IN CAUSAL RELATIONS FOR CLIENTS' BEHAVIOR PROBLEMS

Thousands of studies have shown that the relations between causal variables and behavior problems differ across individuals. Individual differences in causal factors for self-injurious behaviors have been meticulously illustrated by Iwata and others. (See the special issue on functional analysis and self-injurious behaviors, *Journal of Applied Behavior Analysis*, 1994, 27, 1). The authors systematically varied social and nonsocial stimuli while observing their effect on the self-injurious behaviors of 156 patients with developmental disabilities. The authors investigated the role of four classes of reinforcers in maintaining the self-injurious behaviors: (a) social reinforcement (e.g., social attention), (b) negative reinforcement (e.g., escape from an aversive setting), (c) tangible reinforcement (e.g., food, preferred items), and (d) sensory reinforcement (e.g., experience of pleasure). Although all patients evidenced similar self-injurious behaviors, there were significant individual differences in the factors that maintained those behaviors.

Individual differences in the array of causal variables that trigger or maintain the same behavior problem probably result from idiosyncratic learning histories, current environmental contexts, and biological predispositions. For example, Smith (1994) noted that there are important differences between persons in their expectancies about the effects of eating and alcohol intake (see review of alcohol expectancies literature in Jones et al., 2001). This variation in expectancies arises from idiosyncratic learning histories interacting with different levels of biological vulnerability among different persons.

In the aforementioned examples, the most important causal factors for similar behavior problems varied across persons. Consequently, mere diagnosis or problem identification would be insufficient for the clinician to identify the most important causal variables for a client and design the most beneficial intervention program. Diagnosis could help identify a set of the likely causal variables, but additional assessment would be necessary to develop a more precise understanding of the causal relations unique to that client.

As we noted in the previous examples, the concept of *individual differences in causality* for a behavior problem is central to behavioral assessment and the functional analysis because they emphasize an idiographic approach to understanding clients. If causal factors were consistent across persons with the same behavior problem, diagnosis or problem identification would be sufficient to plan the best intervention strategy. However, this is oftentimes not the case, as thousands of studies across hundreds of behavior problems and diagnostic categories demonstrate. Thus, clinicians must be consumers of behavioral science: The research literature is an excellent source of potential causal variables for a behavior problem, and one goal of the pre-intervention behavioral assessment is to identify which of those potential variables are important for an individual client.

## THE DYNAMIC NATURE OF CAUSAL VARIABLES AND CAUSAL RELATIONS

We indicated in Chapter 2 that the functional analysis is *dynamic*: It changes over time because the elements in the functional analysis— the causal variables, functional relations, and behavior problems—are dynamic. In Chapter 4 we discussed how changes in behavior problems can result from changes in the variables that control them. Another way of expressing this is that causal variables, causal relations, and resultant functional analyses are *nonstationary* (Haynes, Blaine, & Meyer, 1995). For example, Patterson and colleagues (2002) noted that, in younger children, aggression is often maintained by tangible reinforcement. However, as a child gets older, aggression is more often maintained by social reinforcement.

On a related issue, we should note that a causal relation for a client could be important within some time frames but not others. A study by Gottman and Krokoff (1989) exemplifies this point. They found that negative interactions between spouses have different effects on martial satisfaction depending on whether these factors are measured concurrently or sequentially. Specifically, they found that the number of negative inter-actions between spouses was positively associated with marital distress when both variables were measured at the same point in time. How-ever, the association between these two variables became negative when marital distress was measured at a later point in time.

The findings of Gottman and Krokoff about the temporal conditions of causal relations emphasize the importance of the *specificity* of the target behaviors and time frame in behavioral assessment and the functional analysis. What is the goal of behavioral assessment with a client and the functional analysis? Is it to explain and remediate the current distress of a couple? Or, is it to identify factors that could lead to an increase in the couple's happiness in the future or in some other contexts? Some of the causal variables associated with these two outcomes will overlap, but some causal variables will be different.

In Chapter 5 we discuss how the magnitude and direction of a causal variable's effect can vary with its duration of action. For example, several studies have noted that a physical or psychosocial stressor can have either beneficial or detrimental effects on a client's physical and psychological health as a function of the duration and intensity of the stressor (see a review of acute and chronic stressors by Asterita, 1985, and a review of PTSD by Bryant, 2006). Brief stressors are more likely to promote enhanced resilience to future stressors, while chronic stressors are more likely to intensify sensitivity to future stressors (of course, many other factors influence the effects of a stressor).

There are several reasons why causal relations can vary across time. First, repeated exposure over time can result in *habituation* (a reduction in the magnitude of causal effects). Second, *sensitization* can occur wherein the causal relationship is strengthened. Third, the causal relationship can change in form (such as from linear to nonlinear).

Changes in causal relations across time can also result from changes in mediating variables. For example, changes in the physiological effects of alcohol (e.g., tolerance) partially arise from changes in glutamate recep-tors and serotonin levels (Khanna, Morato, & Kalant, 2002). Numerous examples from cognitive behavioral therapy outcome research have shown how changes in a person's thoughts and interpretations of interpersonal situations can change his or her probability of experiencing a depressive episode, panic attack, anger, or physical pain (Butler, Chapman, Forman, & Beck, 2006) in stressful interpersonal situations.

Causal relations for a client's behavior problem can also change because of naturally occurring and often-unpredictable variability in the occurrence or form of causal variables. As Bandura (1982) noted, many important causal variables can occur or end by chance or as a function of a person's behavioral repertoire. Examples of this are a chance encounter with a drunk driver, unexpected health problems for a person or someone in her family, a new belief or life goal developed from reading a book or attending a conference, a new stressor at the job of a spouse, a newly developed friendship, or being seated next to an aggressive child in a classroom. Different permutations of these events can occur repeatedly and unpredictably, and can affect many aspects of a person's life.

The strength of a causal relation for a client's behavior problem is also likely to change over time. For example, the client in Figure 2.1, who was experiencing depressed mood as a function of numerous causal variables, could acquire new parenting skills by talking to other parents, the couple's financial problems could increase or decrease with job changes, and marital conflicts could escalate or diminish. Natural fluctuations in life events, chance occurrences of important causal variables, variability in the operation of moderating variables, and clinical intervention can reduce the absolute and relative magnitude of effect of some causal variables and increase the effects of others. These complexities in the causal variables and causal relations operating on peoples' behavior problems show how the functional analysis itself is also dynamic. They also illustrate how it is important to conduct ongoing, time-series assessment with clients. We discuss more about time-series assessment strategies in Chapter 7.


## NONLINEAR CAUSAL RELATIONS

The effects of many causal variables, such as salt intake, internal or external attributions, positive reinforcement from others, amount of alcohol intake, duration of exercise, and the intensity of a stressful event, show nonlinear ∩-shaped or ∪-shaped causal relations with behavior dimensions. A popular example of a nonlinear causal relation is the well-known Yerkes-Dodson Human Performance Curve, which is a ∩-shaped causal relation between stress and performance of a task. As Figure 6.3 illustrates, the magnitude of stress, such as fear of failing, is represented on the horizontal axis while a person's performance, such as exam performance, is represented on the vertical axis. As we can see, performance improves with an initial increase in stress magnitude, but beyond an optimum point it is inhibited with increasing amounts of stress.

Keely, Zayak, and Correia (2008) found a curvilinear relation between anxiety and performance among college students enrolled in a statistics course. Further, and consistent with the notion of dynamic variation in causal relations, they found that the magnitude of curvilinearity varied across time. That is, the students completed a measure of test anxiety prior to each administration of six statistics exams that were taken across a single semester. A significant quadratic relation ("∪-shaped") between anxiety and test performance was observed for the last four tests but not the first two tests. Further, and consistent with the notion that attributes of a causal variable can influence the nature of a causal relation, they found that the inverted "U" relation emerged most strongly when more difficult exams were administered. Thus, the change in the magnitude of curvilinear relations between test anxiety and performance varied as a function of time and test difficulty.

The ∪-shaped and ∩-shaped functional relations are a subset of the *nonlinear (i.e., discontinuous) causal relations.* Many variables change in other ways that are nonlinear. The concept of nonlinearity of a functional relation is relatively simple: Two variables have a nonlinear relation when a unit of change in one variable is associated with a differing, albeit pre-dictable, unit of change in another variable. We illustrated examples of this type of nonlinear relation with the Yerkes-Dodson Human Per-formance Curve in Figure 6.3 and Keeley et al.'s demonstration of the nonlinear relation between test anxiety and test performance. A similar nonlinear causal relation is depicted again in Figure 6.4 and referred to as a *"parabolic function."*

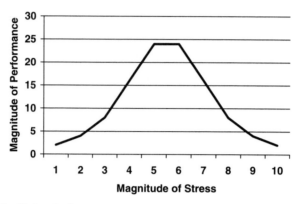

**Figure 6.3** The Yerkes-Dodson Human Performance Curve depicting a ∩-shaped causal relation between stress and performance. As the magnitude of a person's stress initially increases, performance on a particular task also gradually improves up to an "optimal point" at which performance begins to decline with increasing stress levels.

Consider another example of nonlinear causal relations where increases in the frequency of life stressors may have little or no impact on a client's rate or intensity of obsessive thinking when the stressors occur at a low frequency. However, an equal degree of change in the frequency of life stressors can have a stronger effect on the client's obsessive thinking when they occur at a higher frequency. In this example, the functional relation between life stressors and the behavior problem would resemble the "*single discontinuity*" function in Figure 6.4. In essence, the impact of life stressors on the client's obsessive thinking would increase after the frequency of life stressors passed a critical level. Another classic example of a single discontinuity function is illustrated by neuronal action potentials. Specifically, minimal to moderate levels of neuron stimulation produce a linear change in the neuron polarity. However, when neuron stimulation exceeds the threshold for depolarization, there is an abrupt, rapid, and nonlinear reversal of neuron polarity.

Nonlinear causal relations have been proposed in many causal models in psychopathology, including bulimia, alcohol use, schizophrenia symptoms, obsessive-compulsive problems, and PTSD (see extended discussion of nonlinear functions in Haynes, 1992).

Another type of nonlinear functional relation is the *functional plateau*, which is also illustrated in Figure 6.4. An example could be the relationship between positive social exchanges and mood. The

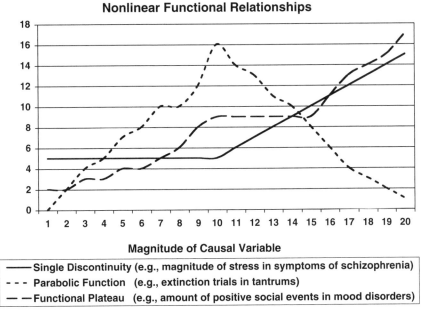

**Figure 6.4** Three nonlinear functional relations between the magnitude of a causal variable (its frequency, intensity, and duration) and the magnitude of a behavior problem.

*Source: From Haynes, 1992, 2003; Haynes et al., 1993; Haynes and O'Brien, 2000.*

functional plateaus would indicate that typical day-to-day fluctuations in positive and negative social interactions might have very little effect on the person's mood. However, periods in which positive or negative exchanges were very low or very high would have a stronger effect on mood.

Causal models of schizophrenia and other behavior problems that propose an interaction between environmental stressors and an individual's physiological or psychological trait vulnerability also include discontinuous causal relations. (For an example of the stress-diathesis model applied to suicide and bipolar disorders, see Grunebaum et al., 2006; illustrated in Figure 6.4 as a *single discontinuity*.) That is, for some persons, environmental stressors have little or no effect on psychotic symptoms until the stressors reach a critical level, after which the magnitude of effect of the stressor increases. Consistent with the principle of *individual differences in causality*, the critical level can vary across persons, probably as a function of their early learning experiences or biological predispositions.

The effects of some psychotropic medications can also be nonlinear. Specifically, some medications have minimal effects until a critical dose level is achieved, and some medications can have the opposite effects at low versus high doses. Similarly, the hyperbolic effect of alcohol consumption on mood and behavior has been well documented (Marlatt, 1985). In this case, small quantities of alcohol often have mood-elevating effects while larger quantities are more likely to have mood-depressing effects.

Nonlinear causal relationships highlight the idea that causal relations are often conditional—in this case the strength of the causal relation varies as a function of the values of the causal variable. As with the example of mood and social reinforcement presented earlier, causal relations that demonstrate functional plateaus are characterized by a mid-range of values in which variation in the causal variable is only weakly associated with variation in the behavior problem. In other words, a variable can have no causal relation with a behavior problem within a particular range of its values, but exhibit significant causal effects if its values fall below or above that range.

What are the implications of nonlinear functional relations for clinical assessment? First, nonlinear aspects of causal relations, along with their dynamic and idiographic nature, emphasize the importance of ongoing assessment and, in clinical research, the use of analytic strategies that go beyond the calculation of commonly used statistical analyses that only yield estimates of linear relations (e.g., bivariate correlations, linear regression). A behavior problem's *state* (a measure of the variable at one point in time) as well as its *phase* (the value of a variable in the context of its value at prior time periods) should be monitored frequently in clinical assessment. The *state and phase of a behavior problem* can be evaluated using visual inspection of scatter plots as well as statistical tests that can estimate nonlinear relations (e.g., multivariate time series analyses). As we discuss in Chapters 7–9, assessment methods, such as self-monitoring, behavioral observations and questionnaires, and psychophysiological measurements, are particularly useful for providing data on nonlinear functional relations.

For some clients, the functional analysis could be more clinically useful if it reflected the nonlinear nature of the causal relations. For example, a causal variable label such as "high level of job stressors" or "increase above typical level of job stressors" might be more informative than "job stressors," because it suggests that the client usually copes well with normal day-to-day variability in job stressors but has difficulty when the level of those job stressors becomes exceptional.

## WHAT ARE THE MOST USEFUL TYPES OF CAUSAL VARIABLES AND CAUSAL RELATIONS IN THE FUNCTIONAL ANALYSIS?

Behavioral assessment strategies and the functional analysis can encompass many types of causal variables across a range of response modes, such as: (a) specific environmental events (e.g., antecedent stimuli, settings, and discriminative stimuli), (b) cognitive events (such as beliefs, expectancies, self-statements, attention, and metacognitions), (c) emotional states, (d) psychophysiological context (e.g., medication state, fatigue, intoxication status, pain), (e) psychosocial context (e.g., recent history of social interaction), (f) response contingencies (such as avoidance functions, positive and negative reinforcement, and escape functions), (g) genetic makeup, (h) early learning history, (i) neurophysiologic factors (e.g., dopamine and serotonin production or uptake), (j) impairments and limitations (e.g., cognitive, neuropsychological, neurophysiological, and physical limitations), and (k) conditioned responses (e.g., conditioned fear responses to some social situations or trauma-related stimuli).

As we mentioned earlier, identifying causal variables and explaining causal relations are a key focus of behavioral assessment. Regardless of the type of causal variables identified, the following four principles guide the behavioral assessment process and strengthen the clinical utility of the selection and description of the causal variables.

1. *Specificity of causal variables.* The causal variable should be precisely defined. This means that vaguely defined constructs such as "frustration," "low self-esteem," and "stress" are inappropriate. Because of their heterogeneous components and inconsistent connotations, they provide insufficient information about clinically useful characteristics of the causal variable. Sometimes, to enhance parsimony and the clinical utility of a functional

analysis, it is necessary to include higher-level, aggregated variables such as "Inappropriate Response Contingencies." In such cases, elements of the causal variable can be defined in other sections of the functional analysis, as on a separate page of a Functional Analytic Clinical Case Diagram. For example "Inappropriate Response Contingencies" can be further defined as "inconsistent rewards for positive behavior, excessive use of time-out, failure to be consistent with stated rewards and punishments, and delayed contingencies for positive and negative behaviors." Notice that the inclusion of all of these variables would clutter an FACCD and decrease its clinical utility, but a failure to define the higher-level variable would also make it difficult for a clinician to know where to focus intervention and what variables to measure when evaluating the effects of intervention.

2. *Noncircular causal variables.* The causal variable should not include elements of the related behavior problem. For example, "Major Depression" is not an appropriate causal variable for "irritability" or "sleep-problems" because these problems are subsumed within and are subsumed within the construct of "depression." "Borderline Personality Disorder" is not a causal variable for self-injurious behaviors because those behaviors contribute to the diagnosis of Borderline Personality Disorder.

3. *Measurable causal variables.* Associated with the concept of "specificity" and the emphasis on a science-based approach to clinical assessment, causal variables should be amenable to measurement. Variables such as "tension," "denial," "frustration," and "arousal" are insufficiently specific constructs that are not readily amenable to precise measurement.

4. *Contemporaneous causal variables.* Because the functional analysis emphasizes clinically useful variables, it is important to identify those that currently account for the variation in a client's behavior problem. Contemporary (i.e. proximal) causal variables often have greater clinical utility than do historical (i.e., distal) causal variables. Historical causal variables such as early life traumas, traumatic brain injury, past illnesses, failure experiences, and childhood deprivations are important for understanding the

emergence of a behavior problem. However, they are less useful in understanding day-to-day variability in the frequency, intensity, or duration of a behavior problem.

We already noted how the relevance of historical causal variables for our clinical judgments could be increased by attending to their sequelae. For example, a historical event such as childhood trauma is less useful for intervention decisions but *"currently occurring, distressing recollections of a childhood trauma"* could be very informative. In a sense, the proximal causal variables that arise from historical experiences can be thought of as mediating variables (see Box 6.2).

---

### Box 6.2 Moderating and Mediating Variables

Two important classes of causal variables in behavioral assessment and the functional analysis are *moderating* and *mediating* variables. The distinction between these two types of variables can be clarified when the conventional use of the words are examined. For example, a legal conflict between two people can be mediated by a third party (i.e., each person talks with a mediator, but they do not talk directly to each other) or moderated by a third party (i.e., the two persons talk with each other with the third party being present and actively intervening whenever the communication becomes problematic or dysfunctional). In the case of mediation, communication between the two persons *goes through* the mediator. In the case of moderation, the communication between the two persons is *affected by* the moderator.

In more formal terms, a *moderator variable* is a variable that affects the strength or form of a relation between two other variables. Moderator variables were illustrated in Figure 3.10, variable X5. For example, "social support" can sometimes moderate the effect of a conflictual divorce on depressed mood. That is, for some persons, social support from friends and family can affect the degree to which a person experiences depressed mood during or following a difficult divorce. Also, "aerobic conditioning" for some persons can moderate the effects of an environmental stressor on sleep problems. Moderator variables are important targets in behavioral assessment and useful components of a functional analysis because they can help the clinician understand the relation between distal causal variables and behavior problems and often are targeted in behavioral interventions.

A *mediating variable* is similar to a *causal mechanism*. It accounts for, or explains, the relation between two other variables. A mediating variable is the means, or way, through which a causal effect occurs. Mediating variables were illustrated in Figure 3.10, variables X2 and X3, and illustrated again in Figures 6.1 and 6.2. For example, the mechanism through which marital conflict influences the aggressive behavior of a child might be: (a) interference with the parent's ability to track the behaviors of the child, (b) a disruption in normal response contingencies delivered by a parent to the child, (c) modeling of aggressive behavior by the parents, (d) an increase in the rate of negative exchanges between a parent and child, (e) a reduction in the support and reinforcement provided to the child for appropriate behaviors, and (f) an increase in aversive stimuli delivered by siblings.

Mediating variables are important because they can indicate alternative strategies of intervention. Interventions that change the mediating variables, even if they do not attend to the distal causal variable, can exert important effects on the behavior problem.[1] Mediator variables are also important in treatment research because they help explain the effects of an intervention strategy.

## An Emphasis on Contemporaneous Causal Relations

Not only are certain types of causal variables more clinically useful than others in a functional analysis, so are certain types of temporal causal relations. Causal variables can differ in their temporal relations with a

[1] Mediating variables are frequent foci of structural equations modeling and other nomothetic research strategies in psychopathology. Unfortunately, the mediating variables selected for study are suggestive but often insufficiently specific to be clinically useful. Examples of some mediator variables identified in 2010 research literature include: stigma, criminality, self-regulation, the family, coping, self-efficacy, mindfulness, burnout, and closeness in relationships.

behavior problem. Some antecedent and consequent causal variables are contiguous and proximal because they occur soon before or after the behavior problem. Others are less contiguous and more distal.

Causal variables across a range of temporal relations can account for a meaningful proportion of variance in a client's behavior problem. The importance of early learning experiences for the development of behavior problems has been well established. Many behavior problems result from learning experiences that have occurred for years, or occurred years previously. Historical causal variables can help identify the patterns, time-course, and contexts that affect the conditional probabilities of behavior problems. A focus on the historical time-course of a behavior problem can also be useful when reoccurrence or relapse is the main dimension of interest. This information can help the clinician to detect triggering or contextual factors that have been associated with recurrence or relapse and, thereby, identify methods of reducing their likelihood or effects.

An important tenet of the behavioral assessment paradigm is that we can best address a client's intervention goals by examining contemporary interactions among causal variables and behavior problems. For example, many studies have shown that a significant proportion of variance in many behavior problems can be accounted for by variance in proximal *response contingencies* associated with them.

Consistent with a natural selection model of behavior change, what happens following a behavior (such as escape from an aversive situation, positive and negative reinforcement, or punishment) affects the future probability or other dimensions of that behavior. Similarly, many behavior problems have been shown to be affected by specific and proximal thoughts, expectancies, and beliefs, or with antecedent or consequent physiological states.

Contemporary causal relations can help explain between-person differences in behavior problems but, in clinical assessment, they are especially useful in explaining within-person variance in behavior problems. For example, proximal causal relations can help explain why some persons, but not others, physically assault their partner or experience prolonged episodes of obsessive thinking (between-person differences). However, they can be even more helpful in explaining why a person shows variation in the likelihood of physical assault or obsessive thinking across times, settings, or contexts (within-person variance).

Proximal social contingencies for a problem behavior and the context within which the behavior occurs have been demonstrated to have strong effects on many behavior problems, such as aggressive behavior, partner violence, recidivism among psychiatric patients living in the community, eating problems, delinquent and antisocial behaviors, social anxiety, and social skills deficits (see overviews in O'Donohue & Ferguson, 2004). For example, parental interactions with an adult child who has been recently released from a psychiatric hospital can significantly influence the frequency and intensity of psychotic symptoms (e.g., Hooley, 2007). Mumma (2004), using time-series measurement designs (taking daily measures of thoughts and mood), has demonstrated how specific thoughts can quickly affect a person's mood.

Behavioral assessment with a client with anorectic eating problems further illustrates the differential role of remote and contemporaneous causal factors. Most causal models of anorexia nervosa implicate a long history of peer, family, and cultural influences. These causal models also emphasize the importance of early learning on associated behaviors, such as obsessive-compulsive behaviors, and the interactions between environmental and biological predispositions (see functional analysis of anorexia nervosa in Lappalainen & Tuomisto, 2005). While acknowledging the importance of these distal causal factors, assessment of a client with an eating disorder is sometimes more clinically useful when it focuses on the client's current thoughts about eating and body weight, current and ideal body image distortions, food aversions and food avoidance behaviors, specific eating patterns, dieting strategies, contextual factors associated with restricted food intake, family and marital interactions regarding eating and body size, and thoughts regarding the consequences of increased caloric intake and weight gain.

A focus on contemporaneous causal factors is especially important in advanced cases of anorexia nervosa because such clients are often malnourished with significant health problems. Following stabilization of caloric intake and weight to more healthy levels, subsequent assessment might examine contemporary functional relations involving depressed mood (which can also be a consequence of malnutrition) and other behaviors, such as obsessive and compulsive behaviors.

Paranoid thoughts and attitudes are also probably learned at an early age (Haynes, 1986). For example, a tendency to view ambiguous events in self-referent terms and/or as personal threats, and to view with suspicion the motivations of others, can undoubtedly be learned from parents. For example, they may instruct and model for a child distrust of others, to suspect hidden meanings in other persons' behaviors, or that the behavior of others is often directed at the child. There may also be biological predispositions to paranoid attributions (Simons et al., 2009).

Despite the explanatory importance of early parent-child experiences and their ubiquitous expression in causal models in psychopathology, they are difficult to measure and address in an intervention. Thus, it may be more effective to focus assessment efforts on contemporaneous causal variables. For example, social isolation can reduce the chance of corrective feedback to a person about his or her thoughts, social skills deficits can contribute to social isolation and interpersonal difficulties, and selective attention, automatic negative thoughts, or hypersensitivity to ambiguous social stimuli can increase the chance of paranoid interpretations of events.

To further illustrate our point, consider cigarette smoking. Peer influences often lead to the initiation of smoking, but its continuation (and relapse after cessation) is often affected by many contemporaneous causal variables, such as family and work stress (smoking can serve as an escape or avoidance of stress-related reactions), depression and anxiety symptoms, physiological dependence, and other linked behaviors, such as concurrent alcohol and caffeine consumption (Kassel, Stroud, & Paronis, 2003).

Our goal here is not to diminish the importance of distal causal variables, such as early learning experiences and neurophysiological processes, but to remind clinicians that a client's behavior problems are often strongly affected by proximal causal variables. Of course, we often want to understand the historical determinants of behavior problems, which can be particularly useful in preventing relapse following successful therapy. However, clinical assessment data and the functional analysis are more likely to be clinically useful if they address questions of contemporaneous utility, such as "Under what conditions is the client more likely to have trouble going to sleep, experience depressed feelings, feel anxious, be reinforced for oppositional behavior, or hit a classmate?"

We noted earlier that clinicians often encounter clients who have been experiencing a behavior problem for a long time. People seldom seek treatment following the initial onset of a behavior problem. They are more likely to seek treatment after long periods of relationship difficulties, depression, headaches, anxiety, substance use, or inability to manage their aggressive and oppositional children. Thus, our assessment often focuses on identifying variables that are maintaining those problems, rather than variables associated with their original onset. Our assessment focus might be directed at the question: "Why is our patient still depressed two years after a difficult divorce?" or "What is happening at home that might be maintaining a child's oppositional and aggressive behavior toward his parents?"

Although we have emphasized contemporary context-behavior inter- actions, the behavioral assessment paradigm also attends to contemporary cognitive (such as outcome expectations and self-evaluative thoughts), emotional, and physiological responses that can influence a behavior problem. Thus, it is important to examine the differential operations of environmental factors, response contingencies, cognitive experiences, affective experiences, and physiological experiences. These are espe- cially important foci when the likelihood of a behavior problem differs across settings. As we discuss in Chapter 9, behavioral observations in the natural environment, self-monitoring, and ambulatory biosensors are powerful assessment methods for identifying contemporaneous behavior- environment interactions and co-occurring cognitive, affective, and physiological variables that may affect a person's behavior problem.

---

### Box 6.3 The Clinician as a Behavioral Scientist

It should be apparent from this discussion of causal variables that the clinician must be a knowledgeable behavioral scientist in order to conduct a competent clinical assessment and construct a valid and useful functional analysis. That is, the clinician must be well informed about the research, assessment strategies, and potential causal vari- ables related to the client's behavior problems. To construct a valid and clinically useful functional analysis of an aggressive child for

example, the clinician must be aware of research indicating that the
aggressive behaviors for some persons with developmental disabilities are especially likely in situations involving aversive demands.
For these persons, the aggressive behavior periodically results in an
escape from those demands and is thereby negatively reinforced. For
other persons, aggressive behaviors are sometimes maintained by
social and tangible rewards. Finally, aggression is more likely when
the parents or others have failed to reinforce alternative, nonaggressive methods of interacting and communicating.

## Contemporary Environmental Causality
## and Bidirectional Causation

Another important concept in causal models of behavior disorders is
*bidirectional causality*—the idea that two variables can affect each other.[2]
The concept of bidirectional causality suggests that a client's behavior
can affect the causal variable, which, in turn, affects the behavior. For
example, a client's depressive behaviors (such as reduced social initiations
and reduced positive responses to others, avoidance of social contact,
slower speech rate, and lowered affect) can eventually cause the client's
family and friends to avoid him or her. Their avoidance and reduced positive interactions with the client can, in turn, increase the client's social
isolation, depressive mood, and depressive behaviors.

Bidirectional causality can also be seen in clients exhibiting paranoid behaviors. In this case, suspicious reactions to others, social withdrawal, misinterpretation of the behavior, and selective interpretation of
ambiguous stimuli, can seem "strange" or hostile to others. In turn, persons
familiar with the client can begin avoiding and conversing surreptitiously
about him or her (stopping the conversations if the client approaches),
which in turn can reinforce the paranoid beliefs of the client.

The presence of bidirectional causality is a common occurrence in
clinical settings but is often incompletely understood by clients. For

---

[2] *Bidirectional causality* is sometimes referred to as circular causality, reciprocal determin-
ism, reciprocal causation, functional interdependence, mutual causation, positive and
negative feedback loop, nonrecursive causal models, and upward and downward causality.

example, in relationship struggles, a client may report that she fears that her partner is withdrawing or becoming "remote." The client may then frequently "check in" (e.g., phoning, texting) in an effort to maintain contact or frequently request reassurance. However, the partner may report the intensified checking and requests for reassurance are experienced as intrusive and aversive, leading to increased avoidance, which leads to an increase in these behaviors by the client. Thus, the client generates an iatrogenic behavioral response (checking and requesting reassurance) that is intended to reduce withdrawal by her partner that, paradoxically, intensifies withdrawal. This pattern is readily discernable to the clinician, but oftentimes incompletely perceived by the client.

Bidirectional causal relations are important in the functional analysis because they indicate two possible points of intervention. If marital conflict and depressed mood have a bidirectional causal relation for a client, an intervention with either could be beneficial to both, depending on the relative strength of relations in both directions. For example, the influence of marital conflict on depressed mood may be stronger than the influence of depressed mood on marital conflict, or vice versa.

One of the complicating aspects of bidirectional causality is that it sometimes creates fuzzy boundaries between a "behavior problem" and a "causal variable." In some instances, both variables in a bidirectional causal relation can be described as either a causal variable or behavior problem (e.g., negative outcome expectancies and social withdrawal). Both variables have causal properties and both can be considered as behavior problems. Which variable is labeled as a "problem" and "cause" will depend on the preferences of the client and clinician, and should, whenever possible, be based on the best estimates of the relative importance of each and the relative strengths of the causal relations between them.

As noted in Haynes and O'Brien (2000), the concept of bidirectional causality also promotes a positive, constructive focus on a client's behavioral skills, self-efficacy, and personal responsibilities during assessment and in treatment. The clinician and client attend to the ways that the client's thoughts or actions may be contributing to his or her behavior problems, and what he or she can do to attain positive intervention goals and maintain positive behavior change over time. Similar to a *task analysis,* and based on the assumptions that behavior problems are a partial function of the client's behavioral repertoire, the clinician can identify the client's skills deficits and the new skills required to address the problems and the intervention goals that are necessary to attain a positive intervention outcome. For example, within a bidirectional causality framework, assessment with a socially anxious and withdrawn client might focus on his specific attitudes, beliefs, self-statements, anxiety sensitivity, expectancies, and behaviors in social situations that prevent him from forming more rewarding friendships.

## SITUATIONS, CONTEXTUAL AND SETTING EVENTS, AND SYSTEMS FACTORS AS CAUSAL VARIABLES

As we noted in Chapter 4, behavior problems are often *conditional*; that is, the probability, magnitude, or duration of a client's behavior problems often vary across situations, settings, contexts, and as a function of transient eliciting and discriminative stimuli. The conditional nature of behavior problems has important implications for identifying their causation.

The term *context* refers to the unique configuration of situational, setting, and person variables that occur at a particular time. Context can refer to a range of conditions and stimuli, from complex social/environmental situations (such as large social gatherings or intimate conversations), to the recent history of reinforcement (such as approval or disapproval by peers), or to states of the person (such as being hungry, angry, intoxicated, fatigued, sleepy, medicated, or in an environment with few social rewards). Context sets the occasion for behavior when there is an associated learning history involved. Consequently, each context will contain unique discriminative stimuli, consequential stimuli, and conditional stimuli, and therefore can be associated with different responses across persons.

Context can be an important causal factor for some clients in that it influences the occurrence or other dimension of a behavior problem. For example, delusional or self-injurious behavior by a psychiatric patient may be more likely to occur when discharge from the hospital is being considered (e.g., the patient may dread returning to an aversive home situation). Domestic violence may be more likely following periods of alcohol ingestion. Chronic pain may be exacerbated in states of depressed mood or sleep loss. Responses to life stressors may be elevated in states of sleep deprivation. Aggressive behavior on a psychiatric unit may be more likely when a patient has not received attention from the staff for a while. A child's oppositional behavior may be more likely with one parent than another.

The contexts that are reliably associated with a behavior problem serve as *marker variables* for the differential operation of unique combinations of causal variables (we further discuss marker variables in Chapter 10). For example, the fact that a client's self-injurious behavior, marital conflict, social anxiety, nightmares, or depressed mood are more likely to occur in some situations than in others suggests that some of the causal variables for those problems covary with those situations.

An emphasis on situational, antecedent, and contextual factors does not preclude the possibility that some persons' behavior problems are not differentially associated with particular contexts. The degree of cross-situational consistency of behavior can vary across behaviors, individuals, and situations. For example, some persons experience paranoid delusions or social anxiety across most social situations, while others are delusional or anxious only in some situations.

The observation that a client's behavior problems and the causal relations relevant to those behavior problems can vary across settings and contexts further guides the behavioral assessment process: It suggests that the clinician should acquire data across relevant settings and contexts. We discuss strategies and methods for these assessment foci in greater detail in Chapters 7-10.

As behavior problems and their causal variables and causal relations are often conditional, so is a functional analysis. A functional analysis for a client's behavior problem can be more valid for certain settings or contexts than for others (such as when the severity and causes of a child's deviant behavior differs between the classroom and home). In some cases, contexts can be considered as moderator variables, in that they affect the likelihood that a particular behavior will occur in response to a particular stimulus.

## Attending to Social Systems Factors in the Functional Analysis

Recall that although we emphasize proximal causal relations, *distal variables* can be important elements of a functional analysis. One particular type of distal causal variable is the *extended social system*. We have noted how many important causal variables involve the behavior of other persons. That is, how parents, staff members, teachers, spouses, coworkers, and friends respond to positive and negative behaviors of a client and how the contexts for the client provided by these persons can strongly affect the client's behavior. Consequently, variables that affect the behavior of these persons in the client's life can be important. Events that disrupt their positive behaviors or increase their negative behaviors can be important components of a functional analysis. In some cases, it is not possible to adequately account for variance in a client's behavior problems and to develop valid functional analyses and effective interventions unless we consider factors operating within the extended social systems in which the behavior problem is imbedded.

Consider the case of an "out-of-control" 7-year-old child who is brought to a clinic by his mother because of multiple, severe, and persistent aggressive behaviors. As expected, an assessment of the contingencies on the child's behavior revealed substantial deficits in parenting behaviors—high rates of maternal reinforcement for negative behaviors, inconsistent negative contingencies for problem behaviors, infrequent reinforcement for positive alternative behaviors, a low rate of positive interactions, verbal threats of abandonment, high rates of noncontingent criticism, and a low rate of expressions of comfort and love by the child's mother.

Two initial questions arise: Is the identification of these immediate and important response contingencies sufficient for a functional analysis? Can we develop an intervention, such as a parent-training or a home-based behavior-management program, based on these important contemporaneous functional relations alone? There certainly are data from multiple sources confirming that, with an appropriately instituted contingency management program, the mother could probably be taught to increase the appropriate use of positive behaviors and decrease the number of negative behaviors and the overall quality of the parent-child relationship could be improved (see Zisser & Eyberg, 2010).

Another question is: Would one expect quick, positive, durable effects from a behavior management training program that focused on only the mother's interaction with the child? The best answer is "it depends." The likelihood of effective intervention depends on the functional relations relevant to the mother's behavioral management strategies. Alessi (1988) labeled these variables "metacontingencies"—contingencies that affect those who deliver contingencies to the client. If the mother is facing multiple and severe difficulties in her life, beginning a behavior management training program for her might be less than optimally effective because she might not attend sessions, attend to learning tasks in sessions, practice new skills at home, or carry out and maintain skills in a consistent manner once they were acquired.

In some cases, decisions about the best intervention strategy could be informed by a functional analysis that included information about social systems factors. In our example, this would involve information about the relationship between the mother and father, the role of the father in the family, the mother's workload, medical and physical problems of family members, and economic issues.

Consider these additional questions: What if the mother was experiencing domestic violence? What if she were working two jobs to help address financial difficulties? What if she was experiencing bipolar behavior problems or was severely depressed? In these cases, additional social system causal variables in the functional analysis might be warranted if they exerted a strong effect on her ability to behave lovingly and reliably deliver appropriate contingencies with her child.

Figure 6.5 is a Functional Analytic Clinical Case Diagram of a case in which there are significant multilevel social systems factors affecting the self-injurious behaviors of a psychiatric patient, such as his head banging and self-hitting. Of course, some of the causal variables for the patient's behavior problems were undoubtedly neurophysiologically based. However, observations on the unit, interviews with staff members, and examination of nursing reports suggested that inappropriate and inconsistent responses from staff members contributed to her problems. As part of the behavioral assessment, the clinician investigated the role of more distal, social-system causal factors, asking the question "Why are there inconsistent and inappropriate responses to the patient by staff members?"

Additional assessment suggested problems with (a) poor staff training, (b) high staff turnover, (c) low pay, (d) inconsistent hospital policies about how to manage self-injurious behavior, (e) insufficient rewards for effective behavior management by staff on the unit, (f) many negative hospital-generated contingencies for staff behavior, and (g) inconsistent supervision. Several distal social system variables are shown in Figure 6.5, and illustrate their relevance for a functional analysis. That is, systems-level changes may be needed to have generalized and long-lasting effects on the way staff members respond to this and other patients.

Social Systems variables have been implicated in many behavior problems. For example, the behavior problems of a client's partner or family members could impede or facilitate the effectiveness of an intervention for substance use disorders. Also, the nature of social interactions in a group home for individuals with developmental disabilities could affect the rate at which a client learns adaptive self-help, cognitive, and physical skills.

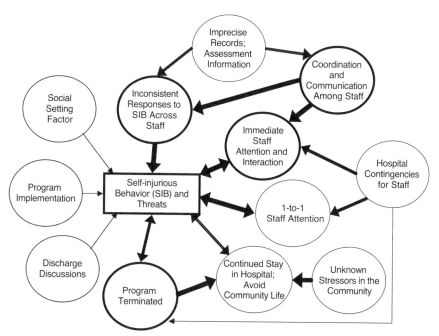

**Figure 6.5** A functional analysis of self-injurious behaviors by a psychiatric inpatient that includes immediate consequences, contextual factors, and social systems variables: Contingencies on hospital workers, training, supervision, and communication from the hospital administrators. Also note the contextual factors, such as discharge discussions.

# AN EMPHASIS ON MODIFIABLE CAUSAL VARIABLES

Modifiability is a central aspect of the clinical utility of a causal variable. As we have discussed previously, important but unmodifiable causal variables can help explain the onset of a behavior problem and explain between-person differences in the occurrence of a behavior problem but they often are less useful in understanding current variance in a client's problems.

Let us return to our earlier case examples. Early childhood sexual abuse was a contributing factor to the anxiety episodes experienced by the client as depicted in Figure 3.13; a family history of bipolar disorders and work stressors experienced by the spouse were contributing factors to the manic episodes of the client depicted in Figure 3.14; and a job injury and financial difficulties were contributing factors to the depressive episodes of the client as depicted in Figure 3.15. In each of these examples, an important causal variable was identified that helped explain the original onset of a behavior problem, but that variable was not amenable to modification—the clinician could not change its occurrence, intensity, or duration.

Causal variables for clients' behavior problems can be difficult to modify for several reasons. First, they can be historical events such as childhood abuse or neglect, physical trauma, and early learning experiences. Second, they can be based on genetic factors or stable physiological characteristics such as spinal cord damage or traumatic brain injury. Third, they can involve difficult-to-modify social or cultural contexts such as living in a violent neighborhood or exposure to very low-weight fashion models. Fourth, they can involve uncooperative social agents such as an uncooperative spouse, parent, or hospital staff member. Fifth, their modification can be a challenge to our current level of intervention technology. Sixth, it can be that change would be unacceptable to the client, such as withdrawal from a violent marriage by a person who has no financial or social resources for independent living.

The estimated modifiability of a causal variable is an important focus of behavioral assessment and of the functional analysis because it affects the expected magnitude of effect that an intervention will have by focusing on that variable (see Figure 3.7). A variable with a strong causal relation to a client's behavior problem is clinically useful only to the degree that the clinician can modify the causal variable. Consequently, the estimated modifiability of a causal variable influences the clinician's decision about the focus of intervention. In some instances, a causal variable that is only weakly related to a behavior problem but is highly modifiable may be a more appropriate intervention target than a causal variable that is strongly related to the behavior problem but is more difficult to modify.

## SUMMARY

Several concepts of causality are especially applicable to the functional analysis and the strategies of behavioral assessment: (a) causal variables have multiple attributes and dimensions that can have differential causal effects; (b) a client's behavior problems are often affected by multiple causal variables; (c) causal variables can have additive and interactive effects; (d) there are individual differences in the type, form, and strength of causal relations; (e) causal relations for a client's behavior problems can be conditional and dynamic; (f) bidirectional causal relations are particularly useful because they provide expanded targets for intervention; (g) causal variables can be described at different levels of specificity and the best level depends on the goals of the assessment; and (h) sometimes noncontiguous causal relations are important, especially social systems factors that affect the behavior of important persons in the client's life.

Understanding causal mechanisms is central to understanding multivariate causal relations. Sometimes, different causal variables share the same causal mechanism. A behavior problem can also be a function of multiple causal mechanisms and a causal variable can operate through multiple causal mechanisms.

Modifiability is another important attribute of causal variables. Modifiability contributes to an evaluation of the relative costs and benefits by targeting causal variables in an intervention. Modifiability can be affected by many factors. Typically an intervention will focus on modifiable causal variables. When historical or unmodifiable causal variables are central to the functional analysis, the clinician should then focus on their sequelae or the contemporary mechanisms through which they affect a client.

# 7

# Principles of Behavioral Assessment

## INTRODUCTION TO MEASUREMENT AND BEHAVIORAL ASSESSMENT

Advances in any science-based discipline partially depend on the degree to which the phenomena of the discipline can be measured. In essence, measurement allows a discipline to evolve by providing the technology for testing hypotheses and theories (Haynes et al., 2011). In behavioral assessment, measurement principally involves the process of assigning values to the attributes of a behavior and of events related to behavior. Examples would include assigning values to the rate, intensity, and duration of a person's manic episodes or alcohol use.

One of the most important psychometric aspects of measurement in behavioral assessment is *precision*—the degree to which a measure is valid and sensitive to change in the measured variable. Without precise measures in behavioral assessment, we cannot adequately identify a client's behavior problems and goals, understand the factors that influence them, or evaluate the degree to which behavior is changed through an intervention Thus, precise measurement provides the foundation for valid functional analyses and clinical judgments pertaining to intervention design. Conversely, measures from assessment that are invalid, nonspecific, or are based on an assessment strategy that fails to measure important variables will limit the validity and utility of the functional analysis and other clinical judgments.

There are many science-based psychological assessment paradigms that emphasize valid measurement, including neuropsychology, psychophysiology, intellectual and cognitive assessment, and personality assessment (see the *Psychological Assessment* series, published by John Wiley & Sons, 2004). However, behavioral assessment is the paradigm most congruent with the underlying concepts of the functional analysis and the psychological assessment paradigm that most strongly emphasizes the importance of precise measurement of clinically useful variables. The principles and methods of behavioral assessment are well adapted to the characteristics of behavior problems and causal relations outlined in previous chapters. In Chapters 7–10, we consider in greater detail particular strategies and methods of behavioral assessment based on these principles.

## BEHAVIORAL ASSESSMENT AS A CONCEPTUAL AND METHODOLOGICAL PARADIGM

Behavioral assessment is a conceptual and methodological paradigm that emphasizes: (a) obtaining precise measures of behavior problems, causal variables, and functional relations; (b) the limits and conditional nature of the psychometric evidence for a measure and the variables that are measured; and (c) deriving valid clinical judgments from measures obtained in clinical assessment. Additionally, and similar to most assessment paradigms in psychology, the overarching goals of behavioral assessment are to describe, predict, and *explain* human behavior and behavior change (Kaholokula et al., 2009).

Behavioral assessment is also a *dynamic, inclusive, science-based* paradigm. It is dynamic in that its methods and strategies are continually evolving to incorporate new findings in theory and research. For example, the behavioral assessment paradigm has expanded with the incorporation of new technological and conceptual developments such as *ecological momentary sampling* and *ambulatory biomeasurement*. It has also evolved in the incorporation of research on functional relations of behavior problems. It is a science-based approach to psychological assessment in the sense that it emphasizes methods of measurement that have been validated for a particular assessment occasion.

## The Conditional Nature of Behavior Problems Across Settings and Contexts

We noted in Chapter 4 that behavior problems are conditional and contextual. Specifically, the rate, duration, and/or intensity of behavior problems vary across settings and contexts. Careful examination of the conditional nature of behavior problems is important because variation in behavior across contexts indicates the operation of different causal variables. The implication of the conditional principle is clear: *In many clinical assessment circumstances, measures should be obtained across multiple settings and contexts to capture the dynamic nature of a behavior problem and its causal relations.* As we discuss further in Chapter 8 and in the case example presented later in this chapter, behavioral interviews focus on evaluating the degree to which a client's behavior problems vary across contexts. In contrast, nonbehavioral interviews and most questionnaires (particularly diagnostic interviews or personality assessment question-naires) emphasize general descriptions of behavior, such as current symptoms and their severity, with little attention to the role of contextual or setting variables. As we discuss in later chapters, the conditional nature of behavior problems emphasizes the utility of assessment strategies that can provide cross-context data, such as self-monitoring, analog observation, and naturalistic observation.

## DATA FROM MULTIPLE SOURCES CAN INCREASE THE VALIDITY OF CLINICAL JUDGMENTS

Each assessment method, instrument, and informant provides unique information about behavior problems and functional relations. Additionally, each assessment method, instrument, and informant is affected by unique sources of error (see Box 7.2). For these reasons, the acquisition of data from *multiple assessment methods* (such as direct observation and interviews), *multiple assessment instruments* (such as multiple rating scales of a child's behavior problems), and from *multiple informants* (such as the client, spouses, parents, staff members, and teachers), can enhance the validity of data and simultaneously diminish the impact of idiosyncratic sources of error. In many assessment contexts, judgments based on aggregated data from multiple, valid sources can improve the validity of clinical judgments (see Box 7.1).

---

**Box 7.1 Aggregating Multiple Measures Using z-Score Transformations**

A $z$-score transformation can be used to form a single composite measure from multiple measures of the same construct when those measures differ in their metric (e.g., aggregating two measures of social anxiety, one that uses a 10-point scale and one that uses a five-point scale; or aggregating observation data and self-report data on pain behavior). A $z$-score (standard score) is the number of standard deviations an observation or datum is above or below the mean of the sample. It converts all measures to the same metric by subtracting the sample mean from a client's raw score on a measure and then dividing the difference by the sample standard deviation. This process allows the clinician to combine measures with different metrics and can attenuate the error uniquely associated with each measure.

The formula for a $z$-score score is

$$Z = \frac{x - \mu}{\sigma},$$

where:

$x$ is a raw score to be standardized;

$\mu$ is the mean of the population (or sample)

$\sigma$ is the standard deviation of the population (or sample)

When two measures of a construct are combined in this manner, the composite measure should provide a more valid measure of the construct, so long as the component measures tap the same construct, are both valid, and do not have overlapping measurement errors (e.g., as when both elicit the same response biases).

---

Assessment methods also differ in their sensitivity to specific response modes and dimensions. Actions, such as praise and criticism among family members, are amenable to observation in analogue or natural environments. Less observable aspects of dyadic communication such as emotions, the experience of pain, expectations, or positive thoughts, are more amenable to self-report methods such as interviews, questionnaires, and self-monitoring. Clinicians sometimes administer standardized assessment batteries to clients without considering the degree to which the methods are appropriate to the particular assessment occasion. Data from such an assessment strategy can be helpful in making clinical judgments, but it may not be the most *cost-beneficial assessment strategy.*

As we have pointed out, assessment instruments have unique measurement errors. For example, one self-report questionnaire of anxiety may provide insufficient coverage of some modes and attributes of anxiety, while another may include excessive coverage of the same components. Some questionnaires targeting a behavior problem may include irrelevant items while others include some terms that exceed the cognitive abilities of respondents or are associated with fatigue-related errors because they are too long.

Some apparent sources of measurement error can also be attributed to the conditional nature of behavior problems. That is, differences between informants in their reports about a client's behavior could be attributed to the fact that they are exposed to the client's behavior in different environments and that the client behaves differently in those environments. De Los Reyes and Kazdin (2005), in discussing the measurement of childhood psychopathology, noted that the correlations between a child's cognitive processes and mood depend on whether the measures are obtained from the same or different informants. The authors also noted that the likelihood that a child would be identified as having a conduct-disorder by a parent is influenced by the parent's level of depression and that a teacher's rating of a child' conduct disorder is influenced by gender of the child and the family's income.

Given these multiple and unique sources of measurement error, there are two important strategies that can be used to improve the validity of measures acquired in clinical assessment. First, it is important to select the most valid measure to use in a particular assessment context. This minimizes the level of error associated with that particular assessment context. Second, *multisource assessment* strategies should be used. As noted earlier, this involves collecting information from more than one source to estimate a targeted phenomenon. True variance can be separated from error variance when measures of the same phenomenon are based on multiple methods, instruments, informants, and settings.

In summary, integrating clinical assessment data from multiple sources can increase the validity of a clinician's judgments about a client by: (a) reducing the impact of unique error associated with each method, instrument, and informant; (b) broadening the settings and contexts from which assessment data are derived; and (c) obtaining measures across response modes and dimensions. The behavioral assessment paradigm particularly emphasizes the importance of basing clinical judgments on assessment methods, such as direct observation of behavior, that supplement a client's self-report. Many assessment scholars have summarized the problems (some of which are outlined in Box 7.2) of relying exclusively on a client's self-report when assessing behavior problems, their causes and correlates, and intervention process and outcome.

The benefits of multisource assessment occur only if the data collected from each measure are valid and do not have similar sources of error. For example, the validity of a clinician's judgments about the causal variables that affect a client's degree of alcohol intake based on interviews with the client, is not increased by interviewing the client's spouse if he or she is biased or is not aware of these causal variables. Similarly, the validity of a clinician's judgments will not be enhanced by using two questionnaires that include highly correlated measurement errors. The addition of less valid data, or data from instruments with similar measurement errors, will reduce the validity of the clinician's judgments.

---

### Box 7.2 Some Sources of Error Associated With Assessment Methods

*Interviews:* Bias in the responses of the interviewee, memory errors, interviewer errors, dissimulation, and state of the respondent.

*Retrospective Self-Report Questionnaires:* Imprecise item wording, biased responding, dissimulation, state of the respondent, imprecise or excessively long time frame for reports.

*Informant Behavior Rating Scales:* Imprecise item wording, rater bias, insufficient exposure to the targeted behavior, and increased impact of more recent behaviors.

*Self-Report Diaries and Ecological Momentary Sampling:* Insufficient adherence to the self-monitoring schedule, excessive client burden, and social desirability effects.

*Ambulatory Biomeasurement:* Reactive effects associated with measurement intrusiveness, errors associated with extraneous events, technological malfunctions, sampling at the wrong times.

*Analog Behavioral Observation:* Reactive effects associated with the observation process, observer errors, imprecise definitions of behavior codes, errors in selecting topics and settings.

*Naturalistic Observation:* Observations made in the wrong settings or at the wrong times, observer errors, reactive effects associated with the observation process, and insufficient number of time samples.

*Psychophysiological Laboratory Assessment:* Reactive effects associated with the laboratory setting, technological malfunctions, movement artifacts, and insufficient time allowed for establishing baseline or recovery to prestressor levels.

## The Dynamic Nature of Behavior, Causal Relations, and the Importance of Time-Series Assessment

We discuss in Chapters 4–6 how behavior problems and the functional relations associated with them are often dynamic—they can change in systematic and unsystematic ways over time. In many cases, "time" can be conceptualized as a marker variable that indicates the operation of other causal variables. However, it can also be conceptualized as a source of error variance (see Box 7.3). For example, a client monitoring aspects of generalized anxiety across time may report that he or she is experiencing a reduction in difficulties with concentration and engaging in social interactions across time. This change across time can reflect the introduction or removal of important causal variables. For example, the reduction of concentration difficulties may reflect the client's use of relaxation strategies (introduction of a moderating causal variable) or a change in workload (removal of a causal variable). The reduction in self-monitored concentration difficulties may also reflect error variance such as diminished adherence to monitoring or a change in the way that the client rates the experience (observer drift).

The dynamic nature of behavior problems creates a measurement and inferential challenge for the clinician. A rule of thumb, however, is that data on a client from a single moment in time, or data from infrequent samples, are insufficient to capture the dynamic aspects of the behavior. The essential risks of using single point measurement or infrequent measurement are that the measure could, by chance, capture a phenomenon at its maximum or minimum, or in increasing, decreasing, or plateau phases.

The dynamic nature of many behavior problems and causal relations has been well documented in many areas of human functioning such as daily or hourly changes in the frequency and form of a client's compulsive behaviors, blood glucose levels, sleep quality, functional impairment associated with pain, and mood. When such variability is present, the behavioral assessment should use time-sampling strategies. For time-sampling strategies to provide a sensitive measure of the dynamic characteristics of the measured phenomenon, the sampling rate must be appropriate for its dynamic characteristics (i.e., its rate and pattern of changes across time). Consider the erroneous inferences that could result if the rapidly fluctuating mood of a client was measured only once per week, or if a questionnaire item provided no time frame (e.g., "I am a moody person"), or if the time frame was insensitive to the dynamic characteristics of the behavior (e.g., "How would you describe your mood during the past month?"). Such measurement time frames would make it difficult to identify the variables associated with the mood fluctuations and impair our ability to track the immediate effects of an intervention.

As these examples suggest, and as we noted in Box 7.3, the time frame of an assessment strategy can affect the specificity and validity of the data obtained. To measure changes across time in clinical assessment, particularly changes in response to an intervention, many commonly used self-report assessment instruments ask respondents to retrospectively rate behaviors or environmental events within a specific time frame, such as one month or one week. Several studies have found that the validity of retrospective reports often decreases as the time frame for responses becomes more distal. That is, reports by clients of behavior for the past day or week are often more valid than their reports for the past month. A more distant or longer time frame can increase the degree to which the data reflect many sources of error, such as a positive response bias, the impact of recent events, and ambient mood on the retrospective report (see Terry et al., 2005).

As with all sources of measurement error, those associated with time frame are also conditional, in that longer time frames may be appropriate for some assessment purposes. For example, for rarely occurring behaviors (e.g., infrequent seizures, migraine headaches), a longer time frame may be necessary as shorter ones are likely to elicit many "0" responses. Lucas and Baird (2006) discuss variables and strategies to enhance accuracy in retrospective recall, such as using specifically identified intervals, targeting easily remembered events, focusing on shorter reference intervals, and providing additional memory prompts.

Recall that differences in measures of a client's behavior obtained at different times can reflect differences in the client's behavior across settings. For example, self-reported measures of a client's level of fatigue would provide biased estimates of a client's average fatigue throughout the day if they were obtained only while the client was at work or only in the afternoons. The data derived from these time-sampling strategies could be an *accurate* measure of the client's fatigue at those times but would provide an *invalid* measure of the client's fatigue in other settings or times. Of course, clinicians are often interested in obtaining measures in selected settings, particularly "high-risk" settings (e.g., right after school for a child with oppositional behaviors, or right after a marital conflict for a client who often injures himself when emotionally distressed). Box 7.3 reviews several time-sampling strategies (see Minke & Haynes, 2003, for a detailed review of sampling concepts and strategies). Each time-sampling strategy has assets and limitations and none are without errors. For example, momentary time samples by nurses of a psychiatric inpatient may miss important contexts associated with the client's aggressive behaviors.

---

### Box 7.3 Strategies for Time-Sampling

*Random time-sampling:* Gathering data at random times within a more broadly specified time frame (the sampling frame), such as randomly sampling a client's mood throughout a day using a programmable device, wristwatch, or diary.

*Systematic time-sampling:* Gathering data at prespecified times within a defined time frame, such as recording a student's level of on-task behavior at the midpoint of each class.

*Event-related time-sampling:* Gathering data during particular times, settings, or contexts (usually those of special clinical interest), such as collecting data on the mood, compulsive behaviors, or alcohol use whenever the client has a distressing exchange with a partner.

*Convenience time-sampling:* Gathering data when it is easier for the client or rater. In self-monitoring methods, clients are often asked to indicate at night, just before going to bed, the amount of time they spent exercising, the number of positive dyadic interactions, or the frequency of their child's tantrums that day. Or, the client may be asked to rate progress toward intervention goals at the beginning of a weekly therapy session. Convenience time-sampling is oftentimes aimed at maximizing compliance with the recording procedure.

---

The dynamic nature of behavior problems and causal relations has several additional implications for clinical assessment. First, multiple time-samples, in clinically relevant settings, will more adequately capture the dynamic nature of behavior and reduce judgment errors associated with the use of only one sample. Chapters 8 and 9 illustrate the application of time-sampling strategies with self-monitoring, ambulatory biomeasurement, naturalistic observation, and analog observation. Second, assessment should be an ongoing process, beginning with the initial meeting with the client and continuing throughout assessment, intervention, and follow-up. Third, we are often interested in the "phase" of a behavior problem and causal variable—whether they are increasing or decreasing—as well as their "state" (i.e., the level or rate of a variable at the time of measurement). Figure 7.1 illustrates how different persons, measured at the same time (a measurement of their state), can be in different phases (e.g., increasing, decreasing, stable, variable). Note how this *time-course context* of a behavior or causal variable can help us predict future behavior and identify the factors associated with behavior change. (See Haynes, Blaine, & Meyer, 1995, for a discussion of state-phase functions in clinical assessment.)

The best sampling rate depends on the characteristics of the variables that are measured and practical issues associated with measurement.

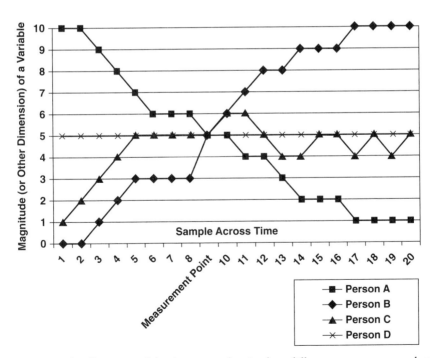

**Figure 7.1** An illustration of the *time-course* showing how different persons, measured at the same time (a measurement of their state), can be in different phases (i.e., A = decreasing, B = increasing, C = variable, and D = stable).

Ideally, highly variable phenomena should be measured several times a day but such rates are often impractical for clients, even with the use of handheld computers. Consequently, daily and weekly measures of variables are often used in clinical and research measurement strategies.

Note how the *time-course context* of a behavior or causal variable can help us identify the causal factors associated with behavior change. If we assume that the variable in Table 7.1 is "alcohol use," the causal relations for the four different persons are likely to be very different. Something is happening to increase alcohol use for Person B and decrease it for Person A, even though their use of alcohol is the same at the measurement point.

## An Emphasis on Lower-Level, Less Inferential, and More Specific Variables and Units of Analysis

The behavioral assessment paradigm emphasizes the clinical utility, and often validity, of more specific, fine-grained measures of behavior, events, and functional relations. Because more molar, less specific, and more heterogeneous constructs, especially psychiatric diagnoses and personality traits, are composed of multiple elements that can differ in importance across persons, the accuracy, specificity, and utility of clinical judgments can often be increased by measuring more specific, lower-level, or more narrowly defined constructs, variables, and units of analysis. As illustrated in Table 4.1, within a behavioral assessment paradigm, clinicians are more likely to measure specific thoughts, social interactions, and sleep of a client diagnosed with "Major Depression" rather than, or in addition, to measure the higher-order construct of "depression," which is composed of an aggregate of those and other variables.

Recall that "specificity" refers to the number of facets or sources of variance in a measure or variable. More specific measures and variables include fewer elements and sources of variance and, therefore, often facilitate more clinically useful judgments. For example, changes in a composite measure of a depressive disorder could reflect changes in different combinations of facets of the disorder (e.g., behavioral actions, somatic, cognitive, interpersonal), and changes in each of these facets could reflect changes in multiple lower-level exemplars of each facet, as illustrated in Table 4.1. Because there are fewer sources of variance, there are also fewer alternative explanations for changes in more specific, compared to more aggregated, measures. Consequently, confidence and specificity in judgments from our assessment data, and our understanding of behavior problems, can often be increased by the use of more specific variables.

As these examples illustrate, "specificity" of a measure is inversely related to its degree of aggregation (we discuss one strategy of aggregating multiple measures of a construct in Box 7.1). An aggregated measure is affected by variance from multiple sources. For example, an aggregated observation measure of "aggression" could include measures of "hitting," and "verbal threats"; an aggregated self-report measure of "quality of life" could include measures of "satisfaction with health," and "satisfaction with family relationships." A limitation of aggregated variables is that they can mask important sources of variance and make it difficult to draw inferences about change in, or functional relations related to, important components of the measure. For example, a composite measure of "social anxiety" can mask important differences in the most problematic behavioral, emotional, or cognitive aspects for clients. For many goals of clinical assessment, such as brief screening and diagnosis, the use of aggregated measures is appropriate. For most clinical applications of behavioral assessment, the use of aggregated variables impedes the goals of the assessment.

## An Emphasis on Contemporaneous Functional Relations and Contemporaneous and Environmental Causal Relations

All clinical assessment paradigms, including behavioral assessment, emphasize the identification and description of clients' behavior problems and intervention goals. Behavioral assessment is unique in its degree of emphasis on the identification of *functional relations* among a client's behavior problems, positive intervention goals, and causal variables. As we noted in Chapters 5 and 6, many clinically useful causal variables for behavior problems are associated with events that occur more closely in time with (i.e., are more proximal to) the client behavior problems or their positive behavior alternatives.

There is a traditional emphasis in the behavior paradigm on the assessment of contemporaneous behavior-environment interactions.

Thousands of studies have documented the importance of immediate antecedent and consequential environmental stimuli in problem behavior onset, maintenance, and cessation (see *Journal of Applied Behavior Analysis* for hundreds of examples, and O'Donohue and Ferguson, 2004). However, it is important to note that this emphasis on behavior-environment interactions does not reduce the importance of understanding how contemporaneous thoughts and emotions can be important causal factors in behavior problems. For example, many cognitive-behavioral causal models of generalized anxiety and panic disorders invoke important cognitive and emotional causal variables (e.g., Gervais & Dugas, 2008).

The behavioral assessment paradigm also acknowledges that noncontemporaneous or distal causal variables can be important in the functional analysis and associated clinical judgments. As we noted in Chapter 6, clients often seek help after they have been experiencing distress for an extended period of time. Consequently, by the time that the client presents for assessment and potential treatment, the variables responsible for the onset of the behavior problem may no longer be operating. Inquiring about these more distal events can provide insight into how the function of the behavior problem has changed across time. An emphasis on contemporaneous causal factors draws the focus of assessment to questions such as "Why is this client still depressed two years after a difficult divorce?" (i.e., "What actions or thoughts are maintaining his depressed mood over such a long period of time") or "What is happening at home that might be maintaining a child's oppositional and aggressive behavior toward his siblings and parents?" or "What can be done to enhance the communication abilities of a child diagnosed with Autism?"

## Assessment of Clients in Their Natural Environment and an Emphasis on the Contemporaneous Measurement of Behavior

Assessment of persons in their natural settings (e.g., home, school, institution) is the iconic strategy of behavioral assessment (e.g., Dishion & Granic, 2004). Collecting real-time data on clients while they are at home, work, school, play, or in institutions can provide valuable information about the form of the client's behavior, the contexts that affect it, immediate antecedent and consequent events that might be maintaining it, and events that impede or facilitate acquisition of positive behavioral alternatives and the attainment of intervention goals. Furthermore, data on a client obtained in his or her natural environments often has *incremental clinical utility* over retrospective self- and other-reports because natural environment data can help to more precisely identify clinically significant behaviors, behavior-environment interactions, and changes across time. Assessment across settings is discussed in more detail in Haynes et al. (2011), and Minke and Haynes (2011).

The improved validity of data obtained in the natural environment is partially due to the errors that occur when clients recall their behavior and associated events in interviews and questionnaires. Chapters 8 and 9 discuss several methods that are especially useful for assessment in the natural environment. Traditional self-monitoring (e.g., with paper and pencil), actometers (that track movements), ecological momentary assessment (self-monitoring involving prompts delivered by hand-held computers), ambulatory biomeasurement (equipment worn by a person that automatically records physiological events), participant observers, external observers, or audio and video recordings can all be used to collect data in the natural environment. Additionally, direct observation of parent–child, couple, teacher–child, client–client, peer, and staff–client interactions in the natural environment is a particularly powerful method of detecting important functional relations. The *Journal of Applied Behavior Analysis* has presented hundreds of examples of direct observation in classrooms, homes, playgrounds, and psychiatric units across a wide range of behavior problems as well as prosocial behaviors.

## An Idiographic Emphasis

The behavioral assessment paradigm is principally aimed at examining the unique modes and dimensions of a person's behavior problems and the unique set of functional relations associated with them. Consequently, the behavioral assessment paradigm is congruent with an idiographic approach to assessment. Haynes, Mumma, and Pinson (2009) described *idiographic assessment* as the measurement of variables and functional relations that have been individually selected, or derived from assessment stimuli or contexts that have been individually tailored, to maximize their relevance for the particular individual.

In idiographic assessment, the methods, strategies, and focus of assessment are individually tailored to reflect the unique aspects of the client's behavior problems and goals, their personal assets and limitations, and associated causal factors. These between-client differences, in turn, affect the sensitivity and utility of different assessment methods and different elements within an assessment instrument. For example, persons with anxiety disorders can differ in the degree to which they exhibit physiological, subjective, cognitive, or overt behavioral responses when exposed to environmental stressors (see overviews in Andrasek, 2006). Matching assessment method to the most important mode and dimension of a client's behavior problem can enhance the clinician's ability to identify important causal factors and measure change in response to intervention.

Within the context of idiographic assessment, the clinician can tailor the specific behaviors to be coded in analogue observation, the specific events and responses to be tracked in self-monitoring, and the specific items presented to clients from questionnaires to match each client's unique behavior problems. Each element in these assessment strategies is selected to provide the most sensitive measure of change over time and of important functional relations and can be used to supplement nomothetically based, standardized assessment instruments.[1]

As Kaholokula et al. (2009) commented, the idiographic emphasis of the behavioral assessment paradigm also encourages sensitivity to the unique aspects of the client and to individual differences that could influence the assessment process and outcome. Differences associated with sex, age, gender, ethnicity, sexual orientation, religious affiliation, and physical and cognitive limitations can easily be reflected in idiographic assessment. The authors also noted how the heightened sensitivity to individual differences encourages: (a) obtaining the client's informed consent for the assessment methods and focus and respect for the rights and autonomy of

---

[1] Because idiographic assessment can involve modification of a standardized assessment instrument, nomothetically based validity evidence for measures from that instrument are not applicable. Nevertheless, idiographic measures can be useful for within-person clinical judgments and some aspects can be generalizable across person (see extended discussion in Haynes et al., 2009).

a client; (b) a positive client-clinician relationship throughout the assessment process; (c) collaboration between the client and clinician in setting assessment and intervention goals; and (d) the clinician's selection of the best assessment strategies, the goals and problems encountered in assessment, the validity of the data collected, and the judgments made from those data.

## Attention to Potential Mechanisms of Causal Action and Alternative Explanations for Hypothesized Causal Relations

Most of the principles underlying behavioral assessment that we have discussed in this chapter are designed to increase the validity and utility of the clinician's judgments about a client's behavior problems and intervention goals, the causal variables that affect them, intervention outcome, and the functional analysis. Recall from Chapters 1 and 5 that in order to *explain* a client's behavior problems, the clinician must collect additional information about causal relations. It is particularly important to consider alternative explanations for the hypothesized causal relations. Examples of some questions a clinician could ask about possible alternative causal mechanisms involved in an apparent causal relation are "Is there another explanation for the relation that I am hypothesizing between the client's pervasive compulsive behaviors and the client's interpersonal distress?" or "Is it possible that an additional important causal variable is involved?" You can see how a premature judgment about a causal relation can lead to a less valid functional analysis and a less-than-optimal intervention decision.

Another important assessment focus is on the relations between distal causal events and current clinical concerns. That is, the clinician should consider the causal mechanisms that are currently operating and how they may account for the effects of a more distal event. For example, how does a client's stressful work experience during the day increase the risk of conflict with his or her partner in the evening? How does a parental conflict in the evening lead to a child's increase in aggressive behavior at school? These questions point to the importance of identifying causal mechanisms and chains associated with the client's behavior problems.

## A Scholarly, Empirically Guided, Hypothesis-Testing Orientation in Clinical Assessment.

It should be evident that clients are best served by a science-based approach to clinical assessment. As we emphasize in Box 6.3, clinicians should be knowledgeable about current research relevant to (a) the nature of a client's behavior problems, (b) the causal variables that can affect them, (c) the psychometric characteristics of measures that are used in the assessment, (d) the process used to derive clinical judgments from the collected information, and (e) treatment research relevant to a client's problems.

Consider the adverse consequences for the client if the clinician were unacquainted with research about possible triggers of a client's migraine headaches, or the influence of setting factors in the communication behaviors of a child with developmental disabilities, or cognitive variables that can affect the duration of a panic episode. Consider the adverse consequences for the client if the clinician were unacquainted with the psychometric limitations of measures and/or how to interpret the measures. Finally, note that lack of familiarity with effective intervention strategies for a particular problem could render the assessment and functional analysis less relevant. That is, if the behavior problems and causal relations are well-specified in a functional analysis, but the clinician has inadequate familiarity with strategies that can be used to modify these relations, then the functional analysis has no utility for treatment decisions.

A book by Hunsley and Mash (2008) reviews and summarizes the research on various behavior disorders and provides many examples of the conditional nature of psychological assessment measures. Chapters in their book focus on various behavior problems often encountered in clinical practice, such as anxiety disorders, mood disorders, adolescent behavior problems, health-related behavior problems, schizophrenia, and couple distress. Within each chapter, frequently used measures are evaluated on the degree to which there is empirical support for their reliability, convergent validity, discriminant validity, content validity, and clinical utility. Consistent with our focus on the conditional nature of psychometric evidence (see Box 7.4), the validity indices for a measure can vary, depending on whether the measure is to be used for brief screening, clinical case formulation, diagnosis, or as an intervention outcome measure.

The important point for the clinician is that in order to construct the most valid and useful assessment strategy for intervention outcome, screening, or the functional analysis, the clinician must be familiar with the research on the client's behavior problems, potential causal variables, and the available measures. The clinician should select those measures that are best suited to the client, his or her situation, and the purpose of the assessment. As we have emphasized before, the clinician should also remember that many assessment instruments provide more than one measure and that *different measures from the same instrument can differ in their degrees of validity*.

In the remaining sections of this chapter, we present another brief case example, adapted from Haynes, Pinson, Yoshioka, and Kloezeman (2008), to illustrate how the principles, methods, and strategies of behavioral assessment are applied to the functional analysis.

---

### Box 7.4 Psychometric Foundations of Behavioral Assessment: The Conditional Nature of Psychometric Evidence

Psychometric concepts and methods provide another foundation for behavioral assessment and are usually covered in graduate and undergraduate courses in psychology, education, and social work. Additionally, many books have been written on the psychometric foundations of psychological assessment. Books by Anastasi and Urbina (1997), Eid and Diener (2006), Furr and Bacharach (2008), Linn (1989), and Nunnally and Bernstein (1994), are scholarly sources on psychometrics. Haynes et al. (2011) discussed psychometric principles applied to clinical assessment. Psychometric foundations of behavioral assessment have been discussed in Cone (1998a), Haynes (2006), Haynes and O'Brien (2000), Silva (1994), and Suen and Rzasa (2004).

Nine elements of psychometrics are especially important in clinical applications of behavioral assessment.

1. *Psychometric evidence for a measure can vary across dimensions of individual difference.* Evidence about the validity, reliability, and utility of a measure can vary as a function of individual differences in clients (e.g., culture and ethnicity, age, sex, economic status, cognitive abilities, or religion). The clinician should consider the degree to which the samples used for psychometric evaluation of a measure are applicable to the client. We provide an example in Chapter 8.

2. *Psychometric evidence for a measure can vary across the clinical judgments that are based on it.* A measure can be valid for only specific clinical applications. For example, psychometric evidence supporting the discriminative validity of a measure does not mean that the same measure would be sensitive to treatment-related changes in a client's behavior problem or that it provides information that is useful for clinical case formulation.

3. *Psychometric evidence for a measure can vary across response modes and dimensions of behavior problems.* A measure can demonstrate good discriminative validity or sensitivity to change for some, but not other, modes or dimensions of a behavior problem. Consider a measure that validly measures the cognitive but not motor activity aspects of a behavior problem.

4. *Measures of reliability are not measures of validity.* Indices of internal consistency or temporal stability can indicate the consistency or stability of measures, but they do not provide information about the extent to which the measure tracks the construct that it is intended to track.

5. *A measure can be inaccurate and valid.* A measure can be inaccurate (e.g., an ambulatory measure of blood pressure that consistently overestimates true blood pressure) but provide valid measures of change over time, between-group differences (i.e., discriminative validity), and functional relations, if measurement error is consistent throughout values of the measured variable.

6. *A measure can be accurate and invalid.* A measure can accurately track the behavior of interest but the measure may not be a valid indicator of the behavior in other contexts (consider an accurate

measure of how a parent responds to a child's oppositional behavior in a clinical setting that does not reflect how the parent responds at home).

7.  *The construct validity of a measure can erode over time.* New knowledge about the characteristics and causes of a behavior problem may not be reflected in the content of older measures of the behavior problem.

8.  *Content validity is a particularly important dimension of psychometric evaluation in behavioral assessment.* Content validity refers to the degree to which the elements of an instrument are relevant and representative of the targeted construct. For example, are the behaviors coded and the time sampling strategies used in a school observation, the topics discussed during analog couple communication, or the probes for a client engaged in ecological momentary assessment of mood, relevant to the problems being addressed, and will they capture the important aspects of the targeted constructs?

9.  *Incremental validity of a measure should be considered when deciding whether to include it in the clinical assessment process.* Will a new or additional measure meaningfully increase the validity or utility of clinical judgments? Also, when selecting measures to use in clinical assessment, does a new measure significantly outperform existing measures?

# A CASE EXAMPLE OF BEHAVIORAL ASSESSMENT PRINCIPLES, STRATEGIES, AND METHODS APPLIED TO A FUNCTIONAL ANALYSIS

## Introduction and First Assessment Session

Carissa Anderson, a married 34-year-old woman, was referred for evaluation at an outpatient mental health clinic, complaining of severe mood "swings." Her psychiatrist referred her for a behavioral assessment after placing her on lithium medication for six months with no significant improvement in her mood swings. Her physician suspected that her mood swings may have been related to marital problems she casually mentioned in a few of her clinic visits.

Mrs. Anderson's assessment process began by obtaining informed consent for the goals and methods of the behavioral assessment, which was done through an initial behavioral assessment interview. The clinician's initial focus was on the identification and specification of her behavior problems (e.g., the dimensions and response modes of her mood swings and other problems) and goals for intervention. This was done in collaboration with Mrs. Anderson to help guide subsequent assessment methods and foci.

Her initial assessment interview was conducted during a period of mood stability, but she recalled experiencing short (two to three days' duration) but frequent (two to three times per month) periods of severely depressed mood alternating with longer periods (three to five days) of highly frenetic, euphoric mood states over the past month. When depressed, she often stayed in bed for most of the day, and felt very tired. She was also consumed by thoughts of being useless and that her life was hopeless, with no future happiness in sight. During her frenetic states, she slept little and felt more energetic. She went on frequent shopping sprees that resulted in the accumulation of excessive bills for clothes and household items (e.g., unneeded high-tech garage door opener and a second huge freezer), talked rapidly and often tangentially, and made grandiose plans for her and her family (e.g., moving to another country, buying a business). During these times, she was frequently unresponsive to feedback from others and became irritable with her husband and teenage daughter, which often led to escalating verbal conflicts within the family. These conflicts and arguments would often last for hours and be closely followed by a depressive episode. Her work as an accountant at a local retail store and her social relations with coworkers were impaired during both her depressive and manic episodes and she had been warned of possible job termination. The interviewer also used a *timeline followback interviewing procedure* (see Chapter 8) to help her better recall information, which revealed a steady pattern of frequent manic and depressive episodes over the past year.

During the initial interview, Mrs. Anderson reported experiencing only a mildly depressive mood state. The clinician understood that some of the information provided by Mrs. Anderson during this initial interview (such as specific impairments) might be conditional. That is, the information she provided about the dimensions and response modes of her behavior problems, and reported events in her life, might be influenced by her current state. Thus, information provided during a manic or depressive state might have been substantially different.

At the end of her first interview, and after probing by the clinician for other concerns, Mrs. Anderson completed well-validated self-report questionnaires that focused on her depressed and manic moods, and a broadly focused behavior problem checklist to identify other concerns. She completed the Quick Inventory of Depressive Symptomatology to identify specific behavior problems associated with depression and manic states (Rush, Gullion, Basco, Jarrett, & Trivedi, 1996). The Adult Behavior Checklist was the broadly focused inventory that was administered in order to assess attention, mood, conduct, anxiety, and worry.

The clinician also asked Mrs. Anderson to keep a daily diary of sleep (sleep-onset latencies; times awake at night and their duration), and to rate her mood four times per day using a 5-point scale ranging from depressed to elated. Because of concerns about her marital relationship, the clinician asked Mrs. Anderson to bring her husband to the next interview. The foci of this interview session and the selection of additional assessment methods were guided by the clinician's knowledge of research on bipolar disorders.

## Second Assessment Session

During the second assessment session, the clinician interviewed Mr. and Mrs. Anderson together and then separately, focusing on factors that could potentially trigger or affect the onset and/or duration of Mrs. Anderson's manic and depressive moods, the effect of her manic and depressive moods on the marital and family relationships, the positive aspects and other concerns about their relationship, and Mr. Anderson's goals and additional concerns. This assessment interview also covered additional individual and couple-related problems, and individual and joint intervention goals. Mrs. Anderson and the clinician also reviewed the self-report and self-monitored data gathered by Mrs. Anderson over the previous week.

At the end of the second assessment session, Mr. and Mrs. Anderson independently completed questionnaires about their relationship satisfaction, areas of conflict and disagreement, and their methods of resolving relationship conflicts. The Dyadic Adjustment Scale (Spanier & Thompson, 1982) was used to measure the dyadic consensus, satisfaction, and cohesion, and the dyad's expression of affection. The Revised Conflict Tactics Scale was used to assess their marital conflict and methods of resolving them (Straus et al., 1996).

After completing the questionnaires, three five-minute analogue observation sessions were conducted. The clinician observed Mr. and Mrs. Anderson discuss and attempt to resolve several issues in their relationship (conflicts over how money should be spent, strategies for dealing with their daughter's disrespectful and oppositional behavior, and how the two of them expressed affection to each other). The Rapid Marital Interaction Coding System (Heyman & Vivian, 1993) was used to code their behaviors on several types of interactions, such as negative attributions, psychological abuse, hostility, withdrawal, acceptance, and humor. Throughout the assessment sessions, the clinician was very attentive to maintaining a supportive and empathic relationship with Mrs. Anderson and her husband, especially given the sensitive nature of the assessment topics.

Between the second and third assessment sessions, the clinician obtained records from the medical center where Mrs. Anderson had previously received treatment for her mood swings. The clinician also conducted a brief telephone interview with her physician to gather his clinical impressions and to follow-up on data in her medical records. In the meantime, Mrs. Anderson continued to self-monitor her mood and sleep patterns, and both Mr. and Mrs. Anderson tracked the frequency and topics of their arguments as well as enjoyable interactions during the week.

## Results of the Behavioral Assessment and the Functional Analytic Clinical Case Diagram

At the third assessment session, the clinician and Mr. and Mrs. Anderson discussed a preliminary clinical case formulation. Using a Functional Analytic Clinical Case Diagram (FACCD) the clinician proposed, and

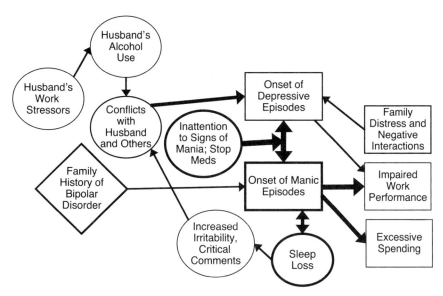

**Figure 7.2** A preliminary FACCD of Mrs. Anderson after two assessment sessions. Note the bidirectional causal relations among some of the variables.

they discussed, several individual problems, couple-related problems, and variables possibly contributing to those problems. The case formulation for Mrs. Anderson, in the form of an FACCD, is presented in Figure 7.2.

Consistent with the problems reported in the initial referral, Mrs. Anderson's most important behavior problems included frequent and severe depressive and manic states, both of which were accompanied by impairments in mood, judgment, physical activity, decision-making, and marital, parental, and occupational functioning. As noted in Figure 7.2, she considered the manic episodes as more important because they lasted longer and had a greater negative impact on her and her family's quality of life. Many, but not all, of Mrs. Anderson's depressive moods were preceded by conflicts with her husband, extended family members, or coworkers. Often, these conflicts occurred during one of her manic states. The precipitants of manic states could not be confidently identified, but they often followed positive events in her life and often closely followed the recovery from depressive states. Medical records and Mrs. Anderson's report also suggested a family history of bipolar disorders (including her mother and one of her three sisters).

Mr. Anderson, partially in response to increasing demands at his job as a construction site supervisor, had been drinking increasing amounts of alcohol immediately upon returning home in the evenings from work (increasing from two or three to about six or eight beers over the last 6 months). During these drinking episodes, he was more likely to be critical of his wife and daughter and to immediately escalate in response to mild verbal provocations from either of them. He had been sleeping fitfully for several months and had also experienced several depressed mood states, each lasting 5 to 6 days. These additional problems and variables are also illustrated in Figure 7.2.

The conflicts that they reported occurring at home were consistent with information from the analog communication assessment. During their discussions, Mr. and Mrs. Anderson frequently disagreed, infrequently agreed, and frequently interrupted each other. The negative emotional tone of the discussion escalated after a few minutes, ending in angry exchanges. Neither one spoke to the other in a supportive, confirming, or empathic manner. Following their discussions, each reported feeling angry, hurt, misunderstood, and blamed the other for their communication difficulties.

Based on this preliminary clinical case formulation, the clinician and Mr. and Mrs. Anderson agreed to start a 12-week treatment program, first focusing on marital enhancement, communication training, problem solving, and discussions of their aspirations for their marriage and their personal lives. To assess the treatment process (i.e., change in target causal variables) and outcomes (i.e., improvement in marital relations), Mrs. Anderson also agreed to continue daily self-monitoring of her mood and sleep pattern, and Mr. Anderson agreed to self-monitor his drinking, sleep, and mood.

Mr. and Mrs. Anderson also agreed on individual intervention sessions to help moderate their problems: Mrs. Anderson would receive treatment for her mood swings, impairment due to her depressive and manic states, and sleeping problems. Mr. Anderson would receive treatment for his alcohol use, stress responses, and sleeping problems. Finally, the clinician, and Mr. and Mrs. Anderson, decided to focus on problems with their daughter in later sessions, if the problems continued.

# SUMMARY

Measurement is central to behavioral assessment. The precision of a measure affects the validity and utility of assessment data. Errors in measures misrepresent a person's behavior and relevant causal relations. As a result, judgments based on the assessment data that reflect significant error variance will be adversely affected.

Behavioral assessment emphasizes the use of specific, lower level definitions and measures of behavior problems, causal variables, and causal relations. Behavioral assessment also emphasizes measurement that captures dynamic, situation-specific, ecologically valid, contemporaneous variation in behavior problems. Finally, behavioral assessment emphasizes the use of multiple methods, observation, multiple instruments, and multiple informants using a science-guided approach based on relevant research.

The case of Mrs. Anderson illustrates the assessment foci, methods, and strategies often applied in behavioral assessment and used to inform the functional analysis. It illustrates the utility and assets of using multiple assessment methods and strategies and the collection of information from multiple sources of data. We elaborate on these assessment methods and strategies, and introduce others, in Chapter 8, 9, and 10.

# Self-Report Methods in Behavioral Assessment

## OVERVIEW OF SELF-REPORT BEHAVIORAL ASSESSMENT METHODS AND STRATEGIES

The case of Mrs. Anderson that we describe in Chapter 7 illustrates how behavioral assessment methods and strategies are consistent with the principles of the behavioral assessment paradigm and the functional analysis. Behavioral assessment emphasizes the use of minimally inferential and clearly defined measures of behavior and related events that have well-developed psychometric properties, are sensitive to change, and appropriate for the characteristics of an individual client and the assessment context. Additionally, the behavioral assessment paradigm encourages the measurement of multiple response modes, dimensions, and attributes of a behavior, using a level of specificity that is most applicable to the problem behavior under investigation and the goals of the assessment. There is an assumption that the most accurate and valid information will be obtained when assessments include multiple informants, multiple measurement methods, and data collection in multiple settings.

In this chapter, we discuss a subset of behavioral assessment methods: those that rely on self-report. There are several types of self-report methods, including behavioral interviews, questionnaires, and self-monitoring using a daily log or an electronic diary. We refer the reader to Hersen (2006a, 2006b), Fernández-Ballesteros (2004), and Fernández-Ballesteros and Botella (2008) for an elaboration on the self-report methods discussed in this chapter.

Self-report assessment methods are used across all psychological assessment paradigms because they can easily be administrated in most settings, are flexible in their clinical applicability and utility, and are relatively cost- and time-efficient compared to direct observational and psychophysiological methods of assessment. Additionally, self-report methods are the only way that a client's cognitive and emotional experiences and subjective appraisal of causal relations can be ascertained. Although there are self-report assessment methods that assess personality traits and unconscious processes, behavioral assessment focuses on more specific and measurable behaviors and events that allow for the specification of a client's behavior problems and of relevant functional relations.

In this chapter, we emphasize *functional* behavioral interviews, questionnaires, rating scales, checklists, and self-monitoring—self-report assessment methods that focus on the specification of clients' behavior problems and their important, modifiable causal relations. In describing these methods, we highlight their clinical utility, assets, sources of error, and psychometric characteristics. As we emphasized in Chapter 7, we also recognize the advantages of using multiple assessment methods and strategies and multiple sources of data to compensate for the limitations of each assessment method.

## FUNCTIONAL BEHAVIORAL INTERVIEWS

With the case of Mrs. Anderson, we illustrated how the functional behavioral interview was used to obtain her informed consent for the assessment process, to identify her assessment goals, to specify her mood and marital discord, to maintain a positive clinician-client relationship, to identify additional assessment methods and strategies, and to generate hypotheses about the causal factors of her behavioral problems. The functional behavioral interview is typically the first step in behavioral assessment and has an important impact on all of the subsequent processes and outcomes of the behavioral assessment. In this section, we describe the functional behavioral interview and its goals, methods and strategies, assets, and liabilities. For more detailed discussions on interviewing, we refer the reader to Sayers and Tomcho (2006) and Beach (2005) for a broad discussion of the principles and methods of behavioral interviewing; Sharp, Reeves, and Gross (2006) for behavioral interviewing with parents of children with behavior problems; O'Neil, Horner, Albin, Sprague, Storey, and Newton (1997) for functional assessment interviewing for a wide-range of behavioral problems; and Barbour and Davison (2004) for a broad overview of clinical interviewing with discussions on structured and semistructured interviewing techniques and on interviewing special populations.

# DESCRIPTION OF THE FUNCTIONAL BEHAVIORAL INTERVIEW

The functional behavioral interview is a type of behavioral interview that focuses on identifying and specifying a client's behavior problems and goals, and relevant *functional relations*, to develop a functional analysis. A particular focus of the functional behavioral interview is on estimating the degree to which a client's behavior problems may be related to different antecedents and consequences and how the problems vary across contexts. Contrast this to other types of clinical interviews, such as diagnostic interviews, that are more often focused on "descriptions" of behavior (such as symptoms, history, and severity), with little attention given to the causal variables that exert important effects on the behavior problems.

The functional behavioral interview is guided by a number of assumptions derived from the behavioral assessment paradigm that we discussed in previous chapters. Beach (2005) elaborates more on the learning principles applied to behavioral interviews and Sayers and Tomcho (2006) provide general guidelines in conducting them.

## The Goals of the Functional Behavioral Interview

The functional behavioral interview has several goals that are consistent with the principles of the behavioral assessment paradigm (see Chapters 4 to 7) and the elements of the functional analysis (see Chapter 2). These goals are listed below.

- To obtain client's informed consent for the assessment goals, methods, and strategies to be used.
- To develop rapport and a collaborative clinician-client relationship and maintain that positive relationship throughout the assessment and intervention process.
- To identify and specify a client's behavior problems and goals.
- To identify and specify the hypothesized causal variables associated with the client's behavior problems and goals.
- To obtain subjective estimates of the strength of relationships among behavior problems, among causal variables, and among causal variables and behavior problems.
- To determine the need for case consultation or whether a referral to another clinician is warranted.
- To identify possible impediments to intervention and to capitalize on the client's strengths.
- To guide the selection of additional assessment methods, instruments, and strategies.
- To provide one source of information about a client in a multisource assessment approach.
- To develop a preliminary functional analysis.
- To design an intervention program.
- To evaluate the process and outcomes of an intervention program.

It should be apparent that many of the aforementioned goals of the functional behavioral interview are overlapping and complementary. For example, the specification of behavior problems, causal variables, and functional relations among them is essential to the development of a functional analysis that, in turn, is critical for intervention design. The functional behavioral interview is also a method of assessment that can be used to evaluate the processes and intermediate outcomes of an intervention, such as identifying failing, ineffective, or potentially harmful components of an intervention; monitoring a client's satisfaction with an intervention; and evaluating the overall effects of an intervention.

It is important to note that the functional behavioral interview is fully compatible with other approaches to assessment that emphasize the need to develop and maintain a positive and collaborative relationship with the client by taking a client-centered approach. A client-centered approach recognizes the client's autonomy, fosters a collaborative and comfortable assessment environment, focuses on the client's needs and goals, and determines whether a referral or consultation is beneficial in meeting the client's needs and goals—all of which are important elements of the functional behavioral interview. Many studies have demonstrated the benefits of using client-centered approaches in therapy (see Norcross, 2002, for more details).

## The Clinical Utility and Assets of the Functional Behavior Interview

The functional behavioral interview can be used across a diverse range of clients, behavioral problems, assessment goals, and settings. Later in this section, we discuss the types of clients and problems for which the functional behavioral interview has limited clinical utility and validity. Additionally, the functional behavioral interview can be used across a range of clinical populations with different diagnoses and behavior problems. It can also be used for a range of assessment goals, such as case conceptualization, intervention selection, and intervention evaluation. Finally, the functional behavioral interview can be applied in the clinician's office; in a client's or informant's home, school, or work; in a clinic or hospital setting; and in the community setting.

## Methods and Strategies of the Functional Behavioral Interview

The functional behavioral interview often involves the collaborative interactions between the clinician and client or other informant about the target behavior problem and intervention goals. Usually these interactions are conducted face-to-face, but can occur over telephone or through the use of computer-based programs (see Box 8.1). A functional behavioral interview is semistructured and uses open-ended and closed-ended queries to specify and quantify the client's behavior problems and their hypothesized causal relations. In the case of computer-based functional assessment interviews, the client or informant responds to a set of preprogrammed queries, and subsequent queries are determined by how he or she responds.

---

### Box 8.1 Computer-Based Functional Assessment Interviews

Several computer-based functional assessment interview programs have been developed. One example is the *Functional Assessment Intervention Program* (University of Utah, 1999). It is designed to conduct a functional behavioral assessment by posing a series of questions about a child's behavior problem. The respondent (e.g., clinician, teacher, or parent) either types a response or clicks a mouse on the pre-programmed answers. There are three sections that are designed to gather information about (1) the child's sociodemographic characteristics and setting, (2) antecedent factors that may influence the behavior problem, and (3) consequences of the behavior problem. After the respondent confirms the antecedents and consequences of the behavior problem, the program formulates hypotheses about the possible functions for the behavior problem (e.g., to obtain attention versus tangible rewards) and the respondent is given the option of confirming each hypothesized function. Finally, the respondent is provided with a list of evidence-based interventions.

Hartwig and colleagues (2004) compared the Functional Assessment Intervention Program to other self-report methods of assessing a child's behavior problem based on the ratings of 59 school psychologists, social workers, and teachers, derived from the Motivation Assessment Scale (Durand & Crimmins, 1992) and the Functional Assessment Interview (O'Neil et al., 1997). They found good interrater agreement and test-retest reliability for both the function of behavior (71% and 81.4%, respectively). Concurrent validity was also demonstrated in which the Functional Assessment Intervention

Program had 69% agreement on behavior functions with Motivation Assessment Scale and 76% with Functional Assessment Interview. In addition, the users preferred the Functional Assessment Intervention Program to the other measures.

Although computer-based interview programs can be time-efficient and user-friendly, they pose several challenges. The direction and degree of questioning is limited to preprogrammed questions. This limits their flexibility and could affect clinical judgments. Computer-based interview programs have been used primarily to identify a limited number of elements of the functional analysis, such as behavior problems and contiguous antecedent and consequential factors. So far, they have not been used to estimate the relative importance of multiple behavior problems and the magnitude of effect of causal variables. For a broader discussion about computerized behavioral assessment we refer the reader to Richard and Lauterbach (2004).

**Interviewing Strategies.** The content of the functional behavioral interview is usually idiographic, in that queries are tailored to the specific goals and behavior problems of a client. Recall how the queries in the cases of Mrs. Sanchez and Mrs. Anderson were individually tailored to their behavior problems and assessment goals. There are forms available to aid clinicians' functional behavioral interviews (see O'Neil et al., 1997, for examples). Many can be obtained over the Internet when "functional behavioral interview form" is used as a search term.[1]

An array of techniques and strategies are used in the functional behavioral interviews. These include open-ended and closed-ended questions, prompts to elicit information, and observation of paralinguistic behaviors (e.g., head nods, gestures, postures); strategies for clarification

---

[1] Some examples of functional behavioral interview forms can be found at: http://www.kipbs.org/new_kipbs/fsi/files/Functional%20Assessment%20Interview.pdf;
http://www.gvsu.edu/cms3/assets/3FF2AC1D-9E7D-0B89-4B0ED2FF1717361F/08-09sibehavior/Parent%20Interview%20Form%20for%20Functional%20Behavioral%20Assessment.doc;
http://www.cow.waisman.wisc.edu/documents/dualdx/FBA_interview.pdf

and elaboration (e.g., reflections, paraphrasing); clinician's monitoring of personal biases and reactions to client's issues; and use of positive feedback to establish and maintain a positive and collaborative assessment experience.

**Queries to Specify Functional Relations.** As we noted earlier, a key difference between a functional behavioral interview and other interviews is its focus on specifying *functional relations*. The queries in the functional behavioral interview are designed to capture the aspects, response modes, and dimensions of a client's behavior problem, their unique causal relations, the most important and modifiable causal variables and relations, contextual and temporal factors, and social and environmental antecedents and consequences.

Here are some examples of functional behavioral interview queries to specify behaviors and identify functional relations:

- To capture antecedent and consequential variables and relations: "How does your father respond to your outbursts?" "What happens when you become anxious?" "What do you do when Lori begins to hit herself?"

- To capture response modes of a behavior problem: "Explain to me what your manic episodes are like for you. How does it feel? What are you thinking?"

- To capture contexts: "Do you become more anxious in certain situations or settings compared to others?" "Are there times when Kira is more likely to act hyperactively?"

- To capture dimensions of a behavior problem: "How many times have you experienced bouts of depression in the last week?" "How often does Pat hit himself during the class?" "On nights that you have worries about being alone, how long does it take before you fall asleep from the time that you put your head on the pillow?"

- To capture relative importance: "On a scale from one to five, with five being the most, how important are your marital problems compared to your work problems?

Notice how, in the examples above, the clinician can design functional behavioral interview queries to collect quantitative data to specifically capture the dimensions of a behavior problem and the relative importance of multiple behavior problems and causal relations. Although the functional behavioral interview queries can have a high degree of specificity, the accuracy of data derived from the functional behavioral interview can be affected by many sources of error due to a client or informant's cognitive limitations, errors in memory, and/or other reporting biases. We elaborate on these sources of error in the next sections.

**Timeline Follow-Back Interviews.** Sayers and Tomcho (2006) argued that there is little research on the content, reliability, and validity of behavioral interviewing, but that there have been many studies that investigated how specific interviewing techniques can influence the accuracy of self-reported data. One semistructured interviewing technique that has been extensively researched is the *timeline follow-back* interview procedure (Sobell & Sobell, 1992). This is a semistructured interview technique using calendars and memory anchors to construct a daily behavior chart during a specific time period, such as a one-year timeline of a client's history of manic episodes, alcohol consumption, and panic episodes. For example, the clinician could ask the client about the occurrence and contexts of episodes of manic mood states or binge eating around their birthday, anniversaries, major holidays, and festivals, and expand reporting from those points. Some studies have found that the data from timeline follow-back procedures can be more reliable and valid than those from other retrospective self-report methods when assessing discrete events and behavior problems, such as a child's exposure to partner violence (Lam, Fals-Stewart, & Kelley, 2009), substance use (Sacks, Drake, Williams, Banks, & Herrell, 2003), and the frequency of panic episodes (Nelson & Clum, 2002).

Assessment instruments and procedures to guide the use of the *timeline follow-back* interview have been developed and evaluated for specific behavior problems. Examples are the *Timeline Follow-Back Interview— Children's Exposure to Partner Violence* to assess children's exposure to daily patterns of intimate partner violence (Lam et al., 2009), the *Timeline Follow-Back Sexual Behavior Interview* for HIV-related sexual behaviors and their antecedents (Weinhardt, Carey, Maisto, Carey, Cohen, &

Wickramasinghe, 1998), and the *Timeline Follow-Back Spousal Violence* interview to assess daily patterns and frequency of spousal violence (Fals-Stewart, Birchler, & Kelley, 2003).

Although the timeline follow-back procedure has been found to be a valid and reliable interviewing strategy in some studies, it may provide less accurate data when compared to other assessment methods. For example, Shiffman (2009) compared the reports of cigarette smoking frequency in 232 smokers based on global retrospective self-reports, the timeline follow-back procedure, and ecological momentary assessment (e.g., self-monitoring in real time using an electronic diary). He found that ecological momentary assessment yielded less bias in estimates of daily number of cigarettes smoked, compared to the timeline follow-back and global reports.

## Limitations of the Functional Behavioral Interview

There are many sources of error in interviews that limit their clinical utility and the validity of interview-derived data. Some sources of error are common to all self-report assessment methods while others are unique to the interview.

**Social Desirability and Dissimulation.** Data gathered from the functional behavioral interview can be biased by a client's discomfort in disclosing personal and socially sensitive information, such as sexual or aggressive behaviors, illegal behaviors, and certain medical conditions. Social desirability can also be an issue when information provided by the informant would place him or her in an unfavorable light. For example, Guinn and colleagues (2010) found that social desirability was associated with dietary recall accuracy for energy intake at school meals among fourth-grade students when compared to direct observations of the students' energy intake.

**Cognitive and Developmental Limitations.** Because the functional behavioral interview often requires retrospective recall, the data collected can also be limited by memory lapses or problems in recall biases (e.g., only remembering negative or positive social interactions). Other cognitive limitations (e.g., dementia, developmental delays) of the respondent can also affect the validity of interview data. A study by Dassel & Schmitt (2008) evaluated the relations between executive skills of spousal caregivers and ratings of their partners' activity of daily living skills. They found a moderate positive correlation between the caregivers' level of executive functioning skills and the accuracy of their subjective reports of partner activities of daily living.

For some clients, the use of the functional behavioral interview is impractical and may result in invalid data. Consider how the validity of data collected from the functional behavioral interview might be diminished with a person experiencing delusions, severe developmental disabilities, or the side effects of psychotropic medication. In cases where the validity of a respondent's recall of information is questionable or unobtainable, it is even more important to employ a multimethod assessment strategy, such as the use of direct observation and collecting data from informants (e.g., teachers and psychiatric staff).

**Interviewing Young Children.** Children should be interviewed cautiously, especially when issues of sexual abuse or trauma are involved. Assessment interviews can inadvertently introduce memories of events that never occurred or influence the recollection of events, such as when two distinct and independent events are coalesced into a single event. Some studies have found that the timing (shortly after an event or later in time) and manner of conducting interviews can shape the memory of young children and lead to unreliable or false reports (Quas et al., 2007; Goodman & Quas, 2008). For more details about the use of clinical assessment interviews with children, we refer the reader to Nader (2008) for trauma-related clinical interviews and Faller (2007) for sexual abuse-related clinical interviews.

An additional concern related to interviewing children is developmental level. Younger children typically do not have capacities for forming well-developed causal inferences nor providing verbal reports on the impact of various antecedent or consequent events on behavior. Further, younger children cannot reliably reflect on, and report, motivations for engaging in certain behaviors. Finally, younger children typically cannot provide well-developed accounts of how contextual factors influence behavior.

**Interviewing Couples and Families.** There are additional considerations when interviewing couples or families. In the case of couples, the clinical research literature is inconsistent on the issue of whether initial assessment of couple distress is best conducted with partners jointly or separately. Arguments for individual interviews include considerations of both validity and safety—particularly when assessing such sensitive issues as partner violence or substance abuse. A partner who is experiencing domestic violence often does not disclose aggressive behavior in conjoint assessment interviews, perhaps due to embarrassment, minimization, or fear of retribution (Ehrensaft & Vivian, 1996). Moreover, the risk of retaliatory aggression against one partner by disclosing the other's violence in conjoint interview supports the importance of conducting inquiries concerning partner violence in individual interviews.

Haynes et al. (1981) found that the convergent validity of data from individual versus joint interviews (comparing verbal reports during the interview with reports on self-report questionnaires) varied with the social sensitivity of the topic. For more sensitive issues, such as satisfaction with sexual interactions, validity was higher for individual interviews relative to joint interviews. For less sensitive topics such as household responsibilities, there was no significant difference in convergent validity between the two types of interviews. Regardless of whether domestic violence is the issue or not, it is probably helpful to conduct interviews separately at some point during the initial assessment. We refer the reader to Snyder, Heyman, and Haynes (2009) for an elaboration of the issues we present here and for a detailed discussion on the assessment of couples.

**Interviewer Experience and Training.** Although more time efficient when compared to direct assessment measures, a functional behavioral interview can be more time intensive and require more training on the part of the assessor than the use of self-report questionnaires. Insufficient training in conducting the functional behavioral interview can lead to imprecise wording of queries and time frames for reporting, ineffective use of many interviewing skills, and a less than optimal client-clinician relationship. These errors can affect the data derived from the interview and diminish the validity of clinical judgments based on them. Studies that have examined the effects of training on conducting behavioral interviews found that modeling (by a skilled interviewer) and behavioral rehearsal were key elements in developing proficiency (see Bootzin & Ruggill,1988).

**Characteristics and Biases of Client and Informant.** The characteristics of the client or an informant can affect the kinds and validity of data collected in an interview. For example, a client's report may be affected by the saliency or recency of behaviors. An interviewee's characteristics such as age, gender, religious and spiritual beliefs, ethnicity, marital status, employment history, and socioeconomic status, to name a few, could also influence the kinds of information reported or not reported in the functional behavioral interview. For example, Ford and Norris (1997) found that age and ethnicity was associated with the reporting of sexual activity among Hispanic women, who were more likely to share such information with younger interviewers.

Informant biases and exposure can also affect the validity of obtained data. For example, a teacher could provide biased information about a student when he or she is angry about the student's disruptive behavior in the classroom. An informant may also have insufficient exposure to the client's behavior to provide accurate information, such as when a recently hired psychiatric staff member is interviewed about the social contexts associated with the delusional behavior of a patient with whom he or she has had minimal exposure.

**Characteristics and Biases of Interviewer.** The interviewer can bias information obtained during an interview because of preconceived notions about a client's behavior problem that influence his or her queries. Biases can also be associated with interviewer characteristics, such as age, gender, or ethnicity. Returning to the study by Ford and Norris (1997), age of the interviewer was associated with reports of sexual behavior among Hispanic women. Tanaka-Matsumi (2004) provides a more detailed discussion on the role of individual differences in behavioral assessment. In Chapter 7 we discuss several additional threats to validity associated with the clinician.

## Summary of the Functional Behavioral Interview

We described the goals, methods, strategies, clinical utility, assets, and liabilities of the functional behavioral interview. We noted that it is an essential component in behavioral assessment and in development of the functional analysis. The functional behavioral interview can be helpful in specifying a client's behavior problems, goals, and functional relations. It also has unique strengths, such as being the major mechanism for establishing rapport with the client, maintaining a collaborative clinician-client relationship, and ensuring that the client has informed consent about the assessment process. We also noted several threats to the validity of data obtained during the functional behavioral interview.

## BEHAVIORAL QUESTIONNAIRES

Self-report questionnaires are often used in behavioral assessment because they are a cost- and time-efficient method of obtaining data on a broad range of behaviors and related events. Hundreds of questionnaires are available that are designed to measure DSM diagnoses, more narrowly specified behavioral problems, social and interpersonal relations, traumatic events, and other social and environmental events. We refer the reader to Hunsley and Mash (2008), who provide ratings on the reliability, validity, and clinical utility of several hundred of the most frequently used questionnaires in clinical assessment.

In this section, we describe the characteristics of behavioral self-report questionnaires that are well-suited for the goals of behavioral assessment and the functional analysis. Throughout this section, we use the term *questionnaires* to collectively refer to self-report inventories, checklists, and rating scales (see Box 8.2). For a more detailed discussion of self-report questionnaires, we refer the reader to Fernández-Ballesteros (2004). Many book chapters on behavioral assessment also include discussions of behavioral questionnaires such as chapters by Haynes and Kaholokula (2008) and Kaholokula, Bello, Nacapoy, and Haynes (2009).

---

**Box 8.2 Definitions for the Different Types of Self-Report Behavioral Questionnaires**

---

The terms *questionnaire, inventory, ratings scale, and checklist* are often used interchangeably in the psychological assessment literature. However, they differ in their content, purpose, and response formats. To distinguish them in this chapter, we provide the following definitions:

*Questionnaires and Inventories:* Synonyms to refer to rating scales and checklists. They are assessment instruments that contain a list of questions or items provided to respondents for the purpose of gathering information about actions, thoughts, beliefs, events, functional relations, physical and psychological states, and intervention goals.

*Rating Scales:* A type of questionnaire that allows the respondent to rate the dimensions of items using an ordinal or ratio scale (e.g., level of anxiety, degree of relaxation, or importance of an intervention goal). For example, a client could be asked to rate the item, "Engages in behavior to get attention, using an ordinal response option ranging from '0 = does not apply' to '4 = often'" (Matson & Vollmer, 1995). The scores of each question or item can be tallied up to provide an aggregate score of a construct.

*Checklists:* A type of questionnaire in which the respondent indicates the occurrence or nonoccurrence of items in a list (e.g., the presence or absence of a life stressor, panic episode, or situations that lead to disruptive behaviors). For example, a child could be asked to place a check in the box next to the item "Completed homework on time." The checks can be tallied to provide an aggregated index of a construct (e.g., aggressive behaviors), or each item could be considered a relevant sample (e.g., hit another child today)

## Characteristics of Self-Report Questionnaires Used in Behavioral Assessment

Although hundreds of self-report questionnaires have been developed, many are not useful for behavioral assessment and functional analysis. There are two principal reasons for this. First, many questionnaires aggregate across items that assess specific behaviors in order to yield a measure of global constructs such as "depression" or "openness to experience." Second, and more important, many questionnaires provide data that are insensitive to the conditional nature of the behavior problems, are poorly constructed, lack psychometric evidence, and are designed to provide aggregated and molar-level data of multifaceted behavior disorders.

For the goals of behavioral assessment and functional analysis, we emphasize the use of questionnaires that provide measures of specific lower-level and more homogenous constructs and the functional relations of a behavior. Additionally, questionnaires that are more closely allied with behavioral assessment will provide data that are sensitive to change in behavior and causal relations over time and across contexts.

**An Emphasis on the Measurement of Lower-Level and More Homogenous Constructs.** Composite measures of behavior are frequently used in psychological assessment. However, their use is typically incompatible with a behavioral assessment and functional analysis. The main difficulty with composite measures is that they aggregate across different modes and dimensions of a behavior. If all of the modes and dimensions of behaviors subsumed within a composite measure were highly interrelated and equivalently affected by a set of causal variables, then the use of such a measure would not be problematic from a behavioral assessment perspective. However, as noted in Chapter 7, this is typically *not the case*. Instead, from a behavioral assessment perspective it is assumed that the modes and dimensions of a behavior problem are often differentially associated with each other and important causal variables.

In Table 8.1, we provide examples of validated self-report questionnaires that provide more homogeneous measures of different facets, response modes, and dimensions of a behavior problem. For example, the *Children's Headache Assessment Scale* (CHAS; Budd et al., 1994) provides a single frequency measure for each of five distinct events surrounding a child's headache experience: (1) its disruptive impact on functioning, (2) social consequences, (3) stress-related antecedents, (4) physical antecedents and quiet coping, and (5) the use of prescription medication. We refer the reader to McGrath (2005) and Smith, McCarthy, and Zapolski (2009) for more discussion on the importance of targeting homogenous constructs in psychological assessment.

**Table 8.1  Examples of Behavioral Questionnaires That Capture the Dimensions, Response Modes, and Functional Relations of a Behavior Problem**

| Questionnaire | Description | Modes and Dimension of Behavior Captured |
|---|---|---|
| • The Motivation Assessment Scale (Durand & Crimmins, 1992) | • Contains 16 items rated by an informant (e.g., parents, teachers, clinic staff) on a seven-point ordinal scale.<br>• The rater specifies the time and setting of observation.<br>• Four subscale scores can be obtained.<br>• Designed for persons with self-injurious behaviors but applied to those with disruptive, aggressive, and stereotypic behaviors. | • Specific behaviors can be rated, such as "hits other people" or "swears at other students."<br>• Four consequential facets: (1) sensory, (2) tangible, (3) attention, or (4) escape motivators.<br>• Assesses the frequency ("0 = never" to "6 = always") of occurrence within a specified setting and time period. |
| • The Questions about Behavioral Function (Matson & Vollmer, 1995) | • Contains 25 items rated by an informant (e.g., parents, teachers, clinic staff) on four-point response scale with N/A option if behavior does not apply.<br>• The rater specifies the time and setting of observation.<br>• Five subscale scores can be obtained.<br>• Designed for persons with mental retardation but applied to those with self-injurious, disruptive, aggressive, and stereotypic behaviors. | • Specific behaviors can be rated, such as "Yells during class discussion" or "bangs own head on table."<br>• Five consequential facets: (1) attention, (2) escape, (3) nonsocial, (4) physical, and (5) tangible reinforcements.<br>• Assesses the frequency (0 = never to 3 = often) of occurrence within a specified setting and time period. |
| • Alcohol Expectancy Questionnaire— Adolescent Version | • Contains 90 items completed by client using a true-false response format.<br>• Seven subscale scores can be obtained. | • Specific expectancies can be endorsed, such as "Drinking alcohol allows people to be in the mood they want |

*Continued*

**Table 8.1** *Continued*

| Questionnaire | Description | Modes and Dimension of Behavior Captured |
|---|---|---|
| (Chrisdansen, Goldman, & Inn, 1982) | • Designed for use with adolescents 12 to 19 years of age.<br>• Adult version available. | to be" and "Drinking alcohol loosens people up."<br>• Seven types of expectancies: (1) global positive changes, (2) enhancement of social behavior, (3) improve cognitive and motor abilities, (4) sexual enhancement, (5) cognitive and motor impairment, (6) increased arousal, and (7) relaxation reduction. |
| • Inventory of Drinking Situations (Annis, Graham, and Davis, 1987) | • Contains 100 items rated by a client using a 4-point ordinal scale.<br>• Eight subscale scores can be obtained.<br>• Designed to assess situations that are most likely to lead to "heavy drinking" for a person. | • Captures heavy drinking within eight high-risk antecedent categories: (1) unpleasant emotions, (2) pleasant emotions, (3) physical discomfort, (4) testing of personal control, (5) urges and temptations, (6) conflict with others, (7) social pressures to drinking, and (8) pleasant times with others.<br>• Assesses the frequency ("1 = never" to "4 = almost always") over the past year. |
| • Inventory of Gambling Situations | • 45 items rated by the client on a 4-point ordinal scale. | • Captures five types of situations that lead to problem gambling: |

**Table 8.1** *Continued*

| Questionnaire | Description | Modes and Dimension of Behavior Captured |
|---|---|---|
| (Weiss & Petry, 2008) | • Five subscale scores can be obtained.<br>• Designed for use with adult, pathological gamblers. | (1) negative affect, (2) luck and control, (3) positive affect, (4) social situations, and (5) gambling cues.<br>• Frequency ("1 = never" to "4 = almost always") during the past year. |
| • The Revised Conflict Tactics Scale (Straus, Hamby, Boney-McCoy, & Sugarman, 1996) | • 78 items rated by a client of self and partner.<br>• Contains 15 subscales measuring minor and severe physical, psychological, and sexual aggression; rates of injury and nonviolent negotiation behaviors.<br>• Designed to measure frequency and type of aggression in a couple. | • Specific behaviors relevant to partner conflict (e.g., "My partner did this to me") and its resolution (e.g., "I explained my side of a disagreement to my partner") are rated.<br>• Frequency ("0 = This never happened" to "6 = More than 20 times in the past year") or had occurred, but not in the past year. |
| • The Children's Headache Assessment Scale (Budd, Workman, Lemsky, & Quick, 1994) | • 44 items rated by parents of child's headache-related behavior on a 7-point ordinal scale.<br>• Five subscale scores can be obtained<br>• Designed to assess children 6 to 16 years of age. | • Captures five factors related to child's headaches: (1) disruptive impact, (2) social consequences, (3) stress antecedents, (4) physical antecedents and quiet coping, and (5) prescription medication use.<br>• Frequency ("0 = never" to "6 = always") over the past two months. |

**An Emphasis on Measuring Multiple Modes and Dimensions of a Behavior Problem.** As noted above, a behavior problem will typically involve multiple response modes that will differ in their dimensions, relative importance, and the degree to which they are related to different causal variables. Thus, in behavioral assessment there is an emphasis on the use of self-report questionnaires that measure the specific modes and dimensions of a behavior problem. For example, a clinically useful questionnaire of "depression" would provide measures of its different response modes (e.g., affective-cognitive and psychophysiological) along multiple dimensions (e.g., severity, duration).

**An Emphasis on Measuring Functional Relations.** The most important characteristic of questionnaires that are compatible with behavioral assessment is their capacity for measuring functional relations. For example, the *Questions about Behavioral Function* (Paclawskyj, Matson, Rush, Smalls, & Vollmer, 2000) and the *Motivation Assessment Scale* (Durand & Crimmins, 1992) provide estimates of the extent to which a behavior problem (mostly used for children's disruptive, aggressive, or self-injurious behaviors) is likely to occur under several consequence conditions. Similarly, the *Inventory of Gambling Situations* (IGS; Weiss & Petry, 2008) provides a measure of the extent to which problematic gambling is likely to occur under specific antecedent conditions.

**An Emphasis on Measures That Are Sensitive to Change.** We already noted how questionnaires that provide homogenous measures of modes and dimensions of behavior are more sensitive to change in the targeted variables than global, nonspecific, heterogeneous measures. In addition, questionnaires that measure the *state* of a behavior (i.e., the current state, such as severity or frequency, of a behavior in a given context) versus those that measure behavior *traits* (i.e., noncontextual, aggregated measures of a presumably stable behavior) can provide measures that are more sensitive to change. Consequently, behavioral questionnaires are more likely to have measurement time frames that are shorter and context specific.

The response format of a questionnaire affects the sensitivity to change of its measures. At one end of the response format scale are dichotomous formats (e.g., yes, no). At the other end of the scale would be ordinal or ratio-level scales, such as providing a value between 0 and 100 on a measure of subjective units of distress where 0 represents absolutely no anxiety and 100 represents extreme panic. Notice that many of the questionnaires we listed in Table 8.1 use a response format that falls between these two extremes because the dichotomous formats tend to be insensitive to the measurement of change. Alternatively, ratio level scales can sometimes introduce additional error variance and/or create an illusion of change. For example, a client may not be able to distinguish among anxiety levels that differ by one or two points (e.g., Is there a discernable difference between a 73 or 74?). Thus, the response format should match the goals of the assessment and simultaneously measure meaningful distinctions in behavior.

**An Emphasis on Relevant Psychometric Evidence.** Throughout this book we have emphasized the use of assessment methods and instruments with psychometric evidence appropriate for a client and the goals and context of the assessment occasion. Thus, the clinician should consider the degree to which the psychometric evidence is relevant to the age of the client, severity of his or her behavior problems, other dimensions of individual difference, and the goals of assessment (e.g., see differential psychometric evidence for measures across diagnostic, screening, intervention outcome, and case formulation applications in Hunsley and Mash, 2008). For example, Schmidt, McKinnon, Chattha, and Brownlee (2006) found that the *Psychopathy Checklist: Youth Version* (Forth, Kosson, & Hare, 2003) had weaker concurrent and predictive validity for girls than for boys, and that predictive validity for boys varied as a function of ethnic background. We note additional aspects of psychometrics in behavioral assessment in Box 7.4.

## The Limitations of Behavioral Questionnaires

Behavioral questionnaires share liabilities with all self-report instruments. To reiterate, potential sources of measurement error include biases in report by the client's or other informants, cognitive and developmental limitations, the emotional state of the respondent, imprecise construction of the items, a rater's insufficient exposure to the target behavior, errors associated with retrospective recall, fatigue associated with long questionnaires, falsification by respondents, social desirability, and reading level of the items and respondent. To reduce the impact of these sources of error, behavioral questionnaires should be augmented with other, more direct, assessment methods whenever possible.

## Summary of Behavioral Assessment Questionnaires

We described the clinical utility, assets, and liabilities of behavioral questionnaires. We discussed several characteristics to be considered when selecting a questionnaire for behavioral assessment. These included the use of questionnaires that provide homogenous measures of the modes and dimensions of a client's behavior problem as well as related functional relations. Additionally, the questionnaire should be constructed so that it is able to measure the state and changes in a behavior. We also highlighted several limitations associated with self-report questionnaires and emphasized the need for supplementary data from direct assessment methods.

## SELF-MONITORING

In the case of Mrs. Anderson, the clinician learned that her mood varied across contexts. This information suggested that different causal variables were influencing her behavior. Subsequently, the clinician sought to identify the variables that could explain the onset, intensity, duration, and direction of changes in her mood. Because her mood changed relatively infrequently, direct observation was not a feasible assessment method. Additionally, she could not identify specific triggering or maintaining factors during the functional behavioral interviews. Thus, the clinician opted to use self-monitoring to help identify the functional relations associated with Mrs. Anderson's mood changes.

In this section, we describe the characteristics, methods, utility, assets, and liabilities of self-monitoring. We highlight electronic assessment tools that allow for more sophisticated data collection. For more discussions of self-monitoring assessment methods, we refer the reader to Cole, Marder, and McCann (2000) for broad overviews of self-monitoring; Sigmon and

LaMattina (2006) for application with adults; Cole and Bambara (2000) for application in school settings; Humphreys, Marx, and Lexington (2009) for application as an intervention strategy; and the Special Section on self-monitoring in *Psychological Assessment* (vol. 11, no. 4, 1999) for general overviews, psychometric considerations, and application across various clinical populations.

## Description of Self-Monitoring

In self-monitoring, the client systematically observes and records his or her own behavior and the occurrence of potential causal variables in real-world settings. Self-monitoring is a self-report assessment method that is especially well suited for measuring the associations between behavior problems and a range of potential causal variables. Data from self-monitoring can be especially useful in clinical case formulation and in evaluating intervention effects.

Self-monitoring has been used with children, adolescents, and adults across a range of behavioral problems. For example, a 15-year-old boy with type 1 diabetes could be asked to self-monitor his daily blood glucose levels and concurrent family interactions (Wysocki, Green, & Huxtable, 1991). A 29-year-old woman could be asked to self-monitor the frequency of her binge-eating and contemporaneous thoughts and emotions (Wilson & Vitousek, 1999).

## Designing a Self-Monitoring Instrument and Strategy

Behavior cannot be measured at all times and conditions. Consequently, the clinician must design a self-monitoring strategy that will allow the client to collect information that will be valid and aid in the design of an intervention. In the sections below, we review principles that guide the design of a self-monitoring system. Additionally, in Box 7.3, we review time-sampling strategies that are relevant to self-monitoring.

When designing a self-monitoring system, several issues need to be addressed. First, the clinician must determine what behaviors, modes of behavior, and dimensions of behavior will be monitored. Second, the clinician must address the settings where monitoring will occur. The third issue is time sampling: How often will the client be instructed to monitor the behavior and for how long? Fourth, the clinician must determine how the client will record behavior and associated variables. Finally, the clinician should consider factors that may facilitate or impede data collection (e.g., competing work requirement or degree of cooperation from family members). As is evident in these considerations, self-monitoring strategies are often individually tailored for a client.

**Selecting Behaviors to Be Self-Monitored.** The clinician must first decide what behaviors are to be self-monitored. In general, behaviors that are likely to be clinically useful will have two important characteristics. First, they should occur at a low to medium level of frequency (e.g., daily alcohol consumption or arguments with a partner). Extremely frequent behaviors or rare behaviors are less suitable for self-monitoring. Second, the occurrence of the behavior should be readily recognized by the client. Thus, discrete and salient behaviors are especially amenable to self-monitoring.

A study by Bauer and colleagues (2009) illustrates the importance of selecting appropriate target behaviors and aspects of target behaviors in self-monitoring. The authors aimed to identify which sleep-wake parameter (e.g., latency to sleep onset, sleep duration, or times awake) were associated with mood changes in patients with bipolar disorders. Over one hundred adult outpatients recorded their daily sleep onset, sleep duration, and time awake for several months. They also recorded their mood and medication use. Using time-series analysis, the authors found that sleep duration was the dimension of sleep most strongly associated with mood changes.

**Selecting Causal Variables to Be Self-Monitored.** Consistent with the emphasis in behavioral assessment on identifying functional relations, the clinician also must determine what hypothesized causal variables should be monitored. Similar to behavior characteristics, the variables most amenable to self-monitoring are those that occur at a low to medium frequency and can be readily identified by the client. Examples could include the verbal or physical responses of others, the social setting, medication use, or the client's emotional state.

## Box 8.3 Critical Event and Critical Period Sampling

*Critical Event and Critical Period Sampling* comprise a class of assessment strategies in which the most important behaviors, contexts, settings, or hypothesized causal relations are selected for measurement. Some examples include a client's recording his or her panic episodes only during their occurrence (rather than whether or not they occurred during specified time periods), a couple rating their distress level only during marital arguments, a parent's rating of a child's oppositional behavior only at bedtime, and a psychiatric staff member's monitoring his or her responses to a patient's social interactions only during recreation periods.

Critical event and critical period sampling are especially compatible with assessment methods such as self-monitoring, naturalistic observation, and the use of hand-held computers. The cost-benefits of this strategy are increased because observers limit their observation time to smaller periods in which the behaviors of interest are most likely to occur. Video and audio recording equipment can also be used to record events during critical events and periods for later evaluation.

**Selecting the Contexts and Times to Self-Monitor.** To capture behavior-environment functional relations, the clinician must select the most appropriate contexts (e.g., when interacting with teacher or parent; home versus school) and times (e.g., before bed; after breakfast, lunch, and dinner; hourly) for self-monitoring. The most clinically useful contexts and times are likely to be those in which the behavior is most problematic, most likely to occur, and/or the monitoring does not place an excessive load on the client. Foster et al. (1999) discuss setting and time-sampling strategies in greater detail.

In *time-sampling*, the client records his or her behavior and related events during selected time periods during the day (e.g., hourly, or when cued to do so; Korotitsch & Nelson-Gray, 1999). In *interval time-sampling*, the client records the occurrences of a target behavior if it occurs at any point during a monitoring interval. For example, a client can perform hourly recordings of whether or not he or she had a positive social interaction. In *momentary time-sampling,* the client records the occurrence of the target behavior at a prespecified moment in time. For example, a client could record whether or not he or she is smoking when cued by a hand-held computer. Data on frequency, duration, onset latency, and severity can be obtained with momentary time-sampling.

**Selecting the Recording Methods for Self-Monitoring.** After determining the target behaviors, causal variables, setting, and time-sampling strategies, the next step is to determine the best recording method. Recording methods should be convenient and reasonably unobtrusive. The most commonly used method of self-monitoring is the *paper-and-pencil* diary. In this method, the client records information using a diary or rating sheet. Many structured daily self-monitoring diaries are available for specific behavior problems, such as gambling (Ladouceur & Lachance, 2006), pain sensations (Satterfield, 2008), and eating behaviors (e.g., *Weekly Eating Behavior Diary*; Tasca et al., 2009). A second method of recording is the *mobile mechanical and electronic devices.* Examples of this include: (a) actometers, which are devices that track physical activity, (b) pedometers to measure walking and running, and (c) physiological measurement instruments (e.g., blood pressure cuff) to measure biological responses. Tryon (2006) discusses the assets, liabilities, and psychometric characteristics of several mechanical and electrical methods of monitoring physical activity.

## Computerized Technology in Self-Monitoring

Hand-held computers and electronic diaries, such as smart phones, pocket computers, and personal digital assistants, promote more sophisticated data collection in the client's natural environment. For example, many mobile computers can serve as a signaling device to cue a client to record data and can provide instructions on what target behavior to record. Rating scales and other questionnaires can be computerized so that a client can also provide dimension ratings of a target behavior, complete a checklist about possible triggers, and record information about the thoughts, emotions, response consequences, and settings associated with the occurrence of the target behavior.

The use of hand-held computers to collect data in real-time reduces some of the problems associated with the other self-monitoring recording methods, such as remembering to record data and errors associated with retrospective recall. Although more costly than paper-and-pencil methods, the use of mobile computers facilitates the collection of highly specific, real-time data from real-world events, with greater *ecological validity* (i.e., the generalizability of measures, and judgments from measures, to the populations, contexts, purposes, or situations that are the primary interest of the assessment). They can make self-monitoring easier for the client and make it easier for the clinician to summarize data and analyze functional relations. They are ideal for time-sampling because they can signal a client to record multiple behaviors, along with associated settings, contexts, and antecedent and consequent events at predetermined or random intervals. For a more detailed discussion on the use of mobile computers, such as electronic diaries, in self-monitoring, we refer the reader to Trull and Ebner-Priemer (2009) and Piasecki, Hufford, Solhan, and Trull (2007).

## Ecological Momentary Assessment

As we noted above, one variation of self-monitoring is the *ecological momentary assessment* (Shiffman, Stone, & Hufford, 2008). The key features common to ecological momentary assessment strategies are: (a) data are collected in real-world settings, as a client goes about his or her daily life, (b) measurement focuses on the client's current state, (c) a specific moment in time or event is specified for data collection, and (d) a client completes multiple measurements of the target behavior and events over time to capture variation across time and contexts.

For example, Shiffman and Paty (2006) used ecological momentary assessment with electronic diaries to examine differences in environmental events and emotions associated with the smoking of light smokers with no apparent nicotine dependence and "heavy smokers" (i.e., smokers with strong nicotine dependence). Each participant used a palmtop computer for two weeks and recorded cigarette smoking occurrences. Each participant also completed questionnaires on situations and affective states occurring during the assessment moment. The electronic diaries randomly signaled the participants to complete an assessment four to five times per day. Participants also recorded the setting (e.g., work, home, bar or restaurant), type of activity (e.g., working, socializing, eating and drinking), the presence of other smokers (e.g., in a social situation where others smoked also), degree of smoking urge, and affective state. The authors found significant differences between light and heavy smokers in situational and affective factors associated with smoking. During smoking periods, light smokers, relative to heavy smokers, were more likely to smoke when they were relaxing and drinking alcohol and when experiencing negative affect.

Shiffman and Paty's study illustrates several aspects of self-monitoring. The self-monitoring involved both critical event and random time-sampling strategies. Because palmtop computers were used, the data were recorded and stored in real-time and measurement occurred in their real-world settings. The resulting data were useful in specifying some of the functional relations associated with smoking. Of particular relevance for the functional analysis, the results illustrated individual differences in those functional relations.

---

**Box 8.4 Emerging Assessment Technologies for Family and Marital Interactions—Electronic Diaries**

---

Snyder et al. (2008) have commented that interviews, questionnaires, and observation data collected in clinics or laboratories are often the methods by which we come to understand how a distressed family or couple interacts in their daily lives. Although these assessment methods can provide useful data about the negative and positive behavioral exchanges, they do not always provide information about the ways that these exchanges unfold in daily life.

Self-monitoring with electronic diaries is a method of obtaining data about couples and families that addresses some of the limitations of interviews, questionnaires, and direct observations. Electronic diaries (e.g., through mobile computers, smart phones, and personal digital assistants) can be used to collect real-time data on the behavior, emotions, thoughts, and the context of a couple's or family's behavior and interactions as they occur in their natural setting.

For example, Janicki, Kamarck, Shiffman, and Gwaltney (2006) used electronic diaries to examine the conflict, positive interactions, and dyadic satisfaction in the daily lives of 245 older couples. The authors found that couples' positive and negative interactions were significantly correlated with ambulatory cardiovascular measures.

Although electronic diaries have multiple sources of potential error (see reviews by Piasecki et al., 2007, and Sigmon & LaMattina, 2006), they have several assets: (a) they reduce the error associated with retrospective reports, (b) they reduce the likelihood of missing data through nonadherence with the assessment protocol, (c) they enable the measurement of the rate of, and functional relations among, multiple variables, (d) they allow for sampling rates and times to be individually programmed, and (e) they are less costly than using external observers.

## The Clinical Utility and Assets of Self-Monitoring

Self-monitoring can be tailored to the unique behavior problems and assessment goals of the client. It can also be used to assess a wide range of cognitive, motor, and affective behaviors as they occur in their natural setting and the causal variables that influence them. Self-monitoring has several additional assets as an assessment method. First, it is a more direct measure of behaviors than functional behavioral interviews and questionnaires because measures of behavior and events are acquired as they occur in real-world settings. Second, it can be more time- and cost-efficient to use than naturalistic observation and analogue observation. Finally, it has strong ecological validity.

**Increasing Validity by Increasing Adherence to Self-Monitoring.** A client's adherence to a self-monitoring protocol can influence the validity of the obtained data. There are several aspects of the self-monitoring strategy that can affect the degree to which a client adheres to the self-monitoring tasks.

One important factor is the type and specificity of behavior problems. To increase adherence, target behaviors and events should be well-defined, more specific, and less inferential, with clear examples provided to the client (Foster et al., 1999). A second factor that affects adherence is the amount of time and effort required for a client to self-monitor. As the number of behaviors to be monitored increases, the validity of the data can be diminished (Epstein, Miller, & Webster, 1976). A third factor is cuing. That is, adherence can be increased with the use of signaling devices. Some examples of signaling devices are electronic diaries, programmable wristwatches, and smart phones with programmable alarm features. A fourth factor is obtrusiveness. Obtrusive methods and instruments can draw unwanted attention and lead a client to stop self-monitoring. A final factor is training. Before using a self-monitoring method the clinician should ensure that the client is familiar with the definitions and demonstrate proficient use of the self-monitoring method.

## The Limitations of Self-Monitoring: Reactive Effects

Many studies have documented that self-monitoring can alter the form and frequency of a behavior. For example, Moos (2008) reported that self-monitoring was associated with a decrease in the rate of cigarette smoking or alcohol consumption. Although reactive effects associated with self-monitoring are a threat to the validity of data acquired, behavior tends to decrease or increase in a therapeutically desired direction. Because of such positive reactive effects, self-monitoring is often used as an intervention strategy itself (e.g., Humphreys et al., 2009). Thus, many of the strategies to increase adherence to self-monitoring can also increase the likelihood of positive outcomes for a client.

## Summary of Self-Monitoring

We described the multiple methods and sampling strategies used in self-monitoring. We also reviewed the clinical utility, assets, and liabilities of self-monitoring, with an emphasis on methods to increase the accuracy of the data obtained. Self-monitoring is an important and powerful self-report assessment method that can capture the functional relations of a client's behavior problem as they occur in his or her natural settings. We highlighted the use of mobile computers to increase the ease and efficiency for a client to collect data and discussed ecological momentary assessment to increase the accuracy of self-monitored data. We also provided other examples of how to increase the accuracy of self-monitoring data, such as targeting specific, well-defined behaviors, having detailed self-monitoring instructions, limiting self-monitoring to a single or a few behaviors at a time, and providing training. Finally, we highlighted the reactive effects often associated with it.

## SUMMARY

Self-report assessment methods can be adapted to be consistent with the principles of behavioral assessment. Interviewing, questionnaires, and self-monitoring methods can provide data that are sensitive to the multivariate, dynamic, multidimensional, conditional, and idiographic nature of behavior problems, intervention goals, and their causal relations.

Functional behavioral interviews, questionnaires, and self-monitoring can provide data that are useful for specifying a client's behavior problems and their causal relations. These assessment methods are particularly useful for gathering information on difficult-to-observe behaviors, such as thoughts and emotions. Compared to direct measures of behavior, they are often more cost- and time-efficient to administer and can be applied across a wide-range of clients, behavior problems, assessment goals, and settings.

The self-report assessment methods we reviewed all have unique assets and liabilities. The functional behavioral interview allows the clinician to investigate many possible behavior problems and functional relationships while simultaneously advancing a positive client-clinician relationship. Behavioral questionnaires can be used to measure the specific modes, dimensions, and functions of a behavior through the use of rating scales and checklists. Self-monitoring can be used for collecting data on a client's behavior problem as it occurs in real-world settings.

# Direct Methods in Behavioral Assessment

## OVERVIEW OF DIRECT BEHAVIORAL ASSESSMENT METHODS AND STRATEGIES

In Chapter 8, we describe the self-report assessment methods of functional behavioral interviewing, behavioral questionnaires, and self-monitoring. We reviewed their clinical utility, assets, and sources of error. We noted that self-report assessment methods are popular because they are easy to administer in most settings, they have a broad and diverse clinical applicability and utility, and they are relatively cost- and time-efficient. They are also particularly useful for collecting data on private, unobservable aspects of behavior, such as a client's cognitive processes, affective responses, and subjective appraisals. However, the validity of self-reported data can be affected by a client's biases, demand characteristics of the assessment occasion, and cognitive limitations influencing the recall or reporting of accurate information. Their validity can also be affected by the client's emotional, physical, and psychological states and motivations.

Assessment methods that allow for the direct observation of a client's behavior in his or her natural environment, or in a contrived setting that approximates the natural environment, can address many of the sources of error inherent in self-report assessment methods. As we discussed in Chapter 7, observational data obtained in natural environments or in analog settings often has *incremental clinical utility* over self-reported data because it permits more precise measurement of clinically significant behaviors, behavior-environment interactions, and changes across time.

Although methods of direct behavioral observation are more time-intensive and costly to conduct compared to self-report assessment methods, they can often provide important information about the functional relations associated with a client's behavior problems that is unavailable from self-report methods. Also, advancements in assessment technology have increased the cost-benefits of direct measurement of overt behaviors and physiological processes associated with a client's behavior problems (e.g., Larkin, 2006; Chatkoff, Maier, & Klein, 2010; Ditzen et al., 2007). In this chapter, we describe behavioral observation methods of assessment in natural and analog settings. We also discuss psychophysiological assessment methods and, in particular, the use of ambulatory biosensors. To set the foundation for our discussion of naturalistic and analog behavioral observation methods, we begin with an overview of the principles and strategies of behavioral observation.

## OVERVIEW OF THE PRINCIPLES AND STRATEGIES OF BEHAVIORAL OBSERVATION

Behavioral observation is the systematic recording of observable behavior. It involves carefully detailed procedures designed to collect reliable and valid data on a client's behavior problem, causal variables, and the associations among them (Hartmann, Barrios, & Wood, 2004; Haynes & O'Brien, 2000). For example, the clinician may record the verbal interactions between a parent and child to identify events that precipitate the parent's critical remarks to the child. Or, the clinician may request the teacher's aide in a classroom to record the number of times that a physically aggressive child hits other students, in order to evaluate the effects of a behavioral management program.

Based on the principle that behavior is strongly influenced by the context in which it operates, behavioral observation allows the clinician to evaluate the situation specificity of behavior. That is, it allows for the identification of context-relevant functional relations that are important to clinical judgment (Hartmann et al., 2004), such as specific events, dimensions and functions of behavior, behavior-environment interactions, and behavior-behavior sequences.

The methods of behavioral observation we discuss in this chapter, whether conducted in naturalistic or analog settings, are based on several tenets of the behavioral assessment paradigm, as follows:

- The systematic recording of behavior as it occurs in the natural environment can yield valid information that is incrementally useful, compared to self-report data, for the goals of behavioral assessment.
- The operationalization and quantification of behavior, causal variables, and functional relations can guide clinical judgments about case formulations, provide data for normative comparisons, and assist the clinician in tracking behavior change across time or conditions.
- Naturally occurring functional relations can often be evaluated by naturalistic observation, but, in some cases, it can be cost-inefficient, and analog observation methods may be more cost-efficient.
- Behavioral observation can be used across a diverse range of populations, behaviors, and settings.
- The validity of data from an observation instrument is affected by the types behaviors selected; the precision of the operational definitions of behavior; the intrusiveness of the observation process, and the degree of training, experience, and supervision of the observer.
- Two important decisions in the observation process involve deciding when and where observations will be conducted to provide the most ecologically valid and clinically useful data.
- Important psychometric dimensions of behavioral observation data are interobserver agreement, content validity of the observation codes, and ecological validity.

A primary goal of behavioral observation is the identification of functional relations related to a client's behavior problems.[1] In pursuit of this goal, the clinician must initially design an observation coding system and time-sampling strategy. The first step in this aspect of behavioral observation is to generate operational definitions of behavior problems and hypothesized causal variables. The clinician must address two questions: (a) What are the behavior problems to be observed? and (b) What are the causal variables and relations to be observed? We review the common functions of behavioral observation that allow the clinician to address these questions, but refer the reader to Hartmann et al. (2004) and to Haynes and O'Brien (2000) for elaboration.

## Defining and Quantifying the Behaviors for Observation

The generation of operational definitions requires that the clinician carefully consider the most valid way to characterize the behavior problem. As Chapter 7 notes, there are many ways to operationalize behavior problems. It can be expeditious, however, to initially consider the relative importance of three response systems: verbal-cognitive behaviors, physiological-affective behaviors, and overt-motor behaviors. Since in behavioral observation we are focused on publicly accessible behaviors, it is important that the behavior problems subsumed within the verbal-cognitive and physiological-affective response systems are operationalized in such a way that they can be directly and reliably observed. For example, a client's physiological-affective response system of "panic" might be operationalized as "rapid speech rate, trembling, pacing, and repeated requests for reassurance." A client's verbal-cognitive response system, such as "guilt," might be operationalized as his or her "verbal statements about having done something wrong or feeling guilty." (Note in these examples that "panic" and "guilt" and "paranoia," described below, could be considered

---

[1] We focus here on "behavior problems," but as we noted earlier, behavioral observation often focuses on the measurement of behaviors that are (a) positive alternatives to behavior problems (e.g., positive rather than critical comments from a spouse), (b) treatment goals (e.g., prosocial play rather than aggressive behaviors by a child), or (c) potential causal events for a client's behavior problems (e.g., critical comments from the client's parents).

"latent variables" that are estimated on the basis of measures from the observable indicator variables.)

To illustrate the development of an operational definition of behavior, we provide an example of a psychiatric inpatient whom staff members reported to be "paranoid." The verbal-cognitive behaviors might be defined as "complaints to staff about his mistrust toward the hospital administration or verbal reports of being suspicious of other patients." The physiological-affective behaviors might be defined as "pacing and angry facial expressions." The overt-motor behaviors might be "moving away from others when they come within touching distance or requests to have others removed from the setting." The dimensions of these behaviors that best match the assessment question are then determined. In this case, the frequency or duration of complaints made by the patient to staff about his mistrust of others could be emphasized in the operational definition.

Taken alone, the operationalization and measurement through observation of a client's behavior problems yields several important outcomes. First, observational data can contribute to the selection of a diagnosis. Second, observational data allows for comparisons of the client's behavior to normative data or to data from other persons in the same setting. Third, it allows the clinician to establish the social significance or the personal importance of the client's behavior problem. Fourth, it allows the clinician to identify the potential functional response classes or behaviors that covary in a given context. Fifth, observation data provide measures that are sensitive to change in behavior across time. Finally, establishing an observation system requires that the clinician and client cooperate in selecting important aspects of the behavior problem.

## Defining and Quantifying the Causal Variables and Relations for Observation

Consistent with our emphasis on identifying functional relations, after specifying behavior problems, the clinician must operationally define and quantify the causal variables hypothesized to be relevant for the behavior problems. There are many ways to describe causal variables and relations, but two general categories can be considered: social/interpersonal events (i.e., interactions with other people or groups of people) and nonsocial/

environmental events (i.e., environmental events and situations other than social interactions). What constitutes nonsocial/environmental events may be less obvious and appear ubiquitous to a clinician. Examples include temperature, lighting, noise level, the presence of food or material objects, the design of the room, or acquisition of an object. Also, as with behavior problems, the dimensions of these categories of causal variables and relations can also be measured.

In selecting potential causal variables to observe, it is useful to remember that sometimes the absence or nonoccurrence of a variable can be causal. For example, the failure of a parent to respond to a child's prosocial behavior can reduce its likelihood of occurrence; a low rate of positive attention from a teacher can increase the likelihood of attention-seeking behavior by a student.

Returning to our previous example, the clinician and staff members would identify and operationally define the causal factors hypothesized to influence the psychiatric patient's "paranoid" behaviors. The social/interpersonal events that could be identified and defined might include the staff members' response to his paranoid behavior (e.g., "redirection" or attempts by staff members to "reason" with the patient), other patients' responses, stressful meetings with family members, or the proximity of certain patients and/or staff members. The nonsocial-environmental events involved could include time-of-day, location on the psychiatric unit, meal composition, sleep cycle or quality, and medication compliance. Recall that different causal variables could influence different response systems of a behavior and can also be measured across multiple dimensions.

## Identifying Functional Relations in Behavioral Observation

The measurement of behavior problems and hypothesized causal variables allows the clinician to identify important functional relations. As we note in Chapters 5 and 6, the clinician will be most interested in identifying the most important functional relations affecting the client's behavior problem and those that can most readily be modified to produce behavior change. Thus, the clinician should decide *a priori* the variables and interactions that are most likely to be important and modifiable.

Two sources of influence guide the clinician in this endeavor: the published research literature and data on the client from other assessment methods. The published research literature in psychopathology can guide the clinician in targeting hypothesized functional relations for a client's behavior problem. For example, Strand's (2000) review of the conduct disorder literature elucidated several factors that maintain conduct problems in children. These data can guide the clinician's selection of potential causal factors for a child exhibiting conduct problems. Preliminary assessment data obtained from functional behavioral interviews and behavioral questionnaires administered to the client and informants can also guide the selection of behavior problems and functional relations. Additionally, the clinician can directly observe behavior problem occurrence within the context of an interview session using informal observation.

In behavioral observation, there is an inherent conflict between the need to be efficient and the need to be comprehensive. An important challenge is to avoid being excessively restrictive in the selection of causal relations. For example, although parents' responsiveness and disciplinary style can affect a child's aggressive behaviors and could be an important target, responses by siblings and peers might also have important causal effects.

## Strategies of Behavioral Observation

After the behavior problems and causal variables have been selected and operationalized, the next step is to design the behavioral observation strategy. In doing so, the clinician must address several questions. First, what time periods and for what durations will observations occur? Second, what data collection strategies will be used? Third, who will be the observers? Finally, in what settings will the observations occur? These are essentially questions about sampling (Minke & Haynes, 2011). The most clinically useful sampling strategy is one that is congruent with the goals of assessment, provides generalizable data, and supports valid inferences. For example, based on observation data, in what settings or times will the clinician be able to draw the most ecologically valid inferences about the client's behavior problem and important functional relations?

**Selecting the Times and Time Frame for Behavioral Observation.** As we have noted throughout the book, behavior and functional relations are dynamic and momentary measurement of behavior is unlikely to provide a valid and sensitive index of its dynamic phase or of important behavior-context relations that are the central elements of the functional analysis and treatment decisions. Consequently, behavioral assessment, particularly behavioral observation in the natural environment, involves a time-series assessment strategy—measuring behavior many times. Time samples can be divided into units that range from milliseconds (e.g., in psychophysiological research evaluating reaction time measures) to days, months, or years. As we described in Chapter 7, time-sampling strategies can include random time-sampling, systematic time-sampling, event-related time-sampling, and convenience time-sampling.

The selection of a time-sampling strategy partly depends on the characteristics of the behavior to be observed. Two important considerations are the rate of the behavior and the extent to which a behavior has discrete beginning and end points. These two aspects of behavior interact to affect the choice of a time-sampling strategy, which we illustrate in Figure 9.1. When a behavior has discrete beginning and end points and occurs at a high frequency, *systematic time-sampling strategies* such as partial interval sampling (e.g., the observer records whether the behavior occurred *at any point* during a specific time frame, such as 10 seconds, a minute, or an hour) are often optimal. When the behavior has discrete beginning and end points and occurs at a low frequency, *event-related time-sampling* (e.g., the observer records the occurrence of the behavior and associated events whenever it occurs) is often optimal. In the case of high-frequency behaviors with ambiguous beginning and end points, *random time-sampling* (e.g., the observer would conduct a brief observation on a random schedule and record whether or not the behavior was observed) is often preferred. Finally, with low-frequency behaviors that have ambiguous beginning and end points, systematic time-sampling such as interval sampling with long windows of observation (e.g., record whether or not the behavior occurred at all during a day) are often preferred (see Suen & Ary, 1989, for a detailed presentation of time-sampling strategies).

| | FREQUENCY OF BEHAVIOR | |
|---|---|---|
| EXTENT TO WHICH THERE ARE DISCRETE ONSET AND ENDPOINTS OF BEHAVIOR | HIGH | LOW |
| HIGH/CLEAR | Examples: Checking behavior for a client with obsessive compulsive disorder, observable self-talking in a schizophrenic patient. | Examples: Stealing items from a store, physical aggression, panic episodes. |
| LOW/AMBIGUOUS | Examples: Symptoms of negative mood states in psychiatric patient; production declines in an assembly worker. | Examples: Premenstrual pain and discomfort symptoms, negative mood states associated with seasonal affective disorder. |

**Figure 9.1** Interaction between frequency and the extent to which a given behavior has discrete beginning and end points.

## Selecting the Subject for Behavioral Observation

Because we are often interested in how the behavior of others affects the client's behavior, the clinician must also decide who, in addition to the client, will be observed. For example, the clinician must determine which students and teachers in a classroom, which patients on a psychiatric unit, which members of a family, or which hospital staff members will be observed. Several subject sampling strategies can be used, depending on the goals of the assessment. *Random sampling* of subjects in which any person in a setting has an equal chance of being selected for behavioral observation is appropriate when the client is a group, such as prior to and during an intervention involving a classroom or a psychiatric unit. *Selective sampling* of subjects is where persons are selected on the basis of their behavior characteristics, such as selecting children in a classroom who are the most aggressive, hyperactive, or socially isolated. Especially for the development of a functional analysis and an analysis of treatment mechanisms, it is important to observe subjects whose behavior is hypothesized to function as a causal variable for a client's behavior problem (e.g., teachers, parents, and intimate partners), and those for whom the ultimate clinical judgments are most important.

## Selecting the Observer for the Behavioral Observation

There are two types of external observers: nonparticipant and participant observers. *Nonparticipant observers* can include the clinician, graduate or undergraduate students, or professionals trained in behavioral observation. *Participant observers*[2] are persons who are normally part of the client's natural environment. They may include a client's family member in a home setting, a teacher or teacher's aide in a classroom setting, a peer or spouse in various natural and clinical settings, or a staff member in a psychiatric hospital. The participant observer is trained in the operational definitions, sampling strategies, data collection strategies, and the rationale and goals of the behavioral observation. The training strategies and developmental and skill level we describe in Chapter 8 for self-monitoring apply to the training of participant observers (see discussion by Hay, Nelson, & Hay, 1980, of the assets and limitations of participant observers).

The decision to use nonparticipant versus participant observers depends on several factors: (a) the complexity of the behavioral observation, (b) the feasibility of collecting data in a given setting by external observers, (c) available resources (time, funding, personnel) for observers, and (d) the expected relative validity and utility of data from each type of observer. For example, nonparticipant observers can collect data across a wide range of behaviors and settings, but they can be more costly for a clinician to recruit, train, and employ. Participant observers are lower cost and less obtrusive because they are a normal part of the client's natural setting, but their observation data may be more prone to error because of their conflicting responsibilities in the setting, less adherence to the time-sampling strategy, and observer bias.

## Selecting the Setting for Behavioral Observation

The selection of the setting for behavioral observation is important, given that a major principle of behavioral assessment is that behavior

---

[2] "Participant observation" also refers to a research method used in cultural anthropology, but the method differs from what is described here. It usually refers to observation by a researcher who collects qualitative data through immersion and intensive involvement in a group (DeWalt et al., 1998).

and functional relations often vary across contexts. The clinician should select settings in which the client's behavior problem and important functional relations are most likely to occur. In a strategy similar to *critical event sampling*, observations can be conducted in "high risk" settings. This sampling strategy can be cost-efficient in terms of identifying clinically useful functional relations, but the degree to which these inferences are generalizable cannot be established without data from a larger array of settings.

## Selecting the Observational Recording Methods and Devices

The clinician must select a method to collect behavioral observation data that is appropriate for the characteristics of the behavior problems and causal variables, the sampling strategies and settings selected, and the assessment context. Many of the data recording methods and instruments that we describe in Chapter 8 apply to behavioral observation. These include the use of paper-and-pencil and electronic methods (e.g., video recorders and hand-held computers). We refer the reader to Chapter 8 for a review and to Hartmann et al. (2004) for examples of technological aids (e.g., time-lapse photography) used in behavioral observation. Many examples of behavioral observation recording forms can be found on the Internet,[3] and Haynes and O'Brien (2000) provide several examples of event and various time-sampling recording forms. With advancements in handheld computer technology, many of these forms can be made electronic and stored on computers. Some examples of behavioral observation software include *The Observer* (Van Haitsman, Lawton, Kleban, Klapper, & Corn, 1997) and *PROCODER* (Tapp & Wehby, 2000). Richard and Lauterbach (2004) provide a list of many computerized software applications for behavioral observation.

---

[3] For examples of event and time-sampling behavioral observation recording forms see:
http://www.kipbs.org/new_kipbs/fsi/files/Obs%20Forms-Event%20Recording%20Form%20_3-9-06_.pdf
http://www.oswego.edu/~mcdougal/web_site_4_11_2005/interval_sampling.htm
http://www.specialconnections.ku.edu/~specconn/page/assessment/ddm/pdf/Momentary_Sample_examplerevised.pdf
http://www.venturacountyselpa.com/Portals/45/Users/IEP%20Forms/Data%20Collection/Specified%20Interval%20or%20Time%20Sampling.pdf

## Statistical Analyses of Behavioral Observation Data

A primary goal of behavioral assessment and behavioral observation is to track behavior change and to identify functional relations associated with a client's behavior problems. Thus, the data-analytic techniques applied to observation data should allow for the identification of (a) rates of behavior and change in behavior rate (or other dimension) over time, (b) covariation between behavior and other events, and (c) order and sequence relations—the degree to which changes in the hypothesized causal variables precede, and are associated, with change in the target behavior. Two approaches to evaluating behavioral observation data are intuitive judgment and statistical testing.

**Intuitive Data Analysis.** The most common type of intuitive data analysis involves "visual inspection" of data, usually plotted in a time-course graph, and subjective estimations of whether or not covariation exists between the behavior problem and its causal variables. It is the easiest means of evaluating behavioral observation data with minimum investment in time and effort by the clinician. It is especially useful for hypothesis generation and for evaluating complex patterns of data. However, intuitive data analytic strategies can lead to unreliable and invalid conclusions. For example, studies have found that intuitive evaluation of data can too often lead to higher rates of Type 1 error— that is, clinicians can incorrectly conclude that a functional relation exists between the target variable and a hypothesized causal variable when, in fact, one does not exist (Chapman & Chapman, 1969; Garb, 2005; Matyas & Greenwood, 1990; O'Brien, 1995). The findings from a study by O'Brien (1995) suggest that a central tendency bias may be operating in which clinicians overestimate the magnitude of weak correlations and underestimate the magnitude of strong correlations when using an intuitive approach to evaluating correlations between a behavior problem and a causal variable. Nevertheless, clinicians should summarize, plot, and examine data: These data can be an important source of hypotheses and suggest additional assessment strategies to use with a client.

**Statistical Analysis of Observational Data.** There are several statistical strategies that can be used to evaluate functional relations from observation data: (a) conditional probability analyses; (b) conventional statistical tests, such as t-tests, Analysis of Variance and regression models; and (c) time-series analysis. The use of these statistical techniques can reduce the likelihood of making a Type I error from behavioral observation data and increase the reliability of inferences from these data. We briefly introduce conditional probability analyses and time-series analysis, but refer the reader to Haynes and O'Brien (2000) for a brief discussion on conventional statistical tests used in behavioral observation.

*Conditional probability analyses* are statistical techniques designed to evaluate the extent to which the occurrence or nonoccurrence of a target behavior is conditional based on the occurrence or nonoccurrence of some other variable, or a comparison of the differences between the overall probability that the target behavior will occur (i.e., unconditional probability) relative to the occurrence of the target behavior given the occurrence or nonoccurrence of some hypothesized causal variable (i.e., conditional probability). Substantial differences between the unconditional and conditional probability or between two conditions would suggest that the target behavior and hypothesized causal variable are functionally related. As we discuss in Chapter 4, covariation between variables is a necessary condition for inferring a causal relation.

To illustrate conditional probability analyses, we provide an example of a contingency table in Figure 9.2, summarizing the interactions between a target behavior and a hypothesized causal variable. The probability that the target behavior occurred, given the occurrence of the causal variable, was 27%. In contrast, the probability that the target behavior occurred given the nonoccurrence of the causal variable was 63%. Thus, it appears that the causal variable is acting to reduce the likelihood that the target behavior will occur. A nonparametric statistical procedure (i.e., chi-square analysis) was calculated to determine the magnitude of the functional relation based on the data in Figure 9.2 (Schlundt, 1985).

*Time-series analysis* is ideal for examining the covariance between a behavior problem and a hypothesized causal variable if a sufficient data set is available. In conducting time-series analyses, repeated measures of the target behavior and one or more hypothesized causal variables are

Target Behavior

|  | Nonoccurrence | Occurrence | |
|---|---|---|---|
| **Causal Variable** — Nonoccurrence | 3 | 5 | 8 |
| **Causal Variable** — Occurrence | 8 | 3 | 11 |
|  | 11 | 8 | 19 |

Calculating unconditional probabilities:
Overall probability of target behavior occurrence = 8/19 = .42
Overall probability of target behavior nonoccurrence = 11/19 = .58
Calculating conditional probabilities:
Probability of target behavior occurrence given causal variable occurrence = 3/11 = .27
Probability of target behavior occurrence given causal variable nonoccurrence = 5/8 = .63
Chi-Square (1) = 12.97, $p < .0001$.

**Figure 9.2** Contingency Table Summarizing Target Behavior-Causal Variable Interactions.
*Source: Adapted from Haynes & O'Brien, 2000.*

taken across time. After the variance attributable to serial dependency is removed, an estimation of the relations among these variables is calculated (Barlow & Hersen, 1984; Wei, 1990). Nominal (e.g., social/ interpersonal events versus nonsocial/environmental events), ordinal (e.g., ranked variables), and interval (e.g., from least to greater on a dimension) scales and ratio assessment data can be analyzed, but different statistical strategies are applied depending on the measurement scales used, such as lag sequential analysis to evaluate functional relations for nominal- and ordinal-scaled measures (Gottman & Roy, 1990). It is beyond the scope of this book to provide detailed descriptions of the mathematical procedures used in time-series analysis. We refer the reader to Shadish, Cook, and Campbell (2002) and Wei (1990) for a broader discussion. It is important to note, however, that time-series methods can provide accurate estimates of the magnitude and reliability of functional relations and of the effects of controlling variables on behavior problems across time lags.

## Psychometric Considerations in Behavioral Observation

**Interobserver Agreement.** An important psychometric characteristic of observation coding systems is *interobserver agreement*, a statistic that reflects the degree to which data collected via a specified sampling strategy, in a particular setting, is consistent among two or more observers (Hops, Davis, & Longoria, 1995). Interobserver agreement is obtained by having two or more persons observe the same client, in the same setting, using the same sampling strategies, and the same operational definitions of target variables (i.e., the same observational system). This is often accomplished by having all persons simultaneously collect data on the client in the actual setting or by observing a video recording of the client.

We provide an example of a 2 × 2 contingency table with calculations of interobserver agreement indices in Figure 9.3. Note the calculation for the different agreement indices. Because occurrence and nonoccurrence agreement indices can be adversely affected by chance agreement, especially when the target variables occur at very low or very high rates (as is the case in Figure 9.3), it is recommended that consistency indicators that correct for this error be used, such as Kappa (k), in addition to standard measures of interobserver agreement. Conceptually, Kappa is the ratio of observed nonchance agreement divided by the highest value that nonchance agreement can attain in a given dataset. Similar to a correlation coefficient, the Kappa values can range from −1 (perfect disagreement) to +1 (perfect agreement) with 0 indicating random agreement. The formulae for obtaining the Kappa in Figure 9.3 are presented in Box 9.1. The Kappa calculated in Figure 9.3 indicates good agreement between the two observers. Thus, the observational system used to obtain the behavioral observation data would be considered reliable.

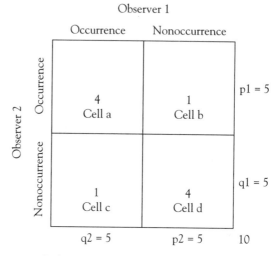

Observer 1

Agreement Indices for Data Presented Above

| Statistic | Value |
|---|---|
| Proportion Agreement = (4 + 4)/(4 + 4) + (1 + 1) | .80 |
| Occurrence Agreement = (4)/(4) + (1 + 1) | .66 |
| Nonoccurrence Agreement = (4)/(4) + (1 + 1) | .66 |
| Chance agreement value = [(.50) (.50)] + [(.50) (.50)] | .50 |
| Kappa (k) = .80 - .50/1 - .50 | .60 |

**Figure 9.3** A 2 × 2 contingency table illustrating interobserver agreement calculations. Formulae used to obtain Kappa are presented in Box 9-1.

---

## Box 9.1 Formulae for Calculating Kappa (k) to Determine Interobserver Agreement

The data from Figure 9.3 are used here to illustrate the formulae for calculating Kappa (k).

*Step 1*: Calculate proportion agreement (po): po = # agreements/# agreements + # disagreements. Example: po = (4 + 4)/(4 + 4) + (1 + 1)

po = 8/10

po = .80

*Step 2:* Calculate proportion of occurrence agreement (poccurrence): poccurrence = # agreement on occurrences/# agreements on occurrences + # disagreements.

Example: poccurrence = $(4)/(4) + (1 + 1)$

poccurrence = $4/6$

poccurrence = $.66$

*Step 3:* Calculate proportion of nonoccurrence agreement (pnonoccurrence): pnonoccurrence = # agreement on nonoccurrence/# agreements on nonoccurrences + # disagreements.

Example: poccurrence = $(4)/(4) + (1 + 1)$

poccurrence = $4/6$

poccurrence = $.66$

*Step 4:* Determine the probability of chance agreements (pe): Multiply the occurrence marginal (i.e., $p1$ and $p2$) and add them to the nonoccurrence marginal (i.e., $q1$ and $q2$).

Where:

$p1$ = proportion of occurrences recorded by observer 1

$p2$ = proportion of occurrences recorded by observer 2

$q1$ = proportion of nonoccurrences recorded by observer 1

$q2$ = proportion of nonoccurrences recorded by observer 2

Example:

$p1 = 5/10 = .50$

$p2 = 5/10 = .50$

$q1 = 5/10 = .50$

$q2 = 5/10 = .50$

Chance agreement value = $[(.50) (.50)] + [(.50) (.50)] = .50$

*Step 5*: Calculate Kappa: k = po – pe/1 – pe

Example:

k = .80 - .50/1 - .50

k = .30/.50

k = .60

*Step 6*: Determine the level of acceptance of Kappa coefficient (see Bryington, Darcy, & Watkins, 2004, for more explanation about Kappa):

Example:

Fair = .40 to .59

Good = .60 to .74

Excellent = ≥ .75

**Content Validity.** In Chapter 7 we introduce the concept of content validity, and Haynes and O'Brien (2000) and Haynes (2001) discussed the importance of content validity in behavioral observation. Content validity refers to the degree to which the elements in an observation instrument are relevant to and representative of the targeted construct. In the case of behavioral observation, in both naturalistic and analog settings, content validity includes the degree to which the behaviors observed, the settings in which observation occurs, and the time frames for observation are appropriate for the goals of assessment. When observing parent-child interactions, for example, are the most appropriate behaviors being observed? Are the settings for observation and instructions to the participants appropriate? Highly reliable data from an observation instrument with low content validity will have diminished clinical utility. Haynes, Richard, and Kubany (1995) outlined steps to increase the likelihood that an assessment instrument will have good content validity.

## Reactive Effects of Behavioral Observation

A major threat to the ecological validity of data acquired in the natural environment is *reactive effects* associated with the observation process. The observation process can be associated with changes in the behavior of the client or other persons in the observation environment. This is especially likely when using nonparticipant observers who are not normally a part of the natural setting. For example, socially desirable behaviors, such as compliments made toward a partner or praise by a teacher given to a student, can increase as a result of being observed. In contrast, socially undesirable behaviors, such as aggression or negative comments, can decrease.

The degree of reactive effects can be affected by several aspects of the observation process: (a) the degree to which the client's natural setting is altered by the observation process, (b) the obtrusiveness of the observation instrument (e.g., placement and obtrusiveness of video or audio recording versus in-person observation), (c) the instructions given to those being observed prior to the observation session, (d) the behavior of observers toward those in the observation environment (meaningful interactions should be minimized), and (e) the number of observation sessions (reactive effects tend to dissipate over time). With time-series data, the reactive effects can sometimes be identified by variability and slope in obtained data (for reviews of reactive effects see Harris & Lahey, 1982; Haynes & Horn, 1982).

# NATURALISTIC OBSERVATIONS

Behavioral observation of a client can occur in settings that range on a continuum from naturalistic to analog. In naturalistic observation, the observer collects data on the behavior of clients and others in the setting in which they naturally occur, without intervening and while minimizing disruptions to the environment. Behavioral observation data collected in naturalistic settings are designed to maximize the ecological validity of information obtained. For example, in a study designed to identify causal relations for severe behavior problems of hospitalized psychiatric patients while on their unit, Lambrechts, Van Den Noortgate, Eeman, and Maes (2010) videotaped the verbal and nonverbal reactions of staff on the patients' psychiatric unit to the patients' self-injurious, aggressive, and stereotypical behaviors (the tapes were later coded by observers).

In this section, we discuss the clinical utility, assets, and limitations of naturalistic observations of a client by external observers. For more discussions of naturalistic observation, we refer the reader to Hartmann, et al. (2004) and Tryon (1998) for general principles and applications of naturalistic observation; Dishion and Granic (2004) for naturalistic observation of social relationships; and Hintze, Volpe, and Shapiro (2002) and Skinner, Rhymer, and McDaniel (2000) for naturalistic observation of children in educational settings.

## Description of Naturalistic Observations

Behavioral observation in the natural environment involves the use of either nonparticipant or participant observers and one of the sampling and recording systems described earlier. Recall how the behavior problems, associated events, and sampling strategies are selected *a priori* and carefully operationalized. In the following sections, we provide examples of naturalistic observations using the two types of external observers.

**Naturalistic Observation by Nonparticipant Observers.** The use of nonparticipant observers in a naturalistic setting, the operationalization of target behaviors, and time-sampling procedures were illustrated in a study by Ryan and colleagues (2004). They examined the effects of orienting and multimodal cuing (i.e., use of visual, physical, and verbal cues to gain a child's attention) on the communicative responses in the classroom of three girls (9, 14, and 16 years old) with Rett's syndrome. The researchers posited that several environmental factors could affect the children's communicative behaviors, such as the degree to which teachers are responsive to the child's attempts at communication (Rhyner, Lehr, & Pudlas, 1990; Sigafoos, Roberts, Kerr, Couzens, & Baglioni, 1994). They also posited that verbal and nonverbal cues given together could serve to facilitate the communicative responses of children with sensory impairments (Rowland, 1990).

In developing their observational coding system, Ryan and colleagues operationally defined several target communicative behaviors and events. For example, they defined "student cue" as "any communication from the student that clearly requires/expects a response," which could be indicated by verbal, nonverbal (e.g., head turning to indicate food not liked) or proximity (e.g., student standing by the door indicating a request to go outside) response. They also specified orienting cues given by teachers, which included visual (i.e., use of objects and/or physical movement to attract girl's attention), tactile (i.e., use of touch to attract girl's attention), and auditory (i.e., use of verbalization and/or noise to attract student's attention) behaviors. Ryan et al. videotaped the girls and their caregivers in their classrooms and adjacent play areas in three two-hour sessions during a structured activity (i.e., one that included an educational outcome), an unstructured activity (e.g., performing a task with no instructions), and a daily living activity (e.g., toileting) initiated by the caregiver. Two research assistants were trained on the behavioral coding system through practice and detailed discussions of the interpretation of the codes while viewing videotape footage prior to actual recording of observations. When the observers reached a criterion level of competency, they independently coded the videotape for occurrence of communicative interactions and orienting cues using 10-second partial interval time-sampling.

Consistent with the emphasis of the behavioral assessment paradigm on individual differences, Ryan et al. found differences between the girls in the activity that provided the most communication opportunity. For the 16-year-old, the most communication opportunities occurred during activities of daily living. For the 14- and 9-year-old girls, structured activities provided the most communication opportunities. Some of their other findings included differences in the rate and type of orientation cues provided across the dyads and that a combination of multiple cues elicited the highest rate of responses from the girls.

**Naturalistic Observation by Participant Observers.** A study by LePage and Mogge (2001) illustrates the use of participant observers in a naturalistic setting. They were interested in testing the reliability and validity of measures on the Behavioral Observation System, a 34-item rating scale measuring psychosis, mania, depression, and behavioral dyscontrol obtained from health service workers of an acute-care psychiatric facility. LePage and Mogge argued that clinical decisions, such as when to start or increase medication, readiness for discharge and outpatient placement, readiness for certain treatment groups, and the need for increased staffing, should be based on valid data from instruments that are feasible to use in health-care environments.

Eighteen health service workers were selected from six different units to serve as participant observers, and all received a one-hour training program on the terms, item-definitions, and rating scales of the behavioral observation system. The health service workers also met weekly with the trainers to help them maintain consistency in their ratings. Examples of items included "Becomes irritable when they cannot get what they want," "Says things that are strange and likely not true," "Suddenly changes topics," and "Does not engage in activities." Each of the 76 psychiatric patients was observed by two health service workers during their work shift. Each health service worker dyad concurrently observed three to four patients during a shift while performing their normal work routine and rated every occurrence of the target behaviors during their shift. High interobserver agreements were found, ranging from 82% to 86%. To measure the internal consistency of each scale in the Behavioral Observation System, Cronbach's alpha were calculated, which ranged from 85% to 89%. To test the validity of the Behavioral Observation System, LePage and Mogge compared the ratings to the patient's psychiatric diagnosis at admission and found a strong association between the two data sources. For example, ratings on the depression scale were significantly higher for patients for whom depression was the primary diagnosis. Their study illustrated how participant observers can be used in naturalistic environments with a high degree of interobserver agreement when there is a well-defined observation coding system and proper training and monitoring in that assessment system.

## The Clinical Utility and Assets of Naturalistic Observations

The studies by Ryan et al. and LePage and Mogge illustrate the clinical utility of naturalistic observations across different client populations and across different settings. They also illustrate the different sampling strategies that can be used, such as critical event sampling, subject sampling, and partial interval time sampling. Because behavior was captured in its natural setting, the data obtained in these studies are assumed to have a high degree of ecological validity. Consider the assets of these observation data compared to the less specific and precise data that would be obtained through retrospective reports from the observers in these studies.

Naturalistic observation can also be used with many populations and target behaviors. Some examples include identifying environmental factors that affect the rate of alcohol consumption in a young adult (Spijkerman et al., 2010), the types of family interactions that affect a child's mood (Messer & Gross, 1995), and factors that affect a clients' fear of test taking, dental surgery, public speaking, and other anxiety-provoking situations (Fonseca & Perrin, 2001).

## The Cost of Naturalistic Observations

Earlier we discussed the reactive effects often associated with direct observation methods. In Chapter 8 we discussed some of the limitations of informants' reports (e.g., biases toward the client can affect the measures obtained) that also apply to the use of participant observers in naturalistic observations. Other limitations of naturalistic observations worth noting are the cost in time and effort to conduct them and the lack of control over target variables.

Compared to other assessment methods, naturalistic observations can be expensive. It usually requires the development of an observational system that matches the client's unique behavior problems and assessment goals, the training of external observers, time to collect data, and, sometimes, complex data analysis. The use of participant observers can reduce the expense of naturalistic observation, although the observers still need to be trained on the observational system and their use can introduce other sources of error (e.g., less reliable data collection because of competing demands).

A limitation that can increase the cost of naturalistic observation is that the clinician often has little control over the occurrence of behavior problems and causal variables when observing clients in their natural setting. Although this problem can be partially addressed with careful sampling strategies and the use of participant observers, naturalistic observation is often costly to use with behaviors that occur infrequently or in infrequently occurring settings and contexts. Consider the challenges of using naturalistic observation to collect data on a client with social anxiety in public speaking settings, or on a client whose panic episodes occur unpredictably a few times a month, or on a couple who have arguments one to two times per week.

### Summary of Naturalistic Observations

Naturalistic observation can provide valuable information on client behavior problems, strengths, and functional relations and can strengthen the ecological validity and clinical utility of the functional analysis and other clinical judgments. It is an assessment method highly congruent with the emphasis in the behavioral assessment paradigm of measuring contemporaneous, well-specified, behavior-environment interactions in a client's natural environment. We described the assets and limitations of naturalistic observations and several factors that affect its utility in clinical assessment. We emphasized the importance of using a well-defined observation coding system, of training participant and nonparticipant observers in order to obtain reliable data, and the implementation of carefully selected time, behavior, and setting sampling. Naturalistic observations with highly trained nonparticipant observers can be helpful in capturing a client's behavior problem, contemporaneous environmental events, and their functional relations in his or her real-world setting.

## ANALOG BEHAVIORAL OBSERVATIONS

Recall that in the case of Mrs. Anderson in Chapter 7, analog behavioral observation in the clinic was used to evaluate the ways in which Mr. and Mrs. Anderson communicated about problematic marital and family issues. The analog observation was designed to test the clinician's hypothesis that one source of marital distress was dysfunctional communication patterns. The functional behavioral interview and behavioral questionnaires were used by the clinician to select the topics for discussion that were more likely to elicit the most informative communication patterns. As the case of Mrs. Anderson illustrates, analog observation is a less costly and time-intensive alternative to naturalistic observations, and is especially cost-beneficial for low-frequency behaviors, such as marital, family, and other interpersonal interactions. In this section, we describe the clinical utility, assets, and limitations of analog observation. For more detailed discussions of this topic, we refer the reader to Heyman and Smith Slep (2004) and the Special Section on analog observation in *Psychological Assessment* (2001; vol., 13, no. 1).

## Description of Analog Behavioral Observations

Analog behavioral observation involves an assessment situation that is designed to increase the likelihood that target behaviors and relevant functional relations will occur (Haynes, 2001; Heyman & Smith Slep, 2004). An important objective of analog behavioral observation is to examine the effects of variables that are hypothesized to influence the onset, maintenance, or termination of a behavior problem. For example, a clinician might request a client who is socially avoidant to initiate a conversation with a confederate or request a parent and oppositional child to clean up a clinic playroom.

The goal of analog behavioral observation is to obtain, in a cost-effective manner, measures of a client's behavior and relevant functional relations that approximates the behavior and interactions that occur in their natural environment. Analog behavioral observation is particularly useful for exploring and testing hypothesis about the functional relations of a client's, dyad's, or family's relational problems. Its main advantage over naturalistic observation is that it allows for the observation of behaviors and functional relations that would be difficult or impractical to observe in the client's natural environment.

## Classes of Analog Behavioral Observation Methods

There are several classes of analog behavioral observation methods: (a) role-plays, (b) experimental functional analysis, (c) contrived situation tests, (d) think-aloud procedures, (e) enactment analog (e.g., family, marital, and peer interaction tasks), (f) response generation tasks, and (g) behavioral avoidance test. Of these, we review the three best suited for identifying the functional relations of a client's behavior problem in a clinical setting: role-plays, enactment analog, and experimental functional analysis. For discussions of other classes of analog behavioral observation methods, we refer the reader to Haynes (1978), Haynes and O'Brien (2000), McFall (1977), Nay (1986), Shapiro and Kratochwill (1988), and Torgrud and Holborn (1992).

**Enactment in Analog Behavioral Observation: Family, Marital, and Peer Interaction Tasks.** Because how a client interacts with others in his or her natural setting is often a focus of behavioral assessment and intervention, the behavioral clinicians often use the enactment method in analog observation. This method involves a client, in the clinic setting, enacting a problematic topic or situation with a person or object from his or her real-world environment for a short period of time (e.g., 5 to 10 minutes). It is often used to assess the verbal and nonverbal interactions of couples, family members, and parent-child dyads. With enactments, the clinician provides basic instructions about the tasks and then observes subsequent interactions. The clinician can then directly observe and measure the antecedents, consequences, and behavioral sequences associated with a behavior problem. The clinician can form inferences based on qualitative observations of the interactions or based on a more formal observation scoring system. The topics and situation in the enactment can be selected from a functional behavioral interview or self-report questionnaire. The case of Mrs. Anderson illustrates an enactment. Recall how Mr. and Mrs. Anderson were asked to discuss their disagreements about family finances.

Another example is the peer interaction task, originally developed by Dishion and colleagues (1996), to assess the antisocial behaviors of preadolescents and adolescents. They had adolescent boys bring a friend to a lab where they were asked to talk for 25 minutes. Although it is difficult to assess antisocial behaviors in natural and analog settings, Dishion et al. were able to measure it by having the boys enact discussions similar to those that occurred in their natural environment. As the boys were talking, Dishion et al. recorded occurrence of discussion topics related to rule-breaking, violating social norms, and positive social reinforcements for antisocial behaviors. A similar peer interaction task could be used in assessing the role of peers in a client's discussion of his or her binge eating or drinking, depressed or manic mood, or disruptive, aggressive, and oppositional behaviors.

**Role-Playing in Analog Behavioral Observation.** In behavioral assessment, "role-play" refers to a person's performance of a particular role, in a particular context, in accordance with the instructions of a clinician. The role and context are selected to be relevant to problems or goals faced by the client in his or her natural environment. Usually, the clinician is interested in assessing a client's social behaviors or skills, such as the client's behaviors or communication skills in a stressful social situation (e.g., asking for a date or initiating and maintaining a conversation) with a confederate (e.g., clinic staff member). Role-playing is a flexible method of assessment because no special setting is needed. The role-playing method also can be helpful in specifying a client's behavior problem and in estimating how the client behaves in his or her real-world setting. However, the usefulness of the role-playing depends on the degree to which it can approximate the client's real world situation, the client's ability and comfort with role-playing, and the specificity of the instructions provided (Nay, 1986).

---

**Box 9.2 Analog Behavioral Observation Data as Measures of Typical Behavior or Skill**

Reactive effects of an assessment process may be especially strong in enactment and role-play analog behavioral observation assessment methods. Consider the clinical assessment context: A clinician instructs a parent to play with a child, or instructs a couple to discuss a source of marital conflict, or instructs a client to converse with a stranger while the clinician watches or records the process. It is easy to see that in some cases the clients may do their best. That is, the data may reflect the client's optimal performance rather than typical performance. Considered as a measure of typical performance, the data would have limited ecological validity. However, these data could still be clinically useful in that it could inform the functional analysis whether or not a "skills deficit" is an important

> causal variable and should be addressed in a behavioral intervention.
> The client can help with this judgment (keeping in mind the many
> sources of error in self-report): Ask the client about how typical the
> performance was to his or her performance in the natural environ-
> ment and in what ways it was similar or different.

**Experimental Functional Analysis.** Often a clinician wants to test
hypotheses about the functional relations relevant to a client's behavior
problem, to inform the functional analysis and treatment selection. A
powerful method for testing hypotheses is the experimental functional
analysis, which involves the clinician systematically manipulating an antecedent stimulus, response consequence, or context to assess the effects of
that manipulation on a client's behavior problem or positive alternatives
to a behavior problem. We discuss experimental functional analysis (i.e.,
"manipulation designs") in greater detail in Chapter 10, but introduce the
basic methods here. Single-subject replication or reversal design strategies,
such as ABA'B' (A = baseline, B = manipulation, A' = a return to baseline conditions (or reversal of contingencies), B' = a reintroduction of the
manipulation) and changing criterion, can be used to examine the direction and strength of the relationship between a hypothesized causal variable
and the client's behavior problem. Experimental functional analyses are a
powerful method of identifying contemporaneous causal relations between
a target behavior and causal variable. It is also a well-researched procedure
and can be readily incorporated into clinical assessment settings.

To illustrate experimental functional analysis, Iwata and colleagues
(1994) and Durand (1990) developed standardized protocols for conducting experimental functional analyses to identify the response contingencies that often help maintain the self-injurious behavior in individuals
with developmental disabilities. Their assessment protocols consist of four
conditions to identify the function of a client's behavior. In the first three
conditions, the client is systematically provided with social attention
(positive reinforcement), tangible rewards (positive reinforcement), or
an opportunity to escape from a negative or aversive task (negative reinforcement) contingent on performance of the self-injurious behavior. In
the fourth condition, the client's self-injurious behavior is observed while

he or she is socially isolated to determine the extent to which intrinsic positive or negative reinforcement (e.g., nociceptive feedback, tension reduction) may be influencing the behavior.

Notice how the results of an experimental functional analysis can inform the functional analysis and the design of an intervention. First, it can help identify the specific causal relations (e.g., attention seeking versus escape) maintaining a client's behavior problem to inform the functional analysis. Second, it provides the foci for intervention. For example, if a client's self-injurious behavior is functioning to elicit attention from others or to obtain a tangible reward, an intervention strategy might involve time-out, noncontingent attention, or differential reinforcement of other behaviors.

In 2003, Hanley, Iwata, and McCord conducted a second comprehensive analysis of the experimental functional analysis literature. In their review, they identified 277 published investigations summarizing the results of experimental functional analyses for 536 individual clients presenting with a wide range of behavior problems. In 95.9% of these cases, the experimental functional analysis yielded a result that indicated one or more of the four types of consequences exerted the strongest effects on behavior. Escape was the most commonly identified reinforcer (34.2%), followed by social attention reinforcement (25.3%), intrinsic/automatic reinforcement (15.8%), multiple reinforcers (14.6%), and tangible reinforcement (10.1%). The development of treatments that matched the function of the problem behaviors was reported to be effective.

As the studies of Iwata et al. (1994), Hanley et al. (2003), and Derby et al. (1992) suggest, most clinical applications of experimental functional analysis have been done with clients who exhibit severe behavior problems or with clients experiencing developmental delays. As we discuss further in Chapter 10, the clinical utility of experimental functional analysis with clients who have other types of behavior problems is promising but has yet to be sufficiently empirically evaluated.

## The Clinical Utility of Analog Behavioral Observations

The three types of analog behavioral observation methods reviewed in this chapter illustrate the clinical utility and congruence of this assessment method with the behavioral assessment paradigm. Analog behavioral observation can be used with adults, children, couples, and families for a wide range of behavioral problems, and to investigate a diverse set of contemporaneous functional relations. This assessment method increases the clinician's ability to observe: (a) specific situations and conditions that are functionally related to a client's behavior problem, (b) behaviors that occur with a low frequency in the natural environment, and (c) patterns and sequences of behavior exchanges across short time periods.

Analog behavioral observation is often used as an idiographic assessment strategy but several analog behavioral observation protocols have also been developed. Although most have been applied in a research context, many can be adapted for clinical assessment. Some examples are the *Rapid Marital Interaction Coding System* (Heyman & Vivian, 1994), the *Behavioral Assertiveness Test-Revised* (Eisler, Hersen, Miller, & Blanchard, 1975), the *Social Skill Behavioral Assessment System* (Caballo & Buela, 1988), the *Standardized Observational Analogue Procedure* for the assessment of parent–child behavior (Johnson et al., 2009), and the *ADHD Behavior Coding System* (Barkley, 1991).

We emphasized the utility of analog behavioral observation for measuring observable behavior, but it can be used also to measure other response systems. For example, after observing a couple having an argument, the clinician can ask the participants about the emotions or attributions that occurred during the argument. Similarly, a person who is role-playing in a stressful social situation can be questioned about his or her thoughts during the situation and data on psychophysiological responses can also be recorded.

## The Limitations of Analog Behavioral Observation Methods

The main limitation of analog behavioral observation is that it is often unclear if the data are ecologically valid:[4] Do obtained data validly measure how the person behaves in his or her natural environment? One reason

---

[4] Analog behavioral observation illustrates how measures can be accurate and invalid. For example, data on the positive behavior of a parent toward a child, derived from observing parent-child interactions in a clinic playroom, could be accurate yet the data may not validly measure the parent's positive behavior toward the child at home.

for the potential limited generalizability across settings is reactivity. Despite reactive changes in the dimensions of a behavior problem, analog behavioral observations often can provide useful clinical information about the triggers and consequences of the behavior or other functional relations. There are several other limitations, some of which we discuss in Chapter 10: (a) a limited number of potential causal relations can be investigated at one time; (b) some types, such as experimental functional analysis, can be cumbersome to use when a behavior is affected by multiple contiguous causal variables; and (c) it is useful mainly for investigating causal variables that operate contiguously with, or are proximal to, a behavior problem.

## Summary of Analog Behavioral Observations

We highlighted three methods of conducting an analog observation in a clinical setting. We noted the clinical utility of using experimental functional analysis to systematically test hypotheses about the contemporaneous causal relations relevant to a client's behavior problem or the intervention effects on a behavior problem. The major assets of analog behavioral observations are the incremental value of the data acquired and its cost-effectiveness compared to naturalistic observations. The major limitation is reactivity, which can threaten the ecological validity of obtained data.

# PSYCHOPHYSIOLOGICAL ASSESSMENTS

Many clients have behavioral problems involving important physiological responses, mediators, and correlates. Some examples include a client who misinterprets his or her increased heart rate in response to an anxiety-provoking stimulus as a "heart attack," which leads to a further acceleration in heart rate (Austin & Kiropoulos, 2008); a client whose blood pressure is adversely affected by chronic work-related stressors (Rau, 2006); and an adolescent with type 1 diabetes whose effective management of it is adversely affected by family stressors (Seiffge-Krenke, 2001).

Psychophysiological assessment, such as measuring blood pressure or heart rate in response to an environmental stressor, can provide direct measures of physiological activity that are an important element of a client's behavior problem. In this section, we consider the rationale, clinical utility, and limitations of several methods of psychophysiological assessment. We refer the reader to Molton and Raichle (2010) for a review of common psychophysiological disorders and their assessment; to Stern, Ray, and Quigley (2001) for psychophysiological measurement; to Wilhelm, Schneider, and Friedman (2006) for psychophysiological assessment in children; and to Lau, Edelstein, and Larkin (2001) for psychophysiological assessment in older adults.

## Rationale for Psychophysiological Assessments

**A Behavior Problem Can Be Associated with Important Physiological Factors.** As we introduced in the previous section and in Chapters 4 and 6, many behavior problems have important physiological aspects. For example, clients with anxiety-related problems often experience increased heart rate, increased perceived heart pounding, and perspiration due to activation of the sympathetic autonomic and neuroendocrine systems (Gorman, Kent, Sullivan, & Copelan, 2000) and concomitant changes in blood pressure, cortisol levels, striated muscle tension and activity, to name a few.

**Differences among Response Systems of a Behavioral Problem.** As we also discuss in Chapters 4 and 6, the overt motor, cognitive, emotional, and physiological response modes of a client's behavior problem can: (a) differ in their time-course (i.e., they can be *dysynchronous*), (b) have a different time-course in response to treatments, and (c) be affected by different causal factors. Consider how a client's change in heart rate (i.e., interbeat interval) can occur within a fraction of a second in response to a stressor while other responses such as overt activity (e.g., avoidance), cognitive processes (e.g., fearful thoughts), and other physiological responses (e.g., blood pressure) are delayed. Also consider how different causal factors might trigger different aspects of a client's behavior problem, such as when the characteristics of a place (e.g., crowded, confined, or small) leads to avoidance, but the misinterpretation of physiological sensations leads to the client's panic episode. Finally, consider how different interventions can have different effects on cognitive, overt-motor, and physiological response modes.

## Description of Psychophysiological Assessments

Psychophysiological methods of assessment usually involve the measurement of physiological variables using noninvasive recording procedures. The goal of psychophysiological assessment is to examine covariance among indices of the central nervous system, the autonomic nervous system, neuroendocrine system, and/or the somatic nervous system with overt behavior (Cacioppo, Tassinary, & Berntson, 2007). Psychophysiological assessments can be performed in the clinic setting, such as when a client's heart rate is monitored while imagining anxiety-provoking stimuli, or under real-world conditions, such as when a client's blood pressure is monitored while going about their daily activity at work and at home.

**An Example of Psychophysiological Assessment.** A study by Alpers and colleagues (2005) illustrates the use of psychophysiological assessment methods within a multimethod assessment strategy. They studied the physiological, affective, cognitive, and behavioral responses of women with driving phobia before, during, and after exposure to a real-world phobic stimulus, and how these responses changed with repeated exposure. They included in their study an age-matched control group of women who did not have a driving phobia.

Based on self-efficacy ratings for driving, suitable exposure situations were selected for each phobic woman that involved driving on one of two multilane, limited access highways: one with moderate traffic mostly through open countryside or one with heavy traffic through a populated suburb. For each of three driving sessions, a sequence of experimental procedures were done that involved a quiet sitting period, an approach drive to the feared situation, actual driving, and quiet sitting again. Before, during, and after driving, biosensors were used to continuously record (a) heart-rate, (b) skin conductance, (c) respiration, (d) hyperventilation, (e) skin temperature, (f) eye blinks, (g) ambient temperature, and (h) body movement. The women also provided ratings of their state levels of anxiety, excitement, tension, heart pounding or racing, breathlessness, and sweating on 10-point Subjective Units of Distress Scales. Overall, Alpers et al. found that the women with a driving phobia, compared to women without, showed greater activation on all physiological and psychological indices and that the differences between groups lessened with repeated exposure. The Alpers et al.'s study illustrates the array of psychophysiological measures that can be used in behavioral assessment, in the natural environment, and in conjunction with self-report measures of cognitive, affective, and somatic variables.

## Psychometric Considerations in Psychophysiological Assessments

In Chapters 7 and 8, we discussed the psychometric issues of accuracy, validity, and sensitivity to change in evaluating an assessment measure—all of which apply to measures derived from psychophysiological assessment instruments. We briefly note some important psychometric considerations relevant to psychophysiological measures.

**Differential Validity of Measures from a Single Instrument.** A single psychophysiological instrument can provide multiple measures that differ in their validity, accuracy, and clinical utility. For example, an instrument for monitoring myocardial functioning might provide measures of heart rate, preejection period, respiratory sinus arrhythmia, and stroke volume that differ in their degree of accuracy (see Hawkley, Burlseson, Berntgson, & Cacioppo, 2003).

**Inaccurate but Valid Measures.** As we noted in Box 7.4, a psychophysiological measure derived from an instrument can be inaccurate and valid. For example, a measure of blood pressure could consistently overestimate "true" blood pressure, but the inaccurate blood pressure measure could provide valid estimates of change over time and of functional relations (presuming that the measurement error is constant across levels of blood pressure). Thus, when data will be used for tracking changes over time or establishing functional relations, the reliability of the measure can be a more important aspect of psychometric evidence than its accuracy.

**High Degree of Sensitivity to Change.** A major advantage of psychophysiological measures is their ability to track rapidly changing physiological and motor responses. This capacity is facilitated by computer-based monitoring systems that typically sample at very high rates (e.g., 200 samples per second). Thus, even with a relatively short period of monitoring, sufficient data can often be collected on functional relations between a causal variable and physiological response.

## The Clinical Utility and Assets of Psychophysiological Assessments

As we illustrated, psychophysiological assessment methods can be applied across a wide range of behavior problems, such as anxiety and mood disorders, aggression, stress, and physiologically-based (e.g., chronic pain) disorders. They can be applied in natural and analog settings and in conjunction with self-report and observation assessment methods. They also allow for measurement of multiple dimensions of behavior and are amenable to time-sampling assessment strategies.

Psychophysiological measures complement self-report and behavioral observation measures because they measure unique aspects of behavior not easily captured by other methods (e.g., most clients cannot accurately self-report their blood pressure or motor activity during sleep). Further, when compared to more easily self-reported psychophysiological responses (e.g., breathing rate and muscle tension), they provide more accurate and sensitive-to-change measures that are less encumbered by the errors associated with self-report (Tomarken, 1995). They are particularly helpful when social desirability or other biases might affect a client's self-report, when assessing infants or young children who cannot provide valid self-report data, and when a client is unable to recognize the effects a stimulus is having on his or her behavior.

## The Limitations of Psychophysiological Assessment Methods

The major liabilities of psychophysiological assessment methods include their cost and the technical knowledge sometimes required to operate the instruments and to analyze the complex data that is obtained. Psychophysiological measures are also susceptible to instrumentation errors and errors associated with movement and other artifacts.

As with all assessment strategies, the clinician must consider the *incremental validity and incremental clinical utility* of psychophysiological data. When psychophysiological responses are an important element of the client's presenting problems, the inclusion of psychophysiological measures can increase the incremental validity, specificity, and clinical utility of a functional analysis and estimates of treatment effects. However, the clinician must also consider their applicability across settings (e.g., home and work, resting and exercise), across populations (e.g., age of client and type of physiological problem), and acceptability to the clinician and client (e.g., how intrusive are the procedures?).

## Ambulatory Biosensor Assessment

Ambulatory psychophysiological assessment can be done in real-time and under real-world conditions to capture the covariances between physiological variables and a client's behavior problem. For example, the assessment of a client with anxiety problems might involve ambulatory monitoring of his heart rate and blood pressure while he self-monitors daily stressors and mood to identify the functional relations amongst these events (Buckley, Holohan, Greif, Bedard, & Suvak, 2004). Many physiological and motor variables can be measured with ambulatory biosensors, including cardiovascular reactivity, cortisol and blood glucose levels, peripheral blood flow, respiration, skin conductance, muscle tension, and physical activity and movement.

In this section, we briefly discuss the assessment with ambulatory biosensors. We discuss the most common methods of biosensor ambulatory assessments: cardiovascular activity, physical activity and movement, and cortisol levels. The assets, psychometric considerations, and limitations of psychophysiological assessments we discussed in the previous section also apply to ambulatory biosensor assessment. We refer the reader to Fahrenberg and Myrtek (2001) for an overview of multimethod ambulatory assessment; to Haynes and Yoshioka (2007) for a broader discussion on the clinical assessment applications of ambulatory biosensors; and to Terbizan, Dolezal, and Albano (2002) and Tryon (2006) for broader discussions of ambulatory assessment instruments and measures.

Ambulatory biosensor assessments comprise a diverse set of strategies to obtain minimally disruptive measures of a client's physiological and motor responses in the real-world setting (Ebner-Priemer & Trull, 2009; Haynes & Yoshioka, 2007). Data on physiological and motor activity can be collected through ambulatory biosensor measures in conjunction with a client's self-monitoring. For example, a client could wear a nonintrusive ambulatory blood pressure device throughout the day while also recording mood. In addition, a client could collect samples of his or her saliva to measure salivary cortisol levels several times throughout the day, in designated situations, or immediately following his or her mood ratings recorded via a handheld computer.

Ambulatory biomeasures can be important components in a multimethod time-series assessment strategy for many behavior problems. They can be particularly useful in the monitoring of treatment-related changes over time and in identifying some of the causes of psychophysiologically related behavior problems. The sampling strategies we present in Chapters 7 and 8 and earlier in this chapter can also be applied to ambulatory biosensor assessments.

**Cardiovascular Activity Measurement.** Cardiovascular activity, such as a client's blood pressure and heart rate, can be measured as the client engages in real-world stressful situations, such as during social interactions, challenging cognitive tasks, or presleep activity. For example, ambulatory biosensors have been used to measure blood pressure and/ or heart rate associated with social situations and mood fluctuations in people with anxiety-related disorders (Beckham et al., 2000) and with negative affect, emotional arousal, and daily stressors (Steptoe, Brydon, & Kunz-Ebrecht, 2005).

High-grade, commercially available instrumentation for ambulatory monitoring of heart rate and blood pressure, such as Accutracker, are often used in psychophysiological research (Ebner-Priemer & Kubiak, 2007; Haynes & Yoshioka, 2007). In measuring cardiovascular activity in the context of clinical assessment, Haynes and Yoshioka (2007) outlined several advantages to using high-grade, commercially-available, ambulatory biosensors: (a) they provide multiple measures of cardiovascular functioning, (b) they provide accurate measures under most circumstances (i.e., stationary and limited movement), (c) they allow for the detection and control of erroneous measures (i.e., by detecting and deleting outliers), (d) they facilitate sophisticated data analytic techniques through data storage systems, and (e) they are sensitive to rapid changes in cardiovascular variables.

Because high-grade instrumentation can be expensive and too technical for a clinician to efficiently use, and too intrusive and cumbersome for a client to use, consumer-grade biosensors are often used. Some examples are ambulatory instruments strapped to a client's wrist or chest to monitor heart rate (e.g., Acumen Cardio Trainer and the Polar a3), or arm to monitor blood pressure (e.g., Omron Automatic BPM with Intellisense HEM-711AC). However, in many cases little information is available on the reliability, accuracy, and validity of consumer-grade ambulatory biosensors, so the clinician is advised to examine the psychometric evidence when considering their purchase.

**Measurement of Activity and Movement.** The movement and activity level of a client as he or she goes about daily life can be measured using actometers. Actometers have been used extensively in assessing clients with mood disorders, hyperactivity, physical impairments, pain, and aging-associated disorders (Tryon, 2006). Actigraphy has also been used extensively in multimethod assessment strategies to identify factors related to insomnia and its treatment outcomes (see Hauri & Wisbey, 1992, and Sadeh, Hauri, Kripke, & Lavie, 1994).

We illustrate the use of actigraphy with the study by Currie, Wilson, Pontefract, and deLaplant (2000). They used the Mini-Motionlogger actometer (by Ambulatory Monitoring, Ardsley, NY) to measure nocturnal movements in patients with insomnia secondary to chronic pain. The actometer was a small monitor that was worn on the patient's wrist while he or she slept at home. It detected movement on all axes and collected data as number of activity counts per 15-second epochs, which was stored in memory for later data analysis. Currie and others (2003) also used the same actometer in examining the sleep patterns of recovering alcoholics with sleep difficulties. They were found to have difficulties in initiating and maintaining sleep (i.e., sleep onset latencies and sleep efficiency), but they were unrelated to length of abstinence or severity of alcohol dependency.

**Cortisol Measurement.** Physiological stress responses are important correlates and causal variables for many behavior problems (see Weyandt, 2006, and Dickerson & Kemeny, 2004, reviews). A commonly used biomarker of stress is cortisol.[5] In Haynes and Yoshioka's (2007) review of published studies from April and May of 2006, they found that cortisol measures had been applied to evaluating treatment outcome in people

---

[5] Cortisol is a naturally occurring corticosteroid hormone produced by the adrenal cortex, which increases in response to environmental stressors.

with Posttraumatic Stress Disorder, the cumulative effects of daily stressors on a person, the effects of stress with sleep chronotypes, the habituation and sensitization effects of repeated stressor presentation, fibromyalgia, the long-term effects of early childhood stressors, and the outcome of cognitive-behavioral stress management programs.

Cortisol can be measured from serum, plasma, and saliva. It is important to use a time-sampling strategy when measuring cortisol because of its high degree of within-day fluctuations. Cortisol is often highest in the mornings, decreasing rapidly for several hours, then increasing over the remainder of the day. The degree of cortisol fluctuation can be affected by stressors but with a delayed causal latency. For example, serum cortisol reaches its maximum level following a stressor in about 30 minutes (Kirschbaum & Hellhammer, 2000). Thus, the time-course sampling is important to maximize the sensitivity of the cortisol measure.

## Summary of Psychophysiological Assessment

We noted how clients sometimes have behavioral problems involving important physiological responses, mediators, and correlates. Many psychophysiological factors, such as blood pressure, heart rate, and striated muscle activity, can be directly measured with biosensors. We discussed the use of biosensors in ambulatory assessment and the three most common physiological factors targeted: cardiovascular, movement and motor, and cortisol activity. Psychophysiological measures complement self-report and behavioral observation measures because they measure unique aspects of behavior not easily captured by other methods and they provide more accurate and sensitive-to-change measures that are less encumbered by the errors associated with self-report. However, they are costly and require technical knowledge to operate the instruments and to analyze the complex array of data.

## SUMMARY

The direct assessment methods and strategies described in this chapter are consistent with the principles of behavioral assessment and the underlying concepts and goals of the functional analysis. Direct observational methods (i.e., naturalistic and analog) and psychophysiological assessments can provide reliable data that have high ecological validity and are less prone to reporting biases inherent in self-reports. They can provide precise data (compared to self-reports) that are also highly sensitive to the multivariate, dynamic, multidimensional, conditional, contemporaneous, and idiographic nature of behavior problems, treatment goals, and their causal relations.

Direct behavioral observations and psychophysiological assessments are consistent with the mandate that behavior is best understood in its natural environment, as it occurs. Although they are more costly and time intensive to conduct than self-report methods, they are ideal for capturing the functional relations of a client's behavior problem as they occur, either in the natural or analog setting, and as they change over time. They can also be used to identify and specify the client's personal strengths and positive treatment goals and can be applied across a wide range of clients, behavior problems, assessment goals, and settings.

Naturalistic and analog observations have unique assets. If the appropriate strategies are used, naturalistic observations can provide assessment data with high ecological validity. Nonparticipant and participant observers can be used to collect data on the client's behavior problem, its causal variables, and their functional relations across different settings. The use of a reliable observational coding system and sampling strategies that match the client's unique behavioral problem and assessment goals are important elements in behavioral observation. Also, recall how analog observations can be a cost- and time-efficient means of directly observing behavior, especially low-frequency behaviors. Data from direct observations can enhance the validity of the clinician's clinical case formulation and the selection of treatment foci and strategies.

Psychophysiological measures complement self-report and behavioral observation measures because they measure important physiological factors associated with a client's behavior problem. Through the use of ambulatory biosensors, psychophysiological responses (e.g., blood pressure, heart rate, cortisol levels, and motor activity), in conjunction with self-report measures, can be monitored in the client's natural environment as he or she goes about his or her daily life. Psychophysiological measures can capture rapidly changing physiological responses with a high degree of sensitivity and, thus, are ideal for time-series assessment strategies.

Throughout this chapter we emphasize a science-based approach to psychological assessment: The collection of data using multiple methods of data collection, from multiple sources, using validated measures to improve the validity of the clinical judgments. A science-based approach to assessment also mandates that the clinician be sensitive to sources of error in data derived from direct observations and measurements. All data from direct observations and psychophysiological measures are affected, to different degrees, by the reliability and validity of the assessment instrument and reactive effects.

CHAPTER

# 10

# Identifying Causal Relations in Behavioral Assessment

In Chapters 7 to 9, we reviewed principles, strategies, and methods of behavioral assessment. We emphasized the use of multiple assessment methods and strategies; the measurement of specific, contemporaneous functional relations for a client's behavior problems and positive intervention goals; and the use of measures with strong psychometric evidence. But, how can the clinician apply these principles, methods, and strategies to identify important causal relations in a challenging assessment context?

Many clinicians base intervention decisions on their subjective judgments about the causes of a client's behavior problems. These judgments can be based on the clinician's personal and clinical experiences; on readings, training, or attendance at recent workshops; and on his or her theoretical orientation. As we noted in Chapters 5 and 6, causal inferences are inherently subjective and they can often effectively guide the clinical assessment process. However, clinical judgments are also subject to many sources of error and bias (Garb, 1998; 2005). A major tenet of this book is that preintervention behavioral assessment, integrated into a functional analysis, can reduce the clinician's judgment errors. Thus, the goal of this chapter is to review the underlying principles, methods, and strategies of identifying causal relations in preintervention behavioral assessment.

In this chapter, we review several methods for deriving causal inferences about clients' behavior problems: (a) rational derivation, (b) self-report instruments that focus on causal relations, (c) marker variables,

(d) time-series assessment strategies, and (e) manipulation strategies in which hypothesized causal variables are systematically varied while the effects on behavior problems and positive intervention goals are measured.

## RATIONAL DERIVATION

*Rational derivation* refers to the process of identifying possible causal variables by applying findings from the psychopathology and treatment research literature. For example, Hanley et al. (2003) outlined several classes of variables that were shown to affect many types of severe behavior problems (e.g., self-injury and aggression) of persons with developmental disabilities. Familiarity with this research literature can help the clinician's search for the causal factors for a client who is presenting with similar behavior problems and cognitive impairments.

Virtually all modern textbooks on psychopathology summarize research on the causes of behavior problems. Oftentimes these textbooks are organized around DSM diagnostic categories and the research literature and causal models are organized within various biological, psychological, and social domains. By identifying a client's behavior problem and understanding the psychopathology research associated with it, the clinician can narrow the array of potential causal variables and, subsequently, sharpen the focus of the assessment.

In Chapter 3, we review the debates concerning the degree to which diagnosis facilitates the identification of causal variables and we will not reiterate those arguments here. However, it is important to recall that, although a diagnosis can be helpful in identifying an array of possible causal variables, it will inadequately identify the specific causal variables that are relevant for an individual client. As we note in our discussion of "The Clinician as Behavioral Scientist" (Box 6.3), the clinician must be knowledgeable of the empirical literature. Without that knowledge, the clinician will be inadequately prepared to know what topics to address in the interview, what questionnaires to use, how to conduct the most useful analog and natural environment observations, or to identify the most profitable context for assessing the client.

# CAUSAL QUESTIONNAIRES AND CLIENT'S CAUSAL ATTRIBUTIONS

As we discussed in Chapter 8, most self-report questionnaires and interviews measure only the occurrence or magnitude of a behavioral problem. They are usually unhelpful in identifying causal variables and relations because they emphasize descriptions, trait scores, and ratings of behavior and insufficiently attend to the associated contexts and functional relations of the targeted behaviors.

---

**Box 10.1 Clients' Attributions of the Causes of Their Behavior Problems**

---

One strategy for identifying causal relations for clients' behavior problems is to simply ask for his or her causal attribution regarding a behavior problem (e.g., "What do you think causes you to become angry at your partner?"). This is a useful strategy for identifying what the client perceives to be the causes of his or her behavior problems. However, many studies on causal attributions and clinical judgment suggest that inferences by clients about the causes of their behavior problems should be interpreted cautiously, due to myriad fallibilities of human memory and cognitive processes.

In addition to memory errors associated with any retrospective self-report, several types of attributional biases are probable when clients are asked to report about the causes of their or others' behavior problems. For example, clients are apt to: (a) underestimate or overestimate the role of situational and dispositional factors depending upon whether he or she is evaluating self versus other's behavior, (b) make erroneous attributions regarding current behaviors because of salient past experiences, (c) bias reports of causality in a self-serving direction, (d) misestimate the strength of covariation between their problems and other events, and (e) report causal attributions that reflect concepts in popular media or what the client has been told by others.

A client's causal attributions can be invalid but functionally related to behavior problems. Consider the effects on the responses of a parent towards the self-injurious behavior of a child when the parent believes that the self-injurious behavior is a function of a brain disease, genetic disorder, or an undiagnosed nutritional deficit. Such a causal attribution could increase the likelihood of ineffective behavioral management strategies and serve to strengthen the child's self-injurious behavior. In such a case, the client's causal attribution would be considered a causal variable in a functional analysis.

Despite many limitations associated with self-reports of causality, questionnaires focusing on causal relations for behavior problems can be useful to the clinician for developing causal hypotheses. The causal attributions of different respondents, whether the client's or other informant's, can sometimes point to different causal relations across contexts. Consider how different causal attributions of a teacher and a parent about the behavior of a hyperactive child (e.g., "He does it to get attention" versus "He easily gets overexcited") indicates possible differences across settings in causal factors for the child's hyperactivity. As we also note in Box 10.1, the causal attribution of a person sometimes explains the behavior of that person in regard to the target behaviors.

## CAUSAL MARKERS

A *causal marker* (or *causal indicator*) is an indirect measure, usually derived from analog assessment, of the strength of a causal relation. Causal markers in clinical assessment are similar to many biomedical diagnostic markers, such as tests for antibodies associated with a virus. The antibodies (the marker variable) indicate the presence of the virus (the true causal variable of interest). Thus, causal markers measure a variable that is correlated with the dimensions of a causal variable or strength of a causal relation, but are not direct measures of the causal variable or relation of interest.

Causal markers are clinically useful when two conditions are met: (a) when the marker variable is highly correlated with the targeted causal variable or relation and (b) when it is easier to measure the marker variable than to measure the causal variable or relation that it indicates. In behavioral assessment, we focus on markers for psychosocial, behavioral, emotional, or cognitive causal variables and relations. For example, it could require months of daily monitoring to evaluate the true functional relations between naturally occurring psychosocial stressors and a client's migraine headaches, obsessive thoughts, sleep problems, or periodic binge drinking. The potential causal role of psychosocial stressors, however, could be indicated by the magnitude of the client's psychophysiological response to a brief psychosocial stressor presented in a clinic or laboratory. In this assessment strategy, the clinician would presume that the degree of response to the laboratory stressor is correlated with (i.e., serves as a marker for) the degree to which the client's behavior problems were triggered by naturally occurring stressors in his or her daily life.

In a sense, all analogue observation and in-clinic assessments exemplify a causal marker assessment strategy. That is, we assume that the way a couple talks to each other in a clinic analog observation session indicates (is a marker of) how the couple talks to each other at home. Similarly, we assume that if in a clinic setting a parent cannot deliver appropriate praise to a child when they are playing together or fails to follow up on instructions to a noncompliant child, the parent is likely to behave similarly at home.

Research conducted by Kohlenberg and colleagues (e.g., Kanter, Tsai, & Kohlenberg, 2010; Tsai, Kohlenberg, Kanter, Kohlenberg, Follette, & Callaghan, 2009) further illustrates the use of analogue observation as a causal marker. Kohlenberg's *Functional Analytic Psychotherapy* is a behavioral account of the therapist-client relationship. A core tenet of Functional Analytic Psychotherapy is that therapists can, and should, systematically manipulate contingencies in order to modify behavior during therapy sessions. Specifically, the therapist can provide reinforcement (typically social reinforcement) to increase adaptive and/or goal behaviors for the client and differential reinforcement of incompatible behavior and/or punishment (typically verbalizations indicating disagreement) to reduce maladaptive behavior or targeted behavior problems.

As an example, therapists employing Functional Analytic Psychotherapy are taught to conduct careful in-session observations of behaviors that are an example of the client's behavior problems in his or her daily living (e.g., negative, global, hopeless verbalizations by a depressed client; or irritating interpersonal behaviors emitted by a client who reports intimacy difficulties) and adaptive or goal-related behaviors (e.g., positive, specific, and hopeful verbalizations by the depressed client; positive interpersonal behaviors emitted by the client who has intimacy difficulties). The former class of behaviors is called "Clinically Relevant Behaviors–1" and the latter class of behaviors is called "Clinically Relevant Behaviors–2." Therapists are trained to consistently and systematically reinforce within-session examples of Clinically Relevant Behaviors–2 (this is an example of differential reinforcement of incompatible behavior and takes the form of therapist agreement, encouragement, supportive statements, etc.) and avoid reinforcing (e.g., through therapist silence) or punishing (in the form of therapist changing the topic, disagreeing, discouraging, correcting, etc.) Clinically Relevant Behaviors–1.

Kohlenberg's work provides a learning-based theoretical framework for components of the therapist-client relationship. Particularly relevant to the current topic, Kohlenberg's research has demonstrated that client behaviors can be systematically modified by therapist contingencies during the therapy session and that these in-session changes are associated with client's behavior change in the natural environment. Thus, these in-session analogue observations can be thought of as markers of "real world" behavior and behavior-consequence relationships.

Perhaps the most common form of causal marker in clinical assessment is the client's verbal reports of causal relations. A clinician can ask a client to indicate his beliefs about causal variables or to report whether a particular causal variable is associated with a behavior problem, as we discussed in Chapter 8. For example, a clinician may ask a client with migraine headaches the degree to which headache onset follows exposure to significant life stressors. In this instance, the client's report of the strength of a causal relationship is interpreted as a marker of a "true" causal relationship that exists in other settings, times, and conditions. As noted earlier, these interview-based marker variables can be useful in clinical assessment but are susceptible to a host of biases and cognitive processing errors (e.g., when events that are consistent with beliefs or expectations are encoded and recalled more efficiently than events that are inconsistent with beliefs and expectations), memory (e.g., recent events and salient events are recalled more consistently than remote and less salient events), and motivations (e.g., a client may not wish to provide information about certain causal variables that he or she may hope to avoid modifying, such as alcohol use).

In order to enhance the validity of a client's self-reports of causation, the clinician can systematically inquire about the key elements of causal inference by envisioning a 2 × 2 table as shown (see Table 10.1) and asking a series of questions that would provide information relevant to each cell. It is particularly important to inquire about Cells B, C, and D because there is a pernicious tendency for clinicians to focus only on Cell A. This tendency to attend to, and inquire about, Cell A has been labeled "confirmation bias" (Nickerson, 1998) and forms the basis for another commonly observed causal inference error known as the "illusory correlation" in which the clinician believes there is a causal relationship between two variables despite evidence against it (Chapman & Chapman, 1969; O'Brien, 1995).

Imagine, for example, a client reports that headaches occur 90% of the time on high stress days (Cell A). If no other information were gathered, the clinician would form an illusory correlation and believe that stress is very strongly associated with headache occurrence. However, suppose the client is asked about Cell B and reports that headaches also occur 90% of the time on nonstressful days. With this additional information, the clinician would learn that stress is not associated with headache occurrence, because the causal variable must be associated with a differential probability, or other dimension, of the behavior problem (of course, we are assuming in this example that moderator variables are not affecting the observed functional relations).

As we discussed in Chapter 9, causal markers are commonly used in psychophysiological laboratory assessment. We often assume that the degree of a person's psychophysiological responses (e.g., heart rate and salivary cortisol) to selected stimuli (e.g., stimuli associated with sexual assault, auto accidents, social rejection, or failure on a task) in the laboratory is strongly correlated with how the person responds to similar stimuli when they occur in his daily life.

Causal markers can be difficult to identify and validate. To be clinically useful, a causal marker must be correlated strongly with the magnitude

**Table 10.1 A 2 × 2 Matrix for Identifying Causal Relations in a Clinical Interview**

| | Hypothesized Causal Variable Present | Hypothesized Causal Variable Absent |
|---|---|---|
| Target Behavior Present | Cell A<br>Evidence Supporting Causation (Necessary Condition)<br>Example: "How frequently do headaches occur on high stress days?" | Cell B<br>Evidence Against Causation<br>Example: "How frequently do headaches occur on nonstressful days?" |
| Target Behavior Absent | Cell C<br>Evidence Against Causation<br>Example: "How frequently are you headache-free on stressful days?" | Cell D<br>Evidence Supporting Causation (Sufficient Condition)<br>Example: "How frequently are you headache-free on nonstressful days?" |

of a causal relation across many persons or across many measurements for one person. For Behavior Problem A (e.g., a client's panic episodes), Variable B (e.g., heart rate reactivity to $CO_2$ inhalation challenge in a laboratory) could be a clinically useful causal marker for Causal Variable C (excessive sympathetic nervous system drive and reactivity in the client's natural environment), but only if B was correlated strongly with the magnitude of correlation between A and C.

The predictive validity of the causal marker must be substantial if it is to be clinically useful. For example, a causal marker that correlates .7 with the strength of a causal relation in the natural environment still would not account for a majority of the variance in that causal relation. In this case, that marker could indicate a weak or moderate causal relation in behavioral assessment with a client when a strong one was truly operating, or vice versa.

To be useful in behavioral assessment, causal markers must also be easily measurable. Causal markers that are difficult or costly to measure would have limited clinical utility in preintervention behavioral assessment.

As with all causal relations, the validity and utility of causal markers can be conditional. That is, a causal marker can strongly correlate with naturally occurring causal relations for some persons, within some contexts, and at some times.

# EXPERIMENTAL MANIPULATION

Perhaps the most powerful method of testing causal hypotheses is by systematically varying the hypothesized causal variable and measuring its effects on the targeted behavior. An experimental manipulation can occur within one assessment session or across several sessions. Manipulation strategies are often used in applied behavior analysis to examine the effects of changing the immediate contingencies for a client's responses.[1] Kazdin (2002) and Shadish, Cook, and Campbell (2002) have discussed several types of experimental manipulations (e.g., A-B-A'-B' and multiple baseline designs) that can be used to evaluate functional relations. Experimental manipulations sometimes take the form of an experimental functional analysis. In this particular application, the aim is to identify contemporaneous functional relations for behavioral problems that are then systematically manipulated in a subsequent treatment program (see Hanley, Iwata, & McCord, 2003, for a thorough review of the experimental functional analysis literature).

A study by Christensen and her colleagues (2007) illustrates the use of experimental manipulation to evaluate the effectiveness of an intervention. The authors examined the outcome of an intervention designed to increase prosocial classroom behaviors in a socially withdrawn child with a learning disability. The school's behavior specialist collected data on the frequency and quality of the child's classroom social interactions. Based on this assessment information, Christensen et al. selected "increased prosocial classroom behaviors" as the primary intervention goal through the use of skill development, self-management with reinforcers, and peer mediation. They subsequently employed an ABA'B' single-subject withdrawal design to evaluate the changes in behavior as a function of intervention.

The first baseline period (A phase) measured the client's prosocial classroom behaviors prior to implementing the intervention. The first intervention period (B phase) lasted for 7 consecutive school days. The

---

[1] The systematic manipulation of hypothesized causal factors to evaluate their effects on selected behaviors is called *single subject* (or *case*) *designs* (or *research*), or *interrupted time-series designs*. When used to identify functional relations that then guide interventions with a client, it is called *experimental functional analysis* (see overview of interrupted time-series designs in Kazdin, 2002).

intervention was then withdrawn for 4 consecutive school days (A' phase). Finally, the intervention was reintroduced (B' phase) and prosocial behavior was measured for an additional 20 days. Briefly, Christensen et al. found that the client exhibited prosocial behavior an average of 48% during the first A phase, but that it increased to an average of 94% during the first B phase. When the intervention was withdrawn (A' phase), the child's prosocial classroom behaviors dropped to 67% and then increased to as high as 97% after reintroducing the intervention (B' phase).

The study by Christensen and her colleagues illustrates the importance of assessment data in formulating causal hypotheses, the functional analysis, and the subsequent design of an intervention. Their study also illustrates some of the key components of experimental functional analysis: The systematic manipulation of an independent variable (e.g., an intervention) while simultaneously examining changes in a dependent variable (e.g., child's prosocial classroom behaviors) over time.

A study by Northrup et al. (1991) also illustrates the use of experimental functional analysis to identify possible causal relations. The authors investigated the degree to which social contingencies maintained the aggressive behaviors (such as scratching, kicking, and hitting others) of three persons with developmental disabilities. After a display of an aggressive behavior by one of the three individuals, the authors systematically presented and withdrew different consequences, such as social attention, escape from the social situations, and tangible rewards. Confirming a basic tenet of the behavioral assessment paradigm, Northrup et al. found individual differences in causal relations in that the aggressive behaviors of each person were most strongly affected by different consequences. They then developed an intervention in which the identified consequence was provided to the child contingent on the performance of nonaggressive alternative behaviors.

If properly done, causal analysis through experimental functional analysis is a powerful clinical assessment strategy because it addresses most conditions for inferring a causal relation discussed in Chapter 5: (a) covariance between two variables is demonstrated, (b) change in the manipulated variable precedes change in the dependent variable, (c) the hypothesized causal relation is logical, and (d) replication of the manipulation effect for a person can reduce the chance of alternative explanations for the covariation (i.e., replication across contexts for a person increases the internal validity of the assessment).

There are limitations associated with experimental manipulation as a clinical assessment strategy, some of which we discussed in Chapter 9. First, systematic manipulation can be time consuming, intrusive, and less acceptable than other assessment strategies to some staff members, therapists, teachers, parents, and clients. Second, manipulation designs are cumbersome and difficult to use for more than one or two hypothesized functional relations at a time. Third, the setting generalizability (i.e., *external* or *ecological validity*) of the functional relations identified in a clinic setting or in a restricted natural environment can be a concern. A strong functional relation identified in the clinical assessment setting may not be a marker for functional relations operating in the person's natural environment. The highly controlled environment associated with manipulation, because it often minimizes other potential sources of influence, can suggest that the hypothesized causal variable is more powerful than it is in the person's natural environment. Fourth, many causal variables (such as physiological variables, severe environmental stressors, and rarely occurring natural events) are not amenable to systematic manipulation during

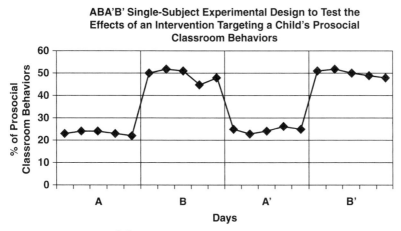

**Figure 10.1**  An ABA′B′ interrupted time-series design that illustrates the effect of systematically manipulating an intervention (such as attention or time-out contingent on a response). When these results are used to guide subsequent interventions, this process is called "experimental functional analysis."

*Source: From Kaholokula et al., 2009.*

clinical assessment. Fifth, because effects are often powerful, experimental functional analyses can mislead the clinician regarding the mechanism of causal action. For example, demonstrating that a token economy system can reduce aggressive behavior in the classroom does not provide insight into causal factors that provoke or maintain aggressive behavior (e.g., it is highly unlikely that "lack of tokens" is an important cause of aggression).

---

**Box 10.2 Manipulation Designs, Causal Mechanisms, and Alternative Explanations: Evidence that "Bad Air" Causes Cholera\***

In the Middle Ages, until the middle of the 1800s, the *miasmatic theory of disease* was a commonly accepted causal model for epidemics such as cholera (Black Death), typhus, or malaria, which were causing millions of deaths in Europe. For some diseases, such as cholera, the illness was assumed to be due to *miasma*, a poisonous vapor filled with particles from decomposed matter.

"Miasmata" was assumed to be identifiable by its nasty, foul smell (which probably emanated from decomposed organic material) and was particularly prevalent around major rivers and stagnant water in London and Paris (two centers of cholera outbreaks). This assumption led to sanitation improvements in major cities and hospitals, which led to a decrease in the severity and duration of the epidemics. Florence Nightingale (1820–1910) was also a proponent of the miasmatic theory and gained fame for her work to sanitize hospitals in order to reduce miasmata (which led to a decrease in hospital-borne diseases).

So, we have an excellent context for ABA′B′ intervention (or a *multiple baseline design* in which some urban areas, followed sequentially and systematically by others, would institute sanitation programs) to test the putative causal variable: miasmata. The outcomes of these real world experimental functional analyses would seem to provide a powerful test of the miasma causal model of disease. The sequence of manipulations and their expected outcomes:

A = No sanitation of rivers and water sources → severe epidemics

B = Improved sanitation of rivers and water sources → significant decrease in epidemics

A′ = No sanitation → significant increase in severe epidemics

B′ = Improved sanitation → significant decrease in epidemics

What is missing, of course, is an examination of the possible causal mechanisms and alternative explanations (see also Box 5.1 on Bubonic Plague). Is a demonstration of a reliable functional relation within an experimental functional analysis sufficient for causal inferences? In many cases, the answer would be "yes." However, a thoughtful behavioral scientist would wonder about the causal mechanism and ask, "*Why* would sanitation efforts result in a reduction in epidemics?" "What is the causal mechanism for the observed functional relation?" "Are there alternative explanations to the miasmatic theory of disease for the observed effects?" It was not until the mid and late 1800s that the role of the cholera bacterium, most often found in contaminated water, was identified as the cause of cholera.

In one sense, and consistent with the arguments of some behavior analysts, the functional relation observed in the manipulation design is clinically useful because it would lead to increased sanitation efforts and decreased disease rates. However, neglecting the "explanation" aspect of causal modeling limits the ability to develop interventions for persons already infected or to intervene to reduce cholera when sanitation problems cannot be easily remedied (e.g., refugee camps and limited clean water supplies following natural disasters) or to strengthen the effects of an intervention.

*This discussion of miasma is based on information from several Wikipedia sites.

Despite these limitations, experimental functional analysis is a powerful and underused clinical assessment strategy. It is a particularly useful strategy for testing causal hypotheses derived from other assessment strategies, such as functional interviews and questionnaires. Experimental functional analysis is particularly underused in validating causal hypotheses in adult outpatient and psychiatric inpatient settings. Given the clinical importance of functional analysis, systematic manipulation is warranted in many clinical assessment cases. Examples of potential uses of experimental functional analysis in clinical assessment include: (a) exposing couples or psychiatric inpatients to carefully controlled social interaction situations in a role-playing format to identify the social stimuli and contexts associated with communication skills and deficits, problematic social perceptions, and emotional responses; (b) exposing clients experiencing anxiety, obsessive-compulsive, and panic problems to a variety of potentially fear-arousing stimuli while measuring subjective and physiological responses; and (c) exposing sex-offender populations to sexual and social interaction situations (by role playing and video presentation) while measuring sexual arousal, overt behavioral, and subjective responses.

## Multivariate Time-Series Measurement Strategies

Although experimental manipulations can be powerful strategies for identifying functional relations, many types of functional relations cannot be conveniently evaluated through systematic manipulation. Causal variables, such as naturally occurring life stressors, negative self-statements, health challenges, family conflict, physiological and emotional states, and social support, can be difficult to manipulate in analog assessment and systematic manipulation could be potentially harmful to clients. Further, the effects of these variables are often delayed, can be prolonged (producing carry-over effects), and sometimes cannot easily be reversed, such as decreasing social support, reinitiating health problems, or reversing positive communication skills.

However, it is important to evaluate these potentially important functional relations in clinical assessment. In such situations, *multivariate time-series regression strategies* can be helpful. This assessment strategy involves the measurement of multiple hypothesized causal and dependent variables across time without manipulation. The assessment goal is to examine time-lagged and concurrent functional relations among hypothesized causal variables and a client's behavior problems.

This assessment strategy was illustrated in a multivariate time-series regression study by Thatcher and Haynes (2001), in which multiple measures were obtained across 60 days from clients with rheumatoid arthritis. The goal of the study was to identify factors associated with "flares" (i.e., an increase above the client's baseline levels in joint pain, joint stiffness, swelling, and fatigue).

Although time-series measurement is usually implemented in the natural environment across many days, it can also be implemented within one assessment session. A within-session time-series assessment strategy is possible when targeted responses occur very frequently or demonstrate considerable variability in magnitude or frequency within an assessment session. Examples of such highly variable responses include some self-injurious or aggressive behaviors of children with developmental disabilities, psychophysiological responses of clients with anxiety and psychophysiological disorders, attention deficits of children in classrooms, and conflictual interactions of married couples in an enactment communication analog behavioral assessment.

There are three interrelated statistical methods of estimating functional relations from time-series data: (a) time-series analysis, (b) conditional probability analysis, and (c) Markov chain analysis.

*Time-series analysis* (Gottman, 1995), as we note in Chapter 9, is a set of data analytic strategies that can assist in identifying functional relations from time-series data. In conjunction with multiple regression analysis, it can help estimate the degree of covariation between variables and the degree of autocorrelation within a variable set while the temporal relation between those variables is specified. Time-series analysis can also help evaluate the role of mediating variables in functional relations, after controlling for variance in the data attributable to autocorrelation.

*Conditional probability analyses* can be used to estimate the probability of occurrence of a behavior problem, given the occurrence of a hypothesized causal variable, as we discussed in Chapter 9 (see Figure 9.2). A significantly elevated conditional probability (the probability that Behavior Problem A will occur given the occurrence of Event B, in comparison with the unconditional probability of the behavioral problem (the overall probability that A will occur), is a necessary but insufficient requirement for a causal relation. The benefits of conditional probability analysis are that it can be simple to apply mathematically, has face validity, and is useful with the types of data often collected in clinical assessment (see Table 10.1). Plus, it can be used to evaluate the causal role of antecedent stimuli, contexts, and consequent events.

*Markov chain analysis models* provide a variety of flexible and useful mathematical techniques for characterizing the probabilities of a behavior when it is presumed that previous states have no effects on future states of a behavior. Markov models are most useful when behavior exhibits stationarity (i.e., a stable and repetitive pattern), measurement processes are consistent across time, and behavior varies in terms of order (the number of events in a sequence required to predict the next event). For instance, a first-order Markov chain requires knowledge of only the immediately preceding event to optimally predict the subsequent event, whereas a second-order chain requires knowledge of two preceding events.

These methods of analyzing multivariate time-series data can be challenging in most clinical assessment contexts. However, *qualitative time-series assessment* can also be helpful in identifying potential functional relations. This process sometimes is referred to as "descriptive procedures" in behavior analysis. Observers monitor the occurrence of specified target behaviors (e.g., "time-on-task" or aggressive behaviors in a classroom) and the events that occur immediately before and following them, and look for obvious patterns in an attempt to identify important sequences. This procedure can be used to examine a large number of potential functional variables, but it is prone to many obvious sources of recording and judgment errors noted in previous sections of this chapter. Nevertheless, qualitative observation analysis of clients can be a rich source of hypotheses about causal relations.

Although the utility of time-series measurement methods in preintervention clinical assessment is hampered by the amount of data that must be acquired for estimating functional relations and the limited number of variables that can reasonably be measured at one time, it is an underused strategy. Further, new data recording technology, such as electronic diaries, can make it much easier to evaluate functional relations.

# SUMMARY OF RECOMMENDATIONS FOR APPLICATIONS OF BEHAVIORAL ASSESSMENT IN THE FUNCTIONAL ANALYSIS

We conclude this and the previous two chapters with a summary of recommendations for the application of behavioral assessment methods and strategies. Additional recommendations for applying behavioral assessment strategies in clinical research and in treatment research specifically can be found in Haynes et al. (2007, 2008). The recommendations listed below are intended to increase the validity and clinical utility of the functional analysis and other clinical judgments by encouraging a science-based, "best practice" approach to clinical assessment.

Recall that the focus and strategies of behavioral assessment are influenced by the tenets of the behavioral assessment paradigm and the elements of the functional analysis outlined in earlier chapters of this book. Both functional analysis and behavioral assessment strongly advocate (a) the identification and specification of the dimensions, response modes, and functional relations of a client's behavior problems and (b) the identification and specification of causal variables and their relations relevant to a client's behavior problems. These are complex and challenging goals in clinical assessment and, thus, we recommend the following twenty principles and strategies of behavioral assessment.

## Clinician Characteristics

1. *Attend to your relationship with the client.* Maintain a positive, supportive, empathic, sensitive, active-listening, and constructive relationship with the client and others during the assessment process.
2. *Obtain informed consent* from clients or responsible other persons for the assessment process. They should understand the methods, purpose, time required, costs, and benefits of the assessment. Informed consent extends to all persons who may participate in the assessment process.
3. *Seek consultation with, or referral to, other professionals* when issues confronted in the assessment process extend beyond your competence.

4. *Maintain a scholarly, empirically guided orientation* in your assessment: Know the research literature on the behavior problems, causal variables, assessment methods and instruments, and potential interventions with which you are dealing. Bring a strong clinical science approach to clinical assessment; remember that you are also a behavioral scientist.

5. *Be careful about your biases and preconceived concepts* about clients, their behavior problems and causal variables. Be open to new information and functional relations, expose your ideas to the possibility of disconfirmation, and understand how your biases could affect your clinical judgments.

6. *Be sensitive to cultural differences across clients* in the expression of behavior problems, their intervention goals, the most effective client-clinician interactions, and potential causal relations. Cultural differences can involve ethnic background, religion, sexual orientation, economic status, sex, age, and physical and mental disabilities and challenges.

7. *Include a positive, constructive approach to assessment.* In addition to identifying behavior problems and their causes, attend to the client's goals, positive values, and strengths.

## Strategies of Assessment

8. *Use multiple assessment methods, instruments, and informants* when they can increase the validity of the clinical assessment data acquired. Do not base the functional analysis or other clinical judgment solely on the basis of self-report data.

9. *Continue to measure* important immediate, intermediate, and ultimate causal and outcome variables throughout the assessment and intervention process.

10. *Observe behaviors and events of interest* to supplement data obtained from self-reports.

11. *Select measures that have been shown to be valid* for the persons, problems, and goals of the assessment. Be sensitive to *limits of validity* associated with the many sources of individual differences and assessment contexts.

12. *Collect precise measures*, those that are specific and valid. Aggregated measures (e.g., personality test scores and trait-based measures) can be used sparingly, but should be supplemented with more precise measures.

13. *Collect measures that are sensitive to change.* Measures should quickly and precisely reflect true changes in the selected behaviors, events, and functional relations.

14. *Assume a hypothesis-testing* approach to assessment. Data from clinical assessment can suggest behavior problems, treatment goals, and causal relations; evaluate hypotheses with additional assessment—search for data that refutes your hypotheses.

15. *Be guided, but not limited, by diagnosis and data on a client's "traits."* Remember that a diagnosis and personality profiles can be useful for describing a possible array of behavior problems, but they are often imprecise, insensitive to individual differences between persons with the same diagnosis or personality trait profile, and may omit important aspects of a behavior problem.

16. *Emphasize the assessment of functional relations* among events and behaviors. Go beyond the mere description of problems and, especially, beyond mere diagnosis.

17. *Be especially sensitive to possible contiguous and proximal causal variables* that can be affecting your client's problems and intervention goals. Be sensitive to, but not distracted by, the importance of past events as causal variables.

18. *Consider possible systems factors* that may be affecting a client and important persons in the client's life.

19. *Examine client behaviors across multiple settings and contexts.*

20. Combine idiographic with nomothetic assessment strategies.

# 11

# Twenty-Two Steps in Preintervention Behavioral Assessment and the Development of a Functional Analysis

## INTRODUCTION

In previous chapters we introduced the basic goals and conceptual foundations of behavioral assessment and the functional analysis. We discussed how behavioral assessment and the functional analysis are designed to help the clinician make intervention decisions by identifying important, modifiable causal variables and causal relations relevant to a client's behavior problems, and how they guide the clinician's strategies for evaluating the effects of intervention. We also stressed the idiographic, multivariate, multi-attribute, conditional, and dynamic nature of behavior problems and causal relations and the importance of a science-based approach to assessment and clinical case formulation.

In Chapter 3 we introduced the Functional Analytic Clinical Case Diagram (FACCD) as a means of visually organizing and efficiently communicating the functional analysis. We first introduced the

FACCD in Chapter 2 with the case of Mrs. Sanchez, as illustrated by Figure 2.1. We also provided many more FACCD examples in Chapter 3. In Chapters 4 through 7, we presented additional examples to further illustrate the science-based assessment strategies that are the foundation of behavioral assessment and contribute to the functional analysis.

We now consider the preintervention clinical judgment process that leads to a functional analysis and guides decisions about subsequent assessment strategies. How does the clinician begin the assessment process and go about constructing a functional analysis to guide intervention decisions? This chapter presents the steps in the initial behavioral assessment process and in integrating multiple judgments into a functional analysis, using the FACCD elements presented in Chapter 3. First, we emphasize several principles pertinent to all steps in the development of a functional analysis, as follows.

- There are many potential judgment errors in clinical assessment and in the construction of a functional analysis. Thus, the clinician should be particularly sensitive to his or her biases, avoid making clinical judgments prior to gathering sufficient data, and use the best science-based assessment strategies.

- As we discuss throughout the book, the validity of all clinical judgments depends on the validity of clinical assessment data upon which they are based. Clinical judgment errors can be minimized with the use of multimethod and multisource assessment strategies to provide measures that are valid, clinically useful, and sensitive to change.

- Although we present the construction of a functional analysis as a step-by-step procedure, in practice, the steps are actually overlapping and iterative. Data pertinent to each of the steps is acquired throughout the assessment process and, at times, the clinician will need to return to an earlier step in order to revise the functional analysis.

# STEP 1: OBTAIN INFORMED CONSENT AND PROMOTE A POSITIVE CLIENT-CLINICIAN RELATIONSHIP

## Obtain Informed Consent

*Informed consent* is a guiding principle of service delivery in all helping professions. In this chapter, we emphasize the ethical aspects of informed consent and its role in the development of the functional analysis. However, there are also legal aspects to informed consent that vary across states and countries. A clinician should, therefore, be knowledgeable of the legal requirements of informed consent that are unique to his or her profession and location.

Informed consent is consistent with the collaborative nature of the behavior assessment process. It also emphasizes the overarching behavioral assessment principle of creating contexts that support client self-determination, client rights, and individual differences. An essential aspect of informed consent involves developing assurances that the client and others have a clear understanding of, and agree to, the goals of the behavioral assessment. Additionally, the client should be informed about the relative costs and benefits of the assessment. Finally, the clinician should create conditions wherein the client is allowed to express concerns and freely choose to participate, or not, in the assessment.

In addition to assuring that the client is informed of the goals, costs, and benefits of assessment, the clinician should provide information about the specific assessment methods that will be used. The consent process should also articulate what other sources of information (e.g., medical records or school records) may be obtained in order to complete the assessment. Finally, the client should be able to determine who will have access to assessment information.

In some cases, because of significant cognitive impairment or limited judgment (e.g., a client's very young age, severe mental illness, intoxication, brain injury, or dementia), the client may not have adequate reasoning and judgment abilities to provide informed consent. In these cases, informed consent should be obtained from a legal guardian who serves the interest of the client.

The principle of informed consent extends to all participants in the assessment process. This includes teachers in classrooms where observations will occur, spouses participating in analog communication assessments, psychologists being interviewed about their referred clients, and nursing staff and administrators in hospitals who will participate in the assessment. For example, if the clinician is conducting observations in a classroom, informed consent should be acquired from the parents, the director of the school, and from the teacher and teacher's aids in the classroom.

## Maintain a Positive, Respectful, and Collaborative Relationship With Everyone Involved in the Assessment Process

The relationship between the clinician and client is an essential aspect of behavioral assessment. Without a positive, collaborative relationship, the assessment process and the amount and validity of information acquired will be adversely affected. Consider the harmful effects on the assessment process and the validity of the functional analysis if the client mistrusts the clinician or believes that the clinician is not empathic, caring, or sensitive to his or her needs.

A positive clinician-client relationship requires that the clinician: (a) be sensitive to, and accepting of, the client on dimensions of individual differences, such as ethnicity, age, sex, sexual orientation, religion, physical and cognitive limitations, and how those differences might affect the methods and outcome of the assessment (Tanaka-Matsumi, 2004); (b) establish and maintain a supportive and collaborative relationship with the client throughout the assessment process, and (c) respect the rights and autonomy of the client, as discussed earlier.

A useful strategy for ensuring a positive relationship is to combine humanistic, person-centered (i.e., Rogerian) interaction styles within a behavioral assessment context. We discuss this in greater detail in Box 1.1 and in Chapter 8, but we note here that empathic statements, reflections of client's expressions, open-ended queries, and statements of acceptance by the clinician can promote client satisfaction with the assessment process *and* enhance the validity of collected data. Further, these relationship-strengthening strategies are compatible with the functional analytic context of specifying behavior problems, treatment goals, and causal relations.

## STEP 2: EVALUATE THE NEED FOR REFERRAL AND THE SAFETY OF THE CLIENT

### Evaluate the Need for Referral or for Additional Assessment

Hays (2008) describes culturally responsive assessment that illustrates how information gained from the initial assessment can suggest the need for referral to other professionals for supplementary assessments. In an example provided by Hays, the initial interview indicated that an older member of the family could be experiencing cognitive impairments that were a result of a recent cerebral vascular accident. Based on this information, the clinician recommended a magnetic resonance imaging of the brain and neuropsychological assessment. Data from these assessments, along with data from the behavioral assessment, helped specify the nature of the client's cognitive impairments and guided subsequent assessment and intervention strategies.

When should a clinician request outside consultation? Our recommendation is that a clinician should seek input from other professionals when a client's behavior problems or possible causal factors lay outside the clinician's domain of competence. Depending on the training and experience of the clinician, input from other professionals could be appropriate when potential problems or causal variables include the following aspects: cardiovascular, neuroendocrine, medication, ethnic and cross-cultural, central nervous system, chronic medical illness, peripheral nervous system, dementia and other cognitive impairments, sex abuse, and developmental disability variables.

The clinician must be a well-informed behavioral scientist to know when to make a referral. That is, the clinician must be familiar with current research that is relevant to the client's behavior problems. For example, in assessment with a client who is complaining of insomnia and daily fatigue, the clinician should be sensitive to the possible role of sleep apnea, endocrine imbalances, dietary factors, stimulus control factors associated with the sleeping environment, sleep schedule shifts, or medication side effects, in addition to the behavioral (e.g., poor sleep hygiene) and cognitive (e.g., excessive worries and rumination) factors often associated with insomnia (see overview in Savard & Morin, 2002).

## Evaluate Client Safety

Is your client safe? This is most often a concern in cases where domestic or other interpersonal violence, abuse of a family member, or self-harm is a concern. Safety procedures and reporting requirements vary across countries and sometimes between regions within a country.[1]

In cases where harm to the client is a concern, the client's safety is the first priority and must be addressed before a more focused behavioral assessment continues. For example, for a client who is reporting depressed affect, anxiety, panic, eating or sleeping difficulties where domestic violence is a reasonable concern, a safety evaluation should be the first priority. If necessary, the clinician should take immediate steps, in collaboration with the client, to insure safety. Such steps could include: (a) escape plans for the client in the case of possible violence (e.g., access to car keys, money, an emergency residence, and phone numbers); (b) establishing frequent contact between the client and others (to widen the client's sources of support and increase the likelihood that abuse can be detected); (c) identification of alternative housing in case the client needs to leave the home; (d) child care plans if a parent leaves the environment; (e) plans for immediate contact with police if harm is imminent; and (f) educating the client about legal options.

There are several methods available to evaluate the occurrence and risk of domestic violence, including timeline follow-back interviewing procedures (e.g., Fals-Stewart et al., 2003) and the Conflict Tactics Scale (Straus et al., 1996). As Snyder et al. (2008) discuss, and as shown in

---

[1] Most regions require the clinician to report instances where there is a substantial chance of harm (and in some cases HIV or other medical conditions would apply). Other regions permit, but do not require, disclosure to medical or law enforcement personnel of a client's intent to harm others. Most regions require immediate reporting if abuse or neglect of a child or elderly person is suspected.

Chapter 8, individual assessment sessions for marital couples are recommended to evaluate the risk of abuse or harm.

## STEP 3: IDENTIFY THE CLIENT'S BEHAVIOR PROBLEMS

After obtaining informed consent, determining the appropriateness of the referral, and insuring the safety of the client, the first step in the functional analytic assessment process is the identification of behavior problems and intervention goals. Referring back to Chapter 4 and our discussion of comorbidity, this early stage of assessment is strongly guided by the knowledge that many clients present with many interacting behavior problems and goals.

### Broadly Survey the Client's Problems and Goals

In this stage of assessment, a broadly focused survey is preferred because it is better able to detect the multiple problems that are presumed to be operating for a given client. Semistructured interviews and diagnostic interviews that permit flexible interviewing about a variety of problems are particularly helpful in identifying multiple problems. Additionally, broadly focused behavior problem checklists can be used to survey areas of concern that may be overlooked in the interviewing process (e.g., Sederer & Dickey, 1996).

Interviewing strategies that move from broadly focused to a more narrowly focused assessment are sometimes called *multiple gating*, or a *funnel approach to assessment*. Multiple gating is often used in structured diagnostic interviews. For example, after the clinician inquires about an array of problems, he or she then asks more detailed questions about problems that the client has identified as relevant to his or her reasons for referral. Keep in mind the overlap in steps; specific information is often obtained during the broad survey stage and additional areas of concern are frequently identified in later stages of specifically focused assessment. Remember also that these tactics are applicable to clients, parents, spouses, teachers, or other professionals (see Chapter 8 and Box 11.1).

## Box 11.1 Sample Interview Probes in the Initial "Survey" Stage of Assessment

"Can you tell me about some of the issues that brought you to the clinic today?"

"So, we have been talking a little about one of your goals in therapy—to be able to concentrate better on your writing. Do you also have some other goals that you would like to discuss?"

"We have been talking about various concerns you have, such as feeling depressed, anxious, and having concerns with your marriage. I know that some of your goals for therapy are to feel better in these areas. Are there some other goals that are important to you?"

### Sample Interview Probes for Greater Specificity After (and Sometimes During) the Initial Survey

"I understand that you want to better manage your diabetes. Could you tell me more about what you are doing now to manage it?"

"I can see how your child's behavior at school is very upsetting. Can you describe what they are like (or give me more examples)?"

"It might be helpful if you carefully walked me through the last time that you experienced a panic attack. Tell me about the situation, how you acted and felt, and what you were thinking"

"You said you would like to be more 'in touch with your feelings,' or be better at 'managing your emotions.' How would you be different if you achieved those goals?"

Note how the clinician's questions and probes illustrated in Box 11.1 have multiple functions. They are designed to: (a) reflect the clinician's understanding and acceptance of the client and maintain a positive clinician-client relationship, (b) summarize some of what has been discussed to seek clarification, validation, and refinement, (c) acquire more specific information about the client's problems and goals, and (d) probe for additional problems and goals.

Mumma (2001), in his Cognitive-Behavioral-Interpersonal Semi-Structured Assessment Interview, offers examples of statements that can be helpful at the initial stage of assessment. His queries focus particularly on cognitive causal variables associated with behavior problems, but are applicable across different classes of causal variables.

---

### Box 11.2 Keeping Track of Information from the Interview

It is important to keep track of information that arises during the interview. Several studies have shown that clinicians make errors, mostly errors of omission, when they attempt to recall the content of an assessment interview. There are several ways to keep track of assessment information, but most involve use of structured notes or some form of a "problem list." A generic form of a problem list might be as shown here.

Date:
Problems and Goals:
Client:

| Description | Importance | Frequency | Duration | Intensity |
|---|---|---|---|---|
|  |  |  |  |  |
|  |  |  |  |  |
|  |  |  |  |  |
|  |  |  |  |  |
|  |  |  |  |  |
|  |  |  |  |  |
|  |  |  |  |  |
|  |  |  |  |  |

Note that additional columns could be included if other information, such as history, previous treatments, etc., were to be included.

---

Problems that might be a focus of intervention can also be identified through self-report questionnaires and checklists. Examples of broadly focused checklists include the Areas of Change Checklist (Gottman, 1999) and the Spouse Observation Checklist (Birchler, Weiss, & Vincent,

1975) to identify problems and goals in marital treatment; the Child Behavior Checklist (e.g., Achenbach, 1991), and the Behavioral Assessment System for Children (Reynolds & Kamphaus, 1992).

Unstructured naturalistic observations or analog observation can also help identify behavior problems in some assessment contexts. For example, qualitative observation of a client's social interactions on a psychiatric unit, observation of couples' problem-solving discussions in a clinic setting, observation of a child in a classroom setting, and observation of social interaction with an adult client with social avoidance or anxiety problems can identify specific behavior problems relevant for a functional analysis. Often, the problems identified via observation supplement those identified in interviews because clients can be unaware of how they are affecting others or how others are affecting them. Observation can also be particularly helpful when the client is limited in his or her ability to use verbal report to convey critical assessment information (e.g., clients with cognitive impairments, memory impairments, impairments due to high levels of distress, or very young clients).

## Is a Functional Analysis Cost-Beneficial?

After the client's behavior problems have been identified and specified, the clinician must decide if additional assessment and case formulation is warranted. The question to address at this point is whether further detailed assessment is needed or whether sufficient information has been obtained to proceed to intervention design. Essentially, a cost-benefit analysis must be conducted. As we discussed in Chapter 3, the cost-benefits of a functional analysis (and any case formulation) are most favorable when: (a) clients have multiple behavior problems, (b) standard interventions for a client have failed, (c) multiple empirically-supported intervention strategies are available, and (d) the clinician must document intervention decisions to other professionals. A situation where a detailed functional analysis is less warranted is when the generation of a basic understanding of the behavior problems and causal variables indicates that a well-developed and empirically-supported protocol targeting the behavior problem are likely to be effective. The rest of this chapter presumes that the clinician has decided to develop a more detailed functional analysis.

## Develop a Functional Analysis and Construct the Functional Analytic Clinical Case Diagram

Recall that causal diagrams can be a useful language for presenting complex functional analyses. Figure 11.1 uses the FACCD causal model diagramming system introduced in Chapter 3 to present the outcome of an initial assessment with a 36-year-old client at an outpatient mental health center. The client had expressed concerns about her arm-cutting (multiple thin cuts with a razor blade, several times per month), frequent short depressive episodes (lasting 1 to 2 days and occurring one to two times per month), and binge drinking episodes (six to eight beers on most weekend nights).

## Challenges in Identifying Clients' Behavior Problems

It can be difficult to fully identify a client's behavior problems. Some clients cannot clearly articulate their problems, concerns, and goals, much less the functional relations among them. They may be experiencing distress, discomfort, and unhappiness but not have sufficient insight, verbal skills, or cognitive abilities to describe specific problems associated with vague, distressing emotional states. Their reports can be

```
┌─────────────┐
│  Frequent   │
│ Arm Cutting │
└─────────────┘

┌─────────────┐
│Frequent, Short│
│ Depressive  │
│  Episodes   │
└─────────────┘

┌─────────────┐
│    Binge    │
│  Drinking   │
│  Episodes   │
└─────────────┘
```

**Figure 11.1** FACCD in the Initial Problem Identification Step of a 36-year-old female client with multiple behavior problems.

imprecise, unreliable, and insufficiently specific for the requirements of a functional analysis.[2]

A further complication is that a client's concerns and goals can change over time. The clinician's ideas and hypotheses about the client can change as assessment and intervention progresses across sessions and, sometimes, they change within a session, as the clinician and client continue to discuss them. The goal of the clinician at this stage is to assist the client in identifying and describing his or her specific problems and goals *as they are presently occurring* so that functional relations can be identified and the best intervention can be selected.

## STEP 4: SPECIFY THE ATTRIBUTES AND RESPONSE MODES OF THE BEHAVIOR PROBLEMS

Once the client's behavior problems and positive intervention goals have been identified, the next step is to gather more specific information about their essential characteristics. What does the client mean by "feeling frustrated and tense all the time," "wanting to reduce aggression by her young child," "feeling depressed around my family," "feeling nervous and irritable," "being bothered by repetitive thoughts that I can't stop," "trouble sleeping," and wanting "a healthier marriage"? These are important but vaguely worded problems and goals that mean different things to different persons. The clinician should not assume that he or she understands what they mean to the client.

As a result of the assessment strategies used in earlier steps, the clinician will already have a preliminary understanding of the components of the problems and goals. However, this is the stage of assessment where it is important to more precisely define each of them. In essence, the goal is to produce an operational definition of each problem that adequately captures both the clinician and client's understanding and facilitates their measurement.

---

[2] Methods of interviewing to help specify problem areas and causal relations are discussed in Chapters 7 and 9 and in books by Haynes and O'Brien (2000), Haynes and Heiby (2004), and Hersen (2006a, 2006b).

The development of an operational definition involves specifica-tion of the behavior problem's *response modes*. In behavioral assessment, response modes are often partitioned into cognitive/verbal, emotional/physiological, and overt/motor categories. For example, if a client reports "depression," to what extent is he experiencing depressed mood, depres-sive thoughts, feelings of fatigue, a reduced level of physical activity, a lack of motivation, increased conflict with others, decreased enjoyment of previously valued activities, or some combination of these factors?

As we discussed in Chapter 4 (see Figure 4.1 for an example of dif-ferent levels of specificity for "depression"), the level of *specificity* is an important consideration in the operational definition of response modes because it affects the clinical utility of the functional analysis. As we noted in Chapter 5, different causal relations operate for different levels of speci-ficity and different modes of a client's behavior problem. It is difficult to identify a functional relation for nonspecific problems, such as "depres-sion" or "anxiety," because different causal relations may be associated with their different components. Which aspects or components are most important for the client? More specific definitions are necessary to design the best intervention for a client. The methods of interviewing to increase specification of behavior problems and positive intervention goals involve the strategies discussed in the previous section and in Chapter 8.

## STEP 5: SPECIFY THE DIMENSIONS OF THE BEHAVIOR PROBLEMS

As we pointed out in Chapter 4, the dimensions of behavior problems are an important component of the functional analysis because different dimensions of the client's behavior problem can be a result of different causal relations. Specifying dimensions of behavior problems involves articulating quantitative aspects of problems and goals—collecting data on the frequency, duration, or intensity (and sometimes cyclicity and latency to onset) of the client's behavior problems. Additionally, it is important to determine which dimensions are the most important for the case for-mulation. For example, for one client the frequency of uncontrollable worrisome thoughts could be the most pressing concern, whereas for another client the intensity and duration of worrisome thoughts could be of greatest importance.

To obtain information on the dimensions of a behavior problem during an interview, the clinician might ask:

"You have been describing how you think and feel during your panic episodes. About how many times a month do you experience those episodes?"

"How long do they last?"

"If you were to rate their severity on a four-point scale (1 being not disruptive at all to 4 being most disruptive), how severe would you rate them?"

With discrete problems, such as panic episodes, migraine headaches, seizures, and eating or drinking binges, timeline follow-back strategies can also be helpful (see discussion in Chapter 8).

Information on the dimensions of a client's behavior problems can also be obtained using observation, ambulatory biomonitoring, electronic diaries, and other forms of self-monitoring. For example, using naturalistic observation, the clinician can estimate the rate of positive social interactions among clients on a psychiatric unit or of children during recess at school. Self-monitoring, perhaps using electronic diaries, can be helpful in estimating the rate, duration, and/or severity of positive social interactions, anxiety, panic, eating, drinking, depressed mood, sleep problems, obsessive thoughts, and pain. Again, we discuss these behavioral assessment methods and strategies in Chapters 8 and 9.

In some cases, it is not necessary to differentiate among dimensions of behavior problems because they share common causal relations. For example, passing beyond a threshold of social stressors may trigger both the onset and affect the duration of a client's obsessive thoughts. Thus, onset and duration are both affected equally by the same causal variable. In other cases, different dimensions of a behavior problem may be associated with different causal factors. Returning to the prior example, it may be that passing beyond a threshold of stressors may affect the onset of obsessive thoughts and compulsive behaviors, whereas the duration of these behaviors is primarily influenced by the presence or absence of

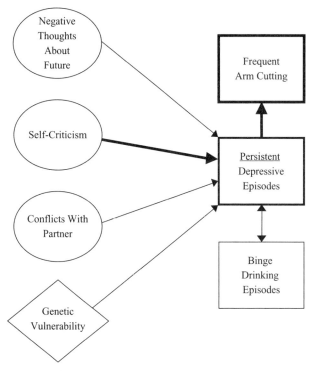

**Figure 11.2** FACCDs illustrating how causal relations for a client's behavior problems can differ across dimensions of the behavior problem. Figure 11.2 shows that the duration of the client's depressive episodes was most strongly affected by her self-criticism.

significant other persons. Consistent with this principle, observe that in Figures 11.2 and 11.3 the strength of causal relations for the depressive episodes of the client depends on whether duration or onset is being considered.

The estimate of which dimensions are most important for the behavior problems of a client will guide further assessment of the causal relations associated with each dimension (see also step 7 on "Importance" of behavior problems). For some clients, the frequency of a problem may be the most important dimension. A client may be experiencing frequent but short duration headaches, or binge eating episodes, or ruminative thoughts, or tantrums. Other clients may have less frequent but longer lasting or more severe dimensions of the same behavior problems.

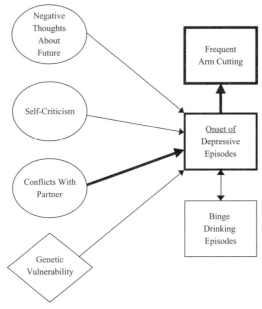

**Figure 11.3** The onset of the same client's depressive episodes was most strongly affected by her conflicts with her partner.

## Box 11.3 Adding Information to the Functional Analytic Clinical Case Diagram

In some cases, it is helpful to add more specific information about behavior problems, positive intervention goals, and causal variables to the Functional Analytic Clinical Case Diagram without rendering it excessively complicated. Additional specification, such as descriptions of behavior problems or descriptions of causal variables, can be done as an attachment and in some software programs as a drop-down menu when one clicks on a variable in the FACCD.

For example, on a separate page following a full FACCD, or at the bottom of an FACCD, the clinician could provide additional information on a variable in the FACCD, such as the examples shown here.

**Frequent Arm Cutting:** *4–5 light scratches with a razor blade, on the inside of arms, 2–3 times/month, for 3 years.*

**Conflicts With Partner:** *Escalating arguments about numerous topics in their relationship, characterized by name-calling, interruptions, disagreements, and anger, lasting for about 30 minutes, terminating in husband's withdrawal.*

## STEP 6: ESTIMATE THE RELATIVE IMPORTANCE OF THE CLIENT'S BEHAVIOR PROBLEMS

We have emphasized that one of the important goals of the functional analysis is to help the clinician estimate the relative degree to which an intervention focused on various causal variables will exert a positive influence on one or more of the client's behavior problems or the attainment of an intervention goal. A rating of the *relative importance* of a behavior problem or goal for the client contributes to this estimate. For example, the relative importance of depressive episodes, self-injury, and binge drinking differ for our client who is depicted in Figures 11.1 and 11.3.

The FACCD in Figure 11.4 illustrates differences in the importance of a client's behavior problems, with three levels based on line thickness of the problem boxes (see also Figure 2.2). These visual representations

Figure 11.4 An FACCD illustrating three levels of importance of a client's behavior problems.

can be also represented by numeric values in order to yield more precise calculations of magnitude of effect. For this client, arm cutting was rated as a more important concern to her than depressive episodes, which were more important than her drinking episodes.

"Importance" of a behavior problem or goal can be estimated in several ways. It is important to note that importance ratings are also conditional because they are based on considerations that vary across clients, behavior problems, and contexts. Several factors that can affect estimates of "importance" were outlined in Chapter 4, including: *(1) The rate and magnitude of a behavior problem, (2) The adverse or negative effects of the behavior problem, (3) The degree of influence on the client's personal distress, (4) The degree of functional impairment associated with a behavior problem, and (5) Behavior problems that interfere with therapy progress.* We reemphasize a few aspects of these here.

1. *The risk of physical harm to the client or others.* Many behavior problems are associated with a substantial risk of harm to the client or to others. Examples include self-injurious behaviors, medication nonadherence by persons with serious medical conditions, domestic violence, physical and psychological aggression, suicidal behavior, child abuse and neglect, and feeding problems of infants.

2. *Rate, severity, or duration of the behavior problem.* As illustrated by the FACCD depicted in Figure 11.4, the relative rate, severity, or duration of a client's behavior problems contribute to estimates of their relative importance. In this case, the client's depressive episodes and binge drinking were judged to be less important (based on her self-reported severity, frequency, and duration) than her self-cutting.

3. *Impact on quality of life.* Some behavior problems have a greater or wider-ranging impact on the client's quality of life than do others. For example, some problems such as severe mood swings, can affect marital relations, economic status, physical health, school and job functioning, and the welfare of the client's children.

4. *Subjective estimates of importance by the client or others.* All elements of the functional analysis and FACCD represent hypotheses by

the clinician, which are often influenced by the client's subjective reports. For example, the client with self-injurious behaviors depicted in Figure 11.4 reported that she was most distressed by her self-cutting, which affected the clinician's judgment about relative importance of the behavior problems. Her subjective estimate was probably based on her sense of the risk of harm, rate, severity, and duration of the three behavior problems, values she placed on the behaviors, and her view of their impact on her quality of life.

One challenge that can arise is when there is a disagreement between the client and clinician about which problems are the most important. For example, suppose that the client's self-injurious behaviors were quite serious, but the client preferred to focus on her mild binge-drinking episodes. Differences between the client and clinician in ratings of problem importance are not uncommon. In such cases of disagreement, the clinician must remain sensitive to the right for client self-determination and the principle of informed consent. Effective intervention requires the client's acceptance and cooperation. If there is disagreement about the importance of intervention targets, the client is less apt to adhere to the clinician's recommendations.

In case of disagreement, the clinician can educate the client about the relative importance of behavior problems, or develop an intervention-focus agreement that addresses the evaluations of both the clinician and client (e.g., "What if we spend four sessions on cutting and then focus on binge drinking?"). As we have discussed, the functional analysis is only one of many factors that affect intervention decisions and, ultimately, clients have an important role in deciding on intervention foci and methods.

5. *Behaviors that impede intervention.* During assessment and intervention, clients often emit problem behaviors and behave in ways that impede or obstruct intervention. As emphasized in Acceptance and Commitment Therapy (see also Hayes, Strosahl, & Wilson, 1999), Functional Analytic Psychotherapy (Kohlenberg & Tsai, 2007), and Dialectical Behavior Therapy

(see also Dimeff & Koerner, 2007), behaviors such as active avoidance of anxiety-arousing situations or thoughts, the client's very low self-efficacy on his or her ability to change, frequent negative self-statements, dissimulation, nonsuicidal self-injury as a way of affecting the therapist and others, verbally aggressive and challenging behaviors toward the therapist, and passive responses to life events can severely limit progress when emitted during the assessment and therapy process. These dysfunctional behavior patterns are important because they must be addressed prior to, or concurrent with, the focus on other problems. Often, they are the same behaviors that cause difficulties in the daily lives of clients.

## STEP 7: IDENTIFY THE EFFECTS OF BEHAVIOR PROBLEMS

As we indicated in step 6, behavior problems are often associated with significant negative effects or sequelae. These sequelae influence the benefits that the client receives from effective intervention of the associated upstream problems. For example, if we can reduce the intensity, frequency, and duration of a client's manic episodes, we might also improve his financial status, work or school performance, and family relationships.

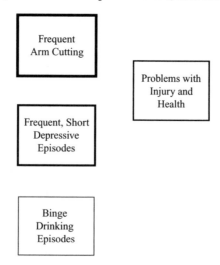

**Figure 11.5** An FACCD illustrating one effect of a client's behavior problems.

All of these effects contribute to our estimate of the relative magnitude of effect of intervention with particular causal variables identified in the functional analysis.

The FACCD depicted in Figure 11.5 illustrates the effects of behavior problems, using the same indicators for importance (box line thickness) with three levels of importance of the problem boxes (see also Figure 3.5).

## STEP 8: IDENTIFY THE FORMS OF FUNCTIONAL RELATIONS AMONG BEHAVIOR PROBLEMS

As we discussed in Chapter 4, a client's multiple behavior problems can have no functional interrelation, they can be only correlated (have no causal relation), or they can have a unidirectional or bidirectional, and nonlinear causal relation. The impact of these functional relations on the estimated magnitude of effect for intervention foci is illustrated in Figure 11.6. In this example, the client's arm cutting and binge drinking were affected by her depressive episodes. That is, there was an increased likelihood that she would cut herself or drink alcohol when she was depressed compared to periods when she was not depressed—her depressed state served as a causal factor for both.

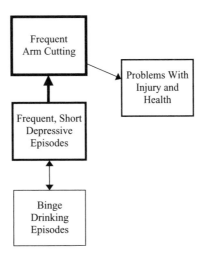

**Figure 11.6** Illustrating the form of causal relations (unidirectional and bidirectional in this case) as well as the relative strengths of causal relations.

Note that the *causal mechanism* for this relation is not shown, so we do not know "why" depressed mood increased the chance of self-cutting. Knowing the mechanism of action could reveal additional avenues for intervention. Note also in Figure 11.6 the *bidirectional causal relation* between depressed states and binge drinking. This suggests that the client was more likely to drink alcohol during her depressed states and, conversely, her use of alcohol increased the likelihood and severity of her depressed states.

There are important implications of the FACCD for an intervention focus with this client. This functional analysis suggests that an intervention that successfully reduced her depressive episodes, or served to moderate the magnitude of effect of her depressive episodes, would also result in a decrease in her arm cutting (and its associated injury and health problems) and binge drinking episodes.[3]

As we point out in a subsequent section (see step 17), the *mechanism of causal action* or *mediating variables* must often be determined in order to select the most effective approach to moderating a causal relation among variables. The clinician must understand "why" depressed states lead to self-cutting in order to weaken the causal link. For example, cutting could serve to distract her from aversive emotional states that arise from negative thoughts and imagery. In this case, cutting would be a negatively reinforced behavior. Alternatively, cutting could bring about pleasant emotional states as a result of past conditioning, imagery, or attention from significant others. In this case, it would serve as a positively reinforced behavior. Because the causal mechanism differs, preferred intervention strategies would also have to use different behavioral principles to exert maximal effects. In the first case, the goal might be to help the client develop alternative strategies for managing and/or tolerating aversive negative emotional states and cognitive rumination (e.g., graded exposure or mindfulness training). In the latter case, efforts might be directed toward removing social attention for cutting and simultaneously enhancing social attention for noncutting behavior (i.e., differential reinforcement of alternative responses).

What if the *direction* or *form* of causal relations among the behavior problems were different? For example, what if the relation between

---

[3] Remember that these illustrations are always schematic simplified models of *incompletely specified* FACCDs because many other causal variables are involved with these behavior problems.

cutting and reduction of aversive emotional states only operated when the client was binge drinking? In that case, an intervention that focuses on binge drinking would also be likely to reduce cutting. This example illustrates an important aspect of behavioral assessment and the functional analysis: small changes in our judgments can have important effects on intervention decisions (i.e., their foci and strategies).

## STEP 9: ESTIMATE THE STRENGTH OF FUNCTIONAL RELATIONS AMONG BEHAVIOR PROBLEMS

Figure 11.6 also illustrates the clinician's estimates of the relative strength of relations among the client's three behavior problems, in a format consistent with the legend in Figure 3.4. As we mentioned earlier, the strength of a causal relation is an important focus in behavioral assessment and indicates the estimated *magnitude of effect* of a variable—the degree to which change in one variable is associated with change in another. Figure 11.6 indicates that a change in the frequency of depressive episodes would have a relatively stronger effect on self-cutting, compared to its effect on binge drinking episodes. The degree of difference between these two causal effects depends on the values associated with the three levels of strength, illustrated in the FACCD by line thickness (or arithmetic values). In this case, we limit relative strengths to three levels, corresponding to strong, moderate, and weak (the absence of an arrow connecting two variables indicates no functional relation). In Chapter 10, we discussed assessment strategies for estimating the magnitude of causal relations between variables.

## STEP 10: IDENTIFY THE CAUSAL VARIABLES ASSOCIATED WITH THE CLIENT'S BEHAVIOR PROBLEMS

The most important and challenging step in developing a functional analysis is the identification of the causal variables that affect the client's behavior problems. The importance of this step derives from the fact that behavioral interventions often emphasize modification of hypothesized

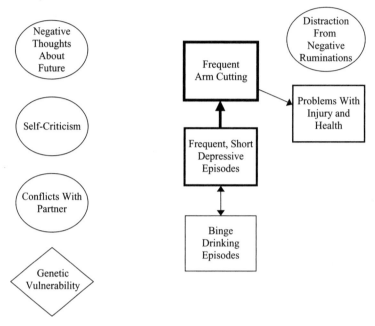

**Figure 11.7** An FACCD that also illustrates multiple causal variables.

causal variables in order to exert a beneficial impact on behavior problems. The challenge of this step arises because, as we discussed in Chapters
4 through 6, causal variables for a behavior problem vary across clients,
and can change across time and differ as a function of the dimension,
mode, or context of the problem.

Figure 11.7 illustrates several causal variables associated with this
client's depressive episodes and arm cutting. Notice how these variables are specified in a manner that is consistent with the focus of many
cognitive-behavioral interventions: they point to intervention strategies
that focus on modifying negative thoughts about herself and the future,
improvement in interpersonal functioning, and learning new strategies
for reducing aversive emotional states and negative ruminations. These
causal variable labels reemphasize a previous point—causal variables
should be identified at clinically useful levels of specificity. Note also the
inclusion of one unmodifiable causal variable—"genetic vulnerability" –
which was based on family history data.

We also discuss assessment strategies for estimating the strength and
direction of causal relations in Chapter 10.

## STEPS 11 AND 12: ESTIMATE THE FORM AND STRENGTH OF RELATIONS BETWEEN CAUSAL VARIABLES AND BEHAVIOR PROBLEMS

After identifying causal variables, the clinician must estimate functional relations between causal variables and behavior problems. These causal and noncausal relations can differ in their form and strength. Figure 11.8 illustrates three levels of strength of relations and unidirectional and bidirectional causal relations.

We mentioned in Chapters 4, 5, and 6, and earlier in this chapter, that the strength of effect of a causal variable can depend on which dimensions or response modes of the behavior problem are affected. We also note that the strength of effect of a causal variable can vary across time, settings, and contexts. Consequently, to increase the overall usefulness of the functional analysis and the FACCD, it is often important for the clinician to specify which aspects, settings, and contexts of the client's behavior

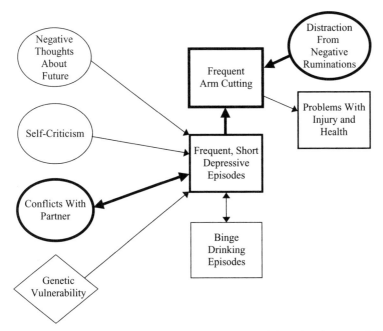

**Figure 11.8** An FACCD that illustrates the strength and form (unidirectional, bidirectional) of causal relations between causal variables and behavior problems.

problems are most important. In Figure 11.8, "conflicts with partner" was judged to have the strongest magnitude of effect on the client's depressive episodes.

As shown in Figure 11.8, we use the same format for illustrating the estimated strength and form of causal relations from causal variables to behavior problems as we did to illustrate the strength and form of causal relations between behavior problems.

Recall the importance of considering "how" a causal relation occurs. In Figure 11.8, how would "conflicts with partner" lead to depressive episodes? What is the causal mechanism? The mechanisms of action can suggest multiple intervention strategies. The mechanisms of action are especially important when a powerful causal variable is difficult to modify (as we discuss in step 13).

## STEP 13: ESTIMATE THE MODIFIABILITY OF CAUSAL VARIABLES

We discussed in Chapter 6 how causal variables could differ in the degree to which they can be modified—the estimated degree to which a causal variable can be changed through interventions. Modifiability contributes to a cost-benefit analysis of the intervention procedures and anticipated intervention effects. It represents the clinician's estimate of the ratio between intervention time and effort and the amount of change that can be effected in a causal variable. Unmodifiable (e.g., an initial traumatic event) or difficult-to-modify (e.g., aversive behaviors emitted by a noncompliant staff member on a psychiatric unit) causal variables can help explain the onset or maintenance of a behavior problem, but are less useful in designing intervention programs.

Figure 11.8 illustrates three levels of modifiability of causal variables (high, moderate, low) and one unmodifiable causal variable depicted as "◊." In this functional analysis, the clinician estimated that "conflicts with partner" would be more modifiable than others because both partners were cooperative and committed to improving their relationship. "Genetic vulnerability," as suggested by a high rate of concordance for depression among multiple family members, is not a modifiable causal variable.

Depending on its relative modifiability and strength of effect, a highly modifiable causal variable that is only weakly related to a behavior problem can be a more useful treatment target than a less modifiable causal variable that is strongly related to the behavior problem. The estimated degree of a variable's modifiability, or the value placed on its modification, varies across behavioral subparadigms. Some paradigms, such as Acceptance and Commitment Therapy (Hayes, Strosahl, & Wilson, 1999), in contrast to some traditional CBT paradigms (e.g., Dryden & Ellis, 2010), posit that the occurrence (frequency, duration, and intensity) of problematic thoughts (e.g., "I am worthless") is essentially uncontrollable and thereby unmodifiable. This paradigm suggests that, while thoughts and emotional states are not controllable, actions are controllable. Thus, the intervention does not focus on directly changing cognitions or emotional states. Instead, efforts are directed at helping the client develop and use behaviors that can permit him or her to achieve valued life goals while simultaneously accepting that negative thoughts and emotional states are inevitable but tolerable. In contrast, the results of many CBT studies suggest that there can also be benefits associated with focusing intervention efforts on clients' thoughts and emotional states.

From a functional analysis perspective, a clinician using acceptance and commitment therapy would provide a low modifiability rating of cognitive and/or emotional variables, whereas traditional cognitive therapists would generate higher ratings for these variables. Additionally, acceptance and commitment therapists would posit that the development and use of certain skills (e.g., accepting the negative cognitive and emotional states and acting effectively in the presence of negative cognitive and emotional states) will moderate the relationship between negative cognitive and emotional states and other problematic behavioral outcomes. The main point here is that a functional analysis and FACCD, within the constraints for specificity and clinical utility, is applicable across paradigms and is neutral about the included elements.

## STEPS 14 AND 15: ESTIMATE THE FORM AND STRENGTH OF RELATIONS BETWEEN CAUSAL VARIABLES AND IDENTIFY CAUSAL CHAINS

Recall that there can be unidirectional and bidirectional causal relations that differ in their magnitudes of effect *among* causal variables. These causal relations are also important when the clinician is deciding where to focus intervention because they point to multiple and interacting causal paths emanating from a causal variable.

We can see from Figure 11.9 that some of the causal variables form *causal chains*—sequences of causal variables that ultimately affect the client's behavior problem. In this case, conflicts between the client and her partner had a direct effect on her depressive episodes. These relationship conflicts also had an indirect effect in that they were elements of causal chains that led to negative thoughts about herself and her future that also contributed to her depressive episodes.

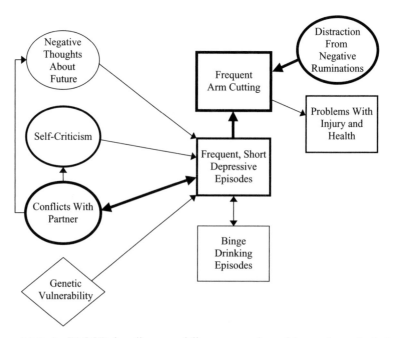

**Figure 11.9** An FACCD that illustrates different strengths and forms of causal relations among causal variables.

The FACCD in Figure 11.9 further illustrates how a causal variable can affect a behavior problem through *multiple causal paths*. The total magnitude of effect of a causal variable is the sum of all causal paths.[4] For another client, a causal chain could include: job stressors → increased negative ruminations about the stressors → substance abuse to reduce obsessions and associated arousal → sleep difficulties from substance use and nighttime ruminations → increased sensitivity to life stressors → increased marital conflict → increased anxiety and panic symptoms.

As we noted in Chapters 1 and 6, causal chains are important elements of the functional analysis because they can indicate several possible points of intervention. Figure 11.9, for example, suggests that we can reduce depressive episodes by reducing partner conflicts or by reducing the effects of these conflicts on the client's negative thoughts.

Marlatt (1985) proposed that a specific chain of events is often associated with relapse following substance abuse treatment. This chain involved the following: exposure of the client to a high-risk situation → decreased perceived self-efficacy → initial use of substance (lapse) → continued substance use (relapse). Consistent with our emphasis on the importance of specifying the dimensions of behavior problems, Marlatt suggested that the causal variables for relapse can be different than those associated with the original use of the substance.

## STEP 16: IDENTIFY MODERATOR VARIABLES ASSOCIATED WITH THE CLIENT'S CAUSAL VARIABLES AND BEHAVIOR PROBLEMS

As we define it in Box 6.2, a *moderator variable* is a variable that alters the strength or the direction of a functional relation between two other variables. We note, as an example, that for some persons "positive social support from friends" can moderate the effects of life stressors on mood, anxiety, or

---

[4]   The analysis of multiple causal paths in a functional analysis is different than the mediational analyses often associated with structural equations modeling. That is, FACCDs are hypothesized models in which the clinician is estimating the relative magnitudes of effects of multiple causal variables. Thus, the sum of effects depicted in an FACCD, and the sum of effects of a causal variable within an FACCD, can be greater than "1."

health problems. Moderator variables can also be environmental events, behaviors by the client, cognitive variables, or physiological processes. They can be particularly important components of a functional analysis when the client's behavior problems are strongly affected by unmodifiable causal variables, such as childhood abuse or neglect, chronic illness or injury, sexual assault or other traumatic life events, an aversive but una-voidable work situation, or brain injury.

A moderator variable can work in several ways—it can increase, decrease, and in some cases reverse the effects of a causal variable. In Figure 11.10, for example, decreases in social support can alter the like-lihood that the client's marital conflicts will lead to depressive episodes. Thus, for this client, the clinician estimated that increasing social sup-port (encouraging contacts with supportive friends and family members) could attenuate the impact of marital conflict on depressive episodes (see discussion of the "direction" of functional relations in step 18).

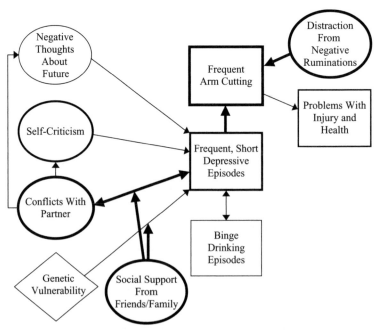

**Figure 11.10** An FACCD that illustrates a moderator variable (social support) that af-fects the degree to which "Conflicts" and "Genetic" factors influence the client's depres-sive episodes.

The usefulness of a moderator variable is inversely related to the modifiability of the targeted causal variables. For the client's depressive episodes illustrated in Figure 11.10, the usefulness of focusing intervention on social support depends partly on the degree to which we can modify the marital conflict and genetic factors. That is, social support would be a particularly useful target in intervention if the client's partner were not cooperative with the intervention process and if the physiological factors associated with the genetic influences could not be addressed.

A moderator variable can also include "context" for the client. For example, the strength of causal relation between marital conflict and depressive episodes could be moderated by the client's concurrent exposure to other life stressors. Thus, under conditions of high stress exposure, the causal relation between marital conflict and depressive episodes may be stronger than when in a context of low stress exposure.

## STEP 17: IDENTIFY MEDIATORS OF CAUSAL RELATIONS ASSOCIATED WITH THE CLIENT'S BEHAVIOR PROBLEMS

As we also explain in Box 6.2, a *mediating variable* is similar to a *causal mechanism*—it explains "how" or "through what means" a causal variable affects a behavior problem. For the client in Figure 11.10, a mediating variable addresses the question of "Why, how, or in what way does couple conflict lead to depressed mood?"

Some mediating variables for the causal relations between couple conflict and depressed mood are already included in the FACCD in Figure 11.10. The FACCD suggests that her relationship conflict leads to depressed mood, in part because it increases the client's self-criticism and negative thoughts about the future (a probable focus of assertive intervention if she sought out Rational Emotive Therapy). With other clients, couple conflict could affect mood because it is associated with reduced positive interactions between the partners, disruption of extramarital social relationships, extended negative and aversive couple interactions, and increased use of alcohol to reduce the stress.

As we note, mediating and moderating variables are important components of the functional analyses because they can suggest multiple intervention foci. We also note several ways through which our FACCD can suggest intervention foci for the client in Figure 11.10: (a) helping the couple reduce the frequency, intensity, or duration of their conflicts, (b) reducing the negative thoughts by the client that follow these conflicts, (c) increasing social support for our client, and (d) by addressing other potential mediators/moderators such as maintaining positive exchanges during periods of conflict, reducing the duration of negative interactions, or reducing the use of alcohol following conflict.

## STEP 18: ESTIMATE THE DIRECTION OF EFFECT OF FUNCTIONAL RELATIONS

Variables can have a positive or negative functional relation. In a *positive functional relation*, an increase in one variable is associated with an increase in the other variable. In a *negative functional relation*, an increase in one variable is associated with a decrease in the other variable. As we discussed in step 16, moderator variables can work in either direction; some moderator variables can strengthen a causal relation while others can attenuate a causal relation.

In an FACCD, variables are presumed to have a positive relation unless accompanied by a negative "−" sign. In Figure 11.11, we have indicated the moderating effects of social support with a "−" sign, indicating that increasing social support is associated with a reduction in the degree to which conflict is associated with depressive episodes.

The direction of a functional relation depends on how the variables are defined or labeled. For example, "social support" could have a negative causal relation, while "decreased social support" could have a positive causal relation, with "depressed mood." The direction of effect would be reversed if the dependent variable were labeled "positive mood."

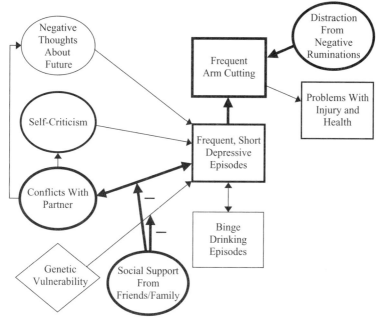

**Figure 11.11** An FACCD that illustrates the direction of effect (negative) of a moderator variable (social support). For this client, increases in social support would decrease the degree to which partner conflict leads to depressive episodes.

---

**Box 11.4 Remembering the Dynamic and Conditional Nature of Causal Relations**

We pointed out in Chapter 6 that causal relations can be dynamic and conditional—they can change over time and can vary across contexts, settings, and values of the variables. We mention this again to caution the clinician against an oversimplified interpretation of an FACCD. We remind the clinician that:

- Causal relations can change over time (e.g., the factors that affect the client's depressed mood can be different in the future).
- Causal relations can differ across contexts (e.g., the factors that affect the client's depressed mood can differ as a function of the client's physical health, social setting, or other factors).

- A causal variable (including a moderator variable) can have multiple effects, which can vary in their direction. For example, an increase in life stressors can result in an increase in negative self-appraisals (a positive causal relation) and, concurrently, lead to a decrease in supportive behaviors from friends (a negative causal relation).
- The overall magnitude of effect of a causal variable is an additive function of all positive and negative causal paths.

## STEP 19: IDENTIFY IMPORTANT SOCIAL SYSTEMS VARIABLES

Most models of case formulation, particularly behavior analytic functional analyses, emphasize temporally contiguous (i.e., closely related in time) antecedent and consequent events and environmental contexts related to a client's behavior problems and positive intervention goals. However, as we discussed in Chapter 6 and illustrate with Figure 6.4, important causal factors sometimes reside with distal events and extended social systems. The chains of causal variables that affect a client's behavior problem often include the behavior of other persons. In turn, the behavior of these persons can be affected by a different set of contexts, stressors, and challenges.

Because they ultimately affect the client, the actions of other persons, and the situations that affect their behavior, can be important components of a functional analysis. In Chapter 6, we discussed an example of the mother of a disruptive child, whose interactions with the child (and her ability to respond effectively to intervention efforts) was affected by domestic violence and other significant life stressors. Similarly, the interactions of psychiatric staff members with clients can be affected by their training, supervision, personal behavior problems, and hospital policies. Sometimes, the development of a valid and clinically useful functional analysis will require that the clinician consider factors that involve the extended social systems in which the behavior problem is imbedded.

The inclusion of social systems variables is particularly relevant in the functional analysis of behavior problems of children, adolescents,

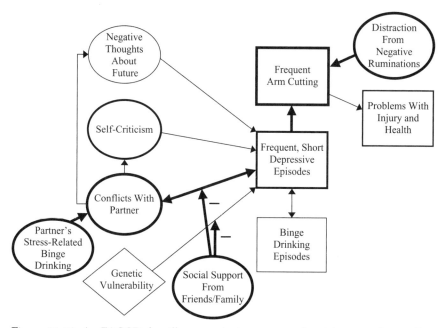

**Figure 11.12** An FACCD that illustrates the importance of social systems factors. For this client, conflicts with her partner were partially influenced by the partner's stress-related binge drinking.

and persons in supervised settings (e.g., institutions, group homes, and extended care facilities). The guiding principle for the functional analysis is: when other persons have an important effect on the client, consider factors that affect the actions of those persons. Figure 11.12 illustrates how "Conflicts with Partner" is affected by her partner's binge drinking, which is in turn a response to stressors in the partner's life.

## STEP 20: IDENTIFY FUNCTIONAL RESPONSE CLASSES

The specification of a client's behavior problems and positive intervention goals, and the variables that affect them, help the clinician determine if the problems and goals form a *functional response class*. We illustrate a functional response class in Figure 3.12, where several behavior problems (drug use, alcohol use, and medication) that differ in form are affected by similar antecedent and consequent factors. In such cases, there is no need to assume separate causal paths, for the behavior problems and modification of a causal variable would affect changes in all elements of the response class.

Functional response classes are important elements of the functional analysis and FACCD because they can increase their parsimony and clinical utility. When several different behavior problems are influenced by the same variables, they can be illustrated together in an FACCD, as shown in Figure 3.12.

Functional response classes are also an important concept in the design of some intervention programs. Clinicians sometimes help clients change actions, thoughts, or physiological states that have the same function as the client's problem behaviors. Examples include helping clients to develop verbal or nonverbal alternatives to self-injury as a strategy to communicate with others, or relaxation or meditation strategies as alternatives to drug use to reduce anxiety and stress.

## STEP 21: INCLUDE HYPOTHETICAL CAUSAL VARIABLES, BEHAVIOR PROBLEMS, AND CAUSAL RELATIONS

As we illustrate in Figure 3.10, clinicians often propose causal variables, behavior problems, or causal relations in a functional analysis without being able to directly collect assessment data that support or disconfirm them. Information obtained during interviews, questionnaires, or observations can provide clues about causal variables that may be affecting the client, but there are insufficient data to validate those hypotheses. Sometimes conflicting data provide information about the operation of other variables. For example, data from interviews and observations can be in disagreement about the degree to which inconsistencies in staff responses contribute to aggressive behavior by a psychiatric client.

For the client in Figure 11.13, there are subtle and conflicting cues that emerge during interviews with the husband and wife about how the client sometimes uses cocaine during her drinking episodes, and that cocaine use increases the likelihood that she will cut herself. Hypothetical

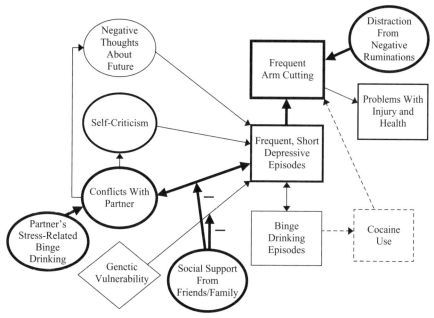

**Figure 11.13** An FACCD that illustrates the inclusion of hypothetical variables and causal relations (related to cocaine use).

elements in a functional analysis can be useful to clinicians because they indicate the need for additional assessment information.

## STEP 22: CONTINUE TO REEVALUATE AND REFINE

As we emphasized in Chapter 1, the functional analysis is a clinician's contemporaneous, hypothesized, tentative, working causal model of a client's behavior problems and positive intervention goals. Although always subjective, we assume that the functional analysis is based on the best available assessment data derived from the best available science-based assessment methods and strategies. However, because of limitations in our assessment technology and biases, limitations in clinicians' and clients' cognitive abilities, and other restraints of the assessment process, the clinician must assume that the functional analysis for a client is imperfect, involves errors of omission and commission, and that it will change across time. These limitations are inherent in all case formulations and emphasize the importance of the following four assessment strategies that can aid in the development, evaluation, and refinement of a functional analysis.

1. Test it! Assume that you could be wrong and collect data that could disprove key elements in the functional analysis. This is a basic tenet of a behavioral science. Do conflicts with her partner really increase the likelihood of a client's negative self-statements? Are a couple's conflicts highly modifiable?

2. When appropriate (such as when it is worded in a constructive manner, would not have adverse reactive effects, and would not violate confidentiality), discuss the functional analysis with the client or other important persons in the client's life. Their feedback could help refine the functional analysis and increase its validity and clinical utility.

3. Assume that the functional analysis will change over time and continue assessing throughout the assessment-intervention process.

4. Address disagreements with the client about the functional analysis in a constructive, supportive, sensitive, and respectful manner. Remember step 1 regarding respecting the client's rights in assessment and intervention decisions and maintaining a positive relationship with the client.

## SUMMARY

This chapter outlines 22 steps in the development of a functional analysis and in the construction of an FACCD. The steps involve:

- Maintaining respect for the client's rights and a positive relationship with the client.
- Insuring the safety of the client and evaluating the need for referral.

- Identifying the client's behavior problems and specifying their response modes, dimensions, importance, and effects.
- Identifying the form, strength, and direction of effects of functional relations among behavior problems.
- Identifying causal variables and estimating their modifiability as well as the form and strength of relations with the client's behavior problems.
- Estimating the form, strength, and direction of effect of relations between causal variables.
- Identifying moderator and mediator variables associated with the client's behavior problems.
- Identifying social systems variables.
- Identifying functional response classes.
- Proposing additional variables and relations.
- Reevaluating and refining the functional analysis.

# References

Achenbach, T. M. (1991). *Manual for the Child Behavior Checklist/4–18 and 1991 Profile.* Burlington, VT: University of Vermont, Department of Psychiatry.

Achenbach, T. M., & Rescorla, L. A. (2001). *Manual for the ASEBA School-Age Forms & Profiles.* Burlington, VT: University of Vermont, Research Center for Children, Youth, & Families.

Alessi, G. (1988). Direct observation methods for emotional/behavior problems. In E. S. Shapiro & T. R. Kratochwill (Eds.), *Behavioral assessment in schools: Conceptual foundations and practical applications* (pp. 14–75). New York: Guilford Press.

Alpers, G. W., Wilhelm, F. H., & Roth, W. T. (2005). Psychophysiological assessment during exposure in driving phobic patients. *Journal of Abnormal Psychology, 114,* 126–139.

American Psychiatric Association. (2000). *Diagnostic and statistical manual of mental disorders,* 4th ed. (DSM-IV, text rev.). Washington, DC: Author.

Anastasi, A., & Urbina, S. (1997). *Psychological testing* (7th ed.). Upper Saddle River, NJ: Prentice-Hall.

Andrasek, F. (Ed.) (2006). *Comprehensive handbook of personality and psychopathology* (pp. 189–206). Hoboken, NJ: John Wiley & Sons.

Annis, H. M., & Graham, J. M. (1995). Profile types on the Inventory of Drinking Situations: Implications for relapse prevention counseling. *Psychology of Addictive Behaviors, 9*(3), 176–182.

Annis, H. M., Graham, J. M., & Davis, C. S. (1987). Inventory of Drinking Situations (IDS): User's guide. Toronto, ON, Canada: Addiction Research Foundation.

Asterita, M. F. (1985). *The physiology of stress.* New York, NY: Human Sciences Press.

Austin, D. W., & Kiropoulos, L. A. (2008). An Internet-based investigation of the catastrophic misinterpretation model of panic disorder. *Journal of Anxiety Disorders, 22*, 233–242.

Baird, S., & Nelson-Gray, R. O. (1999). Direct observation and self-monitoring. In S. C. Hayes, D. H. Barlow, & R. O. Nelson-Gray (Eds.), *The scientist practitioner* (2nd ed., pp. 353–386). Needham Heights, MA: Allyn & Bacon.

Bandura, A. (1982). The psychology of chance encounters and life paths. *American Psychologist, 37*, 747–755.

Barbour, K. A., & Davison, G. C. (2004). Clinical interviewing. In S. N. Haynes & E. H. Heiby (Eds.), *Behavioral assessment* (pp. 181–193). Hoboken, NJ: John Wiley & Sons.

Barkley, R. A. (1991). The ecological validity of laboratory and analogue assessment methods of ADHD symptoms. *Journal of Abnormal Child Psychology, 19*, 149–178.

Barlow, D. H., & Hersen, M. (1984). *Single case experimental designs: Strategies for studying behavior change* (2nd ed.). Needham Heights, MA: Allyn & Bacon.

Barnett, P. A., & Gotlib, I. (1988). Psychosocial functioning and depression: Distinguishing among antecedents, concomitants, and consequences. *Psychological Bulletin, 104*, 97–126.

Bauer, M., Glenn, T., Grof, P., Rasgon, N., Alda, M., Marsh, W., Sagduyu, K., Schmid, R., Adli, M., & Whybrow, P. C. (2009). Comparison of sleep/wake parameters for self-monitoring bipolar disorder. *Journal of Affective Disorders, 116*(3), 170–175.

Beach, D. A. (2005). The behavioral interview. In R. J. Craig (Ed.), *Clinical and diagnostic interviewing* (2nd ed.). Lanham, MD: Jason Aronson.

Beach, S. R. H., Kaman, C., & Fincham, F. (2006). Marital dysfunction. In M. Hersen, J. C. Thomas (Eds.), & F. Andrasik (Vol. Ed.), *Comprehensive handbook of personality and psychopathology: Vol. 2. Adult psychopathology* (pp. 450–465). Hoboken, NJ: John Wiley & Sons.

Beck, A. T., Kovacs, M., & Weissman, A. (1979). Assessment of suicidal ideation: The Scale for Suicide Ideation. *Journal of Consulting and Clinical Psychology, 47*, 343–352.

Beck, A. T., Steer, R. A., & Brown, G. K. (1996). *Manual for the Beck Depression Inventory* (2nd ed.). San Antonio, TX: The Psychological Corporation.

Beckham, J. C., Feldman, M. E., Barefoot, J. C., Fairbank, J. A., Helms, M. J., Haney, T. L., et al. (2000). Ambulatory cardiovascular activity in Vietnam combat veterans with and without posttraumatic stress disorders. *Journal of Consulting and Clinical Psychology, 68*, 269–276.

Beidel, D. C., & Stipelman, B. (2007). Anxiety disorders. In M. Hersen, S. M. Turner, & D. C. Beidel, (Eds.) (2007). *Adult psychopathology and diagnosis* (5th ed.; pp. 349–409). Hoboken, NJ: John Wiley & Sons.

Bentall, R. P., Haddock, G., & Slade, P. D. (1994). Cognitive behavior therapy for persistent auditory hallucinations: From theory to therapy. *Behavior Therapy, 25*, 51–66.

Bergman, R. L., & Piacentini, J. (2005). Targeting discrete response channels in the treatment of childhood specific phobia. *Clinical Psychology: Science and Practice, 12*, 166–169.

Bhuvaneswar, C. G., Baldessarini, R. J., Harsh, V. L., & Alpert, J. E. (2009). Adverse endocrine and metabolic effects of psychotropic drugs: Selective clinical review. *CNS Drugs, 1*, 1003–1021.

Biddle, W. (2002). *A field guide to germs* (2nd ed.). New York, NY: Anchor Books.

Birchler, G. R., Weiss, R. L., & Vincent, J. P. (1975). A multimethod analysis of social reinforcement exchange between maritally distressed and nondistressed spouse and stranger dyads. *Journal of Personality and Social Psychology, 31*, 349–360.

Blalock, H. M. (1971). *Causal models in the social sciences*. Chicago, IL: Aldin-Atherton.

Blechert, J., Ansorge, U., & Tuschen-Caffier, B. (2010). A body-related dot-probe task reveals distinct attentional patterns for bulimia nervosa and anorexia nervosa. *Journal of Abnormal Psychology, 119*(3), 575–585.

Blumenthal, J. A., Burg, M. M., Barefoot, J., Williams, R. B., Haney, T., & Zimet, G. (1987). Social support, Type A behavior, and coronary artery disease. *Psychosomatic Medicine, 49*, 331–340.

Bootzin, R. R., Kihlstrom, J. F., & Schacter, D. L. (Eds.) (1990). *Sleep and cognition*. Washington, DC: American Psychological Association.

Bootzin, R. R., & Ruggill, J. S. (1988). Training issues in behavior therapy. *Journal of Consulting and Clinical Psychology, 56*, 703–709.

Bryant, R. A. (2006). Posttraumatic stress disorder. In F. Andrasek (Ed.). *Comprehensive handbook of personality and psychopathology* (pp. 189–206). Hoboken, NJ: John Wiley & Sons.

Bryington, A. A., Darcy, J. P., & Watkins, M. W. (2004). The estimation of interobserver agreement in behavioral assessment (reprinted by permission of the *Behavior Analyst Today*). *Journal of Early and Intensive Behavior Interventions, 1*, 115–119.

Buckley, T. C., Holohan, D., Greif, J. L., Bedard, M., & Suvak, M. (2004). Twenty-four-hour ambulatory assessment of heart rate and blood pressure in chronic PTSD and non-PTSD veterans. *Journal of Traumatic Stress, 17*, 163–171.

Budd, K. S., Workman, D. E., Lemsky, C. M., & Quick, D. M. (1994). The Children's Headache Assessment Scale (CHAS): Factor structure and psychometric properties. *Journal of Behavioral Medicine, 17*, 159–179.

Bunge, M. (2009). *Causality and modern science*. New Brunswick, NJ: Transaction Publishers.

Butcher, J. N. (2009). *Clinical personality assessment: Practical approaches*. New York, NY: Oxford University Press.

Butcher, J. N., Mineka, S., & Hooley, J. M. (2008). *Abnormal psychology*. Boston, MA: Pearson Education.

Butler, A. C., Chapman, J. E., Forman, E. M., & Beck, A. T. (2006). The empirical status of cognitive-behavioral therapy: A review of meta-analyses. *Clinical Psychology Review, 26*, 17–31.

Caballo, V. E., & Buela, G. (1988). Molar/molecular assessment in an analogue situation: Relationships among several measurements and validation of a behavioral assessment instrument. *Perceptual and Motor Skills, 67*, 591–602.

Cacioppo, J. T., Tassinary, L. G., & Berntson, G. (2007). *Handbook of psychophysiology* (3rd ed.). New York, NY: Cambridge University Press.

Chambless, D. L., & Ollendick, T. H. (2001). Empirically supported psychological interventions. Controversies and evidence. *Annual Review of Psychology, 52,* 685–716.

Chapman, L. J., & Chapman, J. P. (1969). The illusory correlation as an obstacle to the use of valid psychodiagnostic signs. *Journal of Abnormal Psychology, 74,* 271–280.

Chatkoff, D. K., Maier, K. J., & Klein, C. (2010). Nonlinear associations between chronic stress and cardiovascular reactivity and recovery. *International Journal of Psychophysiology, 77,* 150–156.

Chrisdansen, B., Goldman, M., & Inn, A. (1982). Development of alcohol-related expectancies in adolescents: Separating pharmaco-logica from social-learning influences. *Journal of Consulting and Clinical Psychology, 50,* 336–344.

Christensen, A. (1987). Detection of conflict patterns in couples. In K. Hahlweg & M. J. Goldstein (Eds.), *Understanding major mental disorder: The contribution of family interaction research* (pp. 250–265). New York, NY: Family Process Press.

Christensen, L., Young, K. R., & Marchant, M. (2007). Behavioral intervention planning: Increasing appropriate behavior of a socially withdrawn student. *Education and Treatment of Children, 30,* 81–103.

Chorpita, B. F., & Daleiden, E. L. (2009). Mapping evidence-based treatments for children and adolescents: Application of the distillation and matching model to 615 treatments from 322 randomized trials. *Journal of Consulting and Clinical Psychology, 77*(3), 566–579.

Chorpita, B. F., Daleiden, E. L., & Weisz, J. R. (2005). Identifying and selecting the common elements of evidence based interventions: A distillation and matching model. *Mental Health Services Research, 7,* 5–20.

Clarkin, J. F., & Sanderson, C. (2000). Personality disorders. In M. Hersen & A. S. Bellack (Eds.), *Psychopathology in adulthood* (pp. 348–365). Needham Heights, MA: Allyn & Bacon.

Cole, C. L., & Bambara, L. M. (2000). Self-monitoring: Theory and practice. In E. S. Shapiro & T. R. Kratochwill (Eds.), *Behavioral assessment in schools: Theory, research, and clinical foundations* (2nd ed., pp. 202–232). New York, NY: Guilford Press.

Cole, C. L., Marder, T., & McCann, L. (2000). Self-monitoring. In E. S. Shapiro & T. R. Kratochwill (Eds.), *Conducting school-based assessments of child and adolescent behavior* (pp. 121–149). New York, NY: Guilford Press.

Compton, S. N., Burns, B. J., Egger, H. L., & Robertson, E. (2002). Review of the evidence base for treatment of childhood psychopathology: Internalizing disorders. *Journal of Consulting and Clinical Psychology, 70*, 1240–1266.

Cone, J. D. (1979). Confounded comparisons in triple response mode assessment research. *Behavioral Assessment, 11*, 85–95.

Cone, J. D. (1997). Issues in functional analysis in behavioral assessment. *Behaviour Research and Therapy, 35*, 259–275.

Cone, J. D. (1998a). Psychometric considerations: Concepts, contents, and methods. In A. Bellack, & M. Hersen (Eds.), *Behavioral assessment: A practical handbook*. Needham Heights, MA: Allyn & Bacon.

Cone, J. D. (1998b). Hierarchical views of anxiety: What do they profit us? *Behavior Therapy, 29*, 325–332.

Cook, A. J., Brawer, P. A., & Vowles, K. E. (2006). The fear-avoidance model of chronic pain: Validation and age analysis using structural equation modeling, *Pain, 121*, 195–206.

Corsini, R. J., & Wedding, D. (2010). *Current psychotherapies* (9th ed.). Belmont, CA: Brooks/Cole.

Cummings, E. M., & Davies, P. T. (2002). Effects of marital conflict on children: Recent advances and emerging themes in process-oriented research. *Journal of Child Psychology and Psychiatry, 43*, 33–63.

Cummings, E. M., Goeke-Morey, M. C., Pap, L. M., & Dukewich, T. L. (2002). Children's responses to mothers' and fathers' emotionality and tactics in marital conflict in the home. *Journal of Family Psychology, 16*, 478–492.

Currie, S. R., Clark, S., Rimac, S., & Malhotra, S. (2003). Comprehensive assessment of insomnia in recovering alcoholics using daily sleep diaries and ambulatory monitoring. *Alcoholism: Clinical and Experimental Research, 27*, 1262–1269.

Currie, S. R., Wilson, K., Pontefract, A. J., & deLaplant, L. (2000). Cognitive-behavioral treatment of insomnia secondary to chronic pain. *Journal of Consulting and Clinical Psychology, 68*, 407–416.

Cushman, L. A., & Scherer, M. J. (Eds.). (1995). *Psychological assessment in medical rehabilitation* (pp. 3–23). Washington, DC: American Psychological Association.

Dassel, K. B., & Schmitt, F. A. (2008). The impact of caregiver executive skills on reports of patient functioning. *Gerontologist, 48,* 781–792.

Davison, S. N., & Jhangri, G. S. (2005). The impact of chronic pain on depression, sleep, and the desire to withdraw from dialysis in hemodialysis patients. *Journal of Pain and Symptom Management, 30*(5), 465–473.

De Los Reyes, A., & Kazdin, A. E. (2005). Informant discrepancies in the assessment of childhood psychopathology: A critical review, theoretical framework, and recommendations for further study. *Psychological Bulletin, 131,* 483–509.

Derby, K. M., Wacker, D. P., Sasso, G., Steege, M., Northup, J., Cigrand, K., & Asmus, J. (1992). Brief functional analysis techniques to evaluate aberrant behavior in an outpatient setting: A summary of 79 cases. *Journal of Applied Behavior Analysis, 25,* 713–721.

DeWalt, K. M., DeWalt, B. R., & Wayland, C. B. (1998). Participant observation. In H. R. Bernard (Ed.), *Handbook of methods in cultural anthropology* (pp. 259–299). Walnut Creek, CA: AltaMira Press.

Dickerson, S. S., & Kemeny, M. E. (2004). Acute stressors and cortisol responses: A theoretical integration and synthesis of laboratory research. *Psychological Bulletin, 130,* 355–391.

Dimeff, L., & Koerner, K. (2007). *Dialectical behavior therapy in clinical practice: Applications across disorders and settings.* New York, NY: Guilford Press.

Dishion, T. J., & Granic, I. (2004). Naturalistic observation of relationship process. In S. N. Haynes & E. M. Heiby (Eds.), *Behavioral assessment* (pp. 143–161). Hoboken, NJ: John Wiley & Sons.

Dishion, T. J., Spracklen, K. M., Andrews, D. W., & Patterson, G. R. (1996). Deviancy training in male adolescents friendships. *Behavior Therapy, 27,* 373–390.

Ditre, J. W., Heckman, B. W., Butts, E. A., & Brandon, T. H. (2010). Effects of expectancies and coping on pain-induced motivation to smoke. *Journal of Abnormal Psychology, 119*(3), 524–533.

Ditzen, B., Neumann, I. D., Bodenmann, G., von Dawans, B., Turner, R.A., Ehlert, U., & Heinrichs, M. (2007). Effects of different kinds of couple interaction on cortisol and heart rate responses to stress in women. *Psychoneuroendocrinology, 32,* 565–574.

Doss, B. D., & Atkins, D. C. (2006). Investigating treatment mediators when simple random assignment to a control group is not possible. *Clinical Psychology: Science and Practice. 13,* 321–336.

Dryden, W. D., & Ellis, A. A. (2010). Rational emotive behavior therapy. In K. Dobson (Ed). *Handbook of cognitive behavioral therapies* (pp. 226–276). New York, NY: Guilford Press.

Durand, V. M. (1990). *Severe behavior problems: A functional communication training approach.* New York, NY: Guilford Press.

Durand, V. M., & Crimmins, D. B. (1992). *The Motivation Assessment Scale (MAS) administration guide.* Topeka, KS: Monaco and Associates.

Ebner-Priemer, U. W., & Kubiak, T. (2007). Psychological and psychophysiological ambulatory monitoring: A review of hardware and software solutions. *European Journal of Psychological Assessment, 23,* 214–226.

Ebner-Priemer U. W. Kuo, J., Kleindienst, N., Welch, S. S., Reisch, T., Reinhard, I., Lieb, K., Linehan, M., & Bohus, M. (2007). Assessing state affective instability in borderline personality disorder using an ambulatory monitoring approach. *Psychological Medicine, 37,* 961–970.

Ebner-Priemer, U. W., & Trull, T. (2009). Ambulatory assessment: An innovative and promising approach for clinical psychology. *European Psychologist, 14*(2), 109–119.

Eells, T. D. (Ed.). (2007). *Handbook of psychotherapy case formulation.* New York, NY: Guilford Press.

Ehrensaft, M. K., & Vivian, D. (1996). Spouses' reasons for not reporting existing marital aggression as a marital problem. *Journal of Family Psychology, 10*(4), 443–453.

Eid, M., & Diener, E. (2006). *Handbook of multimethod measurement in psychology.* Washington, DC: American Psychological Association.

Eifert, G. T., & Feldner, M. T. (2004). Conceptual foundations of behavioral assessment: From theory to practice. In S. N. Haynes, & E. M. Heiby (Eds.), *Behavioral assessment* (pp. 94–107). Hoboken, NJ: John Wiley & Sons.

Einhorn, H. (1988). Diagnosis and causality in clinical statistical prediction. In D. Turk & P. Salovey (Eds.) *Reasoning, inference, and judgment in clinical psychology* (pp. 51–70). New York, NY: Free Press.

Eisler, R. M., Hersen, M., Miller, P. M., & Blanchard, E. B. (1975). Situational determinants of assertive behaviors. *Journal of Consulting and Clinical Psychology, 29*, 330–340.

El-Sheikh, M., & Flanagan, E. (2001). Parental problem drinking and children's adjustment: Family conflict and parental depression as mediator and moderators of risk. *Journal of Abnormal Child Psychology, 29*, 417–432.

Epstein, L. H., Miller, P. M., & Webster, J. S. (1976). The effects of reinforcing concurrent behavior on self-monitoring. *Behavior Therapy, 7*(1), 89–95.

Essau, C. A. (2003). Comorbidity of anxiety disorders in adolescents. *Depression and Anxiety, 18*, 1–6.

Evers, A. W. M., Kraaimaat, F. W., van Riel, P. L. C. M., & de Jong, A. J. L. (2002). Tailored cognitive-behavioral therapy in early rheumatoid arthritis for patients at risk: A randomized controlled trial. *Pain, 100*, 141–153.

Fahrenberg, J., & Myrtek, J. (Eds.). (2001). *Ambulatory assessment: Computer-assisted psychological and psychophysiological methods in monitoring and field studies.* Seattle, WA: Hogrefe & Huber.

Faller, K. C. (Ed.) (2007). *Interviewing children about sexual abuse: Controversies and best practice.* New York, NY: Oxford University Press.

Fals-Stewart, W., Birchler, G. R., & Kelley, M. L. (2003). The Timeline Followback Spousal Violence Interview to Assess Physical Aggression between Intimate Partners: Reliability and validity. *Journal of Family Violence, 18*(3), 131–142.

Farmer, R. F., & Chapman, A. L. (2008). *Behavioral interventions in cognitive behavior therapy.* Washington, DC: American Psychological Association.

Fernández-Ballesteros, R. (2004). Self-report questionnaires. In S. N. Haynes & E. Heiby (Eds.), *Comprehensive handbook on psychological assessment: Vol. 3. Behavioral assessment* (pp. 194–221). Hoboken, NJ: John Wiley & Sons.

Fernández-Ballesteros, R., & Botella, J. (2008). Self-report measures. In A. M. Nezu & C. M. Nezu (Eds.), *Evidence-based outcome research: A practical guide to conducting randomized controlled trials for psychosocial interventions* (pp. 95–120). New York, NY: Oxford University Press.

Fonseca, A., & Perrin, S. (2001). Clinical phenomenology, classification, and assessment of anxiety disorders in children and adolescents. Cambridge child and adolescent psychiatry. In W. K. Silverman & P. D. A. Treffers (Eds), *Anxiety disorders in children and adolescents: Research, assessment, and intervention* (pp. 126–158). New York, NY: Cambridge University Press.

Ford, K., & Norris, A. E. (1997). Effects of interviewer age on reporting of sexual and reproductive behavior of Hispanic and African American youth. *Hispanic Journal of Behavioral Sciences, 19*(3), 369–376.

Forth, A. E., Kosson, D. S., & Hare, R. D. (2003). *The Psychopathy Checklist: Youth Version.* Toronto, Canada: Multi-Health Systems.

Foster, S. L., Laverty-Finch, C., Gizzo, D. P., & Osantowski, J. (1999). Practical issues in self-observation. *Psychological Assessment, 11*(4), 426–438.

Friesen, M. D., Woodward, L. J., Horwood, L. J., & Fergusson, D. M. (2010). Childhood exposure to sexual abuse and partnership outcomes at age 30. *Psychological Medicine: A Journal of Research in Psychiatry and the Allied Sciences, 40,* 679–688.

Furr, R. M., & Bacharach, V. R. (2008). *Psychometrics: An introduction.* London: Sage.

Gallagher-Thompson, D., Steffen, A. M., & Thompson, L. W. (2008). *Handbook of behavioral and cognitive therapies with older adults.* New York, NY: Springer Science + Business Media.

Garb, H. N. (1998). *Studying the clinician: Judgment research and psychological assessment.* Washington, DC: American Psychological Association.

Garb, H. N. (2005). Clinical judgment and decision making. *Annual Review of Clinical Psychology, 1,* 67–89.

Gervais, N. J., & Dugas, M. J. (2008). Generalized anxiety disorder. In J. Hunsley & E. J. Mash, *A guide to assessments that work* (pp. 254–274). Oxford, UK: Oxford University Press.

Goldstein, G., & Hersen, M. (Eds.) (1999). *Handbook of psychological assessment* (3rd ed). New York, NY: Pergamon-Elsevier Science.

Goodman, G. S., & Quas, J. A. (2008). Repeated interviews and children's memory: It's more than just how many. *Current Directions in Psychological Science, 17*(6), 386–390.

Gorman, J. M., Kent, J. M., Sullivan, G. J., & Copelan, J. D. (2000). Neuroanatomical hypothesis of panic disorder, revised. *American Journal of Psychiatry, 157*, 493–505.

Gottman, J. M. (Ed.) (1995), *The analysis of change*. Mahwah, NJ: Lawrence Erlbaum.

Gottman, J. M. (1999). *The marriage clinic: A scientifically-based marital therapy*. New York, NY: Norton.

Gottman, J. M., & Krokoff, L. J. (1989). Marital interaction and satisfaction: A longitudinal view. *Journal of Consulting and Clinical Psychology, 57*, 47–52.

Gottman, J. M., & Notarius, C. I. (2000). Decade review: Observing marital interaction. *Journal of Marriage and the Family, 62*, 927–947.

Gottman, J. M., & Roy, A. K. (1990). *Sequential analysis: A guide for behavioral researchers*. New York, NY: Cambridge University Press.

Grunebaum, M., Ramsay, S., Galfalvy, H., Ellis, S., Burke, A., Sher, L., Printz, D., Kahn, D., Mann, J., & Oquendo, M. (2006). Correlates of suicide attempt history in bipolar disorder: A stress-diathesis perspective. *Bipolar Disorders, 8*, 551–557.

Guinn, C. H., Baxter, S. D., Royer, J. A., Hardin, J. W., Mackelprang, A. J., & Smith, A. F. (2010). Fourth-grade children's dietary recall accuracy for energy intake at school meals differs by social desirability and body mass index percentile in a study concerning retention interval. *Journal of Health Psychology, 15*(4), 505–514.

Haaga, D. A. F. et al. (1994). Mode-specific impact of relaxation training for hypertensive Hartwig men with Type A behavior pattern. *Behavior Therapy, 25*, 209–223.

Halford, W. K., & Osgarby, S. M. (1993). Alcohol abuse in clients presenting with marital problems. *Journal of Family Psychology, 6*, 245–254.

Hanley, G. P., Iwata, B. A., & McCord, B. E. (2003). Functional analysis of problem behavior: A review. *Journal of Applied Behavior Analysis, 36*, 147–185.

Harris, F .C., & Lahey, B. B. (1982). Subject reactivity in direct observational assessment: A review and critical analysis. *Clinical Psychology Review, 2,* 523–538.

Hartmann, D. P., Barrios, B. A., & Wood, D. D. (2004). Principles of behavioral observation. In S. N. Haynes &. E. H. Heiby (Eds.), *Behavioral assessment* (pp. 108–127). Hoboken, NJ: John Wiley & Sons.

Hartwig, L., Heathfield, L. T., & Jenson, W. R. (2004). Standardization of the functional assessment and intervention program (FAIP) with children who have externalizing behaviors. *School Psychology Quarterly, 19*(3), 272–287.

Hauri, P., & Wisbey, J. (1992). Wrist actigraphy in insomnia. *Sleep, 15,* 293–301.

Hawkley, L .C., Burleson, M. B., Berntgson, G. B., & Cacioppo, J. T. (2003). Loneliness in everyday life: Cardiovascular activity, psychosocial context, and health behaviors. *Journal of Personality and Social Psychology, 85,* 105–120.

Hay, L. R., Nelson, R. O., & Hay, W. M. (1980). Methodological problems in the use of participant observers. *Journal of Applied Behavior Analysis, 13,* 501–504.

Hayes, S. C., Strosahl, K., & Wilson, K. (1999). *Acceptance and commitment therapy: An experiential approach to behavior change.* New York, NY: Guilford Press.

Haynes, S. N. (1978). Principles of behavioral assessment. New York, NY: Gardner Press.

Haynes, S. N. (1986). A behavioral model of paranoid behaviors. *Behavior Therapy, 17,* 266–287.

Haynes, S. N. (1992). *Models of causality in psychopathology: Toward synthetic, dynamic and nonlinear models of causality in psychopathology.* Boston: Allyn & Bacon.

Haynes, S. N. (2001). Clinical applications of analogue behavioral observation: Dimensions of psychometric valuation. *Psychological Assessment, 13,* 73–85.

Haynes, S. N. (2006). Psychometric considerations. In M. Hersen (Ed.), *Clinicians handbook of adult behavioral assessment* (pp. 17–42). Hoboken, NJ: John Wiley & Sons.

Haynes, S. N., Blaine, D., & Meyer, K. (1995). Dynamical models for psychological assessment: Phase-space functions. *Psychological Assessment, 7,* 17–24.

Haynes, S. N., & Heiby, E. (Eds.). (2004). *Behavioral assessment.* Hoboken, NJ: John Wiley & Sons.

Haynes, S. N., & Horn, W. F. (1982). Reactivity in behavioral observation: A review. *Behavioral assessment, 4,* 369–385.

Haynes, S. N., & Jensen, B., Wise, E., & Sherman, D. (1981). The marital intake interview: A multimethod criterion validity evaluation. *Journal of Consulting and Clinical Psychology, 49,* 379–387.

Haynes, S. N., & Kaholokula, J. K. (2008). Behavioral assessment. In M. Hersen and A. M. Gross (Eds.), *Handbook of clinical psychology* (pp. 495–524). Hoboken, NJ: John Wiley & Sons.

Haynes, S. N., Kaholokua, J., & Nelson, K. (1999). Idiographic applications of nomothetically derived treatment programs. *Clinical Psychology: Science and Practice. 6,* 456–461.

Haynes, S. N., Kaholokula, J. K., & Yoshioka, D. (2007). Behavioral assessment in treatment research. In Arthur M. Nezu and Christine Nezu (Eds): *Evidence-based outcome research: A practical guide to conducting RCTs for psychosocial interventions* (pp. 67–94). New York, NY: Oxford University Press.

Haynes, S. N., Mumma, G. H., & Pinson, C. (2009). Idiographic assessment: Conceptual and psychometric foundations of individualized behavioral assessment. *Clinical Psychology Review, 29,* 179–191.

Haynes, S. N., & O'Brien, W. O. (1990). The functional analysis in behavior therapy. *Clinical Psychology Review, 10,* 649–668.

Haynes, S. N., & O'Brien, W. O. (2000). *Principles and methods of behavioral assessment*: New York, NY: Plenum/Kluwer Press.

Haynes, S. N., Pinson, C., Yoshioka, D., & Kloezeman, K. (2008). Behavioral assessment in clinical psychology research. In D. McKay, *Handbook of research methods in abnormal and clinical psychology* (pp. 125–140). Los Angeles, CA: Sage.

Haynes, S. N., Richard, D. C. S., & Kubany, E. (1995). Content validity in psychological assessment. A functional approach to concepts and methods. *Psychological Assessment, 7,* 238–247.

Haynes, S. N., Smith, G., & Hunsley, J. (2011). *Scientific foundations of clinical assessment*. New York, NY: Routledge/Taylor Francis.

Haynes, S. N., & Williams, A. W. (2003). Clinical case formulation and the design of treatment programs: Matching treatment mechanisms and causal relations for behavior problems in a functional analysis. *European Journal of Psychological Assessment, 19*, 164–174.

Haynes, S. N., & Yoshioka, D. T. (2007). Clinical assessment applications of ambulatory biosensors. *Psychological Assessment, 19*, 44–57.

Haynes, S. N., Yoshioka, D., Kloezeman, K., & Bello, I. (2009). Clinical applications of behavioral assessment: Identifying and explaining behavior problems in clinical assessment. In J. Butcher (Ed.), *Oxford handbook of clinical assessment*. Oxford, UK: Oxford University Press.

Hays, P. A. (2008). *Addressing cultural complexities in practice: Assessment, diagnosis, and therapy* (2nd ed.). Washington, DC: American Psychological Association.

Hersen, M. (2001). *Wiley comprehensive handbook of psychological assessment*. New York, NY: John Wiley & Sons.

Hersen, M. (Ed.). (2006a). *Clinician's handbook of child behavioral assessment*. Amsterdam: Elsevier/Academic Press.

Hersen, M. (Ed.). (2006b). *Clinician's handbook of adult behavioral assessment*. San Diego, CA: Elsevier Academic Press.

Hersen, M., & Porzelius, L. K. (Eds.). (2002). *Diagnosis, conceptualization, and treatment planning for adults: A step-by-step guide*. Mahwah, NJ: Lawrence Erlbaum.

Hersen, M., & Thomas, J. C. (Eds.). (2006). *Comprehensive handbook of personality and psychopathology: Adult psychopathology: Vol. 2*. Hoboken, NJ: John Wiley & Sons.

Hersen, M., Turner, S. M., & Beidel, D. C. (2007). *Adult psychopathology and diagnosis* (5th ed.). Hoboken, NJ: John Wiley & Sons.

Heyman, R. E., Eddy, J. M., Weiss, R. L., & Vivian, D. (1995). Factor analysis of the Marital Interaction Coding System (MICS). *Journal of Family Psychology, 9*, 209–215.

Heyman, R. E., & Smith Slep, A. M. (2004). Analog behavioral observation. In S. N. Haynes & E. M. Heiby (Eds.), *Behavioral assessment* (pp. 162–180). Hoboken, NJ: John Wiley & Sons.

Heyman, R. E., & Vivian, D. (1993). *RMICS: Rapid Marital Interaction Coding System: Training manual for coders*. Unpublished manuscript, State University of New York, Stony Brook, NY. (Available at http://www.psy.sunysb.edu/marital)

Hintze, J. M., Volpe, R. J., & Shapiro, E. S. (2002). Best practices in the systematic direct observation of student behavior. In A. Thomas & J. Grimes (Eds.), *Best practices in school psychology IV: Vol. 1, Vol. 2* (pp. 993–1006). Washington, DC: National Association of School Psychologists.

Hooley, J. M. (2007). Expressed emotion and relapse of psychopathology. *Annual Review of Clinical Psychology, 3*, 329–352.

Hops, H., Davis, B., & Longoria, N. (1995). Methodological issues in direct observation: Illustrations with the Living in Familial Environments (LIFE) coding system. *Journal of Clinical Child Psychology, 24*, 193–203.

Howard, I., Turner, R., Olkin, R., & Mohr, D. C. (2006). Therapeutic alliance mediates the relationship between interpersonal problems and depression outcome in a cohort of multiple sclerosis patients. *Journal of Clinical Psychology, 62*, 1197–1204.

Humphreys, K. L., Marx, B.P., & Lexington, J. M. (2009). Self-monitoring as a treatment vehicle. In W. T. O'Donohue & J. E. Fisher (Eds.), *General principles and empirically supported techniques of cognitive behavior therapy* (pp. 576–583). Hoboken, NJ: John Wiley & Sons.

Hunsley, J., Best, M., Lefebvre, M., & Vito, D. (2001). The seven-item short form of the Dyadic Adjustment Scale: Further evidence for construct validity. *American Journal of Family Therapy, 29*, 325–335.

Hunsley, J., & Mash, E. J. (2008). *A guide to assessments that work*. Oxford, UK: Oxford University Press.

Ilkjaer, K., Kortegaard, L., Hoerder, K., Joergensen, J., Kyvik, K., & Gillberg, C. (2004). Personality disorders in a total population twin cohort with eating disorders. *Comprehensive Psychiatry, 45*, 261–267.

Imber, S. D. et al. (1990). Mode-specific effects among three treatments for depression. *Journal of Consulting and Clinical Psychology, 58*, 352–359.

Iwata, B. A., Pace, G. M., Dorsey, M. F., Zarcone, J. R., Vollmer, B., & Smith, J. (1994). The function of self-injurious behavior: An experimental-epidemiological analysis. *Journal of Applied Behavior Analysis, 27*, 215–240.

James, L. R., Mulaik, S. A., & Brett, J. M. (1982). *Causal analysis; Assumptions, models and data*. Beverly Hills, CA: Sage.

Janicki, D. L., Kamarck, T. W., Shiffman, S., & Gwaltney, C. J. (2006). Application of ecological momentary assessment to the study of marital adjustment and social interactions during daily life. *Journal of Family Psychology, 20*(1), 168–172.

Jansen, A. P. D., van Hout, H. P. J., van Marwijk, H. W. J., Nijpels, G., Gundy, C., Vernooij-Dassen, M. J. F. J., . . . Stalman, W. A. B. (2007). Sense of Competence Questionnaire among informal caregivers of older adults with dementia symptoms: A psychometric evaluation. *Clinical Practice and Epidemiology in Mental Health, 3*(Article 11).

Johnson, C. R., Butter, E. M., Handen, B. L., Sukhodolsky, D. G., Mulick, J., LeCavalier, L., . . . McDougle, C. J. (2009). Standardised Observation Analogue Procedure (SOAP) for assessing parent and child behaviours in clinical trials. *Journal of Intellectual and Developmental Disabilities, 34*, 230–238.

Jones, B. T., Corbin, W., & Fromme, K. (2001). A review of expectancy theory and alcohol consumption. *Addiction, 96*, 57–72.

Kahng, S. W., Iwata, B. A., & Lewin, A. B. (2002). Behavioral treatment of self-injury, 1964 to 2000. *American Journal on Mental Retardation, 107*, 212–221.

Kanter, J. W., Tsai, M., Kohlenberg, R. J. (Eds.). (2010). *The practice of functional analytic psychotherapy*. New York, NY: Springer.

Kaholokula, J. K., Bello, I., Nacapoy, A. H., & Haynes, S. (2009). Behavioral assessment and functional analysis. In D. Richard & S. Huprich (Eds.), *Clinical Psychology: Assessment, Treatment, and Research*. Burlington, MA: Elsevier Academic Press.

Kanter, J. W., Tsai, M., & Kohlenberg, R. J. (2010). *The practice of functional analytic psychotherapy*. New York, NY: Springer.

Kassel, J. D., Stroud, L. R., & Paronis, C. A. (2003). Smoking, stress, and negative affect: Correlation, causation, and context across stages of smoking. *Psychological Bulletin, 129*, 270–304.

Kazdin, A. E. (2001). *Behavior modification in applied settings* (6th ed.). Belmont, CA: Wadsworth/Thomson Learning.

Kazdin, A. E. (2002). *Research designs in clinical psychology* (4th ed.) Boston, MA: Allyn & Bacon.

Keane, T. M., Silberbogen, A. K., & Seierich, M. R. (2008). Posttraumatic stress disorder. In J. Hunsley & E. J. Mash (Eds.), *A guide to assessments that work* (pp. 293–318). New York, NY: Oxford University Press.

Keeley, J., Zayak, R., & Correia, C. (2008). Curvilinear relations between statistics anxiety and test performance among undergraduate students: Evidence for optimal anxiety. *Statistics Education Research Journal, 7,* 4–15.

Khanna, J. M., Morato, G. S., & Kalant, H. (2002). Effects of NMDA agonist, NMDA antagonists, and serotonin depletion on acute tolerance to ethanol. *Pharmacology, Biochemistry, and Behavior, 72,* 291–298.

Kirschbaum, C., & Hellhammer, D. H. (2000). Salivary cortisol. In G. Fink (Ed.), *Encyclopedia of stress* (pp. 379–383). San Diego, CA: Academic Press.

Koegel, L. K., Valdez-Menchaca, M., Koegel, R. L., & Harrower, J. K. (2001). Autism. In M. Hersen & V. B. Van Hasselt (Eds.), *Advanced abnormal psychology* (2nd ed., pp. 165–190). New York, NY: Kluwer Academic/Plenum.

Koerner, K., & Linehan, M. M. (1997). Case formulation in dialectical behavior therapy. In T. D. Eells (Ed.), *Handbook of psychotherapy case formulation* (pp. 340–367). New York, NY: Guilford Press.

Kohlenberg, R. J., & Tsai, M. (2007). *Functional analytic psychotherapy: Creating intense and curative therapeutic relationships.* New York, NY: Springer.

Korotitsch, W. J., & Nelson-Gray, R. O. (1999). An overview of self-monitoring research in assessment and treatment. *Psychological Assessment, 11*(4), 415–425.

Krueger, R. F., & Markon, K. E. (2006). A model-based approach to understanding and classifying psychopathology. *Annual Review of Clinical Psychology, 2,* 111–133.

Ladouceur, R., & Lachance, S. (2007). *Overcoming your pathological gambling: Workbook. treatments that work.* Thousand Oaks, CA: Corwin Press.

Lam, W. K. K., Fals-Stewart, W., & Kelley, M. (2009). The Timeline Followback interview to assess children's exposure to partner violence: Reliability and validity. *Journal of Family Violence, 24*(2), 133–143.

Lambrechts, G., Van Den Noortgate, W., Eeman, L., & Maes, B. (2010). Staff reactions to challenging behaviour: An observation study. *Research in Developmental Disabilities, 31,* 525–535.

Lang, P. J. (1995). The emotion probe: Studies of motivation and attention. *American Psychologist, 50,* 519–525.

Lappalainen, R., & Tuomisto, T. (2005). Functional behavior analysis of anorexia nervosa: Applications to clinical practice. *The Behavior Analyst Today, 6,* 166–177.

Larkin, K. T. (2006). Psychophysiological assessment. In M. Hersen (Ed.), *Clinician's handbook of adult behavioral assessment* (pp. 165–185). San Diego, CA: Elsevier Academic.

Last, C. G., Strauss, C. C., & Francis, G. (1987). Comorbidity among childhood anxiety disorders. *Journal of Nervous and Mental Disease, 175,* 726–730.

Lattel, K. A. & Perone, M. (Eds.). (1998). *Handbook of research methods in human operant behavior.* New York, NY: Plenum Press.

Lau, A. W., Edelstein, B. A., & Larkin, K. T. (2001). Psychophysiological arousal in older adults: A critical review. *Clinical Psychology Review, 21,* 609–630.

Laurenceau, J-P, Barrett, L. F., & Rovine, M. J. (2005). The Interpersonal Process Model of Intimacy in Marriage: A daily-diary and multilevel modeling approach. *Journal of Family Psychology, 19,* 314–323.

Leahy, R. L. (2008). The therapeutic relationship in cognitive behavioural therapy. *Behavioural and Cognitive Psychotherapy, 36,* 769–777.

LePage, J., & Mogge, N. L. (2001). The Behavioral Observation System (BOS): A line staff assessment instrument of psychopathology. *Journal of Clinical Psychology, 57,* 1435–1444.

Liberman, R. P., Teigen, J., Patterson, R., Baker, V. (1973). Reducing delusional speech in chronic, paranoid schizophrenics. *Journal of Applied Behavior Analysis, 6,* 57–64.

Lilienfeld, S. O., Waldman, I. D., & Israel, A. C. (1994). A critical examination of the use of the term and concept of "comorbidity" in psychopathology research. *Clinical Psychology: Science and Practice, 1*, 71–83.

Linehan, M. M. (1993). *Cognitive behavioral treatment of borderline personality disorder*. New York, NY: Guilford Press.

Linn, R. L. (Ed.) (1989). *Educational measurement* (3rd ed.). New York, NY: Macmillan.

Loehlin, J. C. (2004). *Latent variable models: An introduction to factor, path, and structural equation analysis* (4th ed.). Mahwah, NJ: Lawrence Erlbaum Associates.

Lucas, R. E., & Baird, B. M. (2006). Global self-assessment. In M. Eid, & E. Diener, *Handbook of multimethod measurement in psychology* (pp. 29–42). Washington, DC: American Psychological Association.

Marlatt, G. A. (1985). Relapse prevention: Theoretical rationale and overview of the model. In G. A. Marlatt & J. R. Gordon (Eds.), *Relapse prevention: Maintenance strategies in the treatment of addictive behaviors* (pp. 3–70). New York, NY: Brunner/Mazel.

Mash, E. J., & Terdal, L. G. (Eds.). (1997). *Assessment of childhood disorders* (3rd ed.). New York, NY: Guilford Press.

Matson, J. L., & Vollmer, T. R. (1995). *User's guide: Questions about behavioral function (QABF)*. Baton Rouge, LA: Scientific Publishers.

Matyas, T. A., & Greenwood, K. M. (1990). Visual analysis of single-case time series: Effects of variability, serial dependence, and magnitude of intervention effects. *Journal of Applied Behavior Analysis, 23*, 341–351.

McFall, R. M. (1977). Analogue methods in behavioral assessment: Issues and prospects. In J. D. Cone & R. P. Hawkins (Eds.), *Behavioral assessment: New directions* (pp. 152–177). New York, NY: Brunner/Mazel.

McGlynn, F. D., & Rose, M. P. (1996). Assessment of anxiety and fear. In M. Hersen & A. S. Bellack, *Behavioral assessment: A practical handbook* (4th ed.). Boston, MA: Allyn & Bacon.

McGrath, R. E. (2005). Conceptual complexity and construct validity. *Journal of Personality Assessment, 85*(2), 112–124.

McKay, D., & Storch, E. A. (Eds.). (2009). *Cognitive-behavior therapy for children: Treating complex and refractory cases*. New York, NY: Springer.

Messer, S. C., & Gross, A. M. (1995). Childhood depression and family interaction: A naturalistic observation study. *Journal of Clinical Child Psychology, 24,* 77–88.

Michelson, L. (1986). Treatment consonance and response profiles in agoraphobia: The role of individual differences in cognitive, behavioral, and physiological treatments. *Behaviour Research and Therapy, 24,* 263–275.

Miklowitz, D. J. (2007). The role of the family in the course and treatment of bipolar disorder. *Current Directions in Psychological Science, 16,* 192–196.

Minke, K., & Haynes, S. N. (2011). Subject, setting, and time sampling. In J. C. Thomas and M. Hersen (Eds.), *Understanding research in clinical and counseling psychology.* Mahwah, NJ: Lawrence Erlbaum.

Mitte, K. (2005). A meta-analysis of cognitive-behavioral treatments for generalized anxiety disorder: A comparison with pharmacotherapy. *Psychological Bulletin, 131,* 785–795.

Molton, I. R., & Raichle, K. A. (2010). Psychophysiological disorders. In D. L. Segal & M. Hersen (Eds.), *Diagnostic interviewing* (pp. 343–369). New York, NY: Springer.

Moos, R. H. (2008). Context and mechanisms of reactivity to assessment and treatment: Comment. *Addiction, 103*(2), 249–250.

Mori, L. T., & Armendariz, G. M. (2001). Observational assessment of child behavior problems. *Psychological Assessment, 13,* 36–45.

Morris, E. P., Stewart, S. H., & Ham, L. S. (2005). The relationship between social anxiety disorder and alcohol use disorders: A critical review. *Clinical Psychology Review, 25,* 734–760.

Mumma, G. H. (2001). *Manual for the cognitive-behavioral-interpersonal semi-structured assessment interview.* Unpublished manual.

Mumma, G. H. (2004). Validation of idiosyncratic cognitive schema in cognitive case formulations: An intraindividual idiographic approach. *Psychological Assessment, 16,* 211–230.

Murphy, C. M., & O'Farrell, T. J. (1994). Factors associated with marital aggression in male alcoholics. *Journal of Family Psychology, 8,* 321–335.

Nader, K. (2008). *Understanding and assessing trauma in children and adolescents: Measures, methods, and youth in context.* New York, NY: Routledge.

Nay, W. R. (1986). Analogue measures. In A. R. Ciminero, C. S. Calhoun, & H. E. Adams (Eds.), *Handbook of behavioral assessment* (pp. 223–252). New York, NY: John Wiley & Sons.

Neacsiu, A. D., Rizvi, S. L., & Linehan, M. M. (2010). Dialectical behavior therapy skills used as a mediator and outcome of treatment for borderline personality disorder. *Behaviour Research and Therapy, 48,* 832–839.

Nelson, W. A., & Clum, G. A. (2002). Assessment of panic frequency: Reliability and validity of a timeline followback method. *Journal of Psychopathology and Behavioral Assessment, 24*(1), 47–54.

Nelson-Gray, R. O., and Paulson, J. F. (2004). Behavioral assessment and the DSM system. In S. N. Haynes and E. H. Heiby (Eds.), *Behavioral assessment* (pp. 470–489). Hoboken, NJ: JohnWiley & Sons.

Nezu, A. M., & Nezu, C. M. (2008). *Evidence-based outcome research.* New York, NY: Oxford University Press.

Nezu, A. M., Nezu, C. M., Maguth, C., & Lombardo, E. (2004). *Cognitive-behavioral case formulation and treatment design: A problem-solving approach.* New York, NY: Springer.

Nickerson, R. S. (1998). Confirmation bias: A ubiquitous phenomenon in many guises. *General Review of Psychology, 2,* 175–220.

Norcross, J. C. (2002). Empirically supported therapy relationships. In J. C. Norcross (Ed.), *Psychotherapy relationships that work: Therapist contributions and responsiveness to patients.* New York, NY: Oxford University Press.

Northrup, J., Broussard, C., Jones, K., & George, T. (1995). The differential effects of teacher and peer attention on the disruptive classroom behavior of three children with a diagnosis of attention deficit hyperactivity disorder. *Journal of Applied Behavior Analysis, 28*(2), 227–228.

Northrup, J., Wacker, D., Sasso, G., Steege, M., Cigrand, K., Cook, J., & DeRaad, A. (1991). A functional analysis of both aggressive and alternative behavior in an outclinic setting. *Journal of Applied Behavior Analysis, 24,* 509–522.

Nunnally, J. C., & Bernstein, I. H. (1994). *Psychometric theory.* New York, NY: McGraw-Hill.

O'Brien, W. H. (1995). Inaccuracies in the estimation of functional relationships using self-monitoring data. *Journal of Behavior Therapy and Experimental Psychiatry, 26,* 351–357.

O'Brien, W. H., & Haynes, S. N. (1997). A functional analytic approach to the conceptualization, assessment, and treatment of a child with frequent migraine headaches. *In Session, 1*, 65–80.

O'Brien, W. H., Kaplar, M., & McGrath, J. J. (2004). Broadly based causal models of behavior disorders. In M. Hersen, S. N. Haynes, & E. M. Heiby (Eds.), *The handbook of psychological assessment: Vol. 3. Behavioral assessment* (pp. 69–93). Hoboken, NJ: John Wiley & Sons.

O'Donohue, W. T., & Ferguson, K. E. (2004). Learning and applied behavior analysis foundations of behavioral assessment. In S. N. Haynes & E. M. Heiby (Eds.), *Comprehensive handbook of psychological assessment: Vol. 3. Behavioral assessment* (pp. 57–68). Hoboken, NJ: John Wiley & Sons.

Ollendick, T. H., & Hersen, M. (1993). Child and adolescent behavioral assessment. In Ollendick, T. H., & Hersen, M. (Eds.), *Handbook of child and adolescent assessment* (pp. 3–14). Boston, MA: Allyn and Bacon.

O'Neill, R. E., Horner, R. H., Albin, R. W., Sprague, J. R., Storey, K., & Newton, J. S. (1997). *Functional assessment and program development for problem behavior: A practical handbook* (2nd ed.). Pacific Grove, CA: Brooks/Cole.

O'Reilly, M., Sigafoos, J., Lancioni, G., Edrisnha, C., & Andrews, A. (2005). An examination of the effects of a classroom activity schedule on levels of self-injury and engagement for a child with severe autism. *Journal of Autism and Developmental Disorders, 35*, 305–311.

Ost, L. G., Jerremalm, A., & Johansson, J. (1981). Individual response patterns and the effects of different behavior methods in the treatment of social phobia. *Behaviour Research and Therapy, 20*, 445–460.

Paclawskyj, T. R., Matson, J. L., Rush, K. S., Smalls, Y., & Vollmer, T. R. (2000). Questions about behavioral function (QABF): A behavioral checklist for functional assessment of aberrant behavior. *Research in Developmental Disabilities, 21*(3), 223–229.

Patterson, G. R. (2002). The early development of coercive family process. In J. B. Reid, G. R. Patterson, & J. Snyder (Eds.), *Antisocial behavior in children and adolescents: A developmental analysis and model for intervention* (pp. 25–44). Washington, DC: American Psychological Association.

Patterson, G. R., & Fisher, P. A. (2002). Recent developments in our understanding of parenting: Bi-directional effects, causal models, and the search for parsimony. In M. Bornstein (Ed.), *Handbook of parenting: Practical and applied parenting: Vol. IV* (2nd ed., pp. 59–88). Mahwah, NJ: Lawrence Erlbaum.

Patterson, G. R., Reid, J. B., & Dishion, T. J. (1992). *Antisocial boys.* Eugene, OR: Castalia.

Patterson, G. R., & Yoerger, K. (2002). A developmental model for early- and late-onset delinquency. In J. B. Reid, G. R. Patterson, & J. Snyder (Eds.), *Antisocial behavior in children and adolescents: A developmental analysis and model for intervention* (pp. 147–172). Washington, DC: American Psychological Association.

Patterson, G. R., Reid, J. B., & Eddy, J. M. (2002). A brief history of the Oregon model. In J. B. Reid, G. R. Patterson, & J. J. Snyder (Eds.), *Antisocial behavior in children and adolescents: A developmental analysis and model for intervention* (pp. 3–21). Washington, DC: American Psychological Association.

Pearl, J. (2000). *Causality: Models, reasoning, and inference.* Cambridge, UK: Cambridge University Press.

Persons, J. (2005). Empiricism, mechanism and the practice of cognitive-behavioural therapy. *Behaviour Therapy, 36,* 107–118.

Persons, J. (2006). Case formulation-driven psychotherapy. *Clinical Psychology: Science and Practice, 13,* 167–170.

Persons, J. B. (2008). *The case formulation approach to cognitive-behavior therapy.* New York, NY: Guilford Press.

Persons, J. B. (2005). Empiricism, mechanism, and the practice of cognitive-behavior therapy. *Behavior Therapy. 36,* 107–118.

Persons, J. B., & Davidson, J. (2001). Cognitive-behavioral case formulation. In K. S. Dobson (Ed.), *Handbook of cognitive-behavioral therapies* (2nd ed., pp. 86–110). New York, NY: Guilford Press.

Piasecki, T. M., Hufford, M. R., Solhan, M., & Trull, T. J. (2007). Assessing clients in their natural environments with electronic diaries: Rationale, benefits, limitations, and barriers. *Psychological Assessment, 19,* 25–43.

Quas, J. A., Malloy, L. C., Melinder, A., Goodman, G. S., D'Mello, M., & Schaaf, J. (2007). Developmental differences in the effects of repeated interviews and interviewer bias on young children's event memory and false reports. *Developmental Psychology, 43*(4), 823–837.

Rau, R. (2006). The association between blood pressure and work stress: The importance of measuring isolated systolic hypertension. *Work & Stress, 20*(1), 84–97.

Rehman, U., Gollan, J., & Mortimer, A. (2008). The marital context of depression: Research, limitations, and new directions. *Clinical Psychology Review, 28*(2), 179–198.

Reynolds, C. R., & Kamphaus, R. W. (1992). *Behavior assessment system for children*. Circle Pines, MN: American Guidance Service.

Rhyner, P .M., Lehr, D. H., & Pudlas, K. A. (1990). An analysis of the teacher responsiveness to communicative initiations of preschool children with handicaps. *Language Speech and Hearing Services in Schools, 2*, 91–97.

Richard, D. C. S., & Lauterbach, D. (2004). Computers in the training and practice of behavioral assessment. In S. N. Haynes & E. M. Heiby (Ed.), *Comprehensive handbook of psychological assessment: Vol. 3. Behavioral assessment* (pp. 222–245). Hoboken, NJ: John Wiley & Sons.

Roberts, M. W. (2001). Clinic observations of structured parent-child interaction designed to evaluate externalizing disorders. *Psychological Assessment, 13*, 46–58.

Rogers, C. R. (1951). *Client-centered therapy: Its current practice, implications, and theory*. Boston, MA: Houghton Mifflin.

Ross, R. G., Heinlein, S., & Tregellas, H. (2006). High rates of comorbidity are found in childhood-onset schizophrenia. *Schizophrenia Research, 88*, 90–95.

Rowland, C. (1990). Communication in the classroom with dual sensory impairments: Studies of teacher and child behaviour. *Augmentative and Alternative Communication, 6*, 62–275.

Rush, A. J., Gullion, C. M., Basco, M. R., Jarrett, R. B., & Trivedi, M. H. (1996). The Inventory of Depressive Symptomatology (IDS): Psychometric properties. *Psychological Medicine, 2*, 477–486.

Ryan, D., McGregor, F., Akermanis, M., Southwell, K., Ramke, M., & Woodyatt, G. (2004). Facilitating communication in children with multiple disabilities: Three case studies of girls with Rett syndrome.

*Disability and Rehabilitation: An International Multidisciplinary Journal,* *26*, 1268–1277.

Sacks, J. A., Drake, R. E., Williams, V. F., Banks, S. M., & Herrell, J. M. (2003). Utility of the Timeline Followback to assess substance use among homeless adults. *Journal of Nervous and Mental Disease,* *191*(3), 145–153.

Sadeh, A., Hauri, P. J., Kripke, D. F., & Lavie, P. (1994). The role of actigraphy in the evaluation of sleep disorders. *Sleep, 18,* 288–302.

Satterfield, J. M. (2008). *Minding the body workbook (Treatments that work).* New York, NY: Oxford University Press.

Savard, J., & Morin, C. (2002). Insomnia. In M. M. Antony & D. H. Barlow, *Handbook of assessment and treatment planning for psychological disorders.* (pp. 523–555). New York, NY: Guilford Press.

Sayers, S. L., & Tomcho, T. J. (2006). Behavioral interviewing. In M. Hersen (Ed.), *Clinician's handbook of adult behavioral assessment* (pp. 63–84). San Diego, CA: Elsevier Academic Press.

Schlundt, D. G. (1985). An observational methodology for functional analysis. *Bulletin of the Society of Psychologists in Addictive Behaviors,* *4,* 234–249.

Schmidt, F., McKinnon, L. C., Chattha, H. K., & Brownlee, K. (2006). Concurrent and predictive validity of the Psychology Checklist: Youth Version across gender and ethnicity. *Psychological Assessment,* *18*(4), 393–401.

Schneiderman, N., Ironson, G., & Siegel, S. D. (2005). Stress and health: Psychological, behavioral, and biological determinants. *Annual Review of Clinical Psychology, 1,* 607–628.

Sederer, L. I., & Dickey, B. (1996). *Outcomes assessment in clinical practice.* Baltimore, MD: Williams & Wilkins.

Seiffge-Krenke, I. (2001). *Diabetic adolescents and their families: Stress, coping, and adaptation.* New York, NY: Cambridge University Press.

Selzer, M. L., Vinokur, A., & van Rooijen, L. (1975). A self-administered Short Michigan Alcoholism Screening Test (SMAST). *Journal of Studies on Alcohol, 36,* 117–126.

Shadish, W. R., Cook, T. D., & Campbell, D. T. (2002). *Experimental and quasi-experimental designs for generalized causal inference.* New York, NY: Houghton Mifflin.

Shapiro, E. S., & Kratochwill, T. R. (1988). Analogue assessment: Methods for assessing emotional and behavioral problems. In E. S. Shapiro & T. R. Kratochwill (Eds.), *Behavioral assessment in schools: Conceptual foundations and practical applications* (pp. 290–322). New York, NY: Guilford Press.

Sharp, W. G., Reeves, C. B., & Gross, A. M. (2006). Behavioral interviewing of parents. In M. Hersen (Ed.), *Clinician's handbook of child behavioral assessment* (pp. 103–124). San Diego, CA: Elsevier Academic Press.

Shiffman, S. (2009). How many cigarettes did you smoke? Assessing cigarette consumption by global report, time-line follow-back, and ecological momentary assessment. *Health Psychology, 28,* 519–526.

Shiffman, S. (1993). Assessing smoking patterns and motives. *Journal of Consulting and Clinical Psychology, 61,* 732–742.

Shiffman, S., Hufford, M., Hickcox, M., Paty, J. A., Gnys, M., & Kassel, J. D. (1997). Remember that? A comparison of real-time versus retrospective recall of smoking lapses. *Journal of Consulting and Clinical Psychology, 65,* 292–300.

Shiffman, S., & Paty, J. (2006). Smoking patterns and dependence: Contrasting chippers and heavy smokers. *Journal of Abnormal Psychology, 115*(3), 509–523.

Shiffman, S., Stone, A. A., & Hufford, M. R. (2008). Ecological momentory assessment. *Annual Review of Clinical Psychology, 4,* 1–32.

Sigafoos J., Roberts, D., Kerr, M., Couzens, D., & Baglioni, A. J. (1994). Opportunities for communication in classrooms serving children with developmental disabilities. *Journal of Autism and Developmental Disorders, 24,* 259–279.

Sigmon, S. T., & LaMattina, S. M. (2006). Self assessment. In M. Hersen (Ed.), *Clinician's handbook of adult behavioral assessment* (pp. 145–164). San Diego, CA: Elsevier Academic Press.

Silva, F. (1994). *Psychometric foundations and behavioral assessment.* Newbury Park, CA: Sage.

Simons, C. J. P., Wichers, M., Derom, C., Thiery, E., Myin-Germeys, I., Krabbendam, L., & van Os, J. (2009). Subtle gene-environment interactions driving paranoia in daily life. *Genes, Brain & Behavior, 8*(1), 5–12.

Skinner, C. H., Rhymer, K. N., & McDaniel, E. C. (2000). Naturalistic direct observation in educational settings. In E. S. Shapiro & T. R. Kratochwill (Eds.), *Conducting school-based assessments of child and adolescent behavior* (pp. 21–54). New York, NY: Guilford Press.

Smith, G. T., McCarthy, D. M., & Zapolski, T. C. B. (2009). On the value of homogeneous constructs for construct validation, theory testing, and the description of psychopathology. *Psychological Assessment, 21*, 272–284.

Smits, J. A. J., O'Cleirigh, C. M., & Otto, M. W. (2006). Panic and agoraphobia. In M. Hersen & J. C. Thomas (Eds.), *Comprehensive handbook of personality and psychopathology: Vol. 2. Adult psychopathology* (pp. 121–137). Hoboken, NJ: John Wiley & Sons.

Snyder, D. K. (1997). *Manual for the Marital Satisfaction Inventory–Revised.* Los Angeles, CA: Western Psychological Services.

Snyder, D., Heyman, R., & Haynes, S. N. (2008). Couple assessment. In J. Hunsley & E. J. Mash, *A guide to assessments that work* (pp. 439–463). Oxford, UK: Oxford University Press.

Snyder, D., Heyman, R., & Haynes, S. N. (2009). Strategies in the assessment of couples. In J. Butcher (Ed.), *Clinical assessment handbook.* Oxford, UK: Oxford University Press.

Sobell, L. C., & Sobell, M. B. (1992). Timeline follow-back: A technique for assessment of self-reported alcohol consumption. In R. Z. Litten & J. P. Allen, *Measuring alcohol consumption: Psychosocial and biochemical methods* (pp. 41–72). Totowa, NJ: Humana Press.

Spanier, G., & Thompson, L. (1982). A confirmatory analysis of the Dyadic Adjustment Scale. *Journal of Marriage and the Family, 44*, 731–738.

Spijkerman, R., Larsen, H., Gibbons, F. X., & Engels, R. C. M. E. (2010). Students' drinker prototypes and alcohol use in a naturalistic setting. *Alcoholism: Clinical and experimental research, 34*(1), 64–71.

Staats, A. W. (1986). Behaviorism with a personality: The paradigmatic behavioral assessment approach. In. R. O. Nelson & S. C. Hayes (Eds.), *Conceptual foundations of behavioral assessment* (pp. 242–296). New York, NY: Guilford Press.

Steele, R. G., Elkin, T. D., & Roberts, M. C. (2008). *Handbook of evidence-based therapies for children and adolescents: Bridging science and practice.* New York, NY: Springer Science.

Steptoe, A., Brydon, L., & Kunz-Ebrecht, S. (2005). Changes in financial strain over three years, ambulatory blood pressure, and cortisol responses to awakening. *Psychosomatic Medicine*, *67*, 281–287.

Stern, R. M., Ray. W. J., & Quigley, K. S. (2000). *Psychophysiological Recording* (2nd ed.). New York, NY: Oxford University Press.

Stewart, D., Law, M., Russell, D., & Ham, S. (2004). Evaluating children's rehabilitation services: An application of a programme logic model. *Child: Care, Health and Development*, *30(5)*, 453–462.

Stiglmayr, C., Ebner-Priemer, U. W., Bretz, J., Behm, R., Mohse, M., Lammers, C. H., . . . Bohus, M. (2007). Dissociative symptoms are positively related to stress in borderline personality disorder. *Acta Psychiatrica Scandinavica*, *117*, 139–147.

Strand, P. S. A. (2000). Modern behavioral perspective on child conduct disorder: Integrating behavioral momentum and matching theory. *Clinical Psychology Review*, *20(5)*, 593–615.

Straus, M. A., Hamby, S. L., Boney-McCoy, S., & Sugarman, D. B. (1996). The revised Conflict Tactics Scales (CTS2): Development and preliminary psychometric data. *Journal of Family Issues, 17*, 283–316.

Sturmey, P. (Ed.). (2009). *Clinical case formulation, Varieties of approaches*. Chichester, UK: John Wiley & Sons.

Suen, H. K., & Ary, D. (1989). *Analyzing quantitative behavioral data*. Hillsdale, NJ: Lawrence Erlbaum.

Suen, H. K., & Rzasa, S. E. (2004). Psychometric foundations of behavioral assessment. In S. N. Haynes, E. M. Heiby (Eds.), & M. Hersen (Series Ed.), *Comprehensive handbook of psychological assessment: Vol. 3. Behavioral assessment*. Hoboken, NJ: John Wiley & Sons.

Tanaka-Matsumi, J. (2004). Individual differences and behavioral assessment. In S. N. Haynes & E. M. Heiby (Eds.), *Behavioral assessment* (pp. 128–139). Hoboken, NJ: John Wiley & Sons.

Tanaka-Matsumi, J., Seiden, D. Y., & Lam, K. N. (1996). The Culturally Informed Functional Assessment (CIFA) Interview: A strategy for cross-cultural behavioral practice. *Cognitive and Behavioral Practice, 3*, 215–233.

Tapp, J., & Wehby, J. H. (2000). Observational software for laptop computers and optical bar code time wands. In T. Thompson, D. Felce, &

F. Symons (Eds.), *Behavioral observation: Computer assisted innovations and applications in developmental disabilities* (pp. 71–81). Baltimore, MD: Paul H. Brookes.

Tarrier, N. (Ed.). (2006). *Case formulation in cognitive behaviour therapy: The treatment of challenging and complex cases.* New York, NY: Routledge.

Tasca, G. A., Illing, V., Balfour, L., Krysanski, V., Demidenko, N., Nowakowski, J., & Bissada, H. (2009). Psychometric properties of self-monitoring of eating disorder urges among treatment seeking women: Ecological momentary assessment using a daily diary method. *Eating Behaviors, 10*(1), 59–61.

Terbizan, D. J., Dolezal, B .A., & Albano, C. (2002). Validity of seven commercially available heart rate monitors. *Measurement in Physical Education and Exercise Science, 6,* 243–247.

Terry, T. P. C., Stevens, M. J., & Lane, A. M. (2005). Influence of response time frame on mood assessment. *Anxiety, Stress & Coping: An International Journal, 18,* 279–285.

Thatcher, I., & Haynes, S. N. (2001). A multivariate time-series regression study of pain, depression symptoms, and social interaction in rheumatoid arthritis. *International Journal of Clinical and Health Psychology, 1,* 159–180.

Tomarken, A. J. (1995). What is the critical evidence favoring expectancy bias theory and where is it? *Behavioral and Brain Science, 18,* 313–314.

Torgrud, L. J., & Holborn, S. W. (1992). Developing externally valid role-play for assessment of social skills: A behavior analytic perspective. *Behavioral Assessment, 14,* 245–277.

Trull, T. J., & Ebner-Priemer, U. W. (2009). Using experience sampling methods/ecological momentary assessment (ESM/EMA) in clinical assessment and clinical research: Introduction to the special section. *Psychological Assessment, 21*(4), 457–462.

Tryon, W. W. (1998). Behavioral observation. In A. S. Bellack & M. Hersen (Eds.), *Behavioral assessment: A practical handbook* (4th ed., pp. 79–103). Boston, MA: Allyn & Bacon.

Tryon, W. W. (2006). Activity measurement. In M. Hersen (Ed.), *Clinician's handbook of adult behavioral assessment* (pp. 85–120). New York, NY: Academic Press.

Tsai, M., Kohlenberg, R. J., Kanter, J. W., Kohlenberg, B., Follette, W. C., & Callaghan, G. M. (2009). *A guide to functional analytic psychotherapy: Awareness, courage, love, and behaviorism*. New York, NY: Springer.

Turk, D. C., & Melzack, R. (Eds.). (2001). *Handbook of pain assessment* (2nd ed.). New York, NY: Guilford Press.

Tversky, A., & Kahneman, D. (1974). Judgment under uncertainty: Heuristics and biases. *Science, 185*, 1124–1131.

University of Utah, Utah State University, & Utah State Department of Education. (1999). *Functional assessment and intervention program*. Longmont, CO: Sopris West.

Van Haitsma, K., Lawton, M. P., Kleban, M. H., Klapper, J., & Corn, J. (1997). Methodological aspects of the study of streams of behavior in elders with dementing illness. *Alzheimer Disease and Associated Disorders, 11*, 228–238.

Wahler, R. G. & Hann, D. M. (1986). A behavioral systems perspective in childhood psychopathology: Expanding the three-term operant contingency. In N. A. Krasnegor, J. D. Arasteh, & M. F. Cataldo (Eds.), *Child health behavior: A behavioral pediatrics perspective* (pp. 146–167). New York, NY: Wiley.

Wahler, R. G., Vigilante, V. A., & Strand, P. S. (2004). Generalization in a child's oppositional behavior across home and school settings. *Journal of Applied Behavior Analysis, 37*, 43–51.

Walitzer, K. S., & Dearing, R. L. (2006). Gender differences in alcohol and substance use relapse. *Clinical Psychology Review, 26*, 128–148.

Ward, L. C., & Thorn, B. E. (2006). The fear-avoidance model of chronic pain: Further thoughts on the process of validating a causal model. *Pain, 121*, 173–174.

Watson, J. C., & McMullen, E. J. (2005). An examination of therapist and client behavior in high- and low-alliance sessions in cognitive-behavioral therapy and process experiential therapy. *Psychotherapy: Theory, Research, Practice, and Training, 42*, 297–310.

Wei, W. W. S. (1990). *Time series analysis: Univariate and multivariate methods* (2nd ed.). Boston, MA: Pearson/Addison Wesley.

Weinhardt, L. S., Carey, M. P., Maisto, S. A., Carey, K. B., Cohen, M. M. & Wickramasinghe, S. M. (1998). Reliability of the Timeline

Followback sexual behavior interview. *Annals of Behavioral Medicine*, *20(1)*, 25–30.

Weiss, L. M., & Petry, N. M. (2008). Psychometric properties of the inventory of gambling situations with a focus on gender and age differences. *Journal of Nervous and Mental Disorders*, *196*(4), 321–328.

Weiss, R. L., & Summers, K. J. (1983). Marital Interaction Coding System–III. In E. Filsinger (Ed.), *Marriage and family assessment* (pp. 85–116). Newbury Park, CA: Sage.

Weyandt, L. L. (2006). *The physiological bases of cognitive and behavioral disorders*. Mahwah, NJ: Lawrence Erlbaum.

Wicks-Nelson, R., & Israel, A. C. (1997). *Behavior disorders of childhood*. Upper Saddle River, NJ: Prentice-Hall.

Widiger, T. A., & Edmundson, M. (2009). Diagnoses, dimensions, and DSM-V. In D. Barlow (Ed.), *Handbook of clinical psychology*. New York, NY: Oxford University Press.

Wilhelm, F. H., & Schneider, S., & Friedman, B. H. (2006). Psychophysiological assessment. Clinician's handbook of child behavioral assessment. In M. Hersen (Ed.), *Clinician's handbook of child behavioral assessment* (pp. 201–231). San Diego, CA: Elsevier Academic Press.

Wilson, J. P., & Keane, T. M. (Eds.). (1997). *Assessing psychological trauma and PTSD*. New York, NY: Guilford Press.

Wilson, G. T., & Vitousek, K. M. (1999). Self-monitoring in the assessment of eating disorders. *Psychological Assessment*, *11*(4), 480–489.

Wise, D. (2006). Child abuse. In M. Hersen (Ed.), *Clinician's handbook of child behavioral assessment* (pp. 549–568). San Diego, CA: Elsevier Academic Press.

Wu, L-T., & Howard, M. O. (2007). Psychiatric disorders in inhalant users: Results from the National Epidemiologic Survey on Alcohol and Related Conditions. *Drug and Alcohol Dependence*, *88*, 146–155.

Wysocki, T., Green, L. B., & Huxtable, K. (1991). Reflectance meters with memory: Applications in behavioral assessment and intervention in juvenile diabetes. Advances in child health psychology. In J. H. Johnson & S. B Johnson (Eds.), *Advances in child health psychology* (pp. 307–319). Gainesville, FL: University of Florida Press.

Zisser, A., & Eyberg, S. M. (2010). Parent-child interaction therapy and the treatment of disruptive behavior disorders. Evidence-based psychotherapies for children and adolescents (2nd ed.). In John Weisz & Alan E. Kazdin (Eds.), *Evidence-based psychotherapies for children and adolescents* (2nd ed., pp. 179–193). New York, NY: Guilford Press.

Zucker, B. G., Craske, M. G., Blackmore, M. A., & Nitz, A. (2006). A cognitive behavioral workshop for subclinical obsessions and compulsions. *Behaviour Research and Therapy, 44,* 289–304.

# Behavioral Assessment and
# Case Formulation

# Author Index

# Subject Index